Cold War Memories:

A Retrospective on Living in Berlin

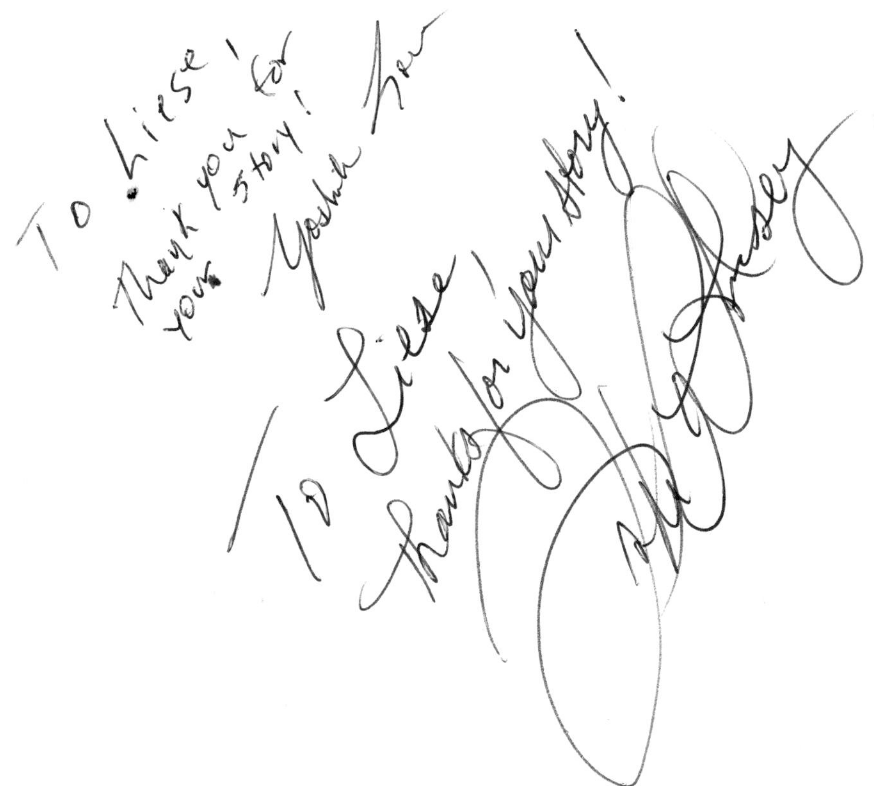

Cover photo by James Miller
Cover design by Trisha A. Lindsey

ISBN-13: 978-0692307885
ISBN-10: 0692307885

To all of the wonderful Brats who sent in their stories and pictures, and who shared their invaluable contacts with us. This project would not have come to fruition without your contributions.

CONTENTS

PREFACE

We could not begin this book without an overview of the actions that led to World War II and to the Allies coming to Berlin at the end of the war. If you attended school in W. Berlin, there was no way to ignore that something monumental had to occur there for there to be a wall surrounding the city. The Wall stretched across the city like a huge snake and you ran into it at the most improbable times, be it out jogging, riding a bike or on the way home from school. Our history teachers were careful to teach us about the war, but also about oppression and how it starts small, and left unchecked, is capable of showing the very worst designs evil human minds can dream up.

Nazi Germany and her allies set up concentration camps, ghettos and extermination camps from the Baltic to the Black Sea. Over 6 million Jews were killed, and numbers estimate from 5 to 11 million others were also killed (including black people, disabled people, homosexuals, Poles, Romani and other Gypsy groups, Jehovah's Witnesses, criminals, Freemasons, Soviet civilians, political prisoners and POWs).

The process of persecution began in stages, with the passing of the Nuremberg Laws in 1935. As early as 1933, concentration camps were built and ghettos constructed in existing cities. Force was used to round up everyone deemed a threat to the state of Germany and the Axis powers. Jewish people and partisans were murdered in mass shootings by a special military branch, the Einsatzgruppen. Victims were regularly taken by train to extermination camps, after working at concentration camps. If they survived the journey, they were then exterminated in gas chambers. By the end of the war, over 6 million Jewish people had been systematically killed throughout most of Europe. People lived around most of these centers of death, and far too many did nothing.

The images the Allied troops met upon liberating these camps were recorded on film, so that the world would never forget. We have included these images as a testimony to the collection of souls targeted and murdered in one of the largest acts of genocide of the 20th century. Into a broken and battered Germany, into Berlin, a city divided between four Allied powers, the first U.S. Dependents arrived and our story began.

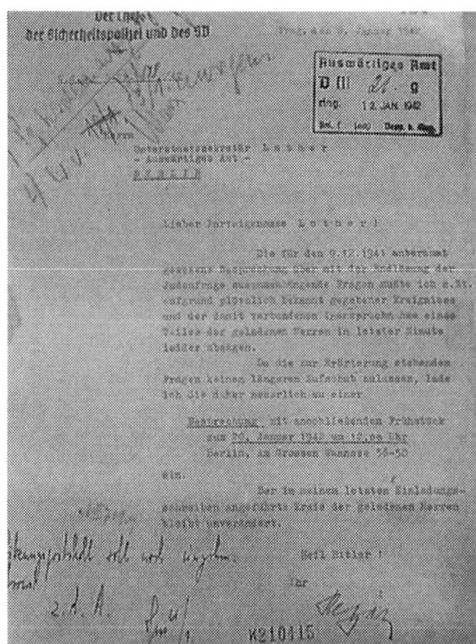

Der Chef der Sicherheitspolizei und des SD

Auswärtiges Amt
D III 21 g
Eing. 12. JAN 1942

Unterstaatssekretär Luther
- Auswärtiges Amt -
BERLIN

Lieber Parteigenosse Luther!

Die für den 9.12.1941 anberaumt gewesene Besprechung über mit der Endlösung der Judenfrage zusammenhängende Fragen musste ich s.Zt. aufgrund plötzlich bekannt gegebener Ereignisse und der damit verbundenen Inanspruchnahme eines Teiles der geladenen Herren in letzter Minute leider absagen.

Da die zur Erörterung stehenden Fragen keinen längeren Aufschub zulassen, lade ich Sie daher neuerlich zu einer

Besprechung mit anschließendem Frühstück
am 20. Januar 1942 um 12.00 Uhr
Berlin, Am Grossen Wannsee 56-58

ein.

Der in meinem letzten Einladungsschreiben angeführte Kreis der geladenen Herren bleibt unverändert.

Heil Hitler!

Ihr

K210415

Final Solution letter, 1942

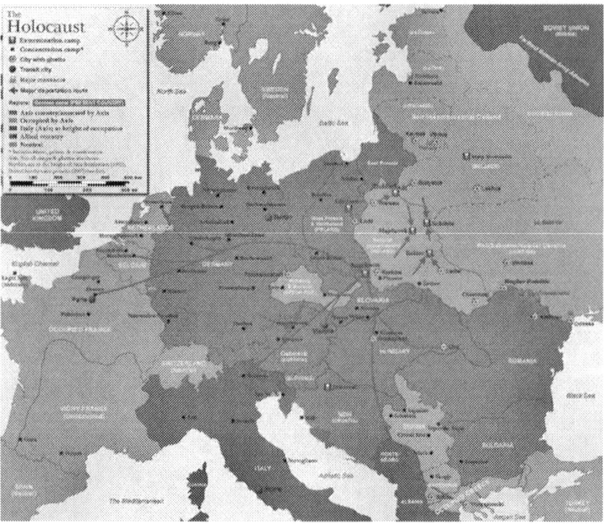

Above: Map of the Holocaust during WW II, 1939-1945. Photo credit: Dennis Nilsson

Mauthausen survivors cheer their liberators: soldiers of the 11th Armored Div. of the U.S. 3rd Army.

A view from inside the Memorial to the Murdered Jews.

The Memorial to the Murdered Jews of Europe consistes of 2,711 concrete stelae or slabs on a sloped field in a grid-like pattern. The square stones differ in height with no rhyme or reason. The architect, Peter Eisenman, said this is to give a sense of confusion and uneasiness. The stelae are black and seemingly systematically placed, giving the feeling of a supposedly ordered system that has lost touch with human reason. The names of all known Jewish Holocaust victims are listed in an atrium underneath the site. Photo: Bill Cunningham

ACKNOWLEDGEMENTS

Special thanks to Jeri Polansky Glass '72 for her tireless efforts in support of this work—her willingness to assist us with contacts, interviewees and introductions was invaluable. We would also like to thank her for her fearless leadership of a rogue group of brats who proudly call themselves the Berlin Brats Alumni Association. Thank you to Cate Speer '85 for creating and maintaining the Berlin Brats Alumni Association website which provided important resources for this project.

Yoshika: Extra special thanks to my family, they mean everything to me! Thank you to my daughter Anastasia for letting me drag her across the country to reunions and Brat gatherings to video interview our Brat classmates. Thank you to my husband Ivan for tirelessly transcribing letters and video interviews and to my son Nathan for the numerous videos he transcribed for us. Thank you to my sister Pleshetta, sons Christian and Ivan III and daughter-in-law Amber for their support for this project.

To my favorite teachers at BAHS who inspire my teaching: Mr. Philip Sullivan and Mrs. Barbara Payne (both have passed) and Mr. Charles Bluem. And to Mrs. Dee Moore, my supervisor and friend at the DYA in Berlin; she inspired me to work with youth because she treated me like I mattered when I didn't think I did.

Trisha: To my exceptional teachers, Mr. Allan Leonard, Mrs. Barbara Payne, Mr. Philip Sullivan, who are all no longer with us and to Ms. Alberta Barlow. I am deeply appreciative to them for their guidance, the way they challenged me, and the belief they instilled in me to never give up, to try and try again. To my Coaches, Mr. Perry Jones, Tom 'Big Ma' Culliton, Mr. Ronald Watt and my dad, Robert Louis Lindsey.

I thank my friends Charlotte, Yoshika and Evelin for their encouragement and prayers over the years. God has blessed me with your friendships. Lastly, I thank my family, who make it possible for me to write: my son Kiernan, my daughter Kaylin and my niece Jasmine. I especially thank my mom and dad, Robert and Trudy Lindsey. I learned to love Berlin due to his antiquing and her job as an East Berlin Tour Guide; and to my sisters Carolyn and Cheryl, I give my thanks. Thanks to Mr. Allen and Lucille Evans, and their sons, Kevin, James and Allen Jr. Miss you Ma and Allen Jr.

INTRODUCTION

These are our stories...the stories of six 'generations' of Berlin Brats over a span of almost fifty years. When we set out to collect and record the history of our Berlin Brat family, we found that they naturally fell into 'generations' roughly by decade. Each decade witnessed major shifts politically and socially. While this was also true in the United States, these changes were very different for the dependents of Americans living in West Berlin–an isolated Outpost of Freedom behind the Iron Curtain.

Since it has been decades since the Berlin Wall came down and Germany was reunified, it is easy to forget that no one in the West ever assumed it would come down—and absolutely not peacefully. We were convinced that nothing short of World War III would bring about the dissolution of the tyranny that separated East from West and held an iron grip upon the many unwilling member states of the Soviet bloc.

This book is written, as are most histories, in an effort to hold onto a piece of history long past. And, it is a warning lest we forget how precious freedom is—for freedom is not free. Additionally, we know that few people are aware that Americans lived in West Berlin, and that fewer still realize that the whole city was over 100 miles inside of Soviet occupied territory. Thus, we lived in an enclave of Capitalism surrounded by Communist East Germany.

So, these are our stories—warts and all. For, any good history retells the good and the bad, the negatives and positives, the sorrows and regrets, lessons learned and opportunities lost. As authors, Trisha and I attempted to edit as limitedly as possible. Retaining each brat's 'voice' and personality was important in a work that records firsthand accounts of human experience. Therefore, grammarians beware, some brats prefer a folksy, sitting-at-the-table approach in their writing style and others are more formal. We love that about this collection of stories—you get to meet each one of us and walk down memory lane from a time and place that no longer exists.

Are we happy that the Wall came down? Ecstatic. Are we sad that West Berlin only exists in our memories? Well, yes and no. We loved our time in Berlin, and we loved our unique time in history and we are thankful for the life-long bonds that we formed despite our transient lifestyles. We are sad that our special place and time no longer exists, but we are grateful that the suffering and fear that necessitated our presence in Berlin is over.

We hope you enjoy reliving our collective history from the arrival of our first Berlin Brat in post-war Berlin 1946 to the last class of 1994 when the Allied Forces withdrew from a reunited Germany.

Chapter 1: Post-war to 1949

"Give service to others if you seek genuine fulfillment. A soul needs goals. A happy soul's goals have objectives that include others. Objective free souls are wandering Dead Sea souls."

– Colonel Gail Halvorsen, The Candy Bomber

First issue

THE GROOPER

VOLUME I, NUMBER 1
BERLIN
28 JULY 1945

Weekly Newspaper, Office of Military Government for Germany (U.S.)

President Roosevelt dead, Truman is successor, Mussolini executed, Hitler kills self, Germany surrenders, V-E day May 8

German chiefs declare war's end in radio message

Challenge citizens to adhere to laws of Allies

New leaders pay homage to the fallen soldiers of the war

Associated Press
May 7, 1945

The Germans have surrendered to the Allies. The war is over.

An announcement on the wavelength of the Flensburg radio carrying German communiques for several days said:

"German men and women! The high command of the armed forces has today, at the order of Grand Admiral Doenitz, declared the unconditional surrender of all fighting German troops."

The announcement was attributed to the new German Foreign Minister, Count Lutz von Schwerin-Krosigk.

"As the leading minister of the Reich government which the admiral of the fleet (Doenitz) has appointed for the winding up of all military tasks, I turn at this tragic moment of our history to the German nation," Schwerin-Krosigk declared.

SAVING THE NATION'S FUTURE

"After a heroic fight of almost six years of incomparable hardness Germany has succumbed to the overwhelming power of her enemies. To continue the war would only mean senseless bloodshed and futile disintegration.

"A government which has a feeling of responsibility for the future of its nation was compelled to act on the collapse of all physical and material forces and to demand of the enemy the cessation of all hostilities.

"It was the noblest task of the admiral of the fleet and of the government supporting him -- after the terrible sacrifices which the war demanded -- to save in the last phase of the war the lives of a maximum number of fellow countrymen.

"That the war was not ended immediately, simultaneously in the west and in the east is to be explained by this reason alone. We end this gravest hour of the German nation and its Reich.

MOURNING THE FALLEN

"In this gravest hour of the German nation and its Reich, we bow in deep reverence before the dead of this war.

"Their sacrifices place the highest obligations on us. Our sympathy goes first to our soldiers. It goes out above all to the wounded, the bereaved and to all on whom this struggle has inflicted blows.

"No one must be under any illusions about the severity of the terms to be imposed on the German people by our enemies. We must now face our fate squarely and unquestioningly.

TOMORROW'S CHALLENGES

"Nobody can be in any doubt that the future will be difficult for each one of us and will exact sacrifices from us in every sphere.

"We must accept this burden and stand loyally by the obligations we have undertaken. But we must not despair and fall into mute resignation.

"Once again we must set ourselves a path through the dark future. These are the factors guaranteeing the best state: unity, justice and liberty.

"From the collapse of the past let us preserve and save one thing -- unity, the ideas of the national community, which in the years of war have found their highest expression in the spirit of comradeship at the front and readiness to help one another in all the distress that has inflicted the homeland.

"Shall we retain this unity and not again split under the stress? Can we get over the future hard times? We must make right the basis of our nation. In our nation justice should be the supreme law and the guiding principle.

"We must also recognize law as the basis for all relations between the nations: we must recognize it and respect it from inner conviction.

"Respect for concluded treaties will be as sacred as the aim of our nation to belong to the European family of nations as a member of which we want to mobilize all human moral and material forces in order to heal the dreadful wounds of which the war has caused.

"Then we may hope that the atmosphere of hatred which today surrounds Germany all over the world will give place to a reconciliation among the nations."

The leaders of the three major Allies, from left to right, British Prime Minister Winston Churchill, [illegible] Premier Joseph Stalin.

A season of sorrow, a season of joy; significant events of past four months

The events over the past few months have certainly reshaped the world's history. April 12 U.S. President Franklin D. Roosevelt passed away. His vice president, Harry S. Truman, was soon sworn in and became the 33rd president of the United States.

The former president had complained of "a terrific headache" while sitting for a portrait in Warm Springs, Ga. The 63-year-old man was pronounced dead of a cere-[illegible]

Roosevelt's [illegible] was followed later in the month with the execution of Italy's former Il Duce, Benito Mussolini.

The former dictator was shot by partisans after which he was taken to Milan in a furniture van and dumped in the street. Residents of the town fought to have the right to spit on their former leader.

May 2, Adolf Hitler and Joseph Goebbels reportedly committed suicide.

Their loss seemed to magnify the futility of the German war effort, and four days later the Germans had surrendered.

Days prior to the anniversary of America's independence, Col. Frank Howley led the liberating troops from the U.S. into Germany's capitol city, Berlin.

EDITOR'S NOTE

The U.S. Forces, headquartered and run by the Group Control Council (the first military headquarters in Berlin) have begun their presence here in Berlin, and it will be our mission here at *The Grooper* to provide American troops with the information and entertainment needed to help ensure that, while temporarily in Berlin, you will have all the news from Berlin, both local and military-oriented.

We will also update you on leisure-time activities and be a vital source of other community information.

Col. Howley leads U.S. troops into city

by Charles Kypper
July 2, 1945

Col. Frank Howley led a contingent of American military personnel into the devastated city yesterday. The Soviets, who had been in sole control of the city since April had refused to allow Americans or the British to enter their sector of occupation.

Having been unable to reconnoiter their sector before finally being permitted to move into it, hundreds of officers and soldiers had to stay amidst the ruins. Many wound up sleeping in the Grunewald, a large [illegible] in the western portion of Berlin. The initial but determined U.S. penetration into the war-ravaged city was only allowed by the Soviet occupation authorities as trade-off.

The U.S. had several bargaining chips when faced with the Soviet refusal to allow the 2nd Armor Division to transit the Soviet zone of occupation and take up its occupation duties in Berlin. Whether the Soviet refusal was due simply to an intransigence born of deep-seated mistrust of the Allies' intentions, to a desire to hold out for a quid pro quo, or to more prosaic reasons, the removal of the 7th Armor Division from the Soviet sector of Germany was the price paid to get American occupation troops in Berlin.

The 7th has moved into garrison in the region northwest of Leipzig, and there President Harry Truman is holding until today. It is the last American unit to be stationed on territory in the Soviet zone.

By July 4, Maj. Gen. Floyd Parks, the American commandant, together with elements of the 2nd Armored Division, will occupy the American sector in the southwestern districts of the city.

Ceremonies will be held to mark the assumption of occupational duties. One is going to be at the Telefunken electronics factory (*now McNair Barracks*). Sherman tanks of the "Hell on Wheels" division will line up opposite two companies of the Soviet Army.

The Grooper: First Edition July 28, 1945 (later renamed The Berlin Observer)

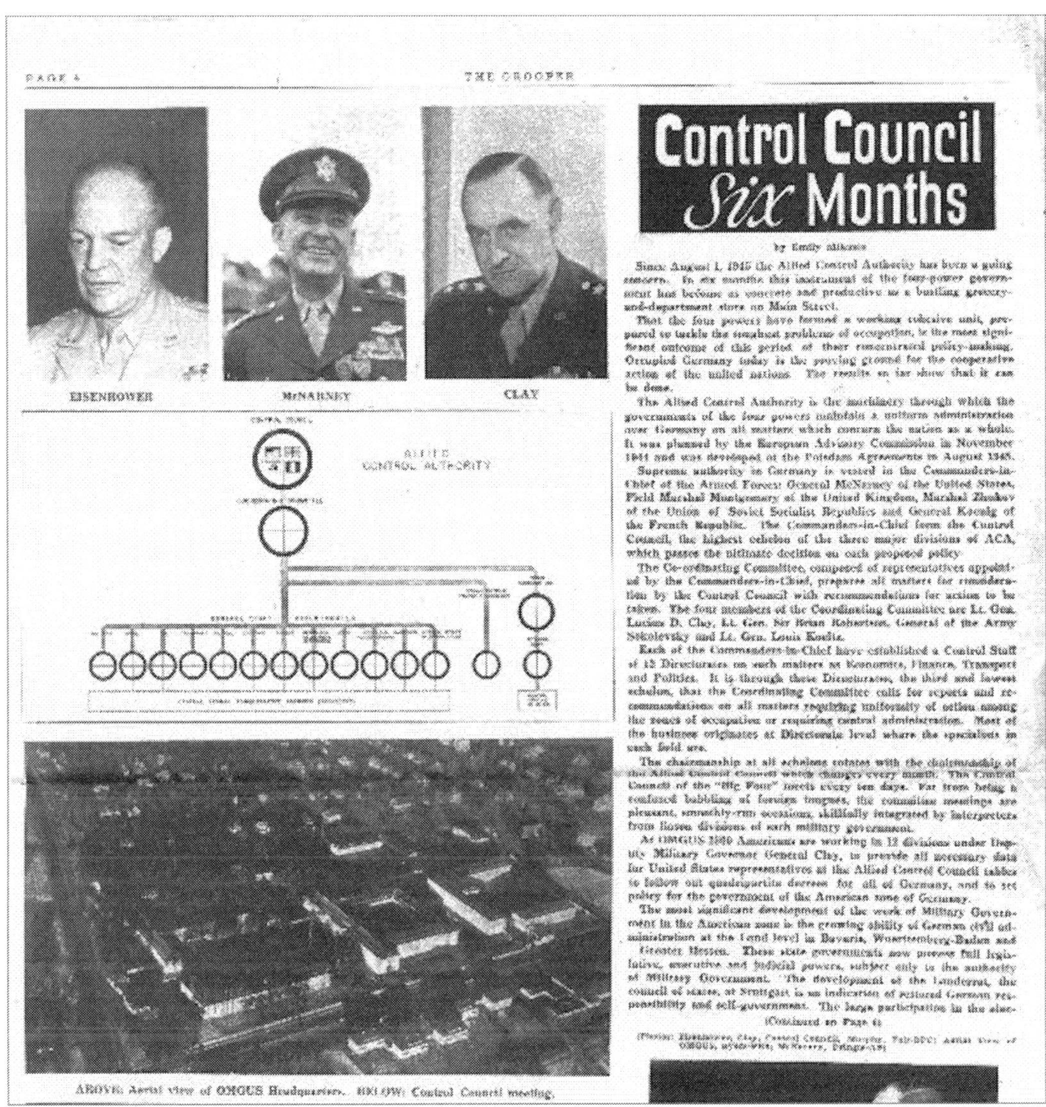

EISENHOWER McNARNEY CLAY

Control Council *Six* Months

by Emily [illegible]

Since August 1, 1945 the Allied Control Authority has been a going concern. In six months this instrument of the four-power government has become as concrete and productive as a bustling grocery-and-department store on Main Street.

That the four powers have formed a working cohesive unit, prepared to tackle the toughest problems of occupation, is the most significant outcome of this period of their concentrated policy-making. Occupied Germany today is the proving ground for the cooperative action of the united nations. The results so far show that it can be done.

The Allied Control Authority is the machinery through which the governments of the four powers maintain a uniform administration over Germany on all matters which concern the nation as a whole. It was planned by the European Advisory Commission in November 1944 and was developed at the Potsdam Agreements in August 1945.

Supreme authority in Germany is vested in the Commanders-in-Chief of the Armed Forces: General McNarney of the United States, Field Marshal Montgomery of the United Kingdom, Marshal Zhukov of the Union of Soviet Socialist Republics and General Koenig of the French Republic. The Commanders-in-Chief form the Control Council, the highest echelon of the three major divisions of ACA, which passes the ultimate decision on each proposed policy.

The Co-ordinating Committee, composed of representatives appointed by the Commanders-in-Chief, prepares all matters for consideration by the Control Council with recommendations for action to be taken. The four members of the Coordinating Committee are Lt. Gen. Lucius D. Clay, Lt. Gen. Sir Brian Robertson, General of the Army Sokolovsky and Lt. Gen. Louis Koeltz.

Each of the Commanders-in-Chief have established a Control Staff of 12 Directorates on such matters as Economics, Finance, Transport and Politics. It is through these Directorates, the third and lowest echelon, that the Coordinating Committee calls for reports and recommendations on all matters requiring uniformity of action among the zones of occupation or requiring central administration. Most of the business originates at Directorate level where the specialists in each field are.

The chairmanship at all echelons rotates with the chairmanship of the Allied Control Council which changes every month. The Control Council of the "Big Four" meets every ten days. Far from being a confused babbling of foreign tongues, the committee meetings are pleasant, smoothly-run occasions, skillfully integrated by interpreters from liaison divisions of each military government.

At OMGUS 1860 Americans are working in 12 divisions under Deputy Military Governor General Clay, to provide all necessary data for United States representatives at the Allied Control Council tables to follow out quadripartite decrees for all of Germany, and to set policy for the government of the American zone of Germany.

The most significant development of the work of Military Government in the American zone is the growing ability of German civil administration at the Land level in Bavaria, Wuerttemberg-Baden and Greater Hessen. These state governments now possess full legislative, executive and judicial powers, subject only to the authority of Military Government. The development of the Länderrat, the council of states, at Stuttgart is an indication of restored German responsibility and self-government. The large participation in the elec-

(Continued on Page 6)

(Photos: Eisenhower, Clay, Control Council, [illegible]; Aerial View of OMGUS, [illegible]; McNarney, [illegible])

ABOVE: Aerial view of OMGUS Headquarters. BELOW: Control Council meeting.

Control Council: the US Command Structure 1946

OMGUS OBSERVER

VOL. II, NO. 21 WEEKLY NEWSPAPER, OFFICE OF MILITARY GOVERNMENT FOR GERMANY (U.S.) ✦ BERLIN, MAY 24, 1946

Select Berlin School House For Dependents' Children

Selection of the public school for minor dependents of US occupation personnel was divulged by the American School Board here this week when the school building at 6—8 Im Gehege, former Gertrauden Schule was chosen.

The school's locale and initial groundwork plans for the model to be established in Berlin were approved by Maj. Gen. Frank A. Keating, Commanding General. BD Headquarters.

Equipped to provide for 450 grammar school students and 150 high school students, the School was chosen for its central location and excellent facilities from a group of 12 buildings that were reviewed by the School Board.

The large modern school requisitioned by OMGUS provides 38 school rooms, eight lavatories, nine laboratories, three lecture, halls, a large gymnasium and playground.

Accomodating pupils of both elementary and high school level, it will be called the American Public Grade School, and the American Public High School of Berlin.

The ultimate School Board shall consist of five members, three to be elected by popular vote of the members of the American Community, one to be appointed by the Deputy Military Governor, OMGUS, and one to be appointed by the Commanding

(Continued on Page 8)

School Selected

(Continued from Page 3)

The term of office of each member shall be one year from the election date or appointment. The first regular school board will be constituted on or before August 1, and subsequent elections will be held on or before May 1 of each year.

Subject to ET directives, the School Board will be responsible for employment of all personnel required for the efficient operation and administration of APS, Berlin.

Their final approval will be necessary for the curriculum of each school, textbooks, provisions for libraries, school buildings and upkeep, student welfare — including adquate recreational and health and the development of community school activities.

While the War Department has stated that it assumes no obligation for the schooling of dependent children, USFET recommended reconsideration of this policy and has submitted a request for funds to support the program.

Non-appropriated funds available to the ET will provide interim funds to carry on initial phases of planning and procurement until such time as specified funds are available.

As an operating agency of USFET, a Dependents Schools Service has been established to plan in detail the school program and to supervise its operation. In serving as the coordinating agency on all school problems, periodic field visits to community schools will be made by supervisors.

In the general outline of the proposed school system, the model schools are to meet or exceed American standards in offering a well-rounded curriculum. Each military community where children of school age are present will have a civilian-staffed school varying in size and type from a one-teacher school for elementary grades to a "graded" school from kindergarten through 12 grades.

The Dependents Schools Service has provided an advisory service to aid parents and students in securing information on private schools and colleges in other countries such as Switzerland, France or England.

A central teacher and placement agency has been established to select teachers, giving first preference to those now in the ET; others will be recruited from the States.

Berlin Observer May 24, 1946- Announcing a New High School for Dependents in Berlin

Thomas A. Robert School October 29, 1946

NEW HIGH SCHOOL IN BERLIN
BERLIN, GERMANY.--THE THOMAS A. ROBERT HIGH SCHOOL, SITUATED AT 6-8 IMGEHEGE STRASSE IN THE OMGUS AMERICAN SECTOR, OPENED RECENTLY WITH AN ENROLLMENT OF 200 STUDENTS. THE SCHOOL OF WHICH EDWIN M. BOYNE, FORMERLY OF THE MICHIGAN GENERAL STATE COLLEGE IS PRINCIPAL WAS NAMED AFTER AN AMERICAN COLONEL WHO WAS KILLED IN LESSAY, NORMANDY, FRANCE. IT HAS 10 AMERICAN TEACHERS AND SEVERAL GERMAN INSTRUCTORS.

KEN815407.......................NEW YORK BUREAU
THIS IS A GENERAL VIEW OF THE MESS HALL IN THE SCHOOL BUILDING WHERE STUDENTS HAVE THEIR LUNCH.
PHOTO BY REGINALD KENNY, ACME CORRESPONDENT.
CREDIT (ACME)
NY CHI CEP 10/29/46 (JS)

The First Berlin Brat Graduate- 1946

American Sector- Kaiser Wilhelm Memorial Church in background, 1946

I was in the first group of students at Thomas A. Roberts High School in Berlin. I arrived in Berlin in 1946 in the early summer and left in 1947 in the fall. So, I was there for almost a year and a half. Being age 17, I only had half a year of high school left before graduation. So I only went to the school as a senior for the last 6 months, from September to December. I left the school in December, which was half of their school year and attended the American University of Berlin. Berlin in those days was a very destroyed city. A very, very, destroyed city. In the summer time in 1946 I remember specifically the stench that was in the city because of the rubble under which hundreds of thousands of people were probably buried. That was not a very pleasant time during that first summer.

In school, I gained some friendships and enjoyed them immensely.

There were only seven or eight students in the graduating class. Most of whom became very close friends. In those days we didn't have much in the way of sports programs. It was mostly social gatherings that we attended. I was involved in music, I played the tenor sax and the drums. I was fairly well known for that. And for dancing; the young ladies I was associated with seemed to thoroughly enjoy the dancing that we did at the officers' club. Between that and studying was about all the activities in those days.

It was not a very formal way of life because of the fact that there was not much in the way of recreational facilities for us. And the fact that being within the Russian zone even though we were in the American Sector, it was difficult to get around. There was not much in the way of transportation, except for the U-bahn, which was the underground metro that was in operation during my time.

Ruins of the Reichstag building, 1946

Other than going down and looking at the destruction and learning what the Hitler regime was all about, there wasn't a great deal of activity, except for the fact that from time to time we were asked to participate in some functions.

For instance, there was an American publication called "Calling all Girls." Three of my friends and I went down with the writers and photographers to the Soviet– I forgot what they call it– inside of the American Sector, just inside the Brandenburg Gate. It was a Soviet facility that honored the Soviet Union and the Soviet Army[Soviet War Memorial]. One was quite aware of the fact that the Soviet soldiers were extremely interested in collecting watches. And you would see from time to time one with three or four, five or six watches if he had been able to gather the Marks that was needed to get them, or cigarettes.

General Clay's wife ran a kind of a barter facility where you could go in with cartons of cigarettes and use them to exchange for things you might want. Bartering in those days with the Germans was something that happened, it was probably not legal from the perspective of the US government, but it went on all the time. And if one had cigarettes, why, one could buy just about anything. We had scrip, which was a currency developed and printed by the U.S. government because we did not get any money in German Marks– we were paid in military scrip.

Unfortunately somebody, I'm not sure who, allowed the Soviet Union to acquire some of these plates... for printing the scrip. The only difference between the American scrip and those that the Soviet Union printed and paid their troops with, was a little dash before the serial number on the scrip. I was quite interested in that because of my love for collecting. I collected American and Soviet scrip, as well as German coins over the period of the Hitler regime which I still have–which is over 66 years.

Soviet War Memorial, Tiergarten

There was a lot of tension because we would get rumors that the Soviets would come into the American Sector and take it over because they didn't like the fact that within the Soviet zone of Germany, the Americans, the British and the French had their own little sectors of Berlin. It was a quadripartite city at that time. There was also a severe problem within the American Sector and I'm sure within the other sectors, with DPs or what are known as displaced persons– people that had been gathered by the German troops and in a lot of cases put in prisons or mental hospitals or other forms of keeping them separate from the German population.

The minute the war was over and these areas were open, these people came out into the population and had no real place to go, because they were Poles, or various other groups that Hitler's regime had taken over. They had been transported hundreds of miles from their homelands. They had no money, no facilities, no place to sleep. When I ended up in the hospital I became very aware of some of the problems of these people: they were fighting, getting weapons, cutting each other with knives and anything they could get a hold of to get money. It wasn't a pleasant time in Germany. You couldn't really supervise martial law, I'm sure there was, I don't remember really. These people were nomads… just there, hiding and going out at night. Whenever there are problems of that type you get murders...any sort of unfortunate situations. I didn't have a curfew despite the dangers.

The class that I was in had a ceremony in June or July of '47, which I did attend, but being the only one that graduated or got their diploma, walking papers or whatever you want to call it at the end of '46 there wasn't any one that was going to have a big ceremony for me.

This account is a transcription of the video interview with Mr. Donald Mathes.

Donald Mathes, Class of 1946
1946-1947

John Wynn class picture 1946-47

A Reminiscence of Berlin Germany in 1946

My father had preceded us to Germany as a "manpower specialist" in the Occupational Military Government, US known as OMGUS. When we received notification that we were to join him in Berlin, we– my mother and we three boys– were living in Dallas, Texas. We received all the necessary inoculations (how very, very many!) from the Public Health Service prior to our driving to New York to board the ship for the trip to Germany. My aunt drove my mother and my two brothers to the New York Port of Embarkation to board the General C. C. Ballou en route to Bremerhaven.

Pleasantly, I remember having the privilege of going to see Finian's Rainbow on Broadway prior to our departure– my aunt had attended Columbia in the early '30's and had some familiarity with New York. As an aside, I especially remember the Murphy bed that pulled down out of the wall in our hotel room, the excitement of eating at the Automat, and of course the obligatory Empire State Building tour and a visit to Chinatown - truly very heady stuff for an eight year old kid from Texas!

Boarding the General C.C. Ballou it seems as though there may have been a problem with our ticketing. We were first berthed below decks separated from my mother and then subsequently moved to a stateroom on the boat deck (the lowest deck below which there was no open railings to the sea). The crew was nice, sharing bottled COKE!– a commodity considered unusual and almost rare at the time.

The crossing was exciting. We– my older and younger brother– played in the upper deck lounge which had as furnishings, large leather covered loungers that had glides permitting us to "race" the heavy chairs by sliding on the linoleum from one side to the other as the ship rolled from side to side almost violently. Friendly seamen fashioned rope harnesses to be tied to my younger brother for his safety while on the deck during the heavy seas.

As we approached the English Channel, we apparently passed through a very heavy weather front that caused the ship to roll severely from side-to-side permitting seawater to come into the interior passage way. The stateroom door jammed. The rope which had secured the metal crib to the bunks in the stateroom came loose and allowed the crib– complete with my younger brother– to wheel freely about the cabin. We unscrewed the lower part of the louvered door in time to see a sailor sloshing down the passage way tying on his life vest and telling us to stay in our cabin!

The next morning we surveyed the damage to the ship. At least one of the large cork/canvas life rafts had come loose and was dangling by a few ropes. A small life boat had come loose at one end and had smashed into the superstructure of the upper decks. We were a real wreck in the eyes of a small child who thought this was terribly exciting! Arriving in Bremerhaven, we were met by my father who escorted us to what I think was a genuine Wagon-Lits sleeper car for the nighttime trip to Berlin.

My next memory was of the Christmas tree at our 61A Im Dol Strasse home. The tree had small candles (not lights!) on the branches. There were, of course, many presents including a train set and so on.

Attending the dependents school was exciting also. There was a fairly large gymnasium with one wall covered with wooden bars/rods running the length and used apparently for exercises of some sort. We merely climbed up and down on them. From this room we were sorted into classes. Our desks were fixed to the floor in rows and resembled the standard school rooms which we had left behind in Texas.

Memories of school trips are sketchy. It seems as though we were given transportation in vans/ambulances marked with the standard Red Cross. We would sit in rows against the walls. If there was any co-mingling with small German children, there was a great reluctance for these other children to board the enclosed ambulances until the dependent children got in!

We had a piano teacher who came to the house for lessons which continued into the spring of '47. There was an apparent polio scare which terminated the piano lessons. We then seemed to have minimal contact with others. I remember in particular the German barber who would come to the house with his hand-operated hair clippers which invariably painfully pulled my hair. When the barber would arrive, he would click his heels, bow slightly in greeting and was most polite!

There were no standing trees in the Tiergarten. Most of the downtown

Berlin streets were impassable with rubble. We would approach an intersection and have to look down the street to determine if it was passable. It seems as though there were a large number of DPs (displaced persons) on the streets cleaning and stacking bricks. For many Germans, transportation was by charcoal powered trucks/vehicles with a hopper mounted behind the cab of the vehicle, unusual three-wheeled conveyances with sort of a ratcheting steering front wheel from time-to-time, and of course bicycles everywhere.

While there were signs at intersections identifying which of the four zones we were entering or leaving, there were no physical barriers or checkpoints to pass through. At night, uniformed US MPs with white helmets patrolled our neighborhood on foot.

Johnny with a school teacher

The black market was incredible. Germans would pass by the house with prized possessions in hand wagons offering them for barter—especially for coffee and/or cigarettes. Army tins of peanut butter and other food items were also highly sought-out commodities. A special treat was the infrequent arrival of real milk from the commissary flown in from Denmark(?).

Sundays were special when we got to go to Truman Hall for lunch. There would usually be a piano, violin and cello playing classical music. By the same token, the infrequent visits to General Clay's office area were exciting with the entry into a walled and gated parking courtyard. We were required to have a cook, a maid, and a fireman (for the coal fired heating system in the basement). The heating system was located at the opposite end of the house from the bomb shelter below the kitchen.

We felt safe going anywhere on our bicycles. The colonel next door had a son about my age. Both he and I once wandered too far on our bicycles on the far side of a large lake in the late afternoon; we were eventually picked up by a Russian weapons carrier– bicycles and all– and driven home with no fanfare!

One poignant event took place when a German woman with a disfigured child spat at me and my friend. She was standing on a street corner and we were on bicycles. At this age I had mastered German to the extent that I often served as a translator for the family in general; I recall that the woman was angry and held us indirectly responsible for the wartime injuries to her child.

Despite the admonitions especially of our mother, we would scour ruins for abandoned weaponry to play with not realizing the dangers to which we were foolishly exposing ourselves. Grease guns made a clattering sound– sort of like tin. Anything we brought home would be confiscated and disposed of quickly never to be seen again. Fortunately we never played with live ammunition!

Although we traveled by car out of Berlin from time to time without severe restrictions, we apparently did have to have travel orders. Our final departure from Berlin was marked by the necessity to travel in a sanctioned Red Cross caravan on the Autobahn en route to Frankfurt– things must have finally become so strained that we were no longer 'welcomed' by the

Russians. The process must have taken a while because we were packed up by Army transportation which constructed fairly heavy wooden shipping crates and cushioned fragile contents with excelsior.

John Thomas Wynn, Class of 1956
1946-1947

The trees are gone but the black market continues at the Tiergarten in the shadow of the Reichstag.

Black Market scene-- Berlin Observer February 16, 1946

Brat Life in Post-War Berlin

Sandra Serbin Dresdner's birthday party January 1947

I flew to Berlin by myself in November 1946. I was 7 years old but my mother was too ill to care for me and my father wanted me in Berlin with him. He had been discharged from active service as a lieutenant in Berlin and immediately got a job with the Allied Control Authority.

The city was largely destroyed– rubble everywhere, with Germans clearing the rubble and behaving in a very servile way toward us. I was aware that we were 'the conquerors,' my childish term for the earliest days of the occupation. I remember I also had most of my clothes made by tailors there– I had a "Bavarian costume" and all of my friends had little suits made from army uniform material. But we also obtained new clothes for me at some sort of bartering location (possibly at the PX) which I believe had been established specifically to provide for increasing numbers of rapidly growing dependent children. Electricity was rationed and of course in the American Sector we got ours at night.

When I first arrived in Berlin, my father was sharing a large house at 4A Am Hirschsprung Strasse--just around the corner from the Thomas A. Roberts school-- with a number of other gentlemen. Homes were assigned to families according to rank, and we soon found a house on Irmgard Strasse in the Zelendorf section and we were also provided with two people in help as well as a 'fireman.' This was a gentleman who lived in the basement and was responsible for keeping the coal furnace going. He also tended a large garden and kept my father's car polished to a high sheen.

Our other help was a maid/cook and my 'governess' Annalise, who took care of me and who would often take me and my friends to the Wannsee to swim or to Titania Palast on Sunday mornings. My understanding was that the army provided this free help to deal with the unemployment problem after the war. I should also add that Titania Palast was the only suitable venue for music or movies and so the operas and concerts were generally held in the mornings while the more popular events were given a more desirable time slot!

We attended the first concert conducted by Wilhelm Furtwängler, the great German conductor who was slated to replace Toscanini at the NY Philharmonic until he was accused of being a Nazi party member. It was an auspicious event, but not politically correct for Americans to attend. Of course he got a standing ovation, but not from the few Americans scattered through the audience who conspicuously held their seats and their hands. Remarkably, years later, I was in touch with another Brat who told me he was at the same concert, he even has the program from that performance!

My birthday was in January; my dad arranged a birthday party for me at Harnack House and invited my whole class. It was like being in a fairy tale compared to my life until then. Suddenly, it was as if we were rich! -- officer's clubs, tennis lessons, riding lessons, horse shows at ARAB (American Riding Association of Berlin) and summer excursions all over Europe. My father was a violinist and a photographer. He bought a fair number of cameras and instruments from Germans living in bombed out, formerly luxurious, apartments on the Ku'damm, with cigarettes and coffee sent to us by family in the States.

When we visited Germans they were always bundled up in their homes against the cold. I remember dimly lit , large apartments with high ceilings and huge windows covered by heavy drapes. Even at that age I recognized a kind of faded glamour and was enchanted by the graciousness of our hosts. Once, when I commented to my father upon leaving about how nice these people were, he said, dismissively, under his breath, "They're all anti-Semites." My father was Jewish of Russian descent, but the fact was that he appreciated all European culture and wanted to imbue me with those same standards.

Sandra reading a birthday card, January 1947

The Allied Control Authority was housed in the Kammergericht building, which I believe was the supreme court of the state of Prussia, and it was located in the American Sector. One entered the building into a large rotunda and from the balcony straight ahead hung the four flags of the four occupying powers. The management of the building itself was rotated monthly among them and the flags were moved as well so that the flag on the end informed you of the country in charge at any given time.

Each month there would be movies, dinner menus and other events provided by that country. In the dining room, the dishes were white with images of the four flags arranged around the rim. I believe that other countries had offices there as well and once my father held a chamber music evening at our house to which he invited an international array of guests. He had asked them to each wear their dress uniforms. I remember coming downstairs and seeing the large marble table in our foyer covered with ceremonial hats from half a dozen countries.

I took piano lessons in Berlin from a Frau Kaufman two times a week. She was very old- a fine pianist really -and she studied as a young girl with Franz Liszt (or at least I was told). I had to practice daily and Annalise sat with me to make certain that I did.

My riding instructor was Herr Kürler. Once I had a bad accident- a horse kicked my leg after I was thrown, breaking it. I was alone at the stable when it happened; I was taken to the hospital in the back of a Volkswagen. I was so scared that my father would be angry– but when he came to the hospital, he said I'd be back on a horse the day my cast came off. I have a picture of myself (in a dress!) on a horse next to Herr Kürler– taken that first day back. I was indeed scared, but learned that very important life lesson.

My favorite horses were Weisse Flieger, (White Flyer, a jumper) Platzregen, (Thunderstorm, an older horse who purportedly escaped three times from his captors during the war and found his way back to the barn which was his home!) and Sundae, the horse who took me to a very proud yellow ribbon at an ARAB horse show. As I recall, a single ride was 50 cents, and a month's membership was five dollars at the American Riding Association of Berlin.

Sandra and Herr Kürler, April 25, 1948

Besides riding, the most wonderful thing about those years was my collie dog Shep. I adored that dog; he came everywhere with me, even to school on a couple of occasions. He met me at the bus stop every day and when I was brought home from the hospital with that broken leg, he would not leave my room and actually growled at Annalise or my father when they came to take care of me.

Shep was a casualty of the Airlift. When the Airlift began in '48 the planes started coming in overhead every three minutes. The airport was right in the middle of the city so we were aware of the constant din. I certainly didn't understand what it was all about except that cordial relationships with Russian friends came to an end.

The only food shortage I recall is of bananas, but in November of 1948 my father decided to bring me home. I recall being told that things were getting "hairy," but it wasn't until I was an adult that I came to learn about the anxiety in the city at that time because winter was approaching and the problem was going to be bringing in enough coal to get through those next cold months.

My father told me we were only allowed to take 70lbs of baggage with us, and Shep weighed almost that much and would be considered baggage. But he promised that on one of the many trips in and out of the city which he was going to have to make, he would bring the dog with him and send him home to me.

And so we left, in one of those troop planes with canvas seats slung along each side. From Frankfurt we made our way to Bremerhaven, from there we sailed home on the USS General George Washington Goethals. The ship docked in Brooklyn and a bus took us into Manhattan through Times Square. The lights were astounding to me; I didn't remember them at all, and had only the hollowed out city of Berlin in my memory by then.

My father never did send Shep to me, and to this day my children point out that I have more pictures of Shep on my wall than of my grandchildren.

Sandra Serbin Dresdner,
Class of 1956
1946-1948

Sandra at the wedding of a British friend, February 1947

Postscript-

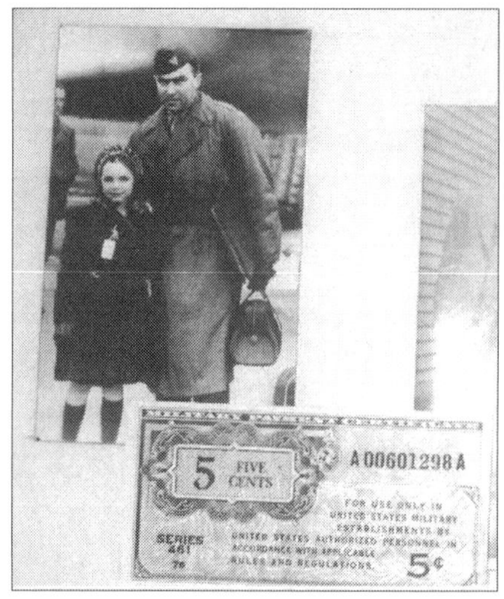

When my father died, I compiled memorabilia from his life. This is a picture which was taken by a reporter for the ***Berlin Observer*** *at the airport in Frankfurt when I arrived. Apparently, I was the youngest dependent to have travelled alone to date. I was to fly to Berlin but the flight terminated in Frankfurt because of the weather.*

Meanwhile my father, who was in Berlin, had been following the flight all the way (it was a three day trip: to Gander [New Foundland], then to Shannon [Ireland], then to Amsterdam, and--surprise!--to Frankfurt) and was mildly frantic because he now had to get to Frankfurt before me. He couldn't fly out either, because of the weather. Ultimately, he took a train, made it in time, and then we proceeded back to the train station for the last leg of the trip.

At the station, I was wandering around the central kiosk and tried to purchase some gum or something with 50 cents I had left over from the dollar my aunt had given me at LaGuardia. For some inexplicable reason, during the layover at Gander I had spent half of it on Christmas Seals. The change I was given looked somewhat strange to me and when I queried the cashier she explained that it was Canadian money, but assured me it could 'buy stuff.' Well, imagine my distress upon learning that that was not true! Thus, learning about military scrip was a first lesson about life in this strange new place. As I recall, it was replaced with new issues more than once—I thought because of counterfeiting. I always was pretty pleased with myself for making that trip alone when I was only seven, but years later when this photograph surfaced, I was mortified to see that I was wearing a tag, and that I had been shipped over like a piece of baggage!

The original Student Body which assembled on October 14, 1946 consisted of thirty-three students. The number has risen slowly but surely to sixty.

Original Student Body- Oct. 14, 1946

The original Student Body which assembled on October 14, 1946 consisted of thirty-three students. The number has risen slowly but surely to sixty.

What was it like living in Berlin during the Cold War?

In October 1947, soon after we arrived, the Thomas A. Roberts School opened. The high school had 30 students. The school grew, as more dependents arrived, but it was never very large while I was there. Our teachers were Americans except for a German physics teacher, who struggled to make us understand that difficult science, lecturing to five or six of us from the front of a high tiered classroom. The class was always just before lunch, which didn't help our attention span. Lunch was good Army food, a hot meal served on metal trays.

There were not enough students in the high school to form sports teams, but there were American Army teams competing with each other in the huge stadium built by Hitler for the 1936 Olympics. Two of our high school classmates, Gloria and Dixie, had been cheerleaders in the States, and Gloria managed to teach a few of us various cheers, adapted from her Wisconsin high school, substituting "Berlin" for "Black River Falls."

Wearing black skirts and white sweaters, we went to the cavernous stadium and led cheering for a tiny group of soldiers. We sat bunched together in the mammoth space hoping to encourage the Berlin football team of U.S. soldiers playing on the field. It was always dark by the time the game was over, and it was always cold.

We took field trips on Saturday or Sunday to German sights of interest, including palaces at Potsdam, where we donned felt slippers and padded around ornate rooms in freezing cold. When Christmastime came, we enjoyed learning German carols, and even put on a performance marching into the school auditorium draped in white sheets singing the carols.

In January, I had a different experience from many of the students in school when I developed an eye inflammation (chorioretinitis) and was put on bed rest at home for 4 months. I was excused from school and, though some lessons were sent home, I couldn't really do them, since I couldn't use my eyes. Through some German friends, my mother found a tutor who came almost every day. She was an elderly lady named Frau von Thieling, the 'von' denoting noble descent.

Frau von Thieling told us that sometime in the 1930's, when they saw where Adolph Hitler was leading Germany, her relatives held a family conference. They concluded that, although they did not like what was happening, they really couldn't do anything about it. If they objected or tried to act against it, they would just end up in the concentration camps themselves. Their families would be persecuted and ruined too. It was better to wait and act when they might be effective. We realized that probably such councils and such decisions must have happened all over Germany.

Frau von Thieling believed that the best solution to the problems facing Germany at that time would be a return to the monarchy. She taught me German grammar, literature and folklore– she would bring me lilacs in bloom, which she said meant friendship. She was a very sweet lady, and I enjoyed her visits and instruction.

My father read to me at times, and I had a radio–but the Armed Forces Network was about all I could get on it in English. A few friends came to visit, but they were busy with school, and I wasn't very interesting company. After a bit, I was introduced to another American teenager, also confined to home by some unidentified illness– Cornelia (Connie or Sudy) McDonald. We were quite congenial and visited each other often, including overnight. She had three brothers, John, Ronald (her twin), and Donald. I enjoyed staying at their house and eating dinner with their family. I kept in touch with Sudy for a while, and I have a lovely soup ladle she sent me as a wedding present, but I have now lost track of all of my friends from Berlin except Jane Schnell '48 and Liz Holmer '48.

Berlin Olympic stadium entrance

Liz Holmer ?? Dixie ?? Ruth? ?? Susy Bevier
Cheerleaders
in front of Thomas A Roberts School

Berlin Olympic Stadium w/ U.S. Football Team

?? Dixie ?? ?? ??
Sue Bevier Liz Holmer

Cheerleaders at Olympic Stadium
Ruth ?? Merrillan ?? Dixie ??

When summer came, and school ended, we took a trip to Switzerland as a family. Our steak dinner on the first evening there -- the first real steak in a year– was a revelation! We had a very good vacation, and ended up enrolling me in the École Supérieure de Commerce in Neuchatel, Switzerland. Fellow Brat Jane Schnell and I went there in September 1947, and had concentrated instruction in French, adding it to the German we had learned in Berlin. We enjoyed being there and living with 14 girls of various nationalities in a home with great food and a lot of freedom.

We returned to Berlin for Christmas 1947 vacation, but by spring of 1948 things were heating up politically, and the Airlift was about to begin. My mother, brother George, and I took a trip to Italy at spring vacation. I then returned to Switzerland, but when Mother and George returned to Frankfurt, she decided that the best place for him was in the States and he flew there. Mother returned to Berlin, expecting to slowly pack up so that she could move to Greece, where my father was now working. But the American Army had different ideas for her.

Very soon after she returned to Berlin, she received a call that the Army was sending men to her house to pack her up the next morning. She remonstrated that she was not ready, and was told "Well, it looks like you and a lot of other folks will be up all night." She did what she could and the next morning the packers came, packed all the furniture, china, household goods, etc. Then flew her and all of it out of Berlin within a day– as a test– she was told, to see how quickly Berlin could be evacuated if necessary.

Mother was flown to Frankfurt, where she was met by my father. They both came suddenly to Switzerland to pick me up and whisk us all home for the summer. We were planning to return in the fall– they to

Greece and me to Switzerland. However, when my father visited the government offices where he had worked before going to Europe for 3 years, he was offered a new position there, so he decided to accept it and stay in the States. My mother was very disappointed about not going to Greece, but accepted what it meant to be, at that point, an "Army wife." I, on the other hand, was left with everything back in Switzerland - my unfinished school year, my clothes, and my boyfriend.

Against the advice of their friends, who were certain war was about to break out in Europe (this was summer 1948, the Airlift was in full swing, and many feared war with Russia), my parents agreed that I could return to Switzerland and finish my school year in December, then come home. I had a good final semester, visiting my Swiss boyfriend Tom on several weekends, coming to know his mother, who was German, and came from Berlin! In the 1920's she had met and married his Swiss father in Berlin, where he had a business. They had to leave Berlin shortly after the Nazis came to power, for a police reported that Tom, aged 5,needed discipline, because he was not saying "Heil Hitler" when he was supposed to.

At the end of the semester, I spent Christmas week in England with friends– George Cole, who had worked with my father in Berlin, and his wife Molly– before sailing home to the States. My connections with Berlin have continued over the years, however. I met my husband, Woody Thomas, because he is a cousin of Berlin Brat Jane Schnell. Woody was born in Berlin while his American parents were there in 1929. His father worked there with the Reparations Commission about payments left over from World War I.

Woody and I made a trip to Berlin in 1999, to visit places each of us had been. We visited the apartment building where Woody's parents had lived in 1929, miraculously unscathed by the war while buildings on both sides had been destroyed in the bombing. We were welcomed by the building's owner and the current tenants of the apartment. We went to the house where I and my family had lived, on Shorlemerallee, off Podbielskiallee. We also took the U-bahn, as I had in 1947, and visited the Thomas A. Roberts School, now a German school again. We were welcomed by the principal, who urged us to look around as much as we liked, to stir up my memories of being there. I hope many of you have had similar experiences.

Merrillan Murray Thomas, Class of 1948
1947-1948

***Further Musings from Merrillan*:**

What did it mean to live in Berlin during the Cold War?

It meant, among other things:
...that the Brandenburger Tor (Brandenburg Gate) was a formidable divider between the American Sector and the threatening Russian Sector of Berlin.

...that we went to the opera in the Russian Sector, but felt a little edgy about it.

...that if anyone called "Stoy!" ("Stop!" in Russian) we were to obey immediately.

....that when we drove to other places in Germany, we drove first through the Russian zone, sometimes in a convoy, and never stopped except at one of the outposts along the Autobahn.

... I remember being served hot tea with condensed milk at a British military post while someone looking very frightened stayed in a car in the parking lot. We were

told later that he was a scientist trying to escape to the West.

...that my father sometimes came home from work exhausted and annoyed that nothing was accomplished in a quadripartite session that day, because the Russians had to refer every tiny decision to the Kremlin.

... that we Americans had good food and plenty of it, even though the meat was always canned and the milk– brought from Denmark– looked revolting in green-glass wine bottles. Yet, a German stranger once collapsed on our front steps from hunger.

... that our cook passed food on to her friends at the backdoor; we knew about it, but let it go. They needed it.

...that by just being there as part of the occupying forces we felt resentment from the German population wherever we went.

...frowning angry looks from Germans standing in line to get tickets for the U-Bahn, while we walked right in flashing our identity cards.

...or at a German doctor's office we walked past sick, resentful people waiting while we were ushered in immediately.

"Teenaging: in Berlin, 1947
Berlin Brat Ann Worrell '52 and friend

Teenaging In Berlin 1947-48

German children watching Airlift planes

What can one say about teen-aged life in Berlin during the Cold War? I arrived in Berlin in July 1947, accompanying my father by auto through the Russian zone. We traveled via the Autobahn and finally reached Berlin's Western Sector (American). Enroute, we were ordered by the Russians to drive straight through, not to stop under any conditions, and exit the Russian zone before dark. Flat tires, engine trouble, no excuse; this would have resulted in a quick trip back to the American zone! We made it!

My mother, sister and brother followed later. My father secured quarters in a beautiful home in the Schlachtensee area that had previously been owned by the Mayor of Berlin until the war's end, when taken over by the American Occupation Forces. I made a beeline to the local teen hangout where we met mornings daily for donuts and coffee. Later, transferred to a teen club (Teen Canteen) established for us. Teen life was much the same as in the other German locations– school, sports, dances and parties and all. I fell madly in love with a beautiful girl named Virginia, with the nickname "Bitty." We went steady until we both left Germany in August 1948.

The Berlin Airlift was an event that went down in history as one of the greatest accomplishments in modern history. Imagine, saving a city totally surrounded and isolated from the world by a major blockade forbidding any land entry into the city from the west. A city without fuel and food most certainly would fall! To respond to this blockade, the Allies decided to fly in the life-sustaining needs of a besieged major city. This then, is a description of the teen life and my personal contribution to the effort.

Berlin Airlift planes on tarmac at Tempelhof Airport

At first it was a minor series of annoying events. Westerners were no longer allowed free access to the Eastern Sector of Berlin. The East was totally blocked out: no one in, no one out. Then more serious actions took place. The Russians, who controlled the power plants for Berlin located within their sector, began cutting off power from evening until late in the morning. Any cooking, bathing, washing, etc. requiring power or heated water had to be done during the "on" hours. Teen life became a blackened series of events. No buses, cabs or trains at night. No electricity for light... so "sleepovers" became the partying times. We still partied, and still came together, but without power, only flashlights and kerosene lanterns.

I remember vividly, my father receiving a telephone call as our family sat down to dinner prior to the total blockade. He took the call and then went to his room, returned with helmet and sidearm and told us he must leave for a while. I told my dad that I was going to go with him. He said no, and for the first time and I'm sure the only time, I stood up to my father and insisted. He finally said OK, but I was to stay with the driver and the car the whole time.

We ended up in a rail yard where a young captain approached my dad and told him the Russians were demanding a railway engine they claimed as theirs. We saw the engine surrounded by armed Russian soldiers and a covered 6 by 6 truck with a machine gun crew in the back aimed at the MPs and others guarding the engine.

The Russian major refused to talk with the American because he was of lesser rank. My father approached him and, through an interpreter, told the Russian major that he (my dad) was a colonel and refused to deal with an officer of inferior rank. This was a standoff until a command car arrived and out stepped a Russian officer, obviously of higher rank. The officer was a general but considered of equal rank with my father. They argued back and forth to no avail. The Russian threatened to open fire and with that my father raised his riding crop into the air and suddenly a deafening noise was heard as American tanks moved into position and directed their weapons toward the Russians. The Russian snorted and ranted but shouted something out loud and they loaded onto their vehicles and departed. I like to call this incident, the first "battle" of the Cold War, and I was there!

The harassment continued until the actual blockade began... when the Russians made an American train turn back at the border, not allowing it to enter the Russian zone. The Airlift began.

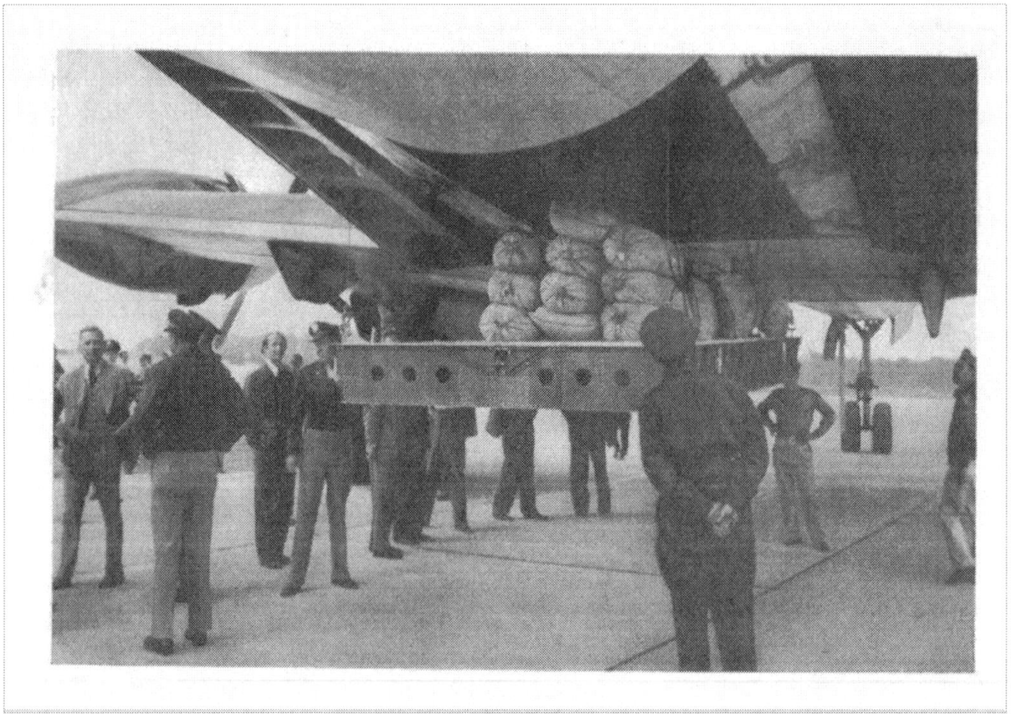

Loaded cargo plane

My father was Transportation Officer in Berlin and in charge of the Tempelhof operation of unloading the planes and seeing that the supplies were transported to designated areas of West Berlin. One day, early on in the "lift," he asked what I was doing after school...as usual, I said "Nuthin," and he replied, "Beginning tomorrow, after school, you will be at Tempelhof helping to unload the cargo. We need all the help we can get."

And so I did. I seemed to have been lucky enough to draw nothing but coal planes. I think I recall unloading flour and other goods, maybe four or five times, but mostly coal. I continued my volunteer work up until the day before I departed to return to the United States.

President Harry Truman and others in Washington D.C. were demanding that the American dependents be evacuated from Berlin ASAP. In fact, I recall he **ordered** us to be evacuated. My mother and several other wives approached the Berlin Commandant and stated flatly that neither the women nor children would leave.

They argued the point that should the American dependents desert the people of West Berlin--that is exactly what the Berliners would believe--and Russian propaganda would most certainly get a lot of mileage on that! Harry Truman backed down and we stayed.

The wives initiated a drive for charity funds by creating a cookbook of donated recipes and called it "Operation Vittles" a cookbook compiled by the Blockaded American Wives of Berlin. It was hard cover and included photos of the Airlift. They also designed note cards depicting the Airlift and sold them as well. I still have a copy of the book in mint condition and one original note card!

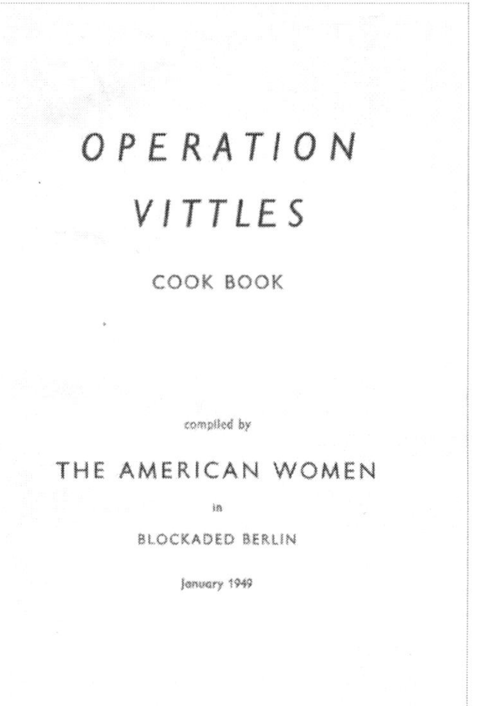

OPERATION
VITTLES
COOK BOOK

compiled by
THE AMERICAN WOMEN
in
BLOCKADED BERLIN
January 1949

Operation Vittles Cookbook- Cover and Title Page

My parents sent me home to attend my senior year and graduate stateside so I would be eligible to be a resident student at the University. My parents sent me home alone, and saw me off as I flew out of Berlin on... of all things...a coal plane! I flew to Rhein-Main, then by train to Bremerhaven, where I boarded a ship to New York, and finally, journeyed by trains west to Eugene, Oregon and my senior year.

I am very proud to have been a part of such an historic event, and I still cherish every moment.

Dan Bunting, Class of 1949
1947-1948
– arrived aboard the "USNS Daniel I Sultan" in April 1946

Dedicated to the happy group of wives who attempted to obtain American meals by slaying the dragons of language, old utensils, ovens sans thermometers, conflicting opinions, etc., ad infinitum . . . and to the many excellent cooks who bore with the puzzling variety in the American diet — the endless series of *"immer was neu ist!"*

"Little Vittles" is what we now call the extra-curricular project of one pilot who began dropping candy, via handkerchief parachutes to the children watching the planes landing at Tempelhof. Thank-you letters began pouring in and more than one asked, "How can we tell which plane is yours?" From then on his plane wiggle-waggled as it circled before landing. There's an unwritten law that says, "For children only!" This was ignored by one grown-up who refused the children entrance to his garden where one little parachute lay. He was immediately and thoroughly dealt with by two hundred assorted German parents and children, thereby clearing up the point forever.

APRICOT SOUFFLÉ

1 C dried apricots
1 C water
4 egg whites (stiffly beaten)
3 T sugar

Soak apricots in water overnight. Cook slowly until tender. Put through sieve. Add sugar to egg whites and beat. Fold in apricot pulp. Pour into buttered casserole, cover and place in pan of hot water. Cook for 1 hour on stove. Before serving, put casserole, with pan of water in oven 5 minutes to brown. (This is also good with a meat course.)

Lucy Smart

34

A late arrival at the cocktail party said, "Dry Martini," to the waiter. The man was back in a flash with three martinis, "Eins—Zwei—Drei!"

BLOCK-ADE

2 cans fruit cocktail
1 C sugar
2 bottles cognac
6 bottles red wine
6 bottles white wine
6 bottles champagne

Put fruit cocktail, sugar and 1 bottle of cognac in glass jar. Allow to ferment for 2 hours. Pour into large container. Add remaining beverage, by bottles, thus: 2 red wine, 2 white wine, 2 champagne, ⅓ cognac. Repeat twice more. Do not stir. 30 minutes before serving add 5 pound piece of ice. Serves: 75.

Dorothy A. Welch

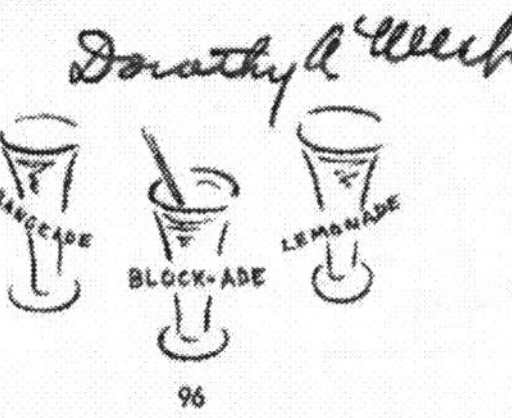

96

FRENCH MILITARY GOVERNMENT

* * *

CHOCOLATE MOULE

1 C sugar
3 eggs separated
4 T and 1½ t cornstarch (or 1 C flour)
4½ squares of chocolate
1 C butter

Mix together sugar, egg yolks and cornstarch or flour. Melt chocolate in small amount of water and add. Cream butter until very soft and add. Beat egg whites until stiff and fold into batter mixture. Pour into 3 inch deep cake pans. Bake. May be iced with frosting made of butter and bitter chocolate.

Oven: 350° Time: 45 minutes

C. Ganeval

77

Operation Vittles Cookbook- Dedication Page (top left) and selected recipes

The Berlin Airlift: An Ode To

T'was 1948 and in Germany, the winter was cold
The Russians had blockaded, a move that was bold.
The Americans, the French, and of course the Brits,
Had met the challenge, and gave Russia the fits.

Their plan was to force the Allies to retreat,
And leave Berlin City for them to mistreat.
The roads had been closed, bridges destroyed,
Railroad tracks dismantled, and totally void.

But their move was too quick, and poorly planned
For the Allies flew over with supplies to land.
They came from all over, the cargo planes,
C-47s, C-54s, and all with great names,
Like "Floozie" and "Dolly," "Marilyn" and "Dames."

Shoulder to shoulder Germans and West Allies
Unloading cargo, and caught the Russians by surprise,
Who would have thought former foes would share
The love for a city; for which they all care.

Day and night the airplanes would fly
Twenty-four seven, but spirits were high.
They carried supplies, food, fuel, how dandy
One pilot alone even "bombed" children candy!

The word spread so fast, everyone tried
Bombing candy too, so no child cried.
Yes, food, fuel, and coal and especially salt
They'd fly in fly out, with no thought to halt.

One glorious day, in May '49, the news was here
The Russians "gave in" after almost a year.
Celebrations exploded, happiness and good cheer,
The blockade was over, Hoorah and hear, hear!
To all who took part, or gave the ultimate price
The gratitude a hundred fold, a thousand and thrice,
For a city was saved and paved the way
For a united Berlin, to be realized one day.
So here's to the Heroes, they know who they are
Berliners remember, they're never too far
They're always remembered with joy and love,
With praise and Thanksgiving, for the gifts from above

Dr. Daniel L. Bunting, Ph.D., Class of 1949 and a "student" Airlift veteran

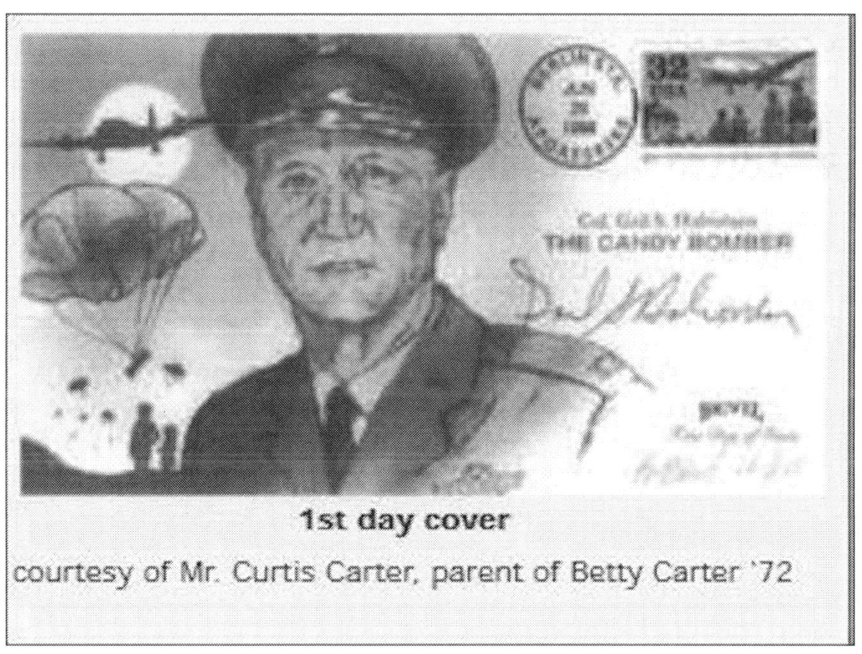

1st day cover

courtesy of Mr. Curtis Carter, parent of Betty Carter '72

2 July 15, 1994
Berlin Observer

Years of grit & glory: the U.S. Army in Berlin

Meals and ideals

Airlift supplies life, liberty, pursuit of happiness

by Dr. Mort Nirenberg and Nicole Hall
Contributing Writers

Berlin's western occupying powers emerged as protective powers after the 1949 airlift. "Operation Vittles" saved 2,250,000 lives faced with the grimness of starvation during the blockade.

A political power struggle between the communist, Soviet sector and the democratic tripartite sectors arose and led to the creation of two competing alliance systems. Increased tension and misinterpretation, along with political and social differences in philosophy would divide Berlin and eventually Germany.

The quadripartite occupation of Germany was created with the intention of democratically securing the country. Yet the fundamental understanding of the "democratic" concept was interpreted differently. As a result, minor decisions which needed to be made by the coalition became chores -- opinions clashed. The provision of supplies to individual zones, the regulation of interzonal commerce and traffic and the cooperation between the zones caused disputes.

Soviet thinking was dominated with strengthening communist politics through the Socialist Unity Party primarily in the Soviet Zone of Occupation.

Rebuilding the war-torn city was not a priority, despite its devastation. In the meantime, the western Allies focused on economic recovery as well as overcoming food and housing shortages.

The Allies decided to act on their own accord. Economic reorganization began with currency reform in the early summer of 1948. A crack in west-east cooperation would soon sever the quadripartite relations.

According to an official American communique of the time "a U.S. . . . military freight train was stopped at Marienborn at approximately 0500, 21 June. Train was not allowed to proceed to Berlin due to the refusal of train commander to permit Soviets to open cars for inspection. At approximately 5 p.m. 22 June, Soviets took over train under threat of arms, attached it to a Soviet locomotive and sent back to Helmstedt -- all this under strong protest of our train commander. ..." The blockade had begun.

On June 23, 1948 the lights dimmed into darkness shortly before midnight. The Soviets cut the electricity. Local power plants could not make up for the energy loss. Six hours later, the complete interdiction of all road and rail traffic between the Western Zones and Berlin follows.

Shortly thereafter, interzonal barge traffic is shut down. The Berlin Blockade is complete -- the Soviets tried to conform western policies to theirs by starving a city.

Berlin children wave at aircraft in a much-reproduced photo which has lost none of its emotional appeal.

From 1948 to 1949 the airborne lifeline that helped feed and clothe the two million residents of West Berlin and the Western Allies stationed in this city, consisted largely of Royal Air Force twin-engine Dakotas with a useful load of just two tons, and America's four-engine C-54 Skymasters with a 14 ton payload.

The planes deployed to Operation Vittles came from as far away as Alaska, Hawaii, Panama, Texas, Montana, the Bermudas, South Africa, Australia and New Zealand. The planes were landing in Berlin every 90 seconds on the average.

The airlift's record day was April 16, 1949 when about 14 thousand tons of supplies arrived aboard 1,383 flights. On that spring day, more than 44 years ago, airplane landed in Berlin every 63 seconds.

It took a work force of 19 thousand, working three eight-hour shifts per day a total of 85 days, to build Tegel Airport whose runway was first operational in November 1948.

Despite the constant droning of aircraft engines and the round the clock hammering and pounding of construction crews, the historical records don't complain much in the way of noise complaints.

The blockade of Berlin was broken not only by the material success of the airlift. In fact, we could argue that the material success reflected the spirit of perseverance.

The determination to preserve Berlin's freedom was shared by those in high places and the so-called common man, woman and child.

This spirit of determination was embodied in such men as General Lucius D. Clay, military governor of the American Zone of Occupation in Germany, Col. (later General) Frank Howley, commandant of American forces in Berlin, and Ernst Reuter, governing mayor of Berlin.

Howley held the commandant's position from December 1947 to August 1949. Thanks to his foresight and forcefulness in ordering large quantities of food and fuel to be stockpiled three months prior to the blockade, Howley helped to avert disastrous shortages during the first weeks of the blockade.

At General Clay's urging, President Harry S. Truman reached the decision to keep United States forces in Berlin and to undertake all steps necessary to overcome the blockade.

General Clay summed up the American position in a letter dated Sept. 6, 1948 to Under Secretary of State William H. Draper, Jr.: "As for us here, we are not discouraged in any sense of the word over our mission to stay in Berlin; in fact, I think each day, we are more proud that we are here."

Clay's pride -- America's pride -- in the Berlin mission was strengthened by the unwavering spirit of the Berliners themselves.

Shortly after the beginning of the blockade Mayor Ernst Reuter spoke for millions of Berliners when he vowed to resist the communist threat. "We lived in such slavery during Adolf Hitler's Reich! We've had enough of it! We don't want a return to it!"

On Sept. 9, 1948, a mere three days after General Clay expressed how proud he was to be in Berlin, more than 300 thousand Berliners came from all four sectors of the city to hear Mayor Reuter's appeal to the world for help.

It wasn't just material help Reuter was asking for but also a "steadfast, indestructible commitment on behalf of those ideals that alone can guarantee our future or indeed secure your own ideals as well!"

When the Soviets lowered the barriers and completely blockaded Berlin on June 24, 1948 (partial, temporary blockades had occurred earlier in the year), most officials were caught off guard. Indecision and unpreparedness had combined to create a serious problem.

First the West had convinced itself that the Soviets would not take the drastic step of blockading the civilian population in West Berlin over the issue of currency reform. When this estimate turned out to be wrong, the Allies doubted whether they could maintain their position in the city.

These doubts were dispelled, however, when it became clear that, even in a war-weary world, the will to stay free had retained its vitality.

With the curtain closing on the Berlin Airlift and Blockade, sounds one act of the Berlin drama. Little did the world know the story hadn't even begun to unfold.

Looking back . . .

"The Candy Bomber," "Uncle Wiggly Wings" and Colonel are just some of the monickers Gail Halvorsen has had over the years.

Halvorsen was made famous during the airlift years by extending the envelope of rations to include candy bars which he air-dropped to waiting, grateful children of Berlin.

The retired Army colonel looks back at his effort today and says, "I volunteered to fly the airlift because I thought it was inhumane of the Soviet Union to starve women and children in West Berlin who already were in need of food.

"By the end of the airlift, I found the German 'Superman' was no different than myself. It's power-hungry men who disrupt human understanding and friendship. It always will be."

Col. (Ret.) Gail Halvorsen recreates his deed of 1948-49 in Bosnia in early 1994.

Halvorsen is now semi-retired and runs a ranch in Provo, Utah.

– Michael Ertel

1945

July 1 -- Col. Frank Howley leads the first American occupying troops into a devastated city.

1948

June -- East Berlin government sanctions supplies into the city, the beginning of the Berlin Blockade.

1949

May -- Allied Operation Vittles, an airlift to airlift food and vital supplies into city, is deemed a success and mission is completed by fall.

Berlin Observer Final Issue- Look Back on the Berlin Airlift

Gail Halvorsen aka The Candy Bomber

BERLIN CANDY BOMBER EPILOGUE by Gail Halvorsen

As I look back at "Operation Little Vittles" and the years that have followed, there is one human characteristic above all others that gave it birth– the silent gratitude of the children at a barbed wire fence in Berlin, July, 1948. They did not beg for chocolate. Flour meant freedom. They would not lower themselves to ask for more. Because not one child begged, thousands received over 21 tons of candy from the sky, or delivered on the ground, over the next 14 months.

Other events are memorable: the excitement as the children chased the parachutes; the letters with heart-felt messages; the drawings; the gifts to crew members on the flight line; the assignment in 1970 for four years as

Commander of Tempelhof Central Airport–a direct result of the Operation; the personal gifts of many descriptions including two Arabian stallions; the personal contact with Peter and Mercedes Wild and other Berlin children now grown; flying with Tim Chopp and crew in "The Spirit of Freedom" since 1994, including the trip to Europe for 69 days in 1998 for the 50th Anniversary celebrations of the Airlift. As a direct result of that trip my high school steady of 1939, Lorraine Pace, found me after all those years and now helps me to carry on after the death of my beloved Alta. So many spiritual and material rewards.

In man's search for fulfillment and happiness, material rewards pale compared to the importance of gratitude, integrity and service before self. Gratitude brings unexpected special blessings, communication is facilitated, understanding is accomplished and progress accelerated. Gratitude, integrity and service to the unfortunate provide more rewards than all things material. They are the foundation upon which hope is born. They provide the strength by which hope endures.

'Uncle Wiggly Wings' connects candies to small parachutes

A victim of the Blockade once told me, "Without hope the soul dies." The Airlift with its dried eggs, dried potatoes, dried milk, coal and even chocolate meant hope for freedom. Freedom was more important than a full stomach or a rare treat. It was hope, not the flour, that gave the West Berliners the strength to carry on. That hope came to full fruition with the fall of the Wall and the reunification of Germany in 1989/1990. Hope prevailed!

General William Tunner was the Airlift genius who made the Airlift a resounding success. The heroes of the Berlin Airlift are the 31 Americans and the 39 British who gave their lives to deliver freedom and democracy to a former enemy. Service to others before self was their mission. It is the only true recipe by which complete fulfillment may be attained in this life. It is one of the core values of the United States Air Force. Today the Air Mobility Command, in the Airlift tradition, launches a mission of mercy every 90 seconds somewhere around the world. The American flag on the aircraft tail is the symbol of hope to those in deep despair from whatever the source of oppression.

October 3, 1948- "Lt. Gail Halvorsen Day" at Tempelhof; Halvorsen throws candy to children from aboard his plane, the "Island of Christmas."

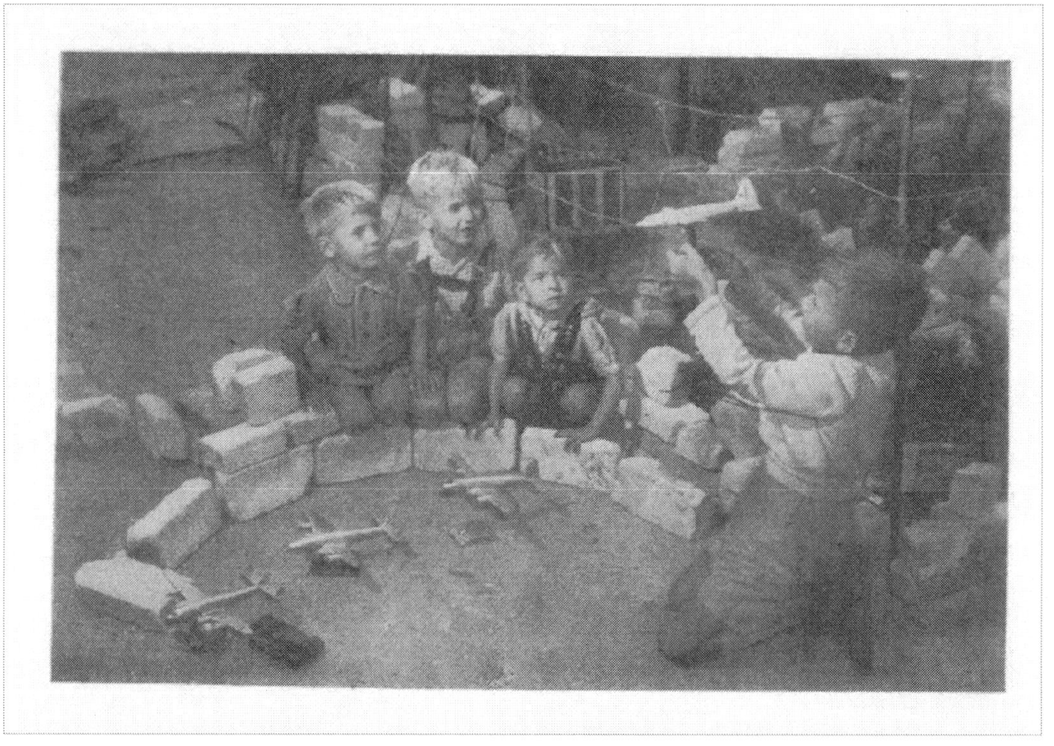

German children play "Airlift"

"Children hold the future of the whole world in their hands. Our children and everyone's children."- Colonel Gail Halvorsen

Chapter 2: The 1950s

"Our policy is directed not against any country or doctrine but against hunger, poverty, desperation and chaos. Its purpose should be the revival of a working economy in the world so as to permit the emergence of political and social conditions in which free institutions can exist."

- General George C. Marshall, from The Marshall Plan Speech

Life in 1950s Berlin

Dad announced he had a choice between Berlin and Alaska. Mom and I voted for Berlin. Knowing how the Army worked, Dad put down his choice as Alaska and we soon made plans to move from Colorado to Berlin. My third grade teacher expressed her concerns about us living "Behind the Iron Curtain" and wrote a good-bye letter that included wishes that someday, "Sheryl will have the home she deserves." Whatever!

The dog, the washing machine, my toy electric oven, the car, and my mom's collection of favorite books got to go to Berlin, but not my collection of comic books. To console me, Dad ordered me a 3 year subscription to Little Lulu comics. It took 10 days for the USS Butner to get to Bremerhaven from NYC. The Duty Train to Berlin was very scary, with the sounds of the mail car being uncoupled and guards boarding the train to check Dad's papers. We traveled at night and were not allowed to raise the window shades. The dog had to stay in quarantine in Bremerhaven, to be retrieved by Dad six weeks later.

Before we could move into our first home on Auf dem Grat, we had to be fingerprinted. Outside that building was our first introduction to German culture-a hurdy gurdy player and his monkey. From our house I was able to walk to Thiel Park and to the Outpost Theater and the PX. For my $1.00 weekly allowance, I could enjoy 2 movies, a grape sucker, and buy one 45 rpm record. On Saturdays, dependent matinees included a cartoon, previews, a serial movie story, and the manager stopping the movie three times to try to quiet down us rowdy Brats.

A year later, we moved to a bigger house on Harnack Strasse. It was a longer walk to and from the theater, so I rode the military bus home. One day I got off at the wrong stop. I found a German policeman who understood little English, but he was able to get me home.

Our third house was at 14 Fischottersteig, a duplex built for US military families. We were the first occupants of that home. On a visit in 2009 we were saddened to see it in disrepair. It appears many of the duplexes were replaced by "Stadt-Villas" (large condos) for the American Embassy.

US dependents were often warned not to cause any 'international incidents.' Although I did my best not to cause any international incidents, one Sunday I dented the rear of a German car with my bicycle in front of the Berlin Command. My parents were not pleased to be called off the golf course, mainly because I was not supposed to be leaving the house that day. The German police were called and I was making a statement to the MP's when my parents arrived. Thankfully, the incident did not take on 'international' proportions.

Dependents had many opportunities for extra-curricular activities. Mom became active with the Girl Scouts. She included German girls in our activities. On a trip to a church in East Berlin, I exchanged addresses with a scout. My pen pal gave her letters to her uncle. He carried the letters across the border and mailed them to me. I, in turn, mailed my letters to her uncle in West Berlin for delivery to her.

American GI's rode on our green school buses; including the buses in the summer that took us from our homes to swimming in Hitler's Olympic pool, back to our homes for lunch, then to TAR for afternoon activities. An enlisted man, LeFevre, who played clarinet with the Berlin Command band, started a band program at the school. I won 200DM playing bingo at the

Harnack House and bought my first clarinet. LeFevre also arranged for some of his fellow band members to accompany us at a recital.

As part of the American Youth Activities program in Berlin, beginners' lessons in the rudiments of swimming have been initiated for the children of the American community. Under the guidance of PFC Jack Parks (in water) the children are receiving instruction in the children's pool at Berlin's Olympic Stadium. (US Army photo)

SEPTEMBER 1952 25

Swimming at the Olympic Pool

Other activities included trips to the American Youth Association (AYA) camps in West Germany and Girl Scout camps in Bavaria. The AYA camp counselors were WACs. The women bounced half dollars off our bunks to make sure they were made up correctly. At Girl Scout camp, we washed in Army helmets supported by tripods made from sticks. The church at Andrews Barracks provided Sunday School and Vacation Bible School activities.

At TAR we were required to take some German language classes in second through sixth grade and German history was added by the time I reached 7th grade. School field trips included the chocolate factory, the Rathaus Schöneberg (with doorless elevators!), the art museum and the tank compound. When dignitaries came to visit on school days, our lessons stopped and we counted the gun salutes to try to guess who was being presented on the parade grounds.

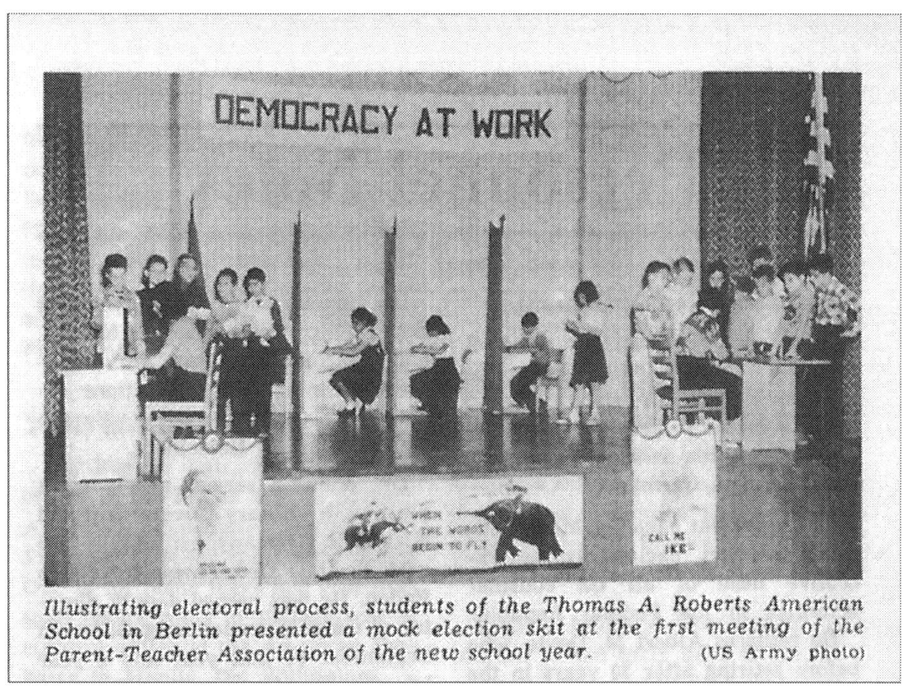

Illustrating electoral process, students of the Thomas A. Roberts American School in Berlin presented a mock election skit at the first meeting of the Parent-Teacher Association of the new school year. (US Army photo)

A typical day for students at the Thomas A. Roberts School (1952)

We were aware of our dangerous surroundings, but had the opportunity to ignore it while having a great time. There was the rubble of reconstruction and rebuilding to see if we chose to leave the comfort of our housing and schools. We didn't have to speak German unless we wanted to.

In 1957, the Russians launched Sputnik and the next year I got on the Duty Train in the night with the shades down to ride back into the 'Free World.' We arrived in New York to a city where no hospital would take in my very sick brother because we had no permanent address. We drove to Fort Dix and watched TV for the first time in 3½ years while my brother recuperated. We arrived in Ohio to a home half the size of the one we left. Army cots and blankets provided us bedding until our furniture arrived.

I had stood in the middle of Fischottersteig looking for Sputnik and wondered if we should be afraid. Then by the 1960's, we were practicing air raid drills in US schools and listening for news about Cuba. The Berlin Wall is now down but we are listening to news from Russia with regained interest. Some things just don't change.

Sheryl Kase Spaulding, Class of 1964
1955-1958

Class of 1959, 8th grade Graduation, May 1955

Living Inside the "Bubble"

As Military Brats, we've all bonded with our fellow Brats because we understand each other and share the unique experiences as a result of our parents' careers. As Overseas Brats, those bonds grow tighter and stronger as we're plunked down in places strange to us. We don't understand the language nor the customs of our host countries, so we tend to grow closer to one another, finding comfort and familiarity in our own kind; at least initially. Take these two situations and throw in a third reason to huddle together even more closely: living inside 'The Bubble.'

That's what Berlin was to me– a bubble of Democracy behind the dreaded Iron Curtain. The Bubble. Fragile and frightening. There were some who could not cope with the feeling of being confined--hemmed in, maybe a grander form of claustrophobia. This feeling intensified when we would hear that the Russians had closed the Autobahn– one of our lifelines to the West. It was a harassing action, which they would cease after strong protestation by the Allies, but it was distressing nonetheless. Whenever it happened the phone in our apartment would ring. Ten minutes later, my dad– in his fatigues— was bounding out the door. How long would he be gone? When would he be back? Only when (and if) the Soviets decided they'd had enough fun, and reopened the Autobahn.

The second lifeline for most of us was the Duty Train, which left Berlin in the evening, chugging most of the night through East Germany— the Soviet zone. All who rode needed special travel orders printed in English and Russian, allowing the bearer passage through "their" territory. The orders were safeguarded by the Train Commander. In the middle of the night the train would stop at Marienborn, the Soviet checkpoint. We were to stay in our compartments at that time. Those who couldn't sleep– and I would wager it was a good number— could hear the trump of heavy boots up and down the passageway. As the train finally whistled into Helmstedt, our checkpoint, I could feel the whole train breathe a collective sigh of relief. After that, sleep came easier all the way to Frankfurt. The Hauptbahnhof welcomed us with the bustle of early morning commuters.

Going back, the procedure reversed, again the oppressive feeling as the West German locomotive surrendered its cars to the East German engine at the border. The countryside appeared as drab and joyless as the expressions of people waiting at the crossings. Only the children would smile and wave, ignoring attempts to suppress them. This in itself was sad. They were too young to grasp the gravity of their circumstance.

As we chug back toward our "bubble," the air takes on a sulfurous taint from the poorer quality of East German coal from the engine. It reminded me of the odor from the lockers in gym class. At last, a sigh of relief, as we pass into the relative safety of West Berlin, and finally squeal to a stop at the train station. On our way in, we could see the stark contrast between East and West. One street, whose center was the border, had bare well-used cobblestones on one side, and overgrown, dingy ones on the other. The Wall had not yet been erected— we left two years before— and Army Special Services was allowed to conduct tours of East Berlin. After all, it was an "open" city. In actuality, it was easier to get into East Berlin than out. Many refugees fled with nothing more than the clothes on their backs– ostensibly going over to the West "just for the day."

The rules on the tours were strict. Do not talk to anybody, especially

East German or Soviet military personnel; absolutely no pictures of same. The offending camera would he confiscated, the film destroyed and the camera itself may never be seen again. Also, the offender could be held for questioning. Not a pleasant thought. With a sort of morbid fascination, we gawked out the bus windows as we passed the Brandenburg Gate.

From there, we rode along Stalin Allee, a street lined with architectural propaganda. This showplace consisted of gleaming facades, fluttering Soviet flags and banners, and the appearance of elegance and complete recovery from the ravage of Allied bombings a little over a decade before. This was nothing more than a two-dimensional Hollywood front. The buildings behind still lay in ruins. The desolation of post-war East Berlin contrasted sharply to the hum of activity and prosperity of the recovering part of the Berlin behind us. Cars were sparse, people scurried about, afraid

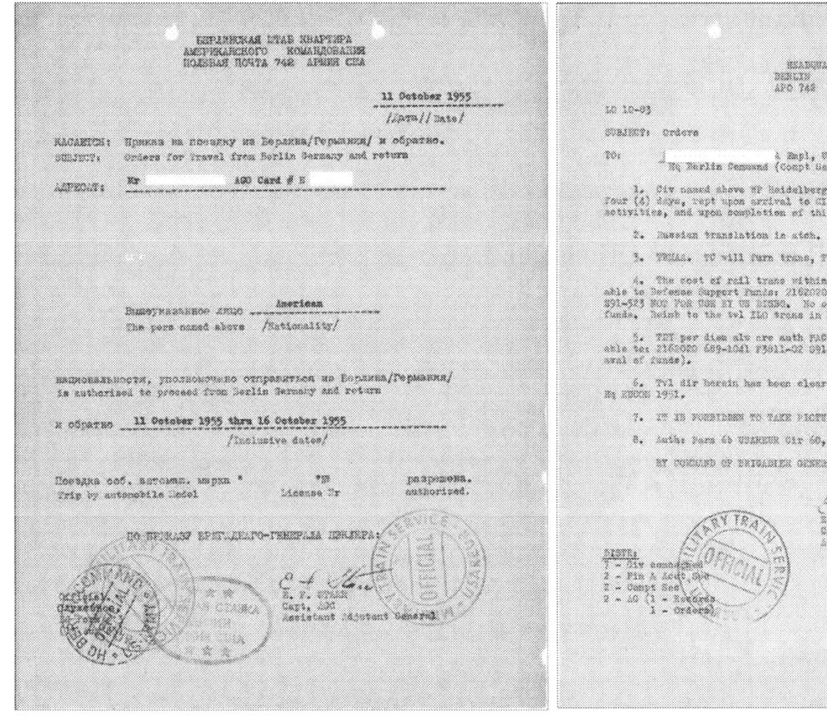

БЕРЛИНСКАЯ ШТАБ КВАРТИРА
АМЕРИКАНСКОГО КОМАНДОВАНИЯ
ПОЛЕВАЯ ПОЧТА 742 АРМИЯ США

11 October 1955
/Дата// Date/

КАСАЕТСЯ: Приказ на поездку из Берлина/Германия/ и обратно.
SUBJECT: Orders for Travel from Berlin Germany and return

АДРЕСАТ: Mr AGO Card # E

Вышеуказанное лицо American
The pers named above /Nationality/

национальности, уполномочено отправиться из Берлина/Германия/
is authorized to proceed from Berlin Germany and return

и обратно 11 October 1955 thru 16 October 1955
/Inclusive dates/

Поездка соб. автомоб. марки " " № разрешена.
Trip by automobile Model License Nr authorized.

ПО ПРИКАЗУ БРИГАДНОГО-ГЕНЕРАЛА [illegible]:

Official:
Служебное:

E. F. STARR
Capt, AGC
Assistant Adjutant General

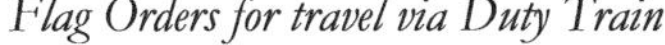

Flag Orders for travel via Duty Train

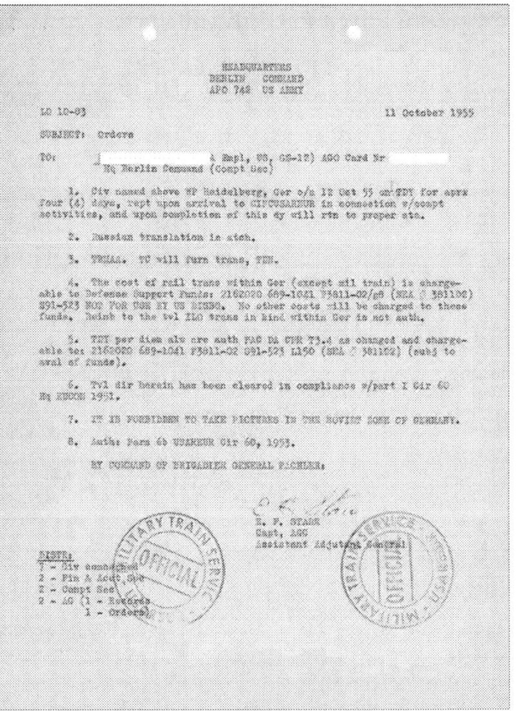

HEADQUARTERS
BERLIN COMMAND
APO 742 US ARMY

[illegible] 10-03 11 October 1955

SUBJECT: Orders

TO: & Empl, US, GS-[illegible]) AGO Card Nr
Hq Berlin Command (Compt Sec)

1. Civ named above WP Heidelberg, Ger o/a 12 Oct 55 on TDY for aprx four (4) days, rept upon arrival to CINCUSAREUR in connection w/compt activities, and upon completion of this dy will rtn to proper sta.

2. Russian translation is atch.

3. [illegible]. TC will furn trans, [illegible].

4. The cost of rail trans within Ger (except mil train) is chargeable to Defense Support Funds: 2162020 689-1041 [illegible] 591-523 [illegible]. No other costs will be charged to these funds. [illegible] within Ger is not auth.

5. TDY per diem alw are auth [illegible] as changed and chargeable to: 2162020 689-1041 [illegible] (subj to aval of funds).

6. Tvl dir herein has been cleared in compliance w/part I Cir 60 Hq EUCOM 1951.

7. IT IS FORBIDDEN TO TAKE PICTURES IN THE SOVIET ZONE OF GERMANY.

8. Auth: Para 6b USAREUR Cir 60, 1953.

BY COMMAND OF BRIGADIER GENERAL [illegible]:

E. F. STARR
Capt, AGC
Assistant Adjutant General

DISTR:
1 - Civ concerned
2 - Fin & Acct Sec
2 - Compt Sec
2 - AG (1 - Records
1 - Orders)

Page 2 (note warning against taking photos)

to stop and talk. Any group of more than three people congregating would be approached, questioned, and who-knows-what-else. Our guide told us that one way to tell which side of the fence we were on was to look for bananas at the fruit stands. They were unobtainable in the East. One had to be blind not to see the differences elsewhere.

A remarkable piece of propaganda was The Garden of Remembrance—a well-maintained park surrounding an impressive monument topped with a massive statue of Mother Russia holding one of her dying sons in her lap. A Russian Pietà, if you will. Inside the circular base was a gallery of mosaics expanding on the theme. From many yards away, I brought my trusty Brownie Reflex to bear. After a final check, I started to press the shutter release. Just then, two Russian soldiers emerged from the gallery. I froze as one of them noticed me lining up the shot. He nudged his comrade and pointed in our direction. Oh, no! Those weren't BB guns slung over their shoulders! I looked at my father, who directed my attention back to the duo. They weren't reaching for their weapons, they were taking off their caps and smoothing their hair; posing for the picture! They looked to be only a few years older than my fourteen years.

"What should I do?" I asked my dad. "Take the picture!" he grinned at me, then at them, nodding. With trembling finger, I found the button and pressed. A click heard around the world, I thought. "Spasibo, Tovarisch!" my father called out. "Thank you, Comrade." The two smiled, shouted back a greeting and went on their way, joking and laughing. From that day on, I felt a little better about living in "The Bubble."

Richard Sobieski, Class of 1960
1956-1959

Stalin Allee hides East Berlin rubble

By Omer Anderson
Photos: Red Grandy
Stars and Stripes Published: February 9, 1954

BERLIN– East Berlin looks drab, dingy and miserable until you hit Stalin Allee. This broad avenue used to be Frankfurter Allee. But the East German communist regime, unable to cope with the misery and backwardness in their sector, needed a propaganda gimmick. So they bought made-in-Moscow Stalin Allee.

For a stretch of about a mile on old Frankfurter Allee, the German Red government has put together a glittering oasis in the midst of the rubble pile that is East Berlin. Stalin Allee is a show street, something to hearten and spur on the wavering Party rank-and-file. It is meant to impress outsiders as an astonishing feat of "Socialist reconstruction."

The Red "miracle mile" is lined with almost solid blocks of eight-story apartment buildings. On the street level are smart shops selling everything from TV sets to fish.

Stalin Allee is a boulevard of weird contrasts. Driving there, you pass through streets lined with rubble piles and the shells of bomb-blasted buildings. Suddenly you round a bend in the road. Up ahead, like an apparition, looms a massive pile of stone and concrete.

Stalin's statue, photographed from the only side permitted by East German police.

Then you drive down a broad boulevard, the lanes separated by a wide, grass-planted traffic island. On either side loom the great blocks of buildings. They have fancy facades with wide terraces and balconies. It is a great show, Stalin Allee.

In the second block is a small park. Close to the sidewalk is a statue of the dead dictator. In real life, Joseph Stalin stood something like 5 feet, 6 inches. But he does much better in stone, towering over in heroic proportions over the avenue. The Reds have thoughtfully provided a wreath of artificial flowers for the base of Stalin's statue. You can pass on a freezing day, but Stalin's flowers look as fresh and cheerful as the benign figure in stone.

Stalinist architecture on E. Berlin's Stalin Allee, 1954

Just so no one will get funny ideas, Stalin's statue is guarded day- and- night by two "people's police." Stars and Stripes photographer Francis (Red) Grandy tried to snap Stalin from, the derriere. Grandy wanted to catch the huge sports center across the street in the background.

But the cops said no. It is forbidden to photograph Stalin's statue from the rear.

Red- and- white propaganda banners festoon the solidly capitalistic facades of Stalin Allee. The boulevard resounds to the blare of music and propaganda messages from loudspeakers hooked to every lamppost: "Boost work norms...defeat the European army…Demand German unification…"

There are some 7,000 persons living in Stalin Allee's 2,600 apartments of two to four rooms. This select population is made up of faithful party hacks and "activists." Consumer goods are scarce in East Berlin. But most of what there is goes to Stalin Allee. If you can't get it on Stalin Allee, East Berlin stores don't have it.

Toward the north end of Stalin Allee is a billboard sign. It is a propaganda sign showing West Berlin under a pall of darkness. But the sun is shining in East Berlin as happy workers take their families on a state-paid vacation. A dog belonging to the happy son of one of the happy workers lingers on the West Berlin sector boundary to relieve himself in the direction of West German Chancellor Konrad Adenauer and a group of Nazi generals. Adenauer and the generals just stare glumly at the happy workers.

If there are happy workers in Berlin, however, they are not on Stalin Allee. For the supreme irony of Stalin Allee is that here started the June 17 anti-Red riots which raced like wildfire through the Soviet Zone.

An East German propaganda sign reproduced in the West Berlin newspaper, *Berliner Zeitung*

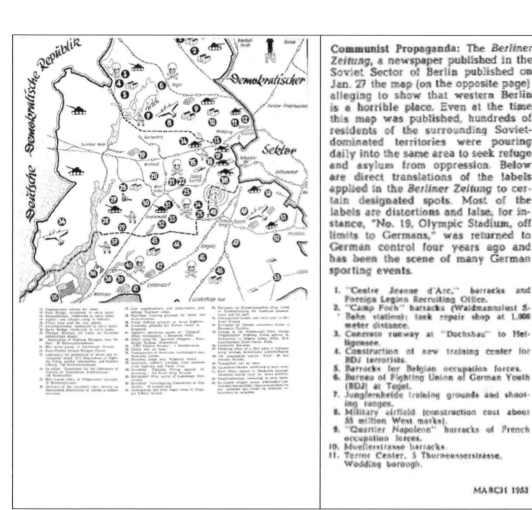

Communist Propaganda: The *Berliner Zeitung*, a newspaper published in the Soviet Sector of Berlin published on Jan. 27 the map (on the opposite page) alleging to show that western Berlin is a horrible place. Even at the time this map was published, hundreds of residents of the surrounding Soviet-dominated territories were pouring daily into the same area to seek refuge and asylum from oppression. Below are direct translations of the labels applied in the *Berliner Zeitung* to certain designated spots. Most of the labels are distortions and false, for instance, "No. 19, Olympic Stadium, off limits to Germans," was returned to German control four years ago and has been the scene of many German sporting events.

1. "Centre Jeanne d'Arc," barracks and Foreign Legion Recruiting Office.
2. "Camp Foch" barracks (Waldmannslust S-Bahn station); tank repair shop at 1,000 meter distance.
3. Concrete runway at "Dachsbau" to Heiligensee.
4. Construction of new training center for BDJ terrorists.
5. Barracks for Belgian occupation forces.
6. Bureau of Fighting Union of German Youth (BDJ) at Tegel.
7. Jungfernheide training grounds and shooting ranges.
8. Military airfield (construction cost about 55 million West marks).
9. "Quartier Napoleon" barracks of French occupation forces.
10. Muellerstrasse barracks.
11. Terror Center, 3 Thurmeusserstrasse, Wedding borough.

MARCH 1953

This kind of misinformation was intended to scare East Berliners into remaining in the East for fear of the dangers listed (such as Terror Center marked with skull and crossbones). The East could not afford the continued economic devastation caused by the brain drain of millions of its citizens fleeing to the West. Between 1950 and 1961, 3.5 million people had fled to the West. The Wall was constructed in 1961in response to this great loss.

Did Anything Important Happen in 1958?

Jan 1st- European Economic Community starts operation

Jan 6th - Gibson patents Flying V guitar

Jan 12th - NCAA adds 2 point conversion to football scoring

Feb 3rd - Royal Teens' "Short Shorts" enters Top 40 chart and peaks at #3

Feb 11th - Ruth Carol Taylor is 1st African-American woman hired as flight attendant, Ithaca NY

Mar 8th- William Faulkner says US schools degenerated to become babysitters

Mar 14th- US performs nuclear test at Nevada Test Site

Mar 14th- USSR performs atmospheric nuclear test

Mar 24th- Elvis Presley joins the army (serial number 53310761)

Mar 27th- CBS Labs announces new stereophonic records

Apr 3rd- Fidel Castro's rebels attack Havana

Apr 18th- A United States federal court rules that poet Ezra Pound is to be released from an insane asylum. Sure looks like Bob Dylan to me.

photo by Alvin Langdon Coburn

Jul 7th - President Eisenhower signed a bill approving Alaskan statehood

Sep 29th- "Summertime Blues" by Eddie Cochran peaks at #8

Oct 14th- The District of Columbia Bar Association votes to accept black Americans as members

Nov 4th - Democrats win US congressional election

Dec 29th - TV soap "Young Dr. Malone" debuts.

The Philips Pavilion photo credit: Wouter Hagens

So, the answer is:

NONE OF THE ABOVE. BUT, Boy Scout Troop 46 was there for the most important occasion of 1958:

The 1958 Brussels World's Fair and Campout of Scouts from all over the world.

It all started out very routinely. Frank Hooven '61 (my best friend) and I boarded the C-47 at Tempelhof early in the morning with the rest of the troop. We sat on the flip down metal seats on either side of the aircraft as it rumbled down the runway. A crewman then handed out the parachutes– almost. I did not get one. Apparently, then being small in stature, I could not wear a parachute.

Was I nervous? Darn right, but then I was invited to the cockpit to talk with the captain. He saluted me, as I was in uniform, and told me not to worry. We would go down with the ship together. I am not too sure why, but I felt reassured.

We landed quite safely at the Brussels airport and were bussed to the campgrounds. Tents were set up, C-Rations distributed and eaten. A most important item, a pack of Lucky Strikes, was pocketed. At 13 I tasted my first refreshing gasp of nicotine and tar. I was hooked until 31 years later. We were all exhausted and slept well that night. Trumpets sounded early the next morning and we were rounded up for our first trip to the Fair. Everything went well and everyone was well behaved.

On the second day, however, Frank and I left the group after arriving at the fairgrounds and went out on our own. This was not considered behavior becoming a military scout from Troop 46. We were confined to the camp grounds for the duration instead of being flown back to Berlin in disgrace. I guess I was not a very good scout. When the English scout bus left that afternoon to return to the Fair, Frank and I were stowaways. It was a wonderful day. We even had a couple beers. Needless to say, when we arrived back at the camp grounds late that night…..well, luckily Troop 46 was returning to Berlin the next morning. I think the "Master" was hoping I would go down with the plane…..he didn't seem to "blame" Frank at all.

Bill "Toby" West, Class of 1961
1953-1962

The only pictures I can find. The French and Finnish Pavilions during the day and the lights at night that Frank and I were not supposed to be seeing.

Teaching in Cold War Berlin

December 18, 1958, was my first day at school. A relaxed place– and I quickly learned why. It was the first day of Christmas vacation! I had been hired to teach at a location where there were no students! Wow! I knew right away that I was going to like this place.

"Boring class, even the teacher fell asleep"-Mr. Longolius, 1962

That changed quickly. Early January I was introduced to classes that were "dynamic," to use a diplomatic term. In junior high, German groups were divided into two sections: Beginners and Advanced. When I arrived, the administrators set up three, introducing an Intermediate class. I thought at first that that term meant their German.

Only later did I find out that the two ladies who had taught German before had decided that with a man coming, "Intermediate" translated into "Hard to Handle." Boy, did I learn the rules of the game fast, and I am still sure that I did not learn all of them. I thought that I spoke English rather well. These classes taught me that I did not. My vocabulary expanded almost daily, which was also true when I was one of the soccer coaches. There seemed to be two different sets of English–classroom English and the real one. Very educational!

I got married almost one year after joining the faculty, in 1959. Since my wife had also gone to school in the United States, language basically was no great problem mixing with the other teachers. We took them shopping–or "antiquing" as the term for fancier shopping mainly of old clocks went–buying cars (with them and from them); we played bridge with them almost every night of the week, and we bowled with them on Tuesday afternoons with the Faculty Bowling League (and Men's Bowling on Fridays after school). We introduced them to "Bowle" (a harmless drink if you stay away from the fruit) and took them on trips to West Germany. In addition, we traveled to the West with students to their games, with the German-American Club and the soccer team. We attended their dances in the cafeteria, and so on.

Due to Allied agreements, travelling with the team was a nuisance. Being German, I was not supposed to use the Duty Train, and while the US did not mind, the Soviets did. So I rode my car to Helmstedt and met the train there, after midnight if I remember correctly, and then went on in it to K-town, Karlsruhe, etc.

I always made it, but one time the shave was more than close. I was in line to be checked at the East German Marienborn checkpoint realizing that I had about 15 minutes to catch the train. At that time, the East Germans only let five cars at a time into their control area, and I was # 6. That is when luck struck. I noticed that the car in front of me belonged to one of my best friends; we changed places, I barely made it to the Helmstedt train station and onto the train. I do not remember how the game went, but with that beginning I am sure we won it.

I consider my time at the school, with the faculty members and the students, to have been the best part of my life. Dramatic, exciting things happened: the Wall was being built and the military confrontation in the heart of Berlin was for real, but looking back now, fortunately, the discipline and self-constraint of world leaders held.

All of us contributed to the victory of the West and of common sense by going on about our lives as normally as possible. Berliners with any kind of memory are still grateful for the fact that the US and the other Western Allies stayed in Berlin and thereby encouraged Berliners to stay. This will be a good lesson, now that the Russian bear has ended hibernation and is hungry again.

Alexander Longolius, Faculty
German Host Nation Teacher, 1958-1967

Six Man Football Champions – TAR football 1951

Junior Senior Prom, 1951

TAR Cheerleading, 1951

Teen - Canteen

This Certifies that

ANN WORRELL

is a member of the

Teen-Canteen, Berlin, Germany

Aug. 1950 DATE

L. Lawson TREASURER

Teen Canteen Card

"Lucky": Bill Toby West '61 and friends

Chapter 3: The 1960s

"Two thousand years ago the proudest boast was 'civis Romanus sum.' Today, in the world of freedom, the proudest boast is 'Ich bin ein Berliner.'"

- President John F. Kennedy, in front of Rathaus Schöneberg

1960 Little League World Series European Champions

Baseball from Berlin to Williamsport and the Missing Brats of 1960

Where are you, my friends? Where are you Alfred, Bruce H, Tim, James H and James I? I have spent the last three months looking for you! Fifty-three years is a long time to not be in touch. I've often thought, "Shame on us for not keeping up with one another over the years." We did not realize that memories become more important as we grow older. Duke, Bruce, Charles, Mike, John, Ed and I have been in contact, and all of us have had a wonderful life and are doing well. Duke, Charles, Ed and I are retired; Mike works for IBM, John is a Baptist pastor and Bruce J owns BHJ Enterprise. Bruce has a family member, David Ash, that is the starting quarterback at University of Texas and Duke is expecting his first grandchild.

It all started on July 23, 1960, when 14 eleven- and twelve-year-old boys were picked to represent Berlin in the German Regional Little League Championship in Bremerhaven. Off we went by train on July 29, 1960 singing our theme song, "Good Timin'" by Jimmy Jones. There were four teams going to Bremerhaven: Bonn, Kassel, Bremerhaven and Berlin. Little did we know we would not be home for more than a month as we went to Bremerhaven, Mannheim, Wiesbaden, New York, Coney Island, Staten Island, West Point, and of course, Williamsport, PA, home of the *Little League World Series!*

THE BERLIN OBSERVER

. . . All Stars

SET TO GO—Pictured on the eve of their departure for Bremerhaven and the Northern District playoffs are the Berlin Little League All Stars. From left to right (first row): Pat Williams, Tim Harrison, Bruce Hampton, Ray Williams, and Charles Spannare. (Second row): Duke Dabia, Hal Ingle, Bruce Jager, Jim Ingle, and Mike Glaser. (Third row): coach Don Thompson, Al Bradley, Ed Cole, John Reale, Ralph Freeman, and coach Bob Meece. —US Army Photo

LL Stars Head for Playoffs; Bisons Falter in League Play

Berlin's 14-man Little League All-Star team leaves today for Bremerhaven to play in the single-elimination Northern District playoffs against teams from Bremerhaven, Bonn, and Kassel, with the winner moving on to the Germany playoffs next weekend.

In league play, Bruce Hampton went 4-for-4 with two singles, a double and a triple to lead the Bulls in a 16-12 slugfest victory over the front-running Bisons, keeping the winner's pennant hopes alive as the Little League season moved into the final week of play.

The Bears started the week off by nipping the Bisons, 7-5, behind an 11-strike out performance by Pat Williams. On the same day the Lions edged the Rams, 9-8, on Charles Spannare's two-run double in the last inning.

Tuesday saw Hal Ingle notch a 12-strike out shutout as the Bisons rebounded to trounce the Bears, 7-0. Ray Williams suffered his first setback of the season Wednesday as the Bisons slipped past the Colts, 11-9. The second game Wednesday saw Spannare slam a homer and double to pace the Lions' 12-8 win over the Bears.

In a return match the next day John Reale fired a no-hitter, striking out 16, as the Colts smacked the Lions, 6-0. Hampton hurled the Bulls to a tight 2-1 win over the Bears, giving up only three hits.

The Rams bested the Lions Saturday, 6-4, in a battle for the cellar.

Ingle moved into the top slot among the hitters last week with a .577 mark. Ralph Freeman of the Bisons continues to lead the long-ball hitters with five home runs. Ed Cole of the Bulls has the best pitching record, 5-1, while Williams' 78 strike outs leads the way.

. . . Trophy

HUNTING—Captain Christian F. Dabia, new BC Special Services Officer, checks an old trophy at the Sports Office with high hopes of adding to BC's already bulging show-

At Bremerhaven, we won 9-6 over Kassel and beat Bonn 23-0 for the championship. We then trekked on to Mannheim for the German Championships. During the first game, we beat Ramstein 9-2. Charles had two hits, Mike and Bruce had 2 hits plus Bruce hit a double. I had three hits and John Reale gave up one earned run. In the final game, we beat Kitzingen 6-1. Ed Cole and Harold Ingle combined for a no-hitter in that championship game, while Duke had an RBI and scored a run. Boy, were we having fun!

We then headed off to Wiesbaden to play teams from Spain, England, France, North Africa, Italy and Turkey. What were we thinking going to the European Championships? We were the smallest command with the fewest dependents! We only had six teams in our league and around 70 boys from which to choose.

It rained a lot at Wiesbaden, so helicopters were brought in to dry the field. They poured jet fuel on the infield and lit it to help it dry. Finally, we could play!

Burning and drying the field

During the first game, John Reale threw a two- hitter, and we beat England 3-0: Duke drove in a run and scored a run. In the second game, we beat Spain 13-0, and Lanky Ed Cole threw a one hitter; Charles had three hits. Now, we were in the championship against France. We were behind 6-5 going into the fifth inning. We scored four runs in the fifth and sixth innings to win 9-6. Ed Cole had one hit relief, and I had three RBI's and scored a run while Duke had two RBI's with a double off the wall; Mike scored twice with one RBI. We were going to be the first team to represent Europe at the *Little League World Series!*

In the last two tournaments that we played as a team, we hit .348, and held the opponents to a .131 batting average. We had a lot of great kids who were great baseball players. Every game somebody else came through for us. We were all friends and we were off to the land of the Big PX

... Real Gone

REALE—Berlin pitcher John Reale plays it cool by leaping the outstretched arms of Ramstein's catcher in the Germany playoff semi-final game which Berlin won, 9-2, on the way to its European Little League championship. —US Army Photo

[Weisbaden was US Air Force HQ, with abundant amenities] and our first soft serve ice cream. "Good Timin'" was playing a lot. We visited New York, Coney Island, Staten Island, West Point and the New York Daily News before heading to Williamsport. We were treated incredibly well by everyone. We lost to Mexico 7-4 after leading until the fourth inning. Ralph Freeman had a home run and Mike had an RBI and a double. During the next game, we beat Canada 6-3. In our last game, we lost to Pearl Harbor 7-2 and finished sixth.

After nearly a month on the road, we were on our way home. As we pulled in on the train August 30th, 1960, there were signs congratulating us; hundreds of parents, friends and supporters met us at the station. We were still playing "Good Timin'." Later, the Berlin Command gave us a banquet, medal, trophy and sports jacket; and the NCO Club gave us each a cashmere coat.

... Champs Return

Berlin All-Stars Back Home After Month of Playoff Games

Delta Nine Nabs Two Wins in ACC Fray

62 Wins Ladies Golf Play

School soon started, our fathers began to be transferred and friends moved. I wound up in San Antonio, Texas and then we moved to Amarillo, Texas when my father retired. We lost contact and grew old. Duke is now in California; Charles is in Pennsylvania. John and Mike are in Virginia, while Bruce J, Ed and I are in Texas.

When I think of my friends now I think, "We few,

we happy few, we band of brothers." Seven of us have reconnected and seven are still lost. Where are you, my friends?

Pat Williams, Class of 1965
1958-1961
In collaboration with some of his teammates!

Mentioned above: Ed Cole '66, Ralph Freeman '66, Harold Ingle '66, John Reale '65, Bruce Jager '66, Charles Spannare '65, Mike Glaser'66 and Christian "Duke" Dubia '66

C'est La Guerre Froid

THE BERLIN OBSERVER

Stout Heart

Berlin All Stars Win European LL Baseball Title; Fly to US for Shot at Coveted World Crown

General Meloy Will Inspect Berlin Troops

... To the Winner

Ray Williams' Clutch Pitching; Plate Power, Sparkling Defense Spells Difference in Playoffs

EM Must Own 2 Army Greens By October 1

CG Launches Unique New AFN Safety Show with Short Address

... Too Little

2nd BG Soldier Saves Child from Drowning

Registration for U of M Term Begins Monday

Berlin Observer- August 19, 1960

"Teen Beat Berlin"

My brother, Jerry and I were relatively new to Berlin High School In December of 1960. We had time during the couple of weeks prior to Christmas and during the holidays to acquaint ourselves with the surroundings and most of the almost 240 students in the school.

By the end of April 1961, I was bold enough to strike up a conversation at the AYA with a girl named Doreen Maloney. Being the suave, sophisticated, mature 15 year old that I was– I tried to impress her with the not-so-factual revelation that I had been a disc jockey back in Indianapolis before coming to Berlin. It wasn't entirely false. A friend of mine and I had played deejay in the basement of his house at Fort Harrison with a Webcor reel-to-reel tape recorder and two GE record players. He, by the way, is a guy named Scott Shannon, who became the most listened to morning disc jockey in New York City and the hottest programmer in all of radio.

Anyhow, Doreen's surprise for me was that her father, Captain Maloney, was the station commander at AFN Berlin and "would you like to go up to the radio station to meet him?" Of course I had to say yes or be caught at my deception and totally blow what I'm sure was a "really cool" impression I had made on her. A couple of weeks later we were in the Office of Captain Jack Maloney at 28 Podbielskiallee, the home of AFN Berlin. I say we, meaning Doreen and me and two friends, Lee Angel '64 and Randy Meyer '64. After introductions to her father we all had a tour of the station, meeting program director Mark White and all of the staff.

Luckily, my conversation with Doreen at the AYA never came up but her father asked that since we were all so interested in the station, if we would consider doing a radio show for the kids at the school. I don't know which of us was the first to reply—but it was an emphatic, 'YES!!!' We were to do the show on Wednesday at 5 o'clock. And so it was....after school on May 17th, 1961 the three of us, Lee, Randy and I, ran to the AYA immediately after school and called a military taxi to take us to the station.

The military taxi was how you got around Berlin when you were 15 or 16 years old and didn't have a car to drive. We had learned this trick from Charlie Johnson '64, a classmate whose father was the Commanding General of Berlin Command. We had seen him do it once to go to the swimming pool at Andrews Barracks, so we figured if he could do it, so could we, and we went all over Berlin when we found out it worked. From the first day, we had full access to the music for "our" show. We probably picked 30 to 40 songs that were either currently popular or had been popular within the last 3 years, but because the show was only going to be 55 minutes long, we ended up cutting it down to about 20 songs, which was still an incredible amount of music for that amount of time. We decided to call our show "Teen Beat" after the Sandy Nelson hit from 1959.

Accent on Youth Radio Show- l to r: Horst Breuer '64, Mikel Fisher '64, PFC Mitch Farrell (producer), Jim Branson '64, Randy Meyer '64

The producer for our show was Staff Sergeant George Hudak, who ordinarily did the 5 o'clock show called "Frolic at Five," and the engineer was a 20 year old PFC named Joey Welz (aka Welzant), who later went on to become the piano player for Bill Haley's Comets (we talked Joey into coming to the AYA to play for all of the kids once and he was GREAT!). We watched another announcer, PFC Jim Stutzman do his show called "American Music Hall," which was a classical program and then from the network at Frankfurt we listened to "Stick Buddy Jamboree," a country music program.

As the clock got closer and closer to 5 o'clock all three of us became extremely nervous and speaking for myself, I felt as though my heart was going to pound through my chest. After 5 minutes of news at 5 o'clock we were going to be ON THE RADIO. We each made a last minute dash to the drinking fountain in the hallway to wash away the cotton ball that had suddenly taken over our mouths. Then it was 5:05 and our theme song was playing and SGT Hudak was explaining to the listeners what was going to happen for the next 55 minutes and had us introduce ourselves.

After we stumbled through the introduction of the first song, we each took turns successively with each song. Sometimes making a dedication for someone at school or using some of the mail SGT Hudak had received to make dedications. After a couple of weeks we started receiving our own mail and used it exclusively. We got mail from GIs, German kids from several different schools, including some in East Berlin and also a lot of requests from kids at the American school. We were a hit with everyone.

During the entire summer of 1961, AFN Berlin was our second home. We spent every possible hour here, making friends with all of the staff and listening to just about every record in their massive library. We were given every possible privilege. To this day it seems unreal to me that they would allow three 15 and 16 year old kids to have the run of the place. Whenever we heard a celebrity was coming in for an interview we were always there, which was how we were able to meet people like Connie Francis, Brenda Lee, Connie Stevens, Paul Anka, and a couple of very popular German singers named Catrina Valenti and Peter Krause.

The following summer Randy and I again did a show on AFN only this time the name was "Accent on Youth." Later, Randy was unable to participate, so it was suggested that we rotate different kids from the school as guest announcers each week. We announced events that were happening in the school and at the AYA and played a lot of records. Our new producer was a young PFC named Mitch Farrell, who became a lifelong friend. After his service was over, he went on to work for Dick Clark at a station in Riverside, California.

The Bats performing in Berlin, ca. 1962

During this same time a band called The Bats came to Berlin from Hamburg. They had been playing in a bar in Hamburg called the Top Ten Club and had come to check out the music scene in Berlin. They ended up staying during the summer of 1962 and played almost exclusively every weekend at the AYA. A young British singer named Tony Sheridan came with them and played at some of their engagements in a few German youth hostels, and once at the Neüe Welt. A few of us guys followed them all over Berlin that summer. On one occasion at the AYA, their manager Jüergen Danckers gave me a copy of a record that Tony Sheridan had made with what he told me were members of The Bats, although on the record it said "Tony Sheridan and the Beat Brothers."

Lee Angel and I were in charge of the jukebox and we decided to put it in the jukebox so everyone could enjoy it. If you know your rock 'n' roll trivia, "My Bonnie (lies over the ocean)," which was a song The Bats played a lot at the AYA, was recorded by Tony Sheridan in Hamburg in 1961 with backing by some guys who later called themselves The Beatles. Today that record sells for about $1500, but God only knows where our copy is.

The Bats came to the AFN studios and recorded about 18 different songs for us to play on "Accent on Youth" and we would play at least one song a week. We were the official Bats Fan Club. They were a band made up of many nationalities. Tony "Tornado" was a black American who played the drums and sang lead, Pete was from Indonesia and played rhythm guitar along with Rolf, who was German. Another German, Rudi, played lead guitar and Colin Melander from England played bass.

I was on top of the world until the 29th of July when we left Berlin for Stuttgart, where I tried to duplicate what we had done in Berlin with a program called "The Kids Next Door" which was a total bust. It lasted maybe a couple of weeks.

The experience that I had doing "Teen Beat"and "Accent on Youth" was probably the most memorable one of my life. Many friendships were cemented and I'll never forget it because I still have several tapes of both radio shows, and listen to them frequently, and also the master copy of The Bats tape. I became a disc jockey for real during the '80s and early '90s after chasing the dream for most of my life and just recently went back to continue my career in radio.

Jim Branson, Class of 1964
1960-1962

Berlin 1961

The might of the Soviet Union was palpable in the surrounded enclave that was West Berlin, at least to those responsible for its survival. While adults scurried about on important missions, my father was a covert operative for the CIA, my friends and I thought of it as more of an adventure. It mattered little to us at the time that our tiny Tank Command was outnumbered 100 to 1. We still used the old cemetery close to it as a make out rendezvous.

But the reality was different for those German teachers at Berlin American High School who had relatives and friends still in the Russian Sector. The Stasi was actively keeping track of those who had family that worked in the West. Informants were everywhere, including in West Berlin.

"The *Ministry for State Security* (German: *Ministerium für Staatssicherheit*, MfS), commonly known as the **Stasi** (literally State Security), was the official state security service of the German Democratic Republic or GDR, colloquially known as East Germany. It has been described as one of the most effective and repressive intelligence and secret police agencies to have ever existed. The Stasi was headquartered in East Berlin, with an extensive complex in Berlin-Lichtenberg and several smaller facilities throughout the city. The Stasi motto was '*Schild und Schwert der Partei*' (Shield and Sword of the Party), that is the ruling Socialist Unity Party of Germany (SED). One of its main tasks was spying on the population, mainly through a vast network of citizens-turned-informants and fighting any opposition by overt and covert measures including hidden psychological destruction of dissidents."*

Such was the situation for one of my favorite teachers, Frau Pietsch.

Whatever artistic ability I have shown over the years was brought to life in her art classes. She was always smiling and had a positive outlook on life as, but she also knew the reality of life in the East.

I can never be 100% positive, but I believe that was one of the reasons my artwork for the 1961 yearbook was shown only in a very small picture of the art class in session. It was too political for the situation that many German citizens, who worked in the West, had to face with regard to what was possible in the East. And besides, the artwork chosen was just fine.

Bill "Toby" West, Class of 1961
1953-1962
*Wikipedia

The 1961 yearbook, Bill's artwork in lower picture, but barely noticeable.

Bill's artwork, not used in yearbook

Berlin Is Still Berlin

I sat up in bed, blinked, rubbed my eyes and listened a little harder. That staccato coughing had to be heavy machine guns, and there was no doubt that the dull rumbling I heard was from prowling tanks, but the question was, ours or theirs?

I soon learned that the sounds that had awakened me that first morning in Berlin in 1959 were only those of an American battle group maneuvering in the Grunewald, a forest where Berliners love to stroll on Sundays. But the incident did underscore the tension of the moment. Khruschev had issued an ultimatum calling for Berlin to be made a "free city" (i.e.,Western troops must withdraw and ties with West Germany disavowed) by May 27, 1959.

The day passed like any other, and I soon adjusted to living in a Cold War battleground in much the same way a construction worker learns to eat his lunch nonchalantly while straddling a girder 15 stories above the ground.

Now, 11 years after I graduated from the American dependent high school there, I was returning to Berlin as a reporter for FAMILY. As the Lufthansa 727 jet made a wide bomber turn and headed for the southernmost air corridor to Berlin, I settled into my seat and glanced at the *International Herald Tribune.*

Flying over the muted green and brown fields that isolate Berlin from West Germany, I wondered if Berliners, German and American alike, had been insulated from the tumultuous changes of the Sixties. *Berlin bliebt doch Berlin,* reads a neon sign on a modern office building in the city center—Berlin is still Berlin. I was curious to see if it were true.

One thing at least had not changed: Berlin was still divided. There was a dividing border but no Berlin Wall in 1959, and any American could hop on the U-Bahn (subway), walk through the gray and nearly desolate streets of East Berlin, still pocked with gutted shells where proud homes once stood, and shake his head sadly at the long lines of listless, silent East Berliners lined up at state-run stores to buy scarce consumer goods. When he returned to the West, he actually would feel that he could breathe easier.

West Berlin offered a sharp contrast. The Kurfurstendamm—"Ku'damm" or "cowpath" to the sardonic Berliners—a broad avenue lined with sidewalk cafes, theaters and chic shops revealed a bustling commercial and cultural life. Modern apartment buildings sprouting where there had been three billion cubic feet of rubble; a functioning democratic city government… it was a showplace, an "Outpost of Freedom in a Red Sea of Tyranny," as U.S. officials were fond of saying.

During this pre-Wall era, our fathers pulled maintenance, drilled and rappelled off rooftops. Our mothers went to teas and kept our bags packed so we could be evacuated quickly if things went awry. And we kids went about our business– dances, sports, school. Sneaking down to a smoky Bierstube (beer hall) at Krumme Lanke to prove ourselves by drinking liters of amber Schultheiss. Going steady: girls draped in over-sized letter jackets and wearing class rings lined with wax.

In short, we lived like kids in the Zone (West Germany) or the States. Our big gripe was that the PX didn't stock enough button-down shirts or crew-neck sweaters and that the music on the teen club jukebox was months behind the States.

But one day, all that changed for me. On the morning of August 13,

1961, I straggled home from a night of hell-raising and found my mother distraught.

"The Russians have closed the border," she said, "There may be trouble." Trying to hide a throbbing hangover, I started to ask what kind of trouble, but a clanking column of armored personnel carriers laden with combat-ready troops lumbered by on Clayallee, and I knew.

My father appeared in fatigues, carrying a sidearm for the first time since we came to Berlin, and then I realized the situation was critical. He was in intelligence, and normally wore civilian clothes.

"It looks bad, son," he said. "Stay in the area. If you hear shooting, get your mother and the kids and go to the basement. They'll try to evacuate the families if possible."

I didn't ask where he would be, when he left for Berlin Command. I didn't know if I'd see him again.

Still, I had never known war, and I couldn't imagine one could be so near. So I told my mother I'd be at the teen club. Instead, I picked up my buddy John Watson, the son of the then U.S. Commander Berlin, Maj. Gen. Albert Watson. We went straight to the Brandenburg Gate.

Along both sides of Straße des 17. Juni (17th of June Street) were amassed thousands of West Berliners chanting, "Kill Walter Ulbricht! " (the East German Communist Party leader). Because my dad was an intelligence officer, I'd been instructed that "under no circumstances are you to ever go into East Berlin." I couldn't even go on tours through the Communist controlled part of the city. John and I flashed our dependent ID cards and were allowed through West Berlin police lines. We approached within 50 yards of the gate. An East German guard stopped us and demanded to see our ID cards. We refused and demanded the presence of a Soviet officer. Eventually, an East German officer appeared, but we refused to show our cards to people the U.S. didn't officially recognize. We were also more than a little bit worried that if they saw our names, we would make excellent hostages. They probably had our father's names and jobs in their files. They certainly would know John's father!

We decided to quickly flash our cards, and the officer saluted us and let us pass into East Berlin! We wandered around the city and quickly came upon two American college women who were traveling in Europe. They were just giggling and bewildered by what was happening. "Is it always like this?" one of the females asked. When they heard that World War III was possibly going to break out, they got a little scared and quickly agreed to stick with us. This was okay with us, because we were high school boys and they were attractive college girls.

On the eastern side of the gate, we could see Vopos (Volkspolizei- East German police) setting up machine guns facing crowds of East Berliners. We took that to signify that they were concerned about their people possibly revolting as they did on June 17, 1953.

We walked to Potsdamer Platz where we saw another platoon of Vopos shattering the pavement with jackhammers. Nearby, trucks were unloading tons of concrete blocks and bags of cement. It was the beginning of the Berlin Wall. At one point, I heard a click. I turned around and one of the college women had snapped a picture of a Russian tank! I assume no one saw her. We went back to the West with great relief.

Finally, after two years of self-imposed isolation from reality, I had an idea of what it meant to live in Berlin. I took the subway to the Oskar-

Helene-Heim stop, strode across Clayallee to the marbled former Luftwaffe headquarters that housed the U.S. Berlin Command, and announced that I wanted to enlist for immediate duty in Berlin.

The kindly recruiting sergeant told me that since I was just 17 I'd have to have written permission from my parents and that in my case I couldn't join a unit on the spot. When my father told me to forget about enlisting, I took my 14-year-old brother aside and told him he'd have to look after our mother, younger brothers and sister because I'd be staying behind with some of my classmates to fight as guerillas. I actually believed it at the time.

THE BERLIN OBSERVER

VOL. 17, NO. 34 • THE NEWSPAPER OF BERLIN COMMAND • FRIDAY, 25 AUGUST 1961

Vice President Pledges American Support

Thousands Cheer Presidential Envoy

Task Force Delta Winding Up Second Week at Wildflecken

BERLIN'S BEST

But within a few tense days, this too passed. President Kennedy sent a battle group from the 18th Inf. Div. in the Zone as reinforcements and as a show of U.S. determination to remain in Berlin. My whole family turned out to join the crowd that lined the avenue from the Autobahn when the convoy arrived. I'd never seen anything like it, except when leafing through odd copies of LIFE magazine showing the liberation of Paris. Near the head of the column was Vice President Lyndon Baines Johnson, yet to be scarred by Vietnam, yet to be crushed by power, standing in a Jeep and waving to 300,000 wildly cheering West Berliners. The Berliners threw flowers, and the troopers stuck them in the camouflage nets on their helmets, grinned, and waved back. I felt a hot rush of chauvinism. We'll show those bastards, I thought. Somehow, flag waving seemed appropriate.

I emerged from my reverie as the 727 burst through the dense low clouds and we landed at Tempelhof Airport, once the pride of the Luftwaffe, later a terminal for the Berlin Airlift, and now a busy commercial airport.

Ret. Army Lt. Col, Lee Ewing, Class of 1961
1959-1961
Excerpted from Family, a supplement of Army Times,
September 20, 1972
Reprinted with permission

Colonel Glover S. Johns, Jr., Commanding Officer of the 1st Battle Group, 18th Infantry, (standing in jeep) salutes Vice President Lyndon B. Johnson as he passes the reviewing stand in front of Berlin Command headquarters. Elements of the battle group paraded through West Berlin within hours of their arrival from Mannheim, Germany. —US Army Photo

As a show of American resolve to remain in Berlin, despite the newly erected Wall, reinforcements from Mannheim march into the city to the cheers of over 300,000 Berliners. LBJ is to the right on the reviewing stand, saluted by Col. Glover S. Johns, Jr, Commanding Officer of the 18th Infantry (standing in jeep).

Spy Games or Reality?

My heart pounded...probably exacerbated by my trying so hard to breathe quietly so no one would hear me. We snuck along the side of the road hunched down, in sort of a walking low crawl. At the first sign of car lights, we'd dive into the ditch next to the road, flattening ourselves against the side, holding our breath.

During one longer than usual steady stream of cars, Nancy passed me a lemon drop, our only food. Maybe it would stop the stomach growls that were loud enough to give our location away. This was the furthest we'd made it into West Berlin without someone spotting us. Not the Stasi with their black boots and weapons cocked and ready. Not a neighbor's dog, barking and sniffing at us like last week. And not our brother yelling, "Mom said you have to come in right NOW!" like last night. Somehow we'd been so immersed in our escape from East Berlin that we hadn't heard Mom's cowbell ring out of the 4th floor apartment window, her signature sound. Each mom in the building had one.

Looking back now I'm not surprised that we played East Berliners on the run instead of, say, Cowboys and Indians. East Berliners had been escaping into the West long before the Wall went up. In fact, that's why it went up in 1961. More than 3.4 million escaped from East Berlin or East Germany into the West from 1950 to 1961. I doubt we kids were aware of any of that until 1961. Once the Wall went up the stories turned into movies in our living rooms.

Our nightly television news was full of scenes we could follow even if we didn't understand every word of the German announcer. For instance, people jumping out of 4th story windows onto the street below into the West

Zone. That was before the East German guards wised up and bricked over all the windows, not just the lower ones. Then there was the guy swimming across the canal with shots pinging the water all around him. There were images of families standing on platforms waving white handkerchiefs to their relatives on the other side.

The Wall became just another part of our world. It didn't impact us kids much. We did go to see it at some point, but it was a number of Strassenbahn stations away. Climbing up on one of the wood platforms to look over the barbed wire on top of brick, we looked into a world that didn't mean a lot to us. Our family was all together on the platform, on one side, not split up by this barrier. The world right around our apartments in the American zone didn't change. I don't remember that we were kept much closer to home in those first weeks or months, but I expect we must have been.

One of the many viewing platforms along the Wall, December 1961

We did eventually question why our other American friends got to go on tours into East Berlin as the years wore on– on buses that stopped through Checkpoint Charlie to have passports checked and recorded. I have no memory of how mom explained that to us but somehow we accepted whatever she told us.

It was only many years later that I discovered the reality of our lives in Berlin. Fast forward to 1972, living in Northern Virginia. Summers between college terms at the University of Virginia, I'd been lucky enough to get one of the better paying jobs in the DC area, as a clerk typist at the Pentagon. By chance I was hired to work in the Office of the Assistant Chief of Staff for Army Intelligence. After the fifth person said to me "Kathie Hotter? Are you related to Joe Hotter who worked in Berlin?" I went home to ask dad, "What did you do in Berlin? Why do all these Intelligence folks know your name?"

Turns out Mom and Dad both worked in the Counterintelligence Corps or CIC in Berlin before they married. Dad had worked in CIC as an Army sergeant during WWII and stepped into an equivalent civilian job in the same office when the war ended. Mom went over to Berlin from Boston to take a civil service secretarial position in 1948, ending up in Dad's office. After marriage and a few years in the States they returned to Berlin in 1955 with two kids in tow and one on the way and Dad stepped right back into his CIC work, not as a bookkeeper as we were always told.

I realize now that our childhood play of running down dark areas from the Stasi had been real-life scenes for my father as he helped important "brain-trust" East Germans escape into the West. Dad of course never talked about this, couldn't apparently, until certain events were declassified. He died before much of that was declassified, before I could ask him questions, or let's face it, before I was old enough to care to ask him questions. My godfather, my dad's nephew, later told me stories Dad had shared with him. Maybe since Ralph lived in Canada and was older, Dad trusted him to keep things secret. Ralph told me stories of dad and colleagues using the closed subway stations to get under the Wall, of running down alleys shooting and being shot at, of getting "one really big one" out…although he never could share the name. He told me Dad was involved with the Nurnberg trials in some way too.

I learned other things years later. When the Wall went up, with the heightened fear of the Russians coming across the border, all the families of CIC agents were to be sent back to the States. Mom and other women balked, refusing to leave their husbands behind. They were told they could stay but to have suitcases packed and by the door at all times, just in case.

Back then, as tensions eased into a new norm, certain aspects of our lives were still different from other Americans in Berlin, all obvious to me now of course. We couldn't "tour" East Berlin for fear of Dad's family members being taken in reprisals.

Back then, when you headed out of Berlin, the train crossed necessarily through East Germany for a long stretch, as Berlin was truly a divided island in the middle of the East. As kids, we were simply excited about the train rides. I can still remember leaning out the window of a train car leaving Wannsee Station with the song playing over the big loudspeakers spaced along the length of the platform– Marlena Dietrich singing "Auf Wiedersehen, Auf Wiedersehen, komm zu mir zuruck." We kids would fight over who got the top bunk to sleep in, always fun because you could lie there with a clear view out the window if you pulled the curtain back.

We didn't pay attention to the fact that when the train stopped at one point, East German guards carrying rifles would board the train, taking everyone's passports for the duration. They'd return them when they left the train at the East/West border. I know now that mom was a nervous wreck the whole time, especially the one time that my brother's passport was not returned immediately with the rest of them. My dad's name was Joseph John Hotter. My brother's name was Joseph John Junior. I realize now that that name was on a list.

Ret. Army Reserve Lt. Col, Kathie Hotter Hightower, Class of 1971
1955-1964

Memorial to Rudolf Urban at Bernauerstrasse. On August 19, 1961 Rudolf and his wife jumped from a fourth story window, he died from his injuries a week later. The building was razed in 1962, remnant of lower floor is seen with boarded windows. Background: The Reconciliation Church, which was cut off by the East barrier along with this building.

The Night the Wall Went Up

I attended Wiesbaden High School from 1961-1965, graduating in 1965. My dad was Air Force and flew the West Berlin Air Corridor from Wiesbaden once a week into Tempelhof. Dad was the flight engineer and had his own window in the Boeing C-97 he flew. Dad had trained prior to WWII as a photographer, his dad being a photographer for a Wichita, Kansas newspaper. So Dad took lots of pictures of the MiGs out his window as they flew back and forth for four years between Wiesbaden and Berlin.

In August 1961 Dad was TDY ('temporary duty') to Berlin for a month. Dad and his friends were great jazz fanatics and the best German jazz clubs were in the Soviet sector. On August 12, Dad and three of his friends were in a jazz club, near the Brandenburg Gate. About 11 pm Dad and a friend decided to go back to base. As they walked through the Brandenburg Gate, they noticed a lot of German and Russian military activity. They thought it was road works, as barbed wire was rolled out.

Dad told this story all his life so I know it well. He and his friend reported the activity to the MPs on duty nearby. Others had reported suspicious activity in other parts of Berlin, so an alert went out that anyone in the eastern sector should evacuate ASAP. However, it was too late that night for Dad's other two friends. They approached Brandenburg Gate about 1am and were told they had to apply to get through and had 48 hours to do so. Well, they did eventually get out.

Anyone who was in the Soviet Sector had 48 hours to show reason for evacuation, since the Wall was being put in place to stem the tide of people escaping to the West. People had no idea what really was about to happen. There were probably about two dozen American servicemen in that jazz club that night and probably dozens more in Gasthauses (taverns) and Bierstubes (beer halls), etc. Everyone eventually got out–under agreement–but some of their German friends who worked on the base were dislocated from their families for over 20 years, as we all know so well.

Two years later we took the train to Berlin from Frankfurt and were told the same as everyone: 'Don't take pictures.' I had a 16mm Minox camera and so of course, being a 15 or 16 year old American teenager, I ignored the warnings. I still have pictures of East German soldiers taken from the train window. I still have some East German coins, and I wedged out a rock from the Wall. I did my bit to take the Wall down. I still have the fist-sized rock in a box in the shed.

Daniel Jenkins, Class of 1965
Wiesbaden High School Alumnus

PAGE 2

Editorial

Berlin's Postwar Years Show Tension Building

The picture of a divided Berlin—half free and half under Communist control—began to emerge almost immediately after World War II as the focal point of international tension.

The United States, Britain, France and the Soviet Union, meeting for the first time in June 1945, agreed to divide the city into four zones of occupation. Berlin was to be governed by the inter-allied Kommandatura consisting of four commandents, each serving in rotation as chief.

Joint administration, however, was not a success. Difficulties arose almost at once when the Soviets insisted on special rights as "host" in Berlin to the three other nations.

This was followed by a series of Soviet refusals to cooperate in programs for the rehabilitation and reunification of all Germany. Before long Moscow had unilaterally imposed its rule on the Soviet sector.

The history of Berlin since that time is a record of tensions—all imposed at Moscow's bidding. Threats, harassment, and direct restrictions have kept Berliners in constant turmoil. Further, Moscow has steadily refused to allow German reunification by free, secret elections.

At Potsdam in July 1945 the United States, Britain and the Soviet Union pledged to treat Germany as an economic whole and to prepare for "the eventual reconstruction of German political life on a democratic basis."

The Soviets broke this pledge regularly during the ensuing years. The East German economy was drained of its resources. Police-state rule in the Soviet zone replaced the empty promise of free political expression.

Early in 1948, four-power administration fell through completely when the Soviet delegation marched out of the Allied Control Council meeting in the divided city.

In June of the same year the Soviet Union began several weeks of sporadic interference in transport facilities, culminating in the Berlin blockade which halted all rail, highway and canal traffic between West Berlin and West Germany.

The Allied answer to the blockade was the famed airlift, which, by its end on May 12, 1949, had supplied West Berliners with more than 2,343,000 tons of food and other necessities.

Public opinion reached a low point in June of 1953, when construction workers in East Berlin began a series of strikes and uprisings which spread rapidly throughout East Germany. The revolt was crushed by Soviet troops and tanks at a cost of nearly 800 Germans killed and 1,740 wounded.

The feeling of East Germans for Communism had made itself felt as early as 1946, when an election of Berlin officials went against Communist candidates by a margin of four to one. Since that defeat, Soviet leaders have consistently rejected all proposals for free elections.

But East Germans found a dramatic means of expressing their opinion of Soviet rule—a stream of refugees crossing into West Berlin and West Germany. The total of this exodus had reached four million by early this month.

This August 1961 article explains what led up to the building of the Wall. The Soviets had to stem the tide of East Germans fleeing to the West. At the time of this article, "The total of this exodus had reached four million by early this month."

"Peace Hostages"

By August 1961, we had been living in Berlin for a few years. The city was magnificent and vibrant, and rebuilding. There were still bombed-out buildings around, but I guess, as kids, we didn't think much about it, though one time my brother was digging in the yard and found an Iron Cross. He brought it into the house and Mom told him to stop digging in case he found something else that we didn't want to find. We all knew that the Russians owned a part of Berlin that we never went into, but the British and French owned part as well. We, as children, felt safe.

My dad was the liaison between the German police and the American State Department. The German police were a paramilitary force in Berlin, and had the same functions of a military group, without the military title. This was due to an agreement after the Second World War that Berlin would not have a German military presence. On a night in August of 1961, my dad got a phone call about activity on the border of the Russian Sector. Russian tanks had surrounded the city. Dad then related that news to the State Department. From that night on, until we left, Dad had dark circles under his eyes, because he never got good sound sleep. The phone rang all night long, relating stories of people trying to escape East Berlin. Sometimes he had to go to an undisclosed place to interrogate escapees to find out if they were spies or what they knew.

The Wall had begun that day in August. The very beginning of the Wall that would surround West Berlin for nearly thirty years was being erected. It first started with tanks, then barbed wire, and finally, the Wall. It seemed like a long process to get it to the Wall stage. When President Kennedy was told about the Russians closing Berlin in, he announced that all American dependents would stay in Berlin, and we would be considered "peace hostages." There would be no evacuation. What I vividly remember about that was my mom. She totally freaked out, thinking that West Berlin would be invaded by the Russians, and everybody knew what the Russians did to Berliners after the Second World War. She was so mad at Kennedy– she who had been his fan–because he "abandoned" us there.

Our Sundays, after that, changed. After church, we would go to the border to see the progress of the Wall. It was so eerie to see windows of buildings on the East side bricked up, so people couldn't jump to freedom. At first, the border was strung with single strands of barbed wire. Then, when we went back, the barbed wire was strung to create a no-man's land, barbed wire on both sides of a mowed area. And towers were built for soldiers to guard the no-man's land so no one could escape without being seen and captured or shot.

Homes near the Wall, windows boarded or bricked up, 1961

On both sides of no-man's land, were people with white handkerchiefs, waving to each other. Dad told us they were families that had been separated by the Russians.

After a few months, cement blocks started to form the Wall. One Sunday, the Wall was done, and barbed wire was strung all on the top of the Wall. The guard towers were barely visible because the Wall was so high. To us kids, this was pretty exciting and scary at the same time. One time, my brother managed to find himself in an unmarked area that was considered East Berlin. My mother grabbed him back just as a guard was pointing his rifle at my brother. As much as the adults must have been affected by this, I don't think we were. We did still go to school, have our friends, and play outside.

After a while, we got used to being enclosed. We knew, as we got older, which subway lines to stay away from (the S-bahn). We took for granted that we couldn't go to East Berlin, and really didn't have any desire to. We had plenty in West Berlin to occupy our time. Taking the Duty Train in and out of Berlin was normal. The sport teams always seemed to look forward to those train trips. Life was really great in Berlin, enclosed or not.

When we came back to the States, people always used to ask, "Did you feel claustrophobic living in Berlin?" I never did. My folks might have, but I didn't. I remember a long bike ride with friends in the spring of 1968, on the wonderful bike paths in Berlin that went around the whole city. I knew we were safe, because of the Wall around us.

Natalie Winter Rogers, Class of 1968
1956-1969

Early guard towers were hastily and crudely made, December 1961

When the Wall Went Up

I was in Berlin when the Wall went up and it's an experience I will **never** forget. I should note that my mother was German and we were fortunate to have been stationed in Berlin at the time because my German grandparents were still alive at that point. I would often spend the weekend with them to help them with some chores in their apartment since they were getting older.

I can still hear the screams and cries that morning when we opened the windows to see what was going on out in the street. People were running, almost aimlessly, up and down the street crying and screaming. It was then that we learned there had been a wall or some other form of barrier put up overnight throughout Berlin, separating the East from the West.

In some spots they'd built an actual wall with barbed wire on top. There were other sections where they'd simply put up a wall of barbed wire but you could clearly see that a large stretch of land had been covered with sand, which had land mines hidden underneath. Then there were lots of soldiers with machine guns. I remember visiting my German cousin and found that they couldn't even use the front door of their apartment because the Wall was immediately outside the apartment doors.

So now back to why people were running in the streets crying and screaming. Imagine your child, spouse, parent…any member of your family happened to go and visit someone in the East Berlin sector that night. These loved ones were now no longer able to return to you. If memory serves me correctly, it was a long time before they would set up checkpoints and allow people from the East to come over to the West to visit.

Now you would think, "Well, why don't they just come for a visit and stay?" Sadly, the answer is simple- there was no way you were allowed to come to the West without having a loved one left behind who would be "dealt with" if you didn't return. So you had no choice but to return after your visit.

Flowers and wreaths lain for those killed attempting to escape to the West

Though it was not the only checkpoint between East and West Berlin, the best known is Checkpoint Charlie, which became infamous over time and was actually where my father served some of his time after he'd done two tours in Viet Nam. My father told us gruesome stories of the poor souls who attempted to flee to freedom but were caught or shot. Eventually, a small store opened here, turned itself into a museum and called itself the Checkpoint Charlie Museum. This museum tells the stories of failed and successful escapes to the West.

I remember there were sections in Kreuzberg where you could see across the water, which was the East and you could see the flowers and wreaths on the West side where people had actually managed to swim and make it all the way to the West only to get shot while climbing out of the water. It was always such a very sad place to visit. Eventually my parents divorced and my mother ended up staying in Berlin because her parents were still alive. She later met a German man who had relatives that still lived in the East. He always enjoyed looking at my Sears and JC Penney catalogs and couldn't get over how you could order all these wonderful things by simply picking up the phone. He was able to sneak one of these catalogs over to his relatives to show it to them. They simply could not understand how this would be possible and told him in a very matter of fact manner that this was nothing but propaganda.

Everyone in the East who was capable of working had to work. Eventually the elderly were allowed to cross over to the West. The feeling was that they were allowed to leave because they were no longer able to work and were now a burden due to medical needs.

I remember visiting Berlin with my daughter, who was only 7 or 8 at the time and allowing her to write her name on the different sections of the Wall throughout Berlin. My stepfather took her to the Brandenburg Gate where she also went to write her name on this very famous Wall only to suddenly have the soldiers come down from the towers on each side with their machine guns, yelling that she could not do this. In this particular case, the Wall had been built well into the East section of Berlin.

I still shudder when I think that they could easily have shot my daughter as well as my stepfather. I am still grateful to these guards for simply yelling and giving them a good scare. I should note that some of the most famous artists in the world came to paint/draw on various sections of the Wall. Some of the artwork was absolutely magnificent.

When I heard on the news that the Wall came down I was in absolute shock. The first thing I did was call my father who was just as shocked as I was. NEVER did either of us think that we would still be around to see this happen. When I spoke to my mother later, I learned that this was apparently not intentional. It all started as a miscommunication of orders to one of the guards. Once it started happening though, there was just no stopping it.

Marion Condon, Class of 1969
1960-1969

East Berlin death strip: rows of Czech hedgehogs (anti-tank obstacles) and sanded areas used to reveal footprints and conceal land mines, 1961.

Postscript from a Time Capsule

When I left Berlin in August of 1963 to go to college, I put my scrapbooks and other special items in an Army issue footlocker. It moved around with my parents until I got married, and they sent it to me in California. It remained in the basement of the houses I've lived in for forty years. I can't remember ever looking through them, though I'm sure Lee Hodges '62 and I must have got them out when she visited several times in the '70s. Chuck Hewins '63 and his wife dropped in for a visit a few years ago and I wanted us to look at them then, but when I opened the books, the pages, glue, and tape had deteriorated. It would have taken more time to plow through them than we had at the time.

When I decided to attend the Berlin Brats reunion in 2003, I knew it was time to open the footlocker to see what was in the "baggage" I'd been carrying around all these years. Monday, March 17, 2003 was the day I'd set aside to begin the project. My husband was out of town on a golf trip so I had a week at the house all to myself to work on it. The U.S. was on the brink of war.

What a journey that week was! I returned to three years of my life that had been stored in the dark corners of numerous basements and hidden beneath the events of the forty years of my life that followed 1960 - 1963. When I first began to look through the "stuff" I asked myself, "Why on earth did I save all this junk?" By the time I finished, I felt I'd been offered a great gift– the opportunity to relive an important time in my life and to see myself as a teenager. I also realized why I'd lugged the footlocker around for so long. As a dependent, you often don't get to return to your neighborhood. You can't revisit your school, run into your high school classmates or members of their family around town and relive your earlier years with your community. Although I hadn't looked at the things I'd saved in years, it was always near me, proof that the things I remembered– and many things I'd forgotten– did happen. Jim Branson '64 suggested that the footlockers many of us have lugged around for years are our "neighborhoods"– a place we can revisit whenever the need for rekindling the memories of our travels strikes us. We don't have a real place– we have footlockers.

At first I was chagrined to see how much time I spent as a cheerleader, at sports events and at the teen club, and how oblivious I seemed to be to the dramatic events that were occurring around me. I remember getting letters from our relatives during our years in Berlin filled with their fear and concern for our safety. It was much harder on them than on us. All they saw was the news broadcasts which showed nothing of our mostly normal day-to-day life.

The day the Wall went up, I went to the border with friends and we watched old women building portions of the Wall while we ate potato chips and dip. I returned home excited about spending a Sunday with my friends to find my parents watching the TV and looking as if someone had just died. In later years I often chastised myself for being so self-absorbed and seemingly unaware of the seriousness of the events so close at hand, but as I have gotten older, and, I hope, wiser, I am glad I got to have a "normal" high school life that enabled us to be wrapped up in our own little world. I am grateful to our parents, teachers and the military for allowing us to be teenagers. There would be plenty of time as adults to feel the weight of the world on our shoulders.

As I followed the war news from Iraq that day, I began hoping that in places around the globe where there are crises, the children and teenagers living there are able to experience some normalcy in their young lives as we did in Berlin in the early 1960's.

Maggie Ellithorpe Stafsnes, Class of 1963
1960-1963

Bernauer Strasse– famous for escapes from the windows of apartments located along this street and via tunnels. Tunnels were dug under the Wall at Bernauer Straasse allowing 57 East Berliners to escape via one tunnel and 29 via another. "Tunnel 29" as it would later be named, became famous because an NBC news crew captured the arrival of the 29 as they exited the tunnel to freedom in West Berlin. This footage was broadcast worldwide.

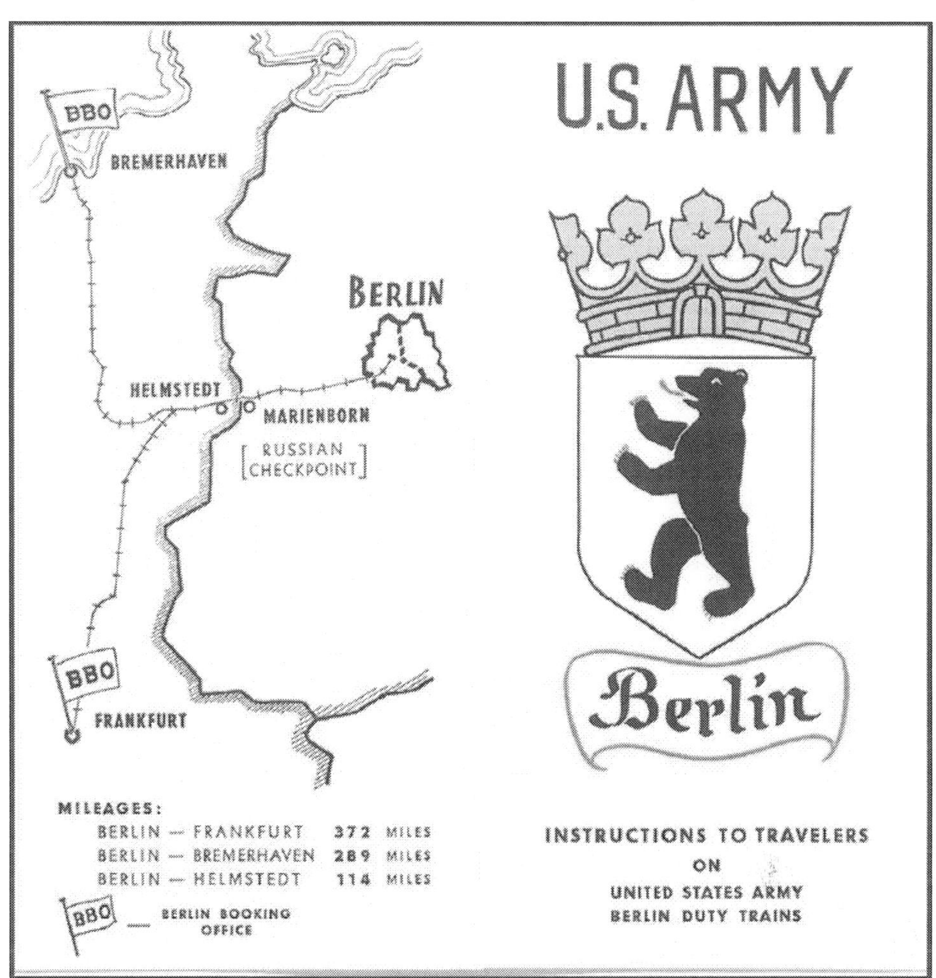

Brief History of the Duty Train

After WWII, Germany was divided through the capital city of Berlin into sectors occupied by the French, British, American, and Soviet governments. To transport soldiers, their dependents, and Us Army civilians in and out of the Allied sectors, the Transportation Corps established the Berlin Duty train in late 1945. The US had a total of four passenger trains that traveled through Frankfurt, Bremerhaven, and Berlin consisting of three compartmentalized sleeping cars, an escort car, and a mail and freight car.

The trains traveled only at night, and the trip averaged nine hours, depending on time spent to check passports and orders. Approximately 80,000 people made the trip each year. Each train was assigned a train commander, a Russian-English interpreter, two military police, a radio operator, and a conductor. The Train Commander was almost always a Transportation Corps Lieutenant, who was responsible for the safety and security of the train during its journey. No one was permitted to get off the train at checkpoints, except for the commander, interpreter, and senior MP. Passport inspection by the Russians took about an hour and if information did not match exactly – a period or a space in the wrong place – a person could be rejected.

–Courtesy of the US Army Transportation Museum

IMPORTANT

CONDUCT ON BOARD MILITARY TRAINS

1. In accordance with USAREUR Circular 550—180, the following actions are prohibited aboard military trains:
   a. Purchase or drinking of intoxicating liquor.
   b. Jumping on or off moving trains.
   c. Pulling emergency brakes (Notbremse) except in case of actual emergency.
   d. Extending the head or limbs out of windows.
   e. Throwing lighted cigarettes, cigars, matches, or any dangerous or unsightly articles from trains.
   f. Taking pictures between Berlin and Helmstedt.
   g. Speaking to or attempting to converse with East German nationals or Soviet personnel while train is in the Soviet Zone of Germany.
   h. Inconsiderate littering of compartments with refuse or food particles.
2. The privacy of an individual's compartment does not exempt him from compliance with the above directions.

REMINDERS

All passengers must be processed by the train commander prior to boarding the train. The train commander is located in the processing booth inside the RTO. Please have your tickets, ID cards, passports and flag orders ready. Do not board the train until authorized to do so by a military policeman or the train commander.

On arrival at your destination, you must check and re-confirm your return booking with the local Berlin Booking Office. If you are traveling on a "space-available" (non-duty) status, there is no guarantee regarding the type of accommodations you will be furnished on your return trip. Duty travelers have priority.

The military crew on board each passenger train is responsible for your safe passage throughout the entire trip. Your cooperation and compliance with the pertinent rules and regulations will insure you a safe and comfortable journey. For those of you who are coming to Berlin, we of the Berlin Brigade wish you a pleasant stay in the "divided city." For those of you leaving, "Auf Wiedersehen" and "Good Luck".

BERLIN DUTY TRAIN STAFF

Train Commander: A commissioned officer of the Berlin Brigade who is responsible for and in command of the Berlin duty train through the Soviet Zone of Germany. The train commander is on board only through the Soviet Zone, i.e. to/from Helmstedt-Berlin.

US Train Conductor: A non-commissioned officer who acts as liaison between passengers and railway operating personnel and who exercises technical supervision over each train to insure the best possible service and comfort to the passengers.

Military Police: MPs are placed aboard Berlin trains to maintain law and order, provide security, and perform other duties as required.

Interpreter: An individual, fluent in Russian, who is designated to act as translator — interpreter for the train commander with Soviet checkpoint officer.

Radio Operator

Porters (Schaffner): West-German employees of Deutsche Schlafwagen-Gesellschaft (roughly equivalent to Pullman Co). Tipping is authorized for the personal services rendered by these individuals.

Conductor (Zugfuehrer): Both East and West German conductors ride on the train in their respective areas.

TRANSPORTATION DIVISION
BERLIN BRIGADE
APO 742

Posted instructions for Duty Train conduct, as well as an explanation of procedures regarding use, safety and security onboard, and at the RTO *(Rail Transportation Office).*

Duty Train Incident of Thanksgiving 1961

In 2007 the US Army Transportation Museum and the Army Transportation Museum Foundation paid tribute to Colonel Norbert Grabowski. He was recognized with a special plaque placed on a Berlin Duty Train guard car that is now housed in the Transportation Museum at Fort Eustis, Virginia. The car has been refurbished and dedicated in his memory. During the memorial service the Berlin Duty Train story was retold. Grabowski was acting as the train commander. The story follows as told by the Army Transportation Museum.

While traveling through East Germany, an East German refugee broke a window and boarded the train. East German and Soviet authorities demanded entrance to the train and the right to seize the passenger at the border crossing. Grabowski, then only a first lieutenant, refused entrance to the East Germans and Soviets for more than 15 hours. Finally, when ordered by US authorities in order to avoid an international incident, Grabowski handed over the refugee. Grabowski served as train commander for only a short time, with the standard tour as train commander being approximately one and a half to two years.

A documentary about the incident reunited Grabowski with the East German he had worked to save. The refugee had served two years in prison for the incident, and lived in East Germany until the Communist regime fell in 1989. Grabowski, according to retired Colonel James Rockey, certainly having been courageous, and others recognizing it, received an Army Commendation Medal for what he did, and in that time it was a rare thing for a lieutenant to be recognized.

Initially he did not know the refugee was on the train. At the time it was an issue of US sovereignty. "If you let them try it one time and no one was there, they will try it anytime they can for publicity, to make the US look bad."

Upon completion of a new addition to the museum, the train will be used to display the film "Stop Train 349," a Hollywood rendition of the incident that tested Grabowski's character when he was a young lieutenant.

by Linda Dinklage, Defense Transportation Journal, September 2007 issue, used with permission

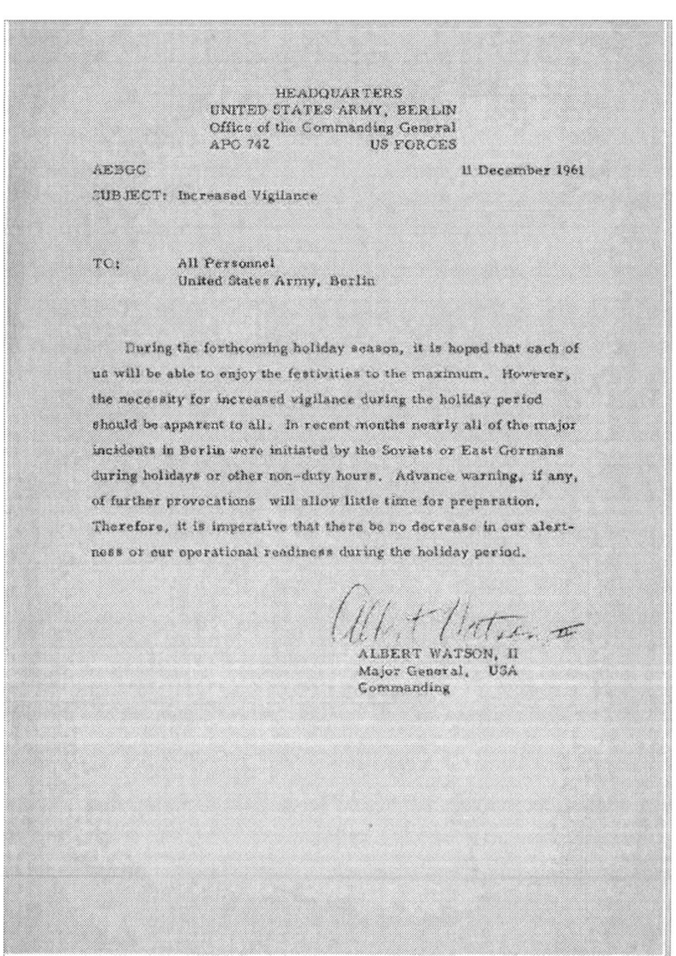

HEADQUARTERS
UNITED STATES ARMY, BERLIN
Office of the Commanding General
APO 742 US FORCES

AEBGC 11 December 1961

SUBJECT: Increased Vigilance

TO: All Personnel
United States Army, Berlin

During the forthcoming holiday season, it is hoped that each of us will be able to enjoy the festivities to the maximum. However, the necessity for increased vigilance during the holiday period should be apparent to all. In recent months nearly all of the major incidents in Berlin were initiated by the Soviets or East Germans during holidays or other non-duty hours. Advance warning, if any, of further provocations will allow little time for preparation. Therefore, it is imperative that there be no decrease in our alertness or our operational readiness during the holiday period.

ALBERT WATSON, II
Major General, USA
Commanding

Berlin Command letter, calling for "Increased Vigilance" during the holiday

BERLIN 1962

This Is "The Night the Lights Went out in Geor"...Berlin. (Sorry Vicki.) When they arrested an innocent man...well, not really. I was guilty as sin. A gang leader bent on the destruction of West Berlin society...well, not really. A small group of us were headed home from a party. I do not remember who gave it or if beer was involved, but it led to a crime spree that would involve the German Police, Military Police, the Provost Marshal and even the CIA.

It all began with a well-aimed soccer kick at a lamp post. Herr Longolius would have been proud. The street light went out. Now this would not happen in the US, but in Berlin, at the time this street had gas mantel lamps. I am not sure why, but I decided to try again to see if it was a fluke. It was not. Two down and what fun.

It was about this time that a German Police car drove past. I got nervous, but it kept on going. A few lamp posts later the MPs arrived. We were taken into custody. Parents were notified. Children picked up. I sat in the brig. I had no parents. Well, not really. They were vacationing for a week in Bavaria. This fact was causing a dilemma for the Military Police. They did not want a dependent on their hands overnight or longer, even if I was 18.

The Duty Officer asked me what I had been thinking. I told him that at the moment, I had not been and asked him to bring me my wallet. He complied and I showed him my "get out of jail free" card. He did a triple take realizing at that point he had no jurisdiction over me, a CIA Brat. I asked him to call the number on the card so someone could pick me up and take me home. Thirty minutes later I was home in my basement room at 5 Ripley Strasse listening to Bill Haley, smoking a cigarette and sipping a beer from my parents' stash.

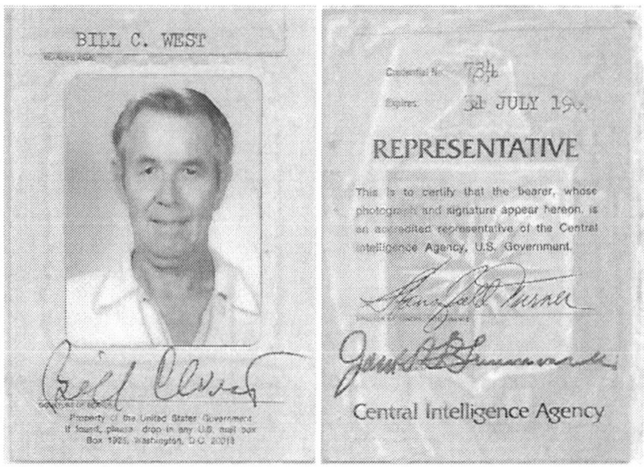

Bill Sr.'s CIA Identification

This sounds like a happy ending. The criminal gets away with the crime. Well, not exactly. When my parents returned there were ramifications. Authorities fined me 50 DM. Everyone else was fined 25 DM. Do you sense a certain injustice here? I was under lockdown for two weeks. Then my father decided I had too much free time on my hands so I was enrolled in the Goethe Institute, a language school. I took two hourly classes a day. One to learn German in German and the other to learn Russian in German. It was here I met Charles, the French Commandant's son who dated Maddie W. This meeting led to further adventures before I returned to the US to attend Denison University in Granville, OH which was also my father's undergraduate alma mater. I will never forget Berlin or the friends I made.

Bill "Toby" West Jr., Class of 1961
1953-1962

The S-Bahn Incident

"I can't believe we just did that!" This is what I said to Wayne Taylor '65, a fellow Berlin American High School Brat, as we stumbled down the steps of the S-Bahn station at the Friedrichstrasse Bahnhof. It all started on a cold Friday evening in January 1962. We were in a partying mood and decided to look for a new watering hole. We were familiar with all of the hot spots like the Resi Bar at Alexanderplatz or the Eierschale Club (Egg Shell), at Breitenbachplatz, so we headed across town over to the British Sector to try out the British NAAFI (Navy Army and Air Force Institute) Club.

When we arrived we were pleasantly surprised to learn that a large mug of cold beer was only 40 pfenning! Needless to say, we drank all night and partied with the British soldiers and their German girlfriends. By the time midnight came, we felt no pain. The NAAFI Club was closing, so we decided to head back to Berlin Command to our apartments to crash. The weather was rather cold but at this point we were not feeling it. We managed to hop on the "autobus" heading back toward the Zehlendorf district, but found that we had to transfer to a different bus near the border at Friedrichstrasse.

By now, the time was approaching 1 am and we had waited for nearly 45 minutes for another bus. The neighborhood was completely dead at that time of the night, so we went in search of another mode of transportation. After walking west on Friedrichstrasse for another 15 minutes, we came upon the infamous S-Bahn railway station. The S-Bahn train was not to be used by Americans as it was maintained and operated by the East German government- the DDR- or in other words, it was strictly "verboten," meaning "off limits." Being that we were not of sound mind or body, due to all of the alcohol and extreme cold setting in, we decided to try the S-Bahn train. After purchasing our tickets and running them through the turnstile, we jumped onto the first waiting train car we saw. It was extremely warm inside the car, which felt so good, that we promptly fell asleep.

I had no clue as to how long we were asleep, but the constant drone of the train motor interrupted by the sudden sound of hissing steam caused me to awaken from my deep sleep. As I peered out the window, I was shocked to see that a Russian soldier, in full battle gear, had defected over to "our side." I started punching Wayne in the shoulder shouting, "Wake up! We got a Russian who just escaped to the West." We were both so excited that we ran off the train, up to the soldier, and grabbed both his hands, shaking them, shouting "Willkommen nach West Berlin Kamerad." The soldier, dressed in a full length long brown overcoat, with his PPSh-41 Kalashnikov machine gun slung over his left shoulder, appeared to be in his late thirties. He also appeared to be in shock! He looked as confused as we were when he turned around and pointed to the writing on the train station wall that said, "Ost Friedrichstrasse." He then regained his composure and shouted at us, "Das ist nicht West Berlin. Das is Ost Berlin."

Wayne and I looked at each other and suddenly realized that we were in deep trouble! We also became instantly sober. Fearing the worst, we stood on the platform thinking

Friedrichstrasse Bahnhof, 1962

about what was going to happen to us, or worse yet– our father's military careers were at stake! At this point, the Russian soldier kept looking up and down the train platform, and as he pulled out a pack of German smokes from his coat pocket, he stated, "Haben Sie Amerikanische Zigaretten?" We reached in our shirt pockets and immediately handed over two packs of Winston cigarettes. The Russian took the cigarettes, dumped out the German smokes and stuffed the American smokes back in the empty German pack. He then stuck out his hand and pointed to his wrist and muttered "Uhr." We seemed to know exactly what he wanted, so we handed over our wrist watches. Suddenly, he glanced up and down the platform once again, and led us over to the train car which we came out of. He then directed both of us to crawl underneath the seats on the floor of the train and stay there!

As we crossed over the border through a wall of barbed wire, we were once again back in West Berlin and FREEDOM! As we ran and stumbled down the steps of the S-Bahn station, we both realized how lucky we were to have been released by that Russian soldier on the other side. Had we been American GI's instead of a couple of teenagers, I am sure that things would have turned out a lot differently! As we found our way to a German taxi, I turned to Wayne and stated, "I can't believe that we just did that!"

Several days later, while doing the laundry, my mother found the S-Bahn ticket in my pants pocket and scolded me for riding on it. I told her what had happened and she replied, "Whatever you do, don't *ever* tell your father what you two did!" ...And you can bet that I never did!!!

Jules DeNitto, Class of 1963
1961-1963

The Spy Who Should Have Stayed Out In the Cold

Most everyone who was living in Berlin when the infamous Wall was constructed on August 13, 1961 was aware that the DDR, or the German Democratic Republic as it was called back then, expanded their spy network exponentially. The main objective was to gather intelligence from the West by any means necessary!

Usually operating under the cover of darkness, many East German agents would sneak over, under or through the concrete and barbed wire fortifications that separated East and West Berlin with the sole purpose of gathering information. Or– if they were extremely lucky– kidnap an American soldier and smuggle him back into East Berlin!

The American authorities at Berlin Command warned all American personnel, especially military soldiers, to be aware of any suspicious persons or activities, and to report any and all incidents when and where they occurred. The city of Berlin, a thriving metropolis of people, stores, buses, and subways, and a night-life filled with hundreds of bars and nightclubs, offered endless hours of excitement and entertainment. It also had an element of danger, which most people paid little or no attention to. Berlin was not immune to its share of incidents!

This is the story of one of East Berlin's Stasi agents (secret police), who slipped into West Berlin on a cool clear night in October 1962, with the intent of successfully fulfilling his mission to acquire any intelligence he could. This well-trained East German spy had no idea what was in store for him, for he was about to meet something that would be the object of his ruin. It was known as a "Berlin Brat."

On the particular night in question, I was with my brother Gary, who had just arrived back in Berlin as an Army soldier. He had enlisted in the Army in Berlin, back in November of 1961. My father was able to pull some strings and get him transferred from an Army post in Busac, France, to Andrews Barracks, in Berlin. Even more amazing, Berlin Command allowed him to live off- post with the family on Taylorstrasse (military dependent housing) during his tour.

It was a time for celebrating, so I proposed that he and I hit the Ku'damm for some partying. I advised him that he should dress in civilian attire as he was still in his Class A Uniform, and it was not wise to travel about at night in Berlin while in uniform. He did not feel it was necessary to change out of his uniform, and we subsequently left for the Kurfürstendamm in downtown Berlin. After visiting a couple of taverns, it was about 9 PM when we entered the famous Smokey's nightclub (a well-known burlesque joint). After a couple of drinks and while enjoying the entertainment up on the stage, I happened to glance across the room when I observed a gentleman focusing his attention on our table instead of the beautiful women up on the stage. Not thinking much about it at that time, I turned my attention back to the dancers on the stage.

About an hour later, we departed that club and while walking up the Kurfürstendamm, I happened to glance behind us and, once again, noticed that same man was walking toward us. It was at this time that I advised Gary of my earlier observations in the club and suggested that we were being followed. He just shrugged it off, stating that I was "imagining things." I was convinced that we were being followed. Across the street was a large department store with several female mannequins in the display window. I suggested to my brother that we cross the street and peer in those windows to see if he follows us.

We immediately ran across the street, in and out of traffic, to the other side and pretended to look at the displays. We were able to see in the reflection in the window that the man had also run across the street and was peering through the windows further down from us. I asked my brother, "Do you believe me now?" My brother was visibly upset and asked, "What are we going to do?" I replied, "I know of a bar in the next block called Captain Bilbo's. Let's go there!"

A couple minutes later, we arrived there and noticed the subject was close behind us. As we walked through the front door, we took a table on the right side of the bar near the hallway that led to the bathrooms. We ordered a beer, and when the waitress served our drinks, we noticed the subject walking through the front door. He suddenly stopped, scanned the bar, and locked his eyes on our table staring at us. He then turned to his left and took a seat on the only remaining empty stool at the bar.

The bar was well-lit, and we got our first real good look at this individual. He was a white male, dressed in all black, with a white shirt and black tie, and had a deep ugly eight inch scar running from across his left eye down to just below his mouth. When he turned toward the bartender to order a drink, his jacket opened slightly revealing a brown shoulder holster containing a black automatic pistol. My brother and I looked at one another, and acting as calmly as I could, I whispered to him, "Don't leave this table. I'm going to walk back to the restroom where there's a payphone, and call Dad."

Within a minute, I was advising my father over the phone of what was happening and our location. He screamed back over the phone, "Don't you leave that G...D...bar for any reason. I'll have someone there immediately." I knew my father would come through as he was also the Sergeant Major of the 7350th Air Police Squadron at Tempelhof Air Base.

I went back to our table and told Gary that help was on the way. As we slowly drank our beer, the subject at the bar was still staring at us with his drink in hand. Approximately 10 minutes later, the door to the bar flew open, and eight uniformed West German Police, accompanied by two Air Force OSI agents, ran in. OSI agent Dutch Schultz– who knew me–shouted, "Point him out to me!" I stood up and pointed directly at the subject in the black suit, whereupon the uniformed police drug him off the bar stool, slammed him on the floor, and removed the gun from his shoulder in one fell swoop. The whole time the subject was screaming profanities in German as they drug him out the door, beating him with their rubber Billy clubs.

When the incident was over, OSI agents Schultz and Al Guidenburger said, "Jules, can't you just keep it simple for once?" as they laughed and walked away. Later investigation revealed that the man in black was in fact an East German agent! After that night, my brother no longer wore his Class A Uniform off-duty again!

Jules A Denitto, Class of 1963
1961-1963

Teddy Roosevelt and the Berlin Wall

Perhaps my most interesting Scout adventure in Berlin began with Teddy Roosevelt and ended with very tired feet!

In 1962, President John F. Kennedy apparently found out that President Teddy Roosevelt, a fitness buff in his own right, had challenged the Marines to hike 50 miles in under 20 hours to prove their fitness. Kennedy used this historical challenge to try to initiate a fitness resurgence in the US. Soon, "Kennedy 50 Mile Hikes" were a craze across the county (and still are). They became the equivalent of the German Volksmarsch and were publicized in all the leading news magazines and newspapers.

In the early 60's, in Berlin, most of our news was from the *Stars and Stripes* newspaper or the Paris edition of *TIME* as well as mail deliveries of *LIFE* and other periodicals. I remember reading with interest about this latest American fad. On Friday 15, 1963 the Berlin Brigade newspaper had an article about an Army officer and several of his sergeants who were going to do the first Kennedy 50 Mile Hike in Berlin. This particular officer had done some work with Troop 46 and so the story caught my eye as well as that of several other Scouts.

Then on Saturday, February 16, we went swimming with the British Scouts at their indoor pool– it was February in Berlin after all. On the ride back, someone- and I really have no idea who- came up with the idea that we should do the Kennedy 50 Mile Hike. We quickly agreed that there was no time to waste since we wanted to try to best the time of the soldiers. Accordingly, we decided to do it beginning early the next morning. I don't remember who all agreed to go on Saturday night but at 4 a.m. on Sunday,

February 17, 1963 only four Scouts showed up at the agreed upon start point in front of Berlin Brigade HQ on Clayallee. They were Ron Bolin '64, Tom Post '64 , Dave Prieto'64 and I.

We quickly plotted out our course and began hiking north towards the upper most point of West Berlin. Our goal: to hike the entire length of the Berlin Wall! As you can see from the pictures, it was snowy, but it was not particularly cold that day. It never got sunny but the exercise kept us warm. After we reached the furthest northern point of the Wall we began to trace its path south. Along the route, we hit many of the famous sites of Berlin, since to make the hike a true 50 miles, we had to take a number of side trips. Thus, the photo of us at the Berlin Airlift Memorial at Templehof.

We carefully plotted our route on city maps and to prove we had been at specific points we had people we met along the way sign and date 3x5 cards. I still have several in my scrapbook. Two of the ones I still have are by Berlin police officers, one is by an English soldier providing security for the Soviet soldiers at the Russian War Memorial and one is on the letterhead of the Kongresshalle (now called the Haus der Kulturen der Welt—House of World Cultures).

At starting point: Berlin Brigade HQ, 4 am February 2, 1963. L to R: Ron Bolin, Tom Post, Dave Prieto and Jim Polley

Somehow I'd forgotten to tell my parents of what we planned so when they got up on Sunday morning- several hours after we'd rendezvoused and left on our hike– they found a note from me and the remains of packages of crackers that'd I taken for "trail" rations. What the other guys told their parents I never knew. We continued to hike throughout the day; taking some short rest breaks and buying some wurst and brotchen to supplement the crackers and other snacks we'd brought with us. Again and again we carefully measured how far we'd come and, possibly more important, how far we still had to go. All this while I, at least, was dreaming of the heroes' welcome we would get when we arrived back at Berlin HQ having shown how fit America's youth truly were.

Shortly after dark we arrived at the US Army train station having done over 40 miles by that time (it gets dark early in February in Berlin). We called our parents and they soon arrived with food, dry socks and a few comments about how nice it might have been if we'd told them what we were going to do before we tried to do it. Despite offers to drive us home we were determined to finish the 50 miles and started out again to cover the last ten. By this time we'd been hiking about 12 hours, it was dark and perhaps more problematic– we were running out of places to hike! So, for the last 10 miles we cut back-and-forth across the American Sector of Berlin, too tired to be bored.

Finally, about 8 p.m. we saw the gates of the US Headquarters on Clayallee, our starting point. In a little over 14 hours, we'd hiked 50 miles, including most of the Berlin Wall, or at least those parts that were accessible. When we arrived at the gate, expecting perhaps the Commanding General to welcome us, there was no one except the gate guard. No band, no ceremony and not even our families. From that point, I had to hike about half a mile home. So with the hike to-and-from the starting point I actually hiked 51 miles.

As for the soldiers I mentioned earlier– that were going to do the first

Kennedy 50 Mile Hike… It turned out that one reason we never gained any recognition was that the soldiers had never completed the hike. In goodwill, the Berliners had showered them with food, beer and schnapps; they became too "full" to finish. We'd apparently not only bested their effort, but also managed to be a bit of an embarrassment in the process.

The next day we were back in school; my only reward was being excused from PE because my legs and feet were sore. Fifty Mile Hikes are a standard part of today's Scouting program but I suspect we took one of the more unusual ones– and didn't even get a patch to show for it.

To learn more about the Kennedy 50 Mile Hikes you can visit the JFK library online, then type in JFK 50 Mile in the search box or visit www.jfk50mile.org.

Jim Polley, Troop 46/Explorer Post 46, Class of 1964
1959-1963

Troop 46 Scouts at Berlin Airlift Memorial at Tempelhof, 1963

THE BERLIN OBSERVER

. . . A Jolly Good Trip

TO MERRY OLD ENGLAND—A trip to Great Britain is about to begin for Boy Scouts of Berlin Troop 46 and their German scout guests. The lads are now near Salisbury attending the European celebration of the Golden Anniversary of the Boy Scouts of America. —US Army Photos

Three years earlier…Troop 46 goes to England for the Golden Anniversary of the Boy Scouts of America, 1960

President John F. Kennedy Visits West Berlin

Excerpt from Kennedy's "Ich bin ein Berliner" Speech-June 26, 1963

"Two thousand years ago the proudest boast was 'civis Romanus sum.' Today, in the world of freedom, the proudest boast is 'Ich bin ein Berliner'

I appreciate my interpreter translating my German!

There are many people in the world who really don't understand, or say they don't, what is the great issue between the free world and the Communist world. Let them come to Berlin. There are some who say that communism is the wave of the future. Let them come to Berlin. And there are some who say in Europe and elsewhere we can work with the Communists. Let them come to Berlin. And there are even a few who say that it is true that communism is an evil system, but it permits us to make economic progress. Lass' sic nach Berlin kommen. Let them come to Berlin.

Freedom has many difficulties and democracy is not perfect, but we have never had to put a wall up to keep our people in, to prevent them from leaving us. I want to say, on behalf of my countrymen, who live many miles away on the other side of the Atlantic, who are far distant from you, that they take the greatest pride that they have been able to share with you, even from a distance, the story of the last 18 years. I know of no town, no city, that has been besieged for 18 years that still lives with the vitality and the force, and the hope and the determination of the city of West Berlin. While the Wall is the most obvious and vivid demonstration of the failures of the Communist system, for all the world to see, we take no satisfaction in it, for it is, as your Mayor has said, an offense not only against history but an offense against humanity, separating families, dividing husbands and wives and brothers and sisters, and dividing a people who wish to be joined together.

Freedom is indivisible, and when one man is enslaved, all are not free. When all are free, then we can look forward to that day when this city will be joined as one and this country and this great Continent of Europe in a peaceful and hopeful globe. When that day finally comes, as it will, the people of West Berlin can take sober satisfaction in the fact that they were in the front lines for almost two decades.

All free men, wherever they may live, are citizens of Berlin, and, therefore, as a free man, I take pride in the words "Ich bin ein Berliner!"

- President John F. Kennedy, in front of Rathaus Schöneberg

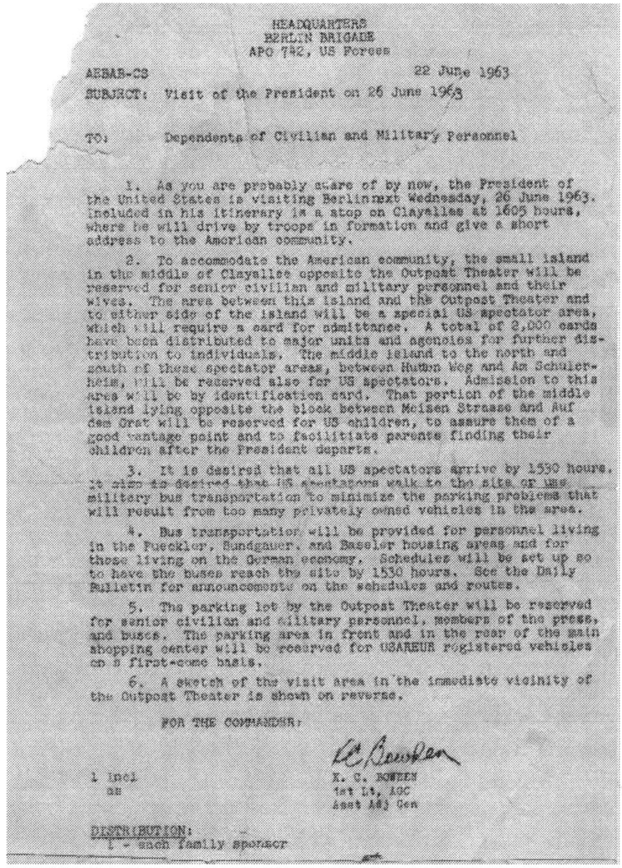

HEADQUARTERS
BERLIN BRIGADE
APO 742, US Forces

AEBAB-CS 22 June 1963

SUBJECT: Visit of the President on 26 June 1963

TO: Dependents of Civilian and Military Personnel

1. As you are probably aware of by now, the President of the United States is visiting Berlin next Wednesday, 26 June 1963. Included in his itinerary is a stop on Clayallee at 1605 hours, where he will drive by troops in formation and give a short address to the American community.

2. To accommodate the American community, the small island in the middle of Clayallee opposite the Outpost Theater will be reserved for senior civilian and military personnel and their wives. The area between this island and the Outpost Theater and to either side of the island will be a special US spectator area, which will require a card for admittance. A total of 2,000 cards have been distributed to major units and agencies for further distribution to individuals. The middle island to the north and south of these spectator areas, between Hutten Weg and Am Schülerheim, will be reserved also for US spectators. Admission to this area will be by identification card. That portion of the middle island lying opposite the block between Meisen Strasse and Auf dem Grat will be reserved for US children, to assure them of a good vantage point and to facilitiate parents finding their children after the President departs.

3. It is desired that all US spectators arrive by 1530 hours. ~~It also is desired that US spectators walk to the site or use~~ military bus transportation to minimize the parking problems that will result from too many privately owned vehicles in the area.

4. Bus transportation will be provided for personnel living in the Pueckler, Sundgauer, and Baseler housing areas and for those living on the German economy. Schedules will be set up so to have the buses reach the site by 1530 hours. See the Daily Bulletin for announcements on the schedules and routes.

5. The parking lot by the Outpost Theater will be reserved for senior civilian and military personnel, members of the press, and buses. The parking area in front and in the rear of the main shopping center will be reserved for USAREUR registered vehicles on a first-come basis.

6. A sketch of the visit area in the immediate vicinity of the Outpost Theater is shown on reverse.

FOR THE COMMANDER:

1 Incl
as

K. C. BOWEN
1st Lt, AGC
Asst Adj Gen

DISTRIBUTION:
1 - each family sponsor

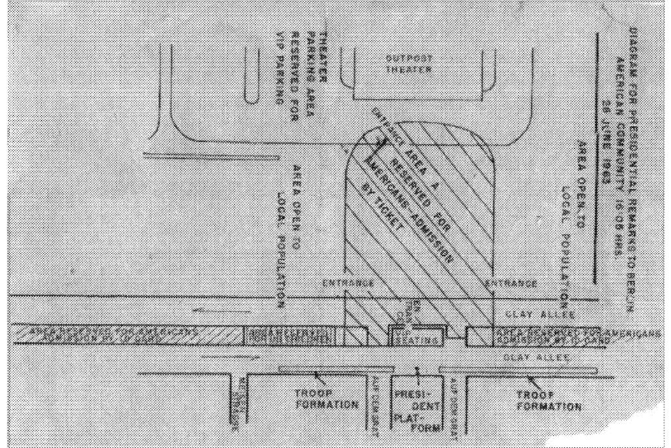

PRESIDENTIAL
REMARKS TO BERLIN AMERICAN
COMMUNITY

CLAYALLEE — 26 JUNE 1963
ADMIT ONE
AREA A

Instruction letter concerning the presidential visit, map of JFK's route, and admission ticket to event

Berlin Command issued a commemorative booklet of JFK's visit to Berlin

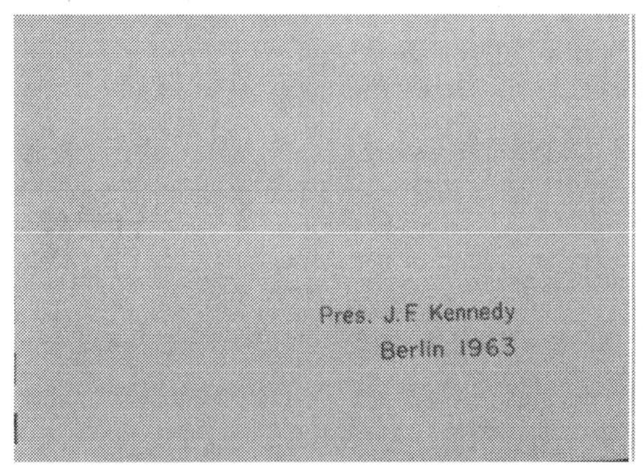

President Kennedy visits the Brandenburg Gate and Checkpoint Charlie during his state visit.

President Kennedy speaks to the German people at Rathaus Schöneberg and the US military community at Clay HQ

I Met JFK- Three Times!

It was June 26, 1963, and graduation day at TAR was fast becoming a memory. All the graduates were embarking on their own careers and or transferring to other parts of the world with their parents. As I was contemplating my own future, my mother reminded me that President John F. Kennedy had arrived in Berlin, and was visiting the American community shortly to give a speech.

I grabbed my camera and we headed out of our third floor apartment on Taylor Strasse, near the Outpost Theater, and crossed over to Clayallee, where the activities were taking place. There was a huge crowd of about 200 to 300 American dependents, soldiers, and VIPs gathered in front of the roped off podium. The President arrived and the crowd was excited as the band was playing and soldiers from Andrews and McNair Barracks were marching past the reviewing stand.

Minutes later, the President gave a rousing speech which lasted about 10 to 15 minutes, and that's when it happened! He stepped from the podium and made his way around the roped security area greeting well-wishers along his route. As he rounded the corner, he walked so close to me that I lunged forward and grabbed his hand, pulling him closer so he could shake my mother's hand. It was at that moment that I snapped a close up photograph of him, flanked by two of his Secret Service agents. I shouted out, "Welcome to Berlin Mr. President," and he replied, "Thank you, it's good to be here."

It wasn't until several days later when the film was developed, that I noticed the look on the Secret Service agent's face—he had focused his full attention on me when I grabbed the President's hand.

A few months later, I left Berlin to live with my sister at McDill AFB in Tampa, Florida and subsequently decided to join the Air Force. On November 18, 1963, I was at an Air Force recruiting station in Tampa, when--in the middle of taking the Oath of enlistment with two other individuals–in walks JFK on an inspection tour! He stayed until we completed the Oath and shook our hands, congratulating us on our entry into the USAF.

I told the President that I had met him a few months earlier in Berlin, and he replied that he was so exhausted from that trip that he did not remember much! I couldn't believe that I met the POTUS two times in 6 months!

First day at Lackland AFB, (11/19/1963)

Then, a mere 48 hours later, I was in my barracks at Lackland AFB in San Antonio, Texas, when my drill sergeant walked in and informed my flight that JFK was coming the next day to inspect the troops...and we'd "better look sharp!" On November 21, 1963, with our heads shaved and our brand new starched green fatigue uniforms, we stood at attention on the parade grounds at Lackland, as President Kenned reviewed the troops.

I was standing at attention in the middle of the formation as he walked past me rather briskly, but then he suddenly stopped, causing the top brass to almost run into him. He then performed what I would describe as a Michael Jackson "Moon Walk" backward to my position, and turned to me stating–with a big smile–"DENITTO, good to see you again. How is the Air Force treating you?" I was stunned and replied, "Very well, Mr. President!"

He then replied, "Well, you go and have a nice career now." I then replied, "Thank you sir!" As he continued on, I overheard the Base Commander whisper to my drill instructor, "Find out who that Son-of-a-b*^% is!" I guess I could describe my feelings after this third encounter with JFK as being on "Cloud Nine!"

The very next day at 1:20 PM, while sitting on my foot locker polishing my boots, a message came over the intercom. "Attention all personnel, The President of the United States was just shot and killed in Dallas." Nov 22, 1963 is a day that I try not to remember, but one that I will never forget!!

Jules A. Denitto, Class of 1963
1961-1963

Last day of Air Police Academy, Lackland, AFB

The Night JFK Was Killed

I was a 14 year old high school student in the American community in Berlin, Germany the night JFK was killed in Dallas, Texas. Most Americans will remember the event as a *day* they will never forget, but over in Europe it was the dark of night when the Armed Forces Radio Network announced the tragedy. I'd been reminded to take the trash out–a routine chore–but I remember looking up through the trees and wondering, as I gazed at the stars, how life would change for me and my family. My memory of the entire period is of darkness, cloudy days and pervasive doom. I was shaken, but still questioned how affected I *should* be by this and how I was *expected* to show the fear and sadness that was growing in me. The engaging young president had only recently visited Berlin making his famous "Ich bin ein Berliner" speech at "City Hall." I missed that, but through careful planning, intricate navigation and furious bike peddling my friends and I had managed to see his motorcade through the suburbs of Dahlem and Zehlendorf and arrive in time to shake his hand at the "Outpost," our local movie theater.

Now he was dead. What of his little girl and toddler son? How about his pretty wife, with whom my mother and so many other women seemed so utterly enthralled? With as much as had happened during the Cuban Missile Crisis, the military donned full battle gear, boots, weapons and helmets, and the few tanks in our small "Brigade" rolled. My weekend driving lessons with my CIA dad were postponed. In the days to come many Berliners, recognizing my BHS letter jacket (Go Cubs!), would stop me along the streets and forest paths and, in their best English, attempt to express their sorrow and condolences to me and other Americans. Berliners were grateful for my country's magnanimity after the war 18 years earlier, its tireless effort during the Airlift bringing in food, fuel and all manner of other supplies to keep an entire city alive, and America's continuous stand against Soviet domination. Solemn lines at the US Embassy on Clayallee– the main street in our suburban section of that great city– stretched for blocks and for hours each day as people waited to sign a condolence book. I was proud to be an American. I would serve my country.

Long lines of mourners wait outside the US Embassy (left) and mourners sign condolence books inside.

I recall vividly the self-propelled howitzers firing their evening salute across the broad avenue, the huge smoke rings expanding upward and crashing against the tall pines by the PX and commissary. Things had, indeed, changed. The assassinations, racial violence and the wrenching experience of Vietnam would follow and cause many to wonder what might have been had this charismatic leader not been taken from us so soon.

(Jerry) Ross Flavel, Class of 1967
1961-1965

Howitzers firing the evening salute, in memoriam, Clayallee HQ

Berlin Mourns for President John F. Kennedy

HEADQUARTERS
UNITED STATES ARMY, BERLIN
APO 742

AEBA-GA 24 November 1963

SUBJECT: Observance of Mourning for Late President John F. Kennedy

TO: See Distribution

1. The purpose of this letter is to provide guidance to all members of this Command, including their dependents, as to our conduct, actions, and the scope of our activities during the 30 - day period of National Mourning for the late President of the United States, John F. Kennedy.

2. The period of Official National Mourning commenced 22 November and will continue to be observed through 21 December 1963. This is a solemn period in which every United States Citizen in Berlin is expected to conduct himself in such a way that he cannot fail to reflect the innermost feelings of all Americans in our hour of National sorrow. The loss of our President is not only a grave loss to all Americans but to the entire free world. This is particularly true here in Berlin where President Kennedy endeared himself in the hearts of all Berliners and stood as a symbol of freedom and friendship. Because their loss approaches our own, the eyes of all Berliners will be upon us and our conduct will be subject to careful scrutiny during this solemn period. This is no time for frivolity but rather is a period for serious reflection and moderation.

3. In observance of the mourning period this command is taking the actions listed below. These actions do not cover every case that will arise. Undoubtedly you will be confronted by numerous situations requiring value judgement on your part. In these areas the command can only provide you with broad guidelines of appropriate behavior. In cases not covered by specific instructions, you should be governed mainly by the dictates of your own conscience as well as the need for discretion, decorum and good taste. If you are in doubt as to the propriety of your actions in some specific situation you are encouraged to seek further guidance from this headquarters. Such queries should be directed to the ACofS, G-1 Berlin Brigade.

4. <u>During the period until the time of interment of President Kennedy on 25 November the Command will observe the following:</u> a. Secretary of Defense has directed that all DOD Personnel will observe Monday 25 November 1963 as a day of mourning. The 25th of November will be a Non-Work Day except for essential activities. All Personnel, except those whose continued presence is directed, will be excused from duty. Civilian employees (US & LN) who are not required to work will be excused without charge to leave or loss of pay.

First page of a 4-page letter instructing military personnel and their families on proper etiquette for the thirty days of mourning for JFK's death

Good Timin' in Berlin: 1961-1965

Robert and the gang, 1965

We arrived a couple weeks before the Wall began construction and actually watched them building the Wall on TV. At that time we lived over in Dahlem, actually not too far from school. We lived on Flanaganstrasse and by the time we left in 1965 we had lived in three different locations. I was one of the lucky ones who actually got to do all of my high school in West Berlin and I have to tell you I had a ball, the best time of my youth. When we arrived, we were probably one of the few black families that had been assigned to Berlin– my sister and I are two years apart--when we began high school there, we were the only black students. It was kind of unusual looking around and not seeing anyone who looked like you, but we quickly adapted to that. That's basically military life, you get assigned somewhere and you find out it's a completely different culture by the time you get there, and you adapt and, that's what we did.

I know my dad went through some hard times just dealing with the stress that came with the territory, at that time it was really the heart-- the deep, deep heart of the Cold War. The standoff at Checkpoint Charlie happened during my time there. We really didn't know whether we were going to war and whatever happened sane minds prevailed and we're all here today; but I can tell you that during those few days, during the showdown at the Wall it was tense. We really did not know whether this world would survive, and I guess that's another one of the experiences that I can chalk up to having lived through and share that same commonality with the guys and the ladies that I went to school with. We'll never forget.

One of the benefits I think that I gained, that really allowed me to do as well as I have in my life is being able to meet and assimilate into the population that was there at the time. As Berlin was a divided city, it had French forces, American forces, English forces, and the Russians. My friends and I would go to the different Sectors of the city and just hang out, try to meet guys over there, hang out with the ladies, and just have a good time. We were frequent guests in the British Sector at the NAAFI club; we were usually the last ones leaving and we would help each other get back on the train to get back over to our section. We were club monsters, we pretty much were known faces at all the clubs in Berlin.

We had many opportunities to meet a lot of American celebrities who came over on tour during concerts– like Chuck Berry and even Chubby Checker (when he was really hot) and a lot of others. We had a chance to actually see The Beatles when they came through; they didn't actually perform in Berlin, but a friend of ours knew about them from performing up in Hamburg and we had a chance to go and meet them at their hotel–

actually it was a hostel they were staying in at the time. We hung out with them for about a day and that was a big deal for us.

My friends and I– we were kind of the terror crowd when we were there. We spent all four of our years raising hell. We got a good education on top of that, but we raised hell. For instance, we snuck across into East Berlin as a challenge just to see what would happen, and we got caught once—it was a minor international incident. It was pretty much swept under the carpet because of the people that were involved– not me, but the other guys that were involved– their parents. Our crowd actually initiated a bomb scare at our high school as an effort to get out of school for that day; it was really stupid but that's what you do when you're young.

Robert and his 'hell raising' crowd

Besides getting in trouble, we did take other issues seriously, we understood the situation that our fathers were put in by being assigned to that city, it was all very serious. I think one of the most significant days while I was there was probably the day that President Kennedy was assassinated. We were at a party that evening, a good friend of ours had a place, and we got a call that everyone needed to come home and we didn't know what the reason was. That night I didn't have a ride back so I caught a cab and I found out when I got in the cab what had actually happened and why the American brigade was put on alert; the cab driver knew but we didn't and I can still remember him that evening. Like people say you always remember where you were the day that Kennedy was shot, I do remember and it was kind of a crazy day.

Other things about my experience in Berlin, I met some great people, stayed in contact with a lot of them, had some great teachers. One of the things that I was impressed by after I left there was the educational system that we were put through. I can't think of better system anywhere in the country, and I've been through a lot. Actually when we do Overseas Brats get-togethers, one questions is, "How many schools have you attended as a military brat?" and I think I hold one of the records. I think I've gone through 29 different schools from Kindergarten until I graduated in Berlin.

Something that has become clear to me is that the education I got in Berlin is by far the best education I could have had anywhere in the country and it's too bad that the educational system in our country isn't up to the same par as that was. It was a great, great education and it also provided me with the tools to be able to move on with my life once I left there, went into the military, got out and started living as a civilian. I still credit my experience in Berlin to the person I've actually evolved into. In fact, I'm retired now, but I was allowed to retire on my own terms because of some of the skill sets that I had been instilled with as a result of living in Berlin.

I currently live in California and we had been seeing stories building up to where the Wall was going to actually be torn down, and I remember the day– because of the time difference we didn't see it until…well I guess it was morning time for us. When I saw it, it kind of gave me a weird feeling knowing that for so many years that had been a symbol of tyranny, of oppression, of lack of freedom–individual freedoms especially– and that it had just maintained itself for so many years and everybody just figured it was a permanent fixture. To see it actually start to come apart and being torn down voluntarily... it was a big deal, it was a really big deal. In a way I wish I'd been there to see it, because I have to tell you, there were a lot of stories about that wall, a lot of stories. Some were extremely sad, some were kind of joyful. For instance, the people who actually made their escape and were successful with it. But, like I said, there were sad times as well. It was just a good feeling seeing it come down; just too bad it took so long.

This account is a transcription of the video interview with Mr. Robert Riddick.

Robert Riddick, Class of 1965
1961-1965

Hanging out in and outside of the AYA.

"A Change is Gonna Come"

Prior to us actually going to Berlin, my dad had orders for Heidelberg and I was in the 7th grade. I finished out the 7th grade at the American School in Heidelberg. That summer, in August, we were told that my dad was transferred to Berlin. Berlin at that point was nothing that was special to us, or something that we were fearful of. It was just another city of the many cities as a military brat that we ended up moving to. We arrived in Berlin in August of 1961. It was at the same time that they were starting to build the barb wire [fence] representing the Wall that was soon to be.

We had to travel through East Germany to get to West Berlin. As we were approaching Berlin– I remember watching in bewilderment with my brothers and sisters in the car– groups of people lined up on both sides of the road in the dead heat of summer with clothes on… three, four or five layers of clothes. They were carrying their satchels, suitcases, whatever they could carry with them. We didn't understand what was going on– we saw these people moving from East to West. Ultimately, we found out that the people were trying to escape from the Eastern Zone to West Berlin for freedom.

I started Berlin American High School– it was at that time Thomas A. Roberts School– in the eighth grade. I was there from eighth grade through my junior year. I had a wonderful time in Berlin. I met a lot of people. I am used to meeting new people almost every couple of years, because all total I went to nineteen different elementary schools and three high schools as a military brat.

Berlin was special because we were set apart from the rest of the world.

As dependent children, we were pretty much given anything we wanted to occupy the time and to make sure that we did not dishonor our parents or the military in any way. They did a really good job of providing us with activities and things to do.

Extracurricular activities for me included sports: I played basketball, I bowled and I played softball. You had to be adventurous to leave the city of Berlin, to travel on the train to go to other military bases to play sports and compete in different sporting events. I was also in the chorus. We got to travel all over Germany with the chorus as well. There were other things on the base that we also liked to do, which included going to the teen club, called the AYA. And of course going to the show. I call it the show– my daughter keeps asking, "What's the show?" I explain that we went to the movies. We had so many wonderful opportunities as military dependents in Berlin. It is a time I will never forget.

Kids Rock to Record Hop; AFN Show Plans Return

Eighty teens gathered at the AYA for AFN's touring rock 'n roll show.

On the flip side of that, we were always protected as African-American families in Berlin. The military didn't allow discrimination, blatant discrimination, or any kind of discrimination. We never felt it in Berlin. And that is why I say we were protected. In 1965, we came back to the States– my brother had already graduated from Berlin American High School– but for me it was my senior year. I ended up going to two different high schools my senior year. I was more or less an outcast, if you will, because I was different.

I was different from the classmates that I was about to graduate with in that I didn't speak the way they spoke. I didn't dress the same way they dressed. We dressed a little differently overseas than in the States. When we came back, we couldn't wear short skirts. They were wearing miniskirts. They were wearing all sorts of fashions that we did not see in Berlin! That part was different. Being around people my age who could not relate to the things I'd just experienced. I didn't feel I was different; I was the same age as they were. I was in the same class, I took the same classes, but it was like 'what is different about me?' I was labeled as being 'proper,' and 'stuck up,' I was labeled this and that. All these things that I wasn't. In my mind, I was just another teenager going to school. I think that was unusual.

Also, in Berlin we had been protected in that, again, there was no discrimination. Whereas I used to visit and have my friends visit me in Berlin, this was no longer true in the States. I had a rude awakening when one of my very closest friends would not allow me to come to her house, because her father said, "We're not in Berlin anymore, we're in the States." and, "No, she can't come to the house." The reasons that were given to me hurt me terribly, but I did get over it.

At one point there were only my brother and myself, another family of brothers called the White Brothers, and another young lady–only 5 African-Americans– and we were treated no different than anyone else. In the early 60's that was something that was unheard of. My time in Germany–and this was my second time in Germany as a child– is something I would never, ever exchange. The experience was so unique and so special.

When we moved to Heidelberg, where I finished out the seventh grade, the teacher made a speech on the last day of class. She said, "It was a pleasure knowing you, Joyce, I didn't know 'negroes' spoke as well as you speak. I didn't know 'negroes' had the ability to pick up a book and read and learn and compete with fellow classmates." I thought it was so odd for her to say that to me. I just live my life the way I've always known it as a military kid. I never forgot what she said to me, even to this day. I'm well into my sixties at this point in my life, but that is something that you never forget.

This account is a transcription of the video interview with Ms. Joyce Perkins.

Joyce Riddick Perkins, Class of 1966
1961-1965

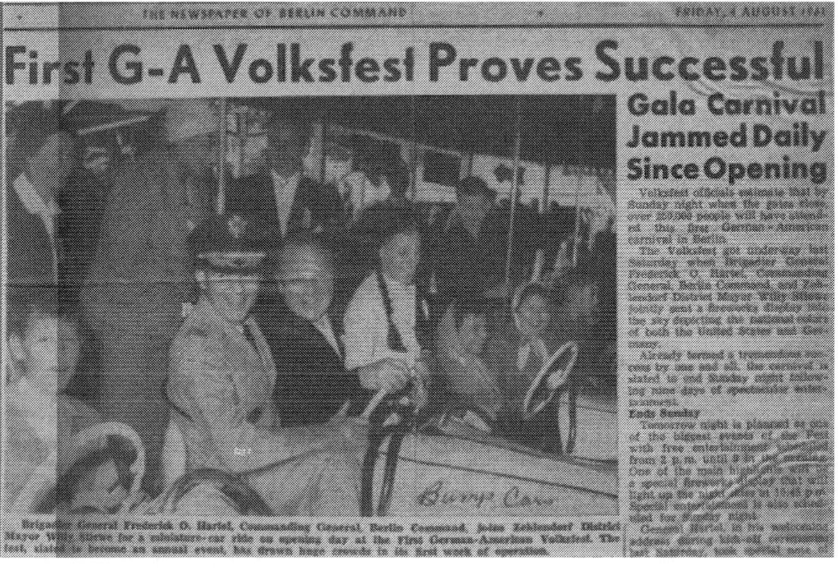

THE NEWSPAPER OF BERLIN COMMAND — FRIDAY, 4 AUGUST 1961

First G-A Volksfest Proves Successful

Gala Carnival Jammed Daily Since Opening

Volksfest officials estimate that by Sunday night when the gates close, over 250,000 people will have attended this first German-American carnival in Berlin.

The Volksfest got underway last Saturday when Brigadier General Frederick O. Hartel, Commanding General, Berlin Command, and Zehlendorf District Mayor Willy Stiewe jointly sent a fireworks display into the sky depicting the national colors of both the United States and Germany.

Already termed a tremendous success by one and all, the carnival is slated to end Sunday night following nine days of spectacular entertainment.

Ends Sunday

Tomorrow night is planned as one of the biggest events of the Fest with free entertainment scheduled from 2 p.m. until 9 in the evening. One of the main highlights will be a special fireworks display that will light up the night skies at 10:45 p.m. Special entertainment is also scheduled for Sunday night.

General Hartel, in his welcoming address during kick-off ceremonies last Saturday, took special note of

Brigadier General Frederick O. Hartel, Commanding General, Berlin Command, joins Zehlendorf District Mayor Willy Stiewe for a miniature-car ride on opening day at the First German-American Volksfest. The fest, slated to become an annual event, has drawn huge crowds in its first week of operation.

The Riddick family arrived in Berlin as the Wall was being built, the first German-American Volksfest took place that summer and ended exactly a week before the Soviets began erecting the Wall.

First Annual German-American Volksfest To Open July 29 Under AYA Sponsorship

Planning has reached the final stages for the First Annual German-American Volksfest to be held at the Sport Center field beginning Saturday, July 29, through Sunday, August 6.

Operating under the sponsorship of the American Youth Association, the event is expected to attract a crowd of approximately 50,000 Germans over the nine-day period.

Featuring a German carnival on the baseball field, the affair will be operated by a volunteer committee now being established, with admission to the field being controlled by the AYA.

One of the fun activities hosted by the AYA was the First German-American Volksfest. The Volksfest is a tradition that lives on in Berlin, celebrated from late July through early August.

Memories of Berlin 1955- 1963

I was born in Berlin in 1955. My dad had been in World War II and fought all the way to Berlin where he stayed for nearly 20 years. After the war, he was an investigator in the Nuremberg Trials and later worked as a CIC agent (Counterintelligence Corps) in Berlin. Since I was so young while in Berlin, most of my memories are sporadic:

• Playing cowboys and Indians in the rolling little hills and forest in front of our base apartment (I believe it was on Flanaganstrasse).

• Going over to the baseball field to see the Berlin Bears play and getting a broken bat from one of the players after a game.

• Attending the German-American school (later renamed the John F. Kennedy Schule) and having Mayor Willi Brandt visit our class one day.

• Going to the Checkpoint Charlie area a day after a couple of people died jumping from buildings to get to the West and seeing wreathes being laid down on that spot.

• Going to the Berlin Zoo one day when this giant Anaconda had just been fed two large pigs and they were traveling slowly down the snake.

• Going to the island of Amrum in the North Sea. My older sister and I were put on a plane to Hamburg where we were met by my dad's German friend and his wife. We then got on a large ship that took us to the island where there were very few cottages and a couple of windmills. After we got off the boat, we had to take a horse-drawn buggy to get to our cottage. The beaches on the island were incredible. We used to go to the sand dunes and hunt for birds eggs which were collected and cooked for breakfast.

• Listening to my mom talk to my relatives about the Berlin Airlift. A relative asked if the steady drum of the airplanes bothered her and she replied, "No, but if the noise stopped, that would be when I'd get worried."

• On that fateful day in November 1963, I was a Cub Scout and we had some sort of awards ceremony going on in a gym. I remember that a man ran in and shouted, "Kennedy's been shot!" and everyone ran out of the building to get to their radios.

• Our family (except my dad) took a trip to Prague, Czechoslovakia when I was about 7 or 8. I remember that the tour bus was stopped at the border by the Russian guards. All the passports were collected and then given back fairly soon, except mine. Although I was just a kid, apparently my dad's name was on one of their lists and the bus sat there for several hours until they realized I was no threat and they finally gave my passport back to my mom. I think she was extremely frightened about the whole situation.

• Probably one of my favorite memories was riding the Duty Train from Berlin to Frankfurt. The train going to Frankfurt left in the early evening, then it would stop in Potsdam where the Russian soldiers with machine guns would check everyone out. (My dad was not allowed to ride the train and had to fly separately from the family.) Once you got to Frankfurt, you disembarked in the Hauptbahnhof. It was an enormous old style train station that had a little section upstairs for American military personnel. There was this fabulous ice cream machine that dispensed ice cream sandwiches and the like. Coming back to Berlin was always the highlight as they would play this great American military music as the train rolled in.

Joe Hotter Jr., Class of 1973
1955-1963

Berlin American High School Opens Its Doors

Sehr geehrter Herr Morasco

Am Montag, dem 30. November 1964, 15 Uhr,
werden wir das Richtfest für das Bauvorhaben

New-High-School

feiern.

Der anschließende Richtschmaus findet pünktlich um
17.15 Uhr in den Berliner Kindl Festsälen,
1 Berlin 44 (Neukölln), Hermannstraße 217, statt.

Wir gestatten uns, Sie ergebenst einzuladen,
und würden uns freuen,
Sie bei der Feier und dem anschließenden Richtschmaus
begrüßen zu können.

Mit vorzüglicher Hochachtung

Arge Amerikanische Oberschule
Strabag Bau-AG. - H. Klammt AG

BRIGADIER GENERAL AND MRS. JOHN H. HAY
request the pleasure of your company
for the
Opening Ceremony of the new Berlin American High School
at
Holzungsweg, corner Am Hegewinkel, Dahlem
Wednesday, 25 August 1965, 1340 hours

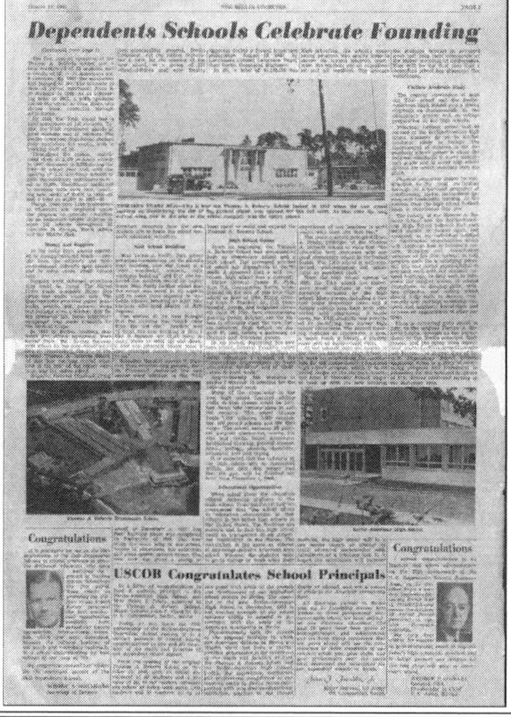

Dependents Schools Celebrate Founding

Congratulations

USCOB Congratulates School Principals

Congratulations

PAGE 2 BERLIN BEAR FACTS

Fifty-Six Graduate In First Class From New Berlin High School

Most Are Set For First Year 'Out In The World'

Clockwise: Invitation to groundbreaking ceremony for new high school, 1964; invitation to Opening Ceremony for new high school, 1965; Berlin American High School in 1965; Celebration of Berlin American High School and TAR, 1966.

Left: Class of 1966- Berlin American High School's first graduating class.

Memories of the Berlin Wall

I first saw Berlin in November 1963. I drove there from Heilbronn where I was teaching with another instructor. It was just a week after President Kennedy had been assassinated, as it was Thanksgiving vacation. One of the most stirring memories of that trip was the Airlift Memorial at Tempelhof. It was decked out with flowers and the words: Wir haben ein freund verloren. The actual trip there was terribly exciting, for any time you drove in the Eastern Sector on a prescribed route, your heart was in your mouth fearing a mistake and dire consequences.

Airlift Memorial at Tempelhof and Ms. Donnocker's 4th grade class at the memorial

I visited Berlin several times before I taught there from 1966-68. To say I was fascinated by the city is putting it mildly!! Of course I saw the Wall several times, and when my parents visited with me, Helen Brady—my principal at TAR–showed us the sights right royally. Her twin sister, Katy, was my principal in Heilbronn. My funniest memory of their trip was when Mother and I ascended one of the lookouts over the Wall, and I suddenly realized she was not behind me. I looked down, it was one of the higher lookouts, and saw her standing very close to a soldier with a most peculiar look on her face. I hurried back and she said, "I'm caught!" I looked down, and somehow the soldier's gun had caught in a pocket of her dress and she was petrified it would go off!!! I told the soldier what had happened. He extricated my mother from his gun and we all had a good laugh (both parents were in their 70s–so quite traumatic for Mother)!!

After I moved to Berlin I taught 4th grade at TAR. When Hubert Humphrey came in 1967, the children were dismissed at noon, and our school locked up tight as a drum as we were located across from the gym where he was speaking. We could see what I think were sharp shooters on the roof of our building. Red, white, and blue banners were hung down the front of the building. High schoolers were seated up front and Humphrey made them the focus of his speech.

By Vice-President Hubert H. Humphrey

Pictorial Record of Recent Berlin Visit

Vice President Hubert Humphrey visits Berlin

Every year, we took the children to the Wall, and I loved the trip–showing the children different spots and letting them touch the Wall when possible. One time we had gotten off our bus and were a few yards away from the Wall, and after ascending the viewing platform, the children begged to touch the Wall at the far end. I was a bit uncertain, but thought, "What can happen, as we're in the West!" So I told them to have a race to the Wall and back and see who was the fastest. They took off like lightning, touched the Wall and raced back. I immediately began to hear loud whirs behind me. I looked around and was surrounded by Japanese tourists, all taking movies of my children tagging the Wall! When we got to the Russian Memorial, I stood in the front and shot movies out of the open door. The Russian guards were grinning at us, and motioning us to come on over!!

Memorial to Peter Fechter: shot while climbing the Wall, bled to death in the death strip in sight of onlookers.

But the most exciting was the second year I was there. Our trip to the Wall was arranged with I-don't-know-how-many buses. I think both 3rd and 4th grades went. I was always early, so I had my class seated on a bus, and we waited and waited and waited. Finally, getting impatient, I told the driver to go ahead; we knew where we were going. We headed straight for Checkpoint Charlie, and a most unusual sight greeted our eyes. We got out of the bus and stood and watched hearse after hearse driving through from East to West with funeral wreaths on top of the hearses! I had never seen anything like it before, and discovered that this was the day the Russians were allowed into the West to lay wreaths at their Russian Memorial! We watched for a long time and then went continued the tour.

When we got back to the school, Helen was standing on the steps with her hands on her hips and a strong look of disapproval on her face. She said, "I knew it was you, Ruth," and told me to report to her office after school!! I was mystified as we'd had a really exciting trip to the Wall! Well, it seems after I'd left the building and boarded the bus, the General phoned the school and told Helen to keep the children in their rooms until further notice! Then he got back to her and told her to tell everyone they were not, under any circumstances, to go to Checkpoint Charlie. So…I really hope some of the children remember that unusual day! I think in reality, Helen was a bit of a rebel, and was secretly amused by our expedition. I was totally unrepentant and said it was something we'd never forget!

I, personally, had many trips through Checkpoint Charlie when we were finally allowed to go using tourist passports, midway through my first year of teaching in Berlin. I'm an opera lover and especially loved going to the Komische Oper and also loved to explore the art museums in the East. Each trip through Checkpoint Charlie was an adventure. One very unusual one was when Helen had her cousin and two of his friends visiting from Rome. They were priests and were studying there. She couldn't take them to the East, so she asked me to.

We took forever to get through Checkpoint Charlie and I began to get very nervous waiting for the third priest to get through. It turned out his passport photo was taken dressed as a priest and I think they almost didn't let him through. The Russians viewed travel documents with great scrutiny. For instance, if you were pictured wearing glasses, you had to be wearing glasses when you presented your documents. I took them everywhere by foot, and when we returned Helen had us over for dinner. We were all so beat we could hardly eat!

The last memorable trip to the opera in the East was probably Christmas 1970 when I was teaching in England. Three of us went to Salzburg, Vienna, and I left them and went to Berlin the last week. Unfortunately, I had come down with the Asian Flu in Vienna and lay in bed almost a week. I got to Berlin in a very weak condition. Teachers in Berlin were great about lending their apartments to fellow teachers when they were away. I stayed in Carol White's apartment. I rested each day and each night went to the opera!!

The night we were to see Fiddler on the Roof is etched in my memory forever. Fellow teacher, Don Priebe drove me to the Checkpoint. He was able to drive through with travel orders, and waited for me around the corner from the last checkpoint. It was a snowy, cold night, and I checked in at the hut where my passport was inspected. I was the only one there!

Snowflakes were falling very hard, the klieg lights that lit up the parking lot were bright and surreal, and the barbed wire on the top of the walls glistened in the lights. A few cars were parked, and there I was, the only object moving in the landscape. It was beautiful and horrifying at the same time, and a bit scary. I managed to get through, met Don and we went to the Komische Oper. There I was, sitting next to some Russian soldiers and if I remember right some German policemen, watching this opera of oppression of the Jews by the Russians. The performance was fantastic but I hardly breathed the whole evening!! The return trip was just as surreal, and when I at last got through and was in Don's car again, I became hysterical. When I was finally able to stop laughing, he asked what I wanted to do. I wanted to go to the top of the Hilton and have a drink!!

After that, I made several trips back, and saw the Wall being torn apart by memento seekers at Easter 1990. Of course, since then, I have seen the new Berlin being rebuilt, but I will never forget the old Berlin, and the Wall.

Ruth Donnocker, Faculty
4th Grade, 1966-1968

My Life in 1960s Berlin

My Father, MSGT Lewis D Walls was a WWII and Korean War Vet when he was on a troop ship headed to Bremerhaven, Germany in 1954. On the way to Bremerhaven, his orders changed; he got off the ship in Southampton, England, where he reported for duty at Molesworth RAF Station near Northampton, England (Army personnel still filled specialties for the US Air Force at that time).

Radio Room of Communications Section. (L to R): PFC Arthur Weitzman, SP3 Nathan Oswell, and Section chief, Msgt Lewis D. Walls

Key NCO

New 3rd Bn Commo Chief's Outpost Tour Tops Career

Once Artilleryman

Lewis' father, MSG Lewis Walls Sr, - Molesworth, AFB 1956

It was in Northampton that my dad met my mother, a German woman; by 1955 they decided to get married. Since my dad was black from Texas and my mother was white from Germany, they had many obstacles to overcome before they could be wed. Among these was the requirement that they sign papers from the Defense Department and State Department saying that they understood that there were about 30 States that had laws against their marriage, including my dad's home State of Texas. They got married and I was born July 28, 1956 in Northampton, England. I lived the first 14 months of my life in England, but have only photos, no actual memories. Our family left England in November of 1957.

We lived in Tacoma, Washington while my dad was stationed at Ft.

Lewis. While there, Dad got orders transferring us to West Berlin in early November, 1963! Two weeks later as we packed, President Kennedy was assassinated!!! Three weeks later, we were at Arlington National Cemetery standing at his grave and we were the only ones there that morning, which was confusing to me, because it seemed as though the country had forgotten him (there was about two feet of snow that morning).

USNS General William O. Darby

We left Brooklyn in January of 1964 aboard an old troop ship, the USNS Darby, which would be taking troops to Vietnam the next year. When we arrived in Bremerhaven after more than a week, I had to be put in a German hospital with measles (which was covered up so as to not have to quarantine the ship). It was a strange experience for me, for they spoke German all of the time and put the thermometer in my butt instead of my mouth!

Brandenburg Gate with Oma

While Dad made arrangements for housing for us, we stayed at my "Oma's" farm in Oberhaverbeck in Niedersachsen. When my dad picked us up to go to Berlin, we took the Autobahn through East Germany. I still remember the stern East German guards pointing their guns at us as they searched my dad's car! We lived for a few weeks in an apartment in downtown Berlin until we moved to Taylorstrasse, right next to Thomas A Roberts School, which had kindergarten through 12th grade in it (the JFK Schule and Berlin American High Schools opened the following years).

Since we had no American TV in the years I lived there (1964 to 1967), we played outside a lot and besides sports, the main thing we did was marbles in the grassy and sandy strip that divided the parking lot. That strip is pictured here, most importantly though, it shows how close we military brats were. I'm in the back with the striped shirt.

Above: The Taylorstrasse gang hangin' out
Below: Softball Team, 1966

I first played organized sports in Berlin, learning to swim in the Olympic swimming pool from the 1936 Olympics, in the British Sector. Also pictured here is my softball team, the Cardinals, in 1966. I'm on the right in the back row.

At TAR we had German classes and Current Event classes. I first heard of Vietnam in show and tell when a new classmate brought a pair of black pajamas, a cross bow and some Ho Chi Minh sandals! In Current Events class we were given–what was obvious to me even at that time (2nd grade)—a West German propaganda pamphlet that was very graphic called "Criminal Acts at the Barbed Wire."

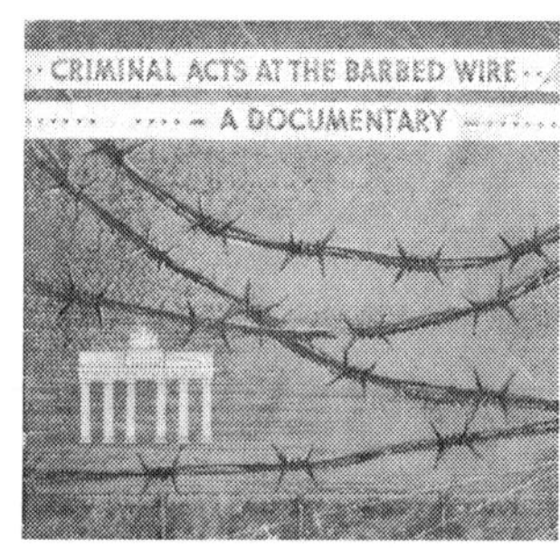

Propaganda Pamphlet

We left Berlin from Tempelhof in January of 1967, expecting America to be the same, but you can imagine the culture shock I experienced since I left the States right after the Kennedy assassination and returned with the Vietnam War all over TV and the newspapers, Hippies and LSD on the front of LIFE Magazine, and demonstrations for Civil Rights and against the War in Vietnam all across the country.

To this day I have vivid and fond memories of living overseas and I am glad that after more than 45 years I can finally share them with people who understand.

Lewis D. Walls Jr., Class of 1974
1964-1967

Clockwise from top: Lewis and his Oma in London, 1956; The Walls children: Mary Ann, Lewis and Deola, 1966; Pop Warner football, 1966; TAR playground on a snowy day, 1966

Snowballs for "Freedom"

The wall went up in August 1961. The Cuban Missile Crisis was in 1962. In 1964 the Cold War was in full swing. It was not lost upon a 15 year old boy in Berlin, Germany over a hundred miles inside Soviet controlled East Germany, that Communists and the Soviet Union–the USSR– did not have America's best interests steering their actions. They represented (even then) what President Reagan would later refer to as the "evil empire."

So, it was certainly not beyond credulity that fearless, if clueless, guys such as myself and a few similarly minded fellow adventurers– the sons of heroes of WWII– would want to strike a blow for truth, justice and the American Way! Now, dear reader, understand that the typical German boy of our age could doubtless soundly, but only literally, kick our butts. By literally, I do, in fact, mean literally–with their legs & feet. They could run circles around any of us on the soccer field. But baseball— that's another-story-entirely. We could throw at least twice as far as local boys our age.

Well, it was a lovely February day in Berlin's southwest suburbs. A break in the cold winter weather had transformed the snow to a consistency perfect for snowmen, which, as it happens and as any denizen of regions either significantly north or south of the tropics knows, is also ideal for the formation of the 4 to 6 inch diameter spheres known as snowballs.

Stay with me here. Get four or five guys with about four pre-packed and ready snowballs each, and with speed, coordination and descending trajectories for each throw– then between 16 and 20 such missiles can be airborne at once with time to duck before initial impact.

"Now, for an agreed upon target." Hmmm...well, given what I've stated in paragraph two.. and the fact that we found ourselves with little to do along the Teltow Canal, a decision on the subject didn't elicit a lot of debate. The Teltow Canal was a cleared, barbed wired, well-guarded and patrolled boundary between the American Sector of West Berlin and East Germany. The two hapless border guards, VoPos (Volkspolizei), may have known what hit them, but were at a loss as to from whence the assault had been launched. It being our max range– only two snowballs actually made direct contact. But twenty "rounds" impacting within seconds of each other in close proximity does make an impression. The AK's came off their backs and they knelt as one put his binoculars to his eyes. But we could tell he was looking way too close in. We waited hidden behind a snow bank for a while. Finally we stood up and left with a friendly wave...but not before they'd re-shouldered their weapons.

Ross Flavel, Class of 1967
1961-1965

A young VoPo or East German Policeman– VoPos helped erect the Wall (aka the 'Anti-Fascist Protection Rampart').

Living in Two Worlds

We lived in Berlin from 1955 to 1964. It was a little like living with one foot in Germany and one in the States. We had a taste of America from life connected to the military, namely access to the military commissary, so we had Cheetos, root beer, popsicles and American ice cream (in the only flavors back then: vanilla, chocolate and strawberry). The ice cream came in those one-portion little cartons that you could eat out of with a spoon, making it easy for us kids to get our own dessert. We ordered hamburgers and hot dogs at the snack bar on post. We could watch American movies at the post theatre. It cost 10 cents to get in and for 15 cents you could get a bag of popcorn and a Charms lollypop that lasted through the entire feature. We had a library on post full of the same books we'd have had back in the states: *A Wrinkle in Time, The Borrowers…The Oz books*. We had a bowling alley and little league baseball teams.

We immersed ourselves in German life too, riding our bikes to the German candy store for HARIBO Gummibärchen, plastic baby bottles full of tiny pearl candies, and my favorite, a marshmallow dome on a wafer coated in chocolate. The fact that it was called a Negger Kusse didn't really hit me back then, ironic really especially since my best friend at school was African American. I was just saying a German word I'd learned after simply pointing to them at first. Never thought of it translating to [N- word] Kiss. Just as I knew our closest Strassenbahn (subway) station was Onkel Tom's Hutte, never connecting it to a book about an important historical issue in our native country.

We enjoyed Wiener Schnitzel, Frikadeller (the German version of a hamburger) and Bratwurst at neighborhood stands. Our black and white televisions only played German stations of course-- other than very limited, occasional AFN (Armed Forces Network) shows, mostly public service announcements about security and stuff. We grew up on a few American shows, like Bonanza, the Donna Reed Show and Father Knows Best, only they were dubbed in German. It felt like watching scenes from a foreign country.

Because my brother and I went to German kindergarten and later to the brand new Deutsch-Amerikanische Gemeinschaftschule (later renamed the John F. Kennedy Schule), we were exposed to German children's books as well as English. The original Grimm's fairy tales are much more violent and gory than the watered-down versions here in the States. We learned life lessons from Struwwelpeter (or Shockheaded Peter), like the kid who dies of starvation, turning from fat to skin & bones, when he refuses to eat what his mom serves; the kid who falls off the dock and drowns because he always has his head in the air; the kid who gets his fingers cut off because, hmmm, I can't remember the life lesson in that one....maybe playing with scissors?

Our holidays were a mix, celebrating both American and German holidays. We went trick-or-treating in the American stairwells. But we also celebrated Laternenmass, carrying lighted lanterns door-to-door singing songs for treats. We put our shoes out on Dec. 6, St. Nikolaus Day, to be filled with candy or coals, depending on whether we'd been good or bad, but celebrated Christmas American style too (which of course is really based on German Christmas traditions). We didn't celebrate Mardi Gras but we joined right into the just as wild, German Fasching. On New Year's Eve we had our family's tradition of root beer floats and sparklers, but we also took on a fun German one. We'd buy tiny pewter figurines, lucky pigs, four leaf clovers, and ladybugs. We would place them in a spoon over a candle flame until they melted and then pour them into a glass of cold water. This would tell your fortune for the year from the figure that resulted. A bit like reading tea leaves.

We simply didn't see our German worlds and American worlds in Berlin as different, just all our world. What we did see as exotic was the United States. We got to go to the States on "home leave" every two years, flying on the military Flying Tigers, MAC flights as we called them, short for Military Air Command. The flights had to stop for refueling partway, at Keflavik, Iceland, or Shannon AFB, Ireland.

We dressed up for flying back then, all of us kids wearing hats even. No pajama pants or sweat suits, no pillows in our arms, no flip flops. No pants even for us girls–dresses only of course. And Dad in a full suit with tie and hat. Even my brother had to wear a suit and tie and a little newsboy-type hat. Flying was serious business, a big event. The dresses didn't stop us from enjoying the giant trampolines set into the ground near the Rhein-Main AFB lodging where we waited for flights.

The flights all landed at McGuire AFB, Ft. Dix, New Jersey. We'd get a Greyhound bus to Braintree, Massachusetts where Mom's brother lived. Uncle Sammy was a Voc-Tech teacher at the high school, teaching auto mechanics and auto body work. His students were always working on a bunch of different cars and he'd loan us one– always a station wagon. We'd make the trek from Massachusetts to Troy, New York to visit Mom's sister and family and then on to Regina, Saskatchewan, Canada to visit Dad's family.

Those were the days of picnicking at rest stops along the way, with easy-to-transport-and-fix peanut butter and jelly sandwiches, apples and chips as the mainstay. No easily available fast food places back then, plus it wouldn't have been part of the budget on any regular basis. Not even a consideration. The rest stop picnic tables were well-used back then, not sitting empty except for a few smokers as they seem to be today.

Also exotic to us, were the Big Boy Restaurants with that easily sighted statue out front: a chubby, Cheshire-Cat-grinning boy, wearing red and white checked overalls. "Big Boy, Big Boy, Big Boy" we'd all chant from the back until we wore our folks down.

It seems funny to think this now, but we also found backyard BBQs exotic. At Mom's brother's place in Braintree, we had our first BBQ--hamburgers and hot dogs–cooked on the grill outside with "pop" to drink. Having lived in apartment buildings up to that point, it was one more new experience. The US was the foreign country to us back then.

Ret. Army Reserve Lt. Col, Kathie Hotter Hightower, Class of 1971
1955-1964

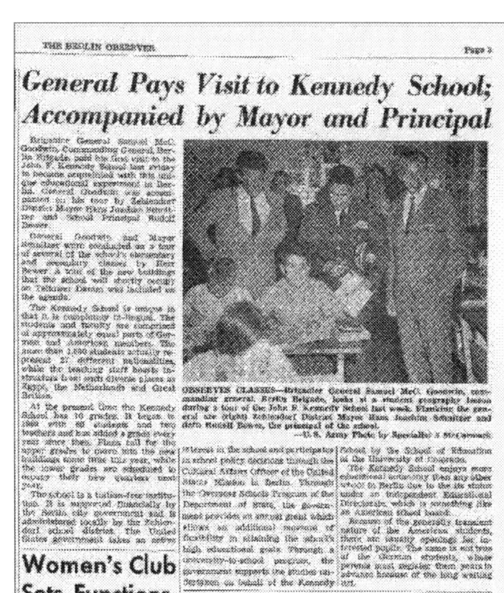

General Pays Visit to Kennedy School; Accompanied by Mayor and Principal

Women's Club Sets Functions

The JFK Schule was founded in 1960; it is a bi-lingual international school with classes taught in both German and English.

Ski Season in Berlin 1965

We were sitting in the AYA after school and the topic was skiing. It was our senior year, we were living in Berlin, Germany, which has the topography of a pancake and it was ski season. Sure, cross country skiing was an option in Berlin, but that did not require a road trip and it ain't downhill. I mean really, from Berlin we had access to some of the greatest downhill skiing locations in the world, and they were just a train ride away. And for all we knew by the next Ski Season we could find ourselves enrolled, at no cost, in a US government subsidized "advisory" project in tropical Southeast Asia which included all transportation, room and board, dress alike clothing, medical care and any necessary activity equipment. But no skiing.

We would have to go low budget to gain parental approval and it could not conflict with our primary life purpose of graduating from good old BAHS that spring. So we needed a plan. First we would take the Duty Train from Berlin to Frankfurt. It was a free overnight hotel room and when we woke up we'd be half way to our destination, Garmisch-Partenkirchen. Garmisch, the sight of the 1936 Olympics would offer us world class down-hill skiing. Plus the US government had created a fantastic ski resort by the famous Zugspitze, the highest mountain (10K ft) in Germany. But the bigger plus was that the US government subsidized the cost for US citizens. The cost of everything from ski lift tickets to skis and boots to pants and coats. This was a US government program in which we wanted to be enrolled and dressed alike. The program in the tropics, not so much.

Once in Frankfurt we had to get to Munich by train, so we rode in 3rd class for next to nothing. In Munich we just needed to get to the airport by public transportation– not to catch a flight at the airport, but to pick up what became the star of our trip: the CAR. This infamous CAR was an older high mileage Taunus, shared by numerous Pan Am personnel when they were in Munich on layovers or business. One of our guys having a Pan Am dad qualified us for use of the CAR, sort of.

We drove this fine no-cost vehicle to Garmisch-Partenkirchen, where we checked into Frau Shaffer's pension, which cost us less than the US government-operated luxury hotel. We had arrived safely and our budget was working. Our rooms included a breakfast of hot chocolate and breads (plus all we could carry in our pockets). During the day we traded cigarettes with various street vendors around town for lunch. We planned to splurge every day on a good evening meal. This was truly going to be that ever elusive "$75.00 per person-four-day- European Ski Trip."

We picked up our ski gear that first evening. We wanted to be ready at first light to attack the mountain. We were ready, but overnight the weather changed. Temperatures were dropping fast and so was visibility due to fog. But we were committed, so the next morning we went skiing. When we called it a day we realized it was so cold with wet snow we had ice in our hair. Hey, we were on a senior road trip, the trails and lifts were empty…so we skied.

Overnight the weather cleared a little bit, so early in the morning we attacked the mountain again. But during that second day the fog started rolling in fast and it began to snow and ice. The mountain was becoming hazardous. The safety patrol closed the ski lifts and then they closed the ski runs. It was OK with us because we needed to go over to Oberammergau and have a lunch of the famous craft beer at the Wolfe Hotel. It was worth the trip. The weather continued to deteriorate and the forecast was bad. So we had to make a decision. Either go home or move the party. We, of course as high school seniors, decided to move the party. After all, just across the mountains from Garmisch was Innsbruck, Austria. Innsbruck, where exactly one year before the 1964 Winter Olympics had been held! We could ski Innsbruck the next morning and ski two different Olympian slopes on one ski trip! So we made a High School decision and decided that the weather could be better to the south and off we went. We also knew we might blow our budget, but the thought of skiing two Olympic slopes took away any realistic and reasonable thinking.

We drove in the ice and snow all day arriving late in the afternoon quietly united in weather denial. Finally, in late afternoon we met with reality. Innsbruck had closed its ski slopes before we even arrived and had announced they would also be closed until noon the following day. Time for another decision. We of course decided not to spend money on the outrageously expensive hotels of Innsbruck but to drive all night over the mountains and arrive in Munich, drop the CAR off at the airport, get to the Bahnhof in time to catch the cheap train to Frankfurt and get on the free Duty Train hotel ride home to Berlin. A good plan when you believe you are invincible.

So we had a big dinner and filled the CAR with gasoline. We did not realize at the time, but these two actions may have been the two smartest decisions we made that day. We took off for Munich, not quite as enthusiastic as we had been when we were going to ski Innsbruck, but soon we would have all the excitement we would need. First came more snow. Then ice started mixing with the snow. We were OK and taking it slow and steady, plus the Austrians really knew how to keep their roads cleared. Next, the windshield wipers were slowing down, becoming sporadic and the rubber blades were just smearing the snow. Our solution was to roll down the front windows and use our gloved hands to wipe the ice off the windshield. It was working but we were freezing.

Then the car began to sputter and gasp like it was out of fuel. We had a full tank. So we turned around to drive back to a village we had just driven past and the car's engine worked like a champ. So we thought maybe the fuel pump was our problem. Good guess. The car would work great when we were driving downhill…or backing uphill. Remember we were invincible male high school seniors. We decided that we would back our way over the mountains to Germany.

So we began one of the more interesting segments of this road trip. This car did not have USA license plates, so silly excuses were going to be out of the question if a police or border patrol agent tried to save us from ourselves. We stayed in the right lane, put the car in reverse and began a very slow trip over the mountains. The two of us in the back seat served as windshield wipers for the rear window and the front seat passenger's job was to tell the driver when to flash the lights at cars coming up behind us (or to our front and headlights). We did not have much illumination on the back of the CAR. It was a pre-backup-light-

and-emergency-flasher model year. Since we could only go in reverse, the car had only one gear and it was slow, but it was now front wheel drive so it was somewhat sure footed. This was all the good news we could rationalize. The really bad news was it was snowing and icing and the other drivers on the road did not know what was happening.

Needless to say every driver we met thought they were the first to see us and tell us we were doing something wrong. We received numerous salutes, horn blasts and comments on our intellect, family tree and what we should do with certain body parts. The good news is all of these comments were in the German language which took them longer to deliver than we were in their vicinity, so we did not get to fully appreciate the commentary. But in reality all of those drivers were just as scared as we were. We even wondered if we passed another car full of high school seniors on a road trip.

The 1965 yearbook was not dedicated to the four of us on our skiing road trip, so obviously we made it back. We left the CAR at the Munich airport with a warning to the next driver; we caught our trains and arrived back in Berlin. The hard part was not to tell anyone about the crazy drive to Munich because we knew how fast that story would make it home. We were still seniors and had the desire to take several more road trips.

Graham Beachum, Class of 1965
1964-1965

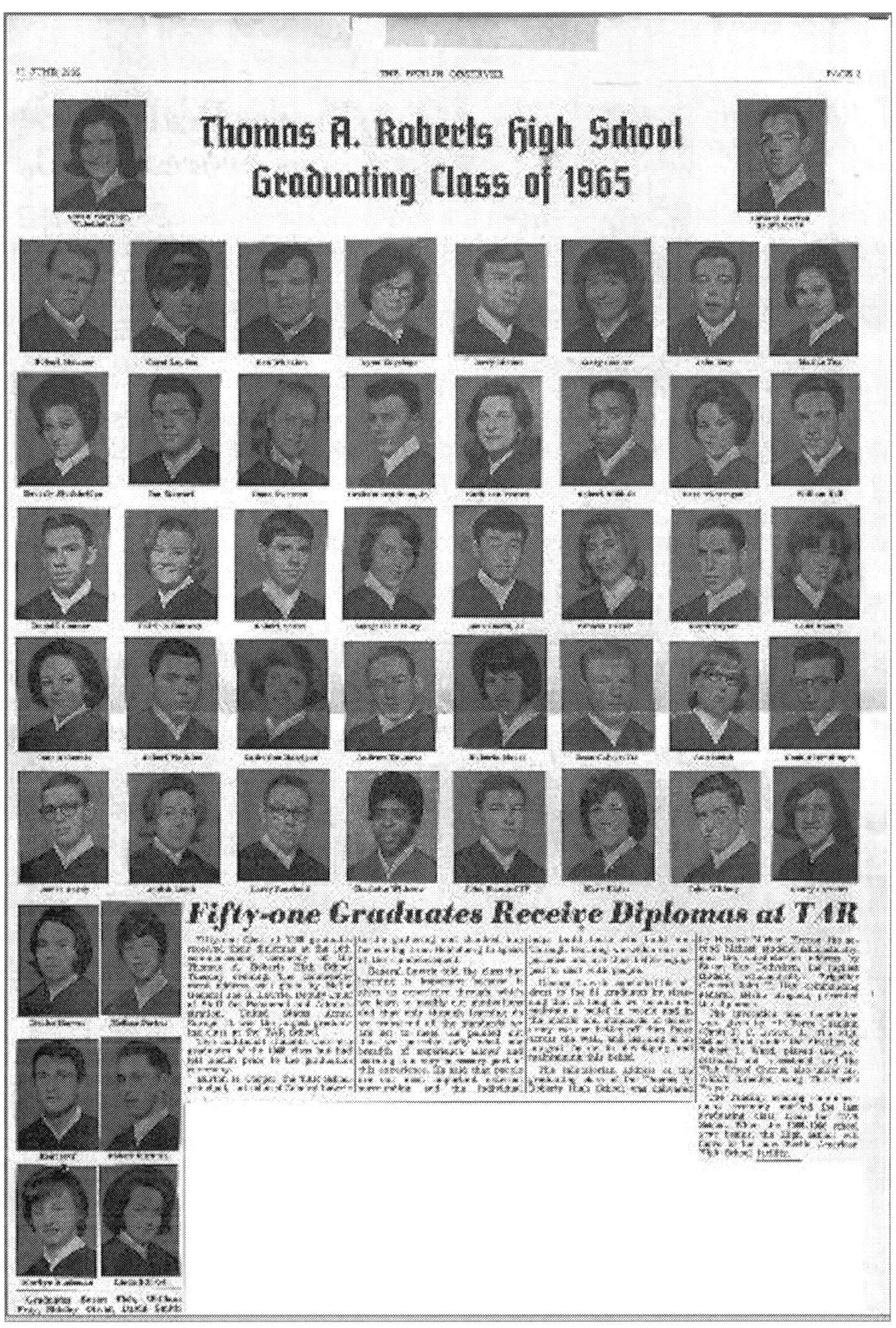

Thomas A. Roberts High School Graduating Class of 1965

Fifty-one Graduates Receive Diplomas at TAR

The Class of 1965—including Graham and his fellow Senior Ski Trip buddies.

Indestructible Teens

Everyone Knows that American Teens See Themselves As Being Indestructible; Everyone Else Sees Them as STUPID!

It was a dank, grey day–*oh, no! not in Berlin…say it isn't so!*– when I asked Skip to tell me again about the bunker that some kids had found some years earlier, before my arrival. The best that he could do was to say that he thought that it might be in the French Sector and that it was in some sort of park. As an indication of the desperation that drives some people to do incredibly stupid things when they are bored, we hatched a plot to go looking for that bunker. I was able to con my parents out of our inconspicuous red and white Chevy station wagon--it was a behemoth. It was only barely able to navigate the smaller streets of the city, especially when cars were parked on either side of the street…with their wing mirrors extended.

We had gotten together a smallish band of similarly disaffected youth in search of adventure and had begun to drive aimlessly around a part of what had once been a huge city (before the DDR had cordoned off a major part of it). It was an outing which had all the earmarks for catastrophic failure from the get go…no map of the city, no more than one working flashlight, no idea of where we were going and nobody who had actually been there before, or who had even seen the park. Also, we were precariously short on the kinds of sustenance that the typical teenage boy needs every 15 minutes or so. This was well before the heyday of American junk food, Mickey Ds on every other corner, power bars and any other logical food item that we might have prepared ourselves with. And before the time of GPS and cell phones.

That made it all the more astounding that we actually were able to find a park with a tall hill in the middle of it, which looked like it might serve as our quest. We parked the car and started walking up the winding pathways to the top of the hill where we arrived at a carefully fenced off–with barbed wire– enclosure. Germans are quite fond of strolling in public areas so it was difficult to climb the enclosure and start poking around in the bushes without looking like what we actually were, which was scofflaw jerks determined to earn the necessary DRs (Delinquency Reports) which would get us sent back to the States pretty much over night.

We gained an entrance to a sloping area littered with bricks and dirt and it was pitch black inside. Also, by touch and using the rather inadequate light form our flashlight, it was obvious that there had been some attempt to fill in this edifice with war debris. Of particular concern were the ends of rebar metal sticking down at about eyeball level. I began to descend the fairly steep slope and started to lose my footing before I started to slide on the seat of my pants to slow down. I asked whoever was holding the flashlight to shine it down the slope toward me and it became apparent that we were on the edge of a descending precipice where a ladder of sorts had been made from iron--u-shaped brackets–that had been placed in the concrete of the descending, vertical wall.

When we all gathered at the edge of this Hole to Hell, someone kicked a brick into the maw and it took forever before it made a sound as it finally reached the bottom. Being a sort of a chicken and feeling in a command position, I suggested that we get the heck out of there and plan a return better equipped for another assault on this objective. As we climbed out of the darkness and belly crawled through the hole and back into the limited light of a Berlin day, we saw a gaggle of young, German boys watching us with curiosity while we strolled back down the hill, in the middle of the park.

When we assembled a week or two later, we had rope, more flashlights, food, some colas and some of us thought it better to dress in boots, fatigue jackets and other very inconspicuous attire so that we would look like typical Germans out for a weekend stroll…only with coils of rope and other suspicious equipment over our shoulders. As I recall, it was a time before "I Spy" or any other shows where one might mimic sleuth and stealth tactics. In any case, we would not have had access to U.S. television shows at that time in Berlin. I believe that the very first James Bond movie had been released, because I recall seeing it at the Outpost Theater, but none of us was wearing Bond-like tuxedos. We were pretty well winging it when it came to what was necessary for this adventure.

This time, we designated a lookout as we climbed over the enclosure fence. We were shocked to find the entrance blocked by new piles of dirt so we began digging with our hands only to discover that there were multiple lengths of barbed wire which had been passed back and forth to block out the entrance before they were covered with the dirt. Those crafty Teutonic workmen! Some serious and deliberate determination to commit trespass eventually got us slipping between the strands of barbed wire and back inside the, as yet, incompletely explored chamber.

We surveyed the scene with much greater illumination. We were at the point of "I double dare you," trying to find a group member who would attempt to climb down the iron bracket ladder– all of us with rapidly diminishing resolve. Just then, our lookout hollered into the entranceway, "Polizei!" We scrambled back up the slope in time to see two of those silly green and white VW Beetle police cars with flashing blue lights gingerly driving along the walking paths to the top. They were circling in opposite directions so as to make it more likely to catch the interlopers. All of us broke into a wild run down the hillside but Germans are very clever utilizers of barbed wire and strands of it had been laced at ankle height here and there to protect the plantings and to keep law-abiding citizens on the pathways.

There was a fair amount of swearing as several of us tumbled and rolled only to get back up and try to keep going downhill while remaining out of sight of the police. Miraculously, we all breathlessly assembled near that inconspicuous red and white boat of a car, tossed equipment and ourselves inside and I drove like the proverbial bat as we fled that darkened hell, all the time nursing scratched ankles and torn clothing. Evading detection was made somewhat easier by the fact that the police vehicles were barely able to turn around in the narrow walking paths but we did not stay around long enough to actually watch any of that. I drove back toward Dahlem, hoping that I could avoid clipping wing mirrors and scratching my dad's car…or worse.

It was not long after, that Juergen, a German friend, showed me an article in a local newspaper. It detailed how a German boy had been quite seriously injured in a fall inside an old war construction, which was located underground in the area of the park where we had been. Juergen, of course, knew of our excursion since we were far too stupid to keep from repeating all of the details of the experience to anyone who would listen to us. It is remotely possible that it was coincidence but we began to feel as if our own irresponsibility had influenced and contributed toward that poor guy's fall.

So, we were left with some lingering guilt and we had none of the fantastic things that we had dreamed of liberating from that bunker…no Nazi flags, abandoned militaria, portraits of Der Führer or anything…but slowly healing barbed wire scratches.

Ross Calvert, Class of 1965
1963-1966

The guys and the red and white Chevy behemoth

He's Not Heavy...

Let me set the stage for you, I was not your average military brat, for even though my father was Army, he was old school Negro. We always lived in mostly black neighborhoods and hung around mostly black people. Then we received orders to go to Germany; though we did not know what lay ahead, away we went. We arrived in Berlin midway through basketball season in 1965. After enrolling in school I started to practice with the junior varsity team and was told that if the varsity team made the playoffs they would take me along. That was my first clue that I had some skills.

But the real test was adjusting to my new environment. Now my class was loaded with kids from all walks of life and for the most part they were very friendly. But this was all new– for my contact with other races was very limited, to say the least. But I was not alone; for whatever reason, Coach Jim Rice took me under his wings and made me the man I am today. He taught me that people are just people no matter what color they are and being blessed with a talent like mine would draw them to me. But it was up to me as to how I nurtured those relationships. Track season is where his teaching came into play, for I really found my niche in life, and people started to recognize me not only as a good sportsman but as a person.

That season I made it to the finals and got three gold medals. Of course, now at that age, my hormones were out of control, but there was a shortage of women of color so what was I to do? And the one young lady that I tried to talk to was too cute and full of herself and blew me off but as it would happen, God sent a lovely white angel name Darlene R. '67 and the rest was history. I remained with her until I left Germany.

Summer in Berlin was wonderful. I got to explore this new land and its people and watch them adjust to another black man in their country. When the new school year started, so did a whole new set of adventures. During football season I made the team and was a starter on both offense and defense. Back then we played iron man football. And, it turns out that I was also very good in this sport as well– I made both the offensive and defensive All-Conference teams.

Traveling on the Duty Train were some of the best times that we teens could have. Once, the train was stopped and boarded by East German guards because one of our players mooned the guards. I won't name any names, but they know who they are. We would always bring items to trade with the guards without anyone knowing it. I still have some of my old items that I traded to get.

I had lots of friends on the football team and we had a special bond, but a comment made by one of them brought me back to reality. We discussed keeping in touch and maybe visiting each other when we got back to the States, but were reminded that that would not be a good idea. For, where they were from in Alabama I would not be accepted. This really shook me up and I realized that this fantasy was only for a short time. Hanging out with my white friends…openly dating a white girl…would more than likely get me killed back in the United States.

We had a wonderful football season– made it to the finals but lost the championship to Bremerhaven in the cold and snow. Next came basketball season, and boy was that a season! We were favored to take the whole thing and came very close. We lost in the first round to Verdun, France and ended up getting 3rd place. I was the only one to make the All-Tournament team that season, but a number of my teammates made All-Conference.

McCalley Wins USDESEA Track Medal

by Jim Van Dyne

Above are the four winners of the Karlsruhe-Berlin meet.

As we came back to track season I realized that this would be it for me– for my father was being sent back to the States. I believe I won one or two more gold medals, but the best part was that our assistant coach had ordered a new car and I got to drive back from Ludwigshafen to Berlin with him! Somewhere along the way I was told that I had been named the first Athlete of Year and that was a great honor. Driving through the East was a real experience, going through the checkpoints and all was an adventure. Finally, came the time to say goodbye to all the friend that I had been blessed with. I don't know how anyone else felt, but I must say as a man of color this was the turning point in my life. It made me realize that a man is a man, and we all deserve respect and love. Had it not been for my experiences in Germany I'm not sure how I would have turned out.

Thank you Berlin, and Jim Rice for making me the man that I am today.

Larry McCalley, Class of 1968
1965-1967

Cubs Open Track Season With Win; McCalley Wins 3 Events in Tri-Meet

OBSERVER Sports

Sports Shorts For BBde

All-Star Football Set For June

BERLIN ROD AND GUN CLUB NEWS

McCalley, all around great athelete

On the Verge of Creating an International Incident

It was a little kept secret fact that a number of members of the Class of '65 (as well as some of the other classes) were in the habit of sampling the cross-cultural pleasures to be found at the NAAFI (Navy, Army, Air Force Institute) Club in the British Sector. As I recall, the British military members enjoyed very low cost potables. Though drinks had to be paid for in paper scrip at the time, a pint of lager was something like four pence (could that possibly be true?). We also consumed great quantities of mixed drinks called the James Bond and the Pimms #- something- or- other cocktail.

The NAAFI was an interesting place to try to practice being an inoffensive American teenager while surrounded by British troops. It also offered the advantage of being off the beaten paths likely to be used by coaches. Several dollars were more than adequate to exchange for British scrip and to get fairly well lubricated in an evening and still have enough money for the return U-Bahn trip to Dahlem.

On one ill-fated occasion as our time in Berlin was winding down, I pointed out the large Union Jack flag flying from the roof of the NAAFI building as we crossed over from the U-Bahn stop and I carelessly said, "That flag will be mine tonight!" At the end of the evening, I could only convince one other cohort of the vital necessity of going after that prize. We rode the elevator to the top floor, found a stairway to the roof, mounted it and found another stairway to the top of a smaller platform where the actual flagpole was located. It was pretty frightening going to the top because the Brits, proud as they are of their standard, had it illuminated with spotlights. Also, that flag was huge and it looked so normal sized from many floors below on the street!

I detached the flag after lowering it more rapidly than the traditional slow drop at the end of the day and quickly rolled it up into a ball that I could stick under my letter jacket. Remember when I said that it was really huge? There was not going to be room for both Ross and the Union Jack inside my letter jacket so, respectfully as I could under the circumstances, I dropped the balled up flag over the side of the roof to the ground many floors below. Do you know what a parachute looks like when it unfurls during a descent? That flag was draped across the shrubbery for many square meters of (respectful) display.

We quickly reentered the top floor, took stairs down several flights, took an elevator back up a flight and, then another elevator down several flights, etc. so as to be able to fool absolutely nobody, probably. We emerged on the ground floor trying our best to look inconspicuous as we left the building. Amazingly, the flag was still draped and more amazingly, various passersby paid it no attention at all.

I re-balled the flag, leapt over hedge works and beat a hasty retreat for the U-Bahn station while stuffing the flag inside my jacket (which I had to carry under my arm after snapping it closed). I guess I looked a bit like a ventriloquist carrying a chubby and headless dummy.

I arrived home with my prize and had to hide it in our basement party room. It was large enough to drape down the one wall, cross the floor and go all the way up the opposite wall. Various friends, who listened respectfully to the whole saga of its liberation, admired it. My parents usually avoided that party room, as it was a "kids' place." But my dad was quite proud of what I had done with a Sousaphone that he had bought at a property disposal sale. I had mounted a flashing, red light down inside the large brass bell of the horn. I had additionally strung some wire up through the missing valve and attached a small speaker to the other end so that music could play from my Symphonie jukebox upstairs and actually emit from the weird, flashing instrument.

On the occasion of the last party that my parents held before our pack out, I heard my dad ask another Lt. Col. to come and see what his crazy kids had done downstairs. I panicked because the other man was on the Allied Staff and, if anyone could have heard about the disappearance of the gigantic Union Jack, it would have been this man! With highball glasses in hand, they went to the basement and grinned bemusedly at the whole room, being careful to walk respectfully over the part of the flag that lay on the floor and… I survived to tell the tale!

Ross Calvert, Class of 1965
1963-1966

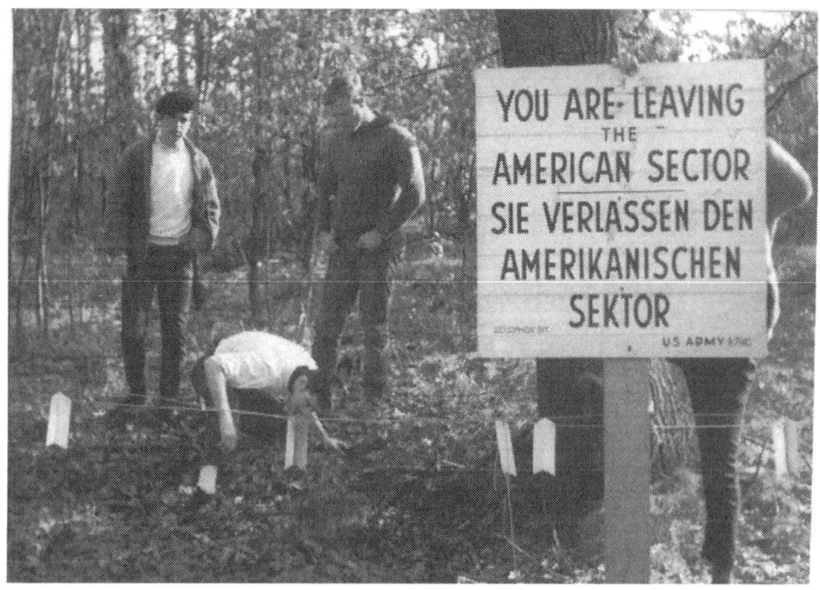
YOU ARE LEAVING
THE
AMERICAN SECTOR
SIE VERLASSEN DEN
AMERIKANISCHEN
SEKTOR
US ARMY

Ross and pals on the 'verge of creating (another?) international incident'

My Year in Berlin

Our experience was kind of unique because we were only stationed in two places—with my stepfather who was in the military. We were in Ankara, Turkey, before Berlin, which was a very interesting experience. He came home and said, "Now we're going to be going to Germany." Of course, we just wanted to go home; we were very homesick. We went to Berlin and it was the most amazing experience of my life.

I remember the first day in one of my classes, we were new to being Brats– I just remember the impact of how everyone was so welcoming. They know they have to make friends quickly. They're only going to be there a very short time. That was very new to me. It was a great experience.

We lived on the economy. A lady named Mrs. Steinhoyer lived upstairs. It was a beautiful, German brick house that had survived the war. It had cobblestone streets. I would take the city buses to school every day. I found our experience was unique because we were not your classic Army Brats.

The reason I felt that we were not the classic Army Brats is that everyone I'd met had been military brats from when they were very young, and they'd been stationed in many different countries. This was a very new experience. I was only in the eighth grade at the time. So, I was aware of the history, but I wasn't aware of the intensity with which we would be living.

I remember going on a field trip during class, they talked about the night the Wall went up. That was really impactful to me because it made me realize that if you lived on one side of the street and the Wall went up, you could now be in East Berlin. If you lived on this other side of the street, you were now in West Berlin. How horrifying that must have been! People were reaching through the fence to their boyfriend and family...

When we first got there, we stayed at a place down at the Wannsee and learned later that one of the places at the Wannsee was where Hitler, and his men came together to come up with "The Final Solution." You were living history.

I thought high school life would be different, because of the unique place in which we lived. Yet, when we were at that school you felt like you were back in the States. Everything was the same; there were football teams and cheerleaders. We would go to the AYA every Saturday and go dancing. I always thought it would make a really interesting film, because it was so surreal that you were able to have this experience.

When we left I remember going down to the train station and seeing how close to the Wall we were. Despite being in a closed-in city, I remember the freedom– I was just 14 years old–how safe the city was. We would go downtown, to the Europa center, or to the AYA, we'd take the buses or the U-Bahn to Krumme Lanke station and get currywurst. Sometimes walking home there would be Black Watches in the bushes, men in long black coats with German Shepherds, just watching. Yet, we were carefree. But in the States my daughter wasn't allowed to go across the street alone at night.

Page 8 / The Berlin Observer / November 30, 1973

THE ULTIMATE DESTINATION of an U-Bahn train is always shown above the windshield of the lead car. This train on Line 2 is headed for Krumme Lanke, which is two stops below the Oskar-Helene-Heim U-Bahnhof across Clayallee from Berlin Brigade Headquarters. This same train going in the opposite direction will be headed for Wittenbergplatz on the Kurfürstendamm. The name of each U-Bahn station is clearly posted along the tracks within the station, and a conductor announces the name of the station when the train stopped. So there should be no difficulty in knowing you have reached your destination. (Photo courtesy of

U-bahn train headed to Krumme Lanke station: two stops past the Berlin Brigade HQ at Oskar-Helene-Heim station

My stepdad was a Russian linguist, but whatever he did we were not allowed to go into East Berlin. Some of my friends were [allowed]. It was really scary; I was always afraid I would somehow get on the S-Bahn and end up in East Berlin. Life there was intriguing, as if we were living a spy movie. So when I went back a few years ago and we drove through the Brandenburg Gate [vehicular traffic is no longer allowed through the gate—only foot traffic], I just got goose bumps thinking, "I'm in East Berlin, on Unter den Linden."

I stayed in a hotel in East Berlin; it is actually quite beautiful on that side of the city. Of course, we went to a spot where they had saved a portion of the Wall, and stood thinking about the night it came down. I was there for work and they had this young man that was driving me. I said, "I want to go find the school!" Now it is actually a German high school. We found the school and we found my house. I lived in Zehlendorf, on Hohenstrasse. He helped me find the house. At the end, I told him, "I want to thank you so much for helping me find these places." But he said, "No, this is great for me. I'm from East Berlin, I was twelve when the wall came down." Our two worlds collided–we both had experienced two sides of the same coin, living in East and West Berlin. It is absolutely amazing that we got to relive that history together.

It was just this amazing, unique experience. I've talked to many Berlin Brats, who have been stationed in a lot different places, but for some reason Berlin has this special pull on their lives that no other place does.

This account is a transcription of the video interview with Ms. Barbara Hermes Hannegan.

Barbara Hermes Hannegan, Class of 1971
1966-1967

Living in Berlin: 1967-1973

It was February, 1967; I was 12 years old and living in Atlanta, Georgia. My father and mother had just told me we were moving to Germany. Times were turbulent; it was the height of the Civil Rights Movement. Four years earlier, JFK was assassinated in Dallas, Texas. My parents decided it was time to act on their dreams. My dad had a successful financial/real estate business and my mother was pursuing a career in opera.

I remember boarding the Pan Am Jet Clipper with my parents and my three year old brother. It was a long ride, but very exciting for me. I had no idea what Germany was or even where it was, but I was all for an adventure! One of the first amazing things to happen to this little southern girl was seeing the Aurora Borealis, or the Northern Lights. My father woke me and told me to look out the plane window. It was the one and only time I have ever seen them. It was magical and awesome.

I stepped off the plane and entered into another world, or so I thought. It even smelled different. It smelled like fresh dirt, green lush trees and delectable foods I had yet to taste. We had rented a small townhouse near the corner of the American Berlin Brigade housing and a few streets over from the high school. I was not able to attend that school. We were there for my mother to study opera under the tutelage of Elizabeth Grümmer.

I was enrolled into John F. Kennedy International School. I was excited that there were some American kids that went there. Some had dads that were missionaries; some were with John Deere or diplomats. But the most fun was meeting the kids in the housing area of the brigade. For the next two years, I was actively seeing Berlin, learning to ice skate, finding my favorite kiosk with bratwurst mit pommes frites, shopping for clothes and shoes and learning the language.

My dad finally got a job working as a civilian in the Berlin Brigade and I was able to enroll in Berlin American High School. I was issued dog tags as well as an identification card, I was on cloud nine! My teachers, both at JFK School and BAHS were the most wonderful, loving caring and encouraging people ever. I was so blessed and had the time of my life. I made so many friends and was able to travel and see places like England, Italy, Spain, and North Africa.

Because I was living on the economy at first, I made many friends who were German. Our landlord's father came to supper one evening and in the course of dinner, he handed me a basket of rolls. I noticed that he had numbers tattooed on his arm. I didn't know what tattoos were and I asked him what they meant. The next hour was a very sobering history lesson I will never forget. This gentle and kind man was a concentration camp survivor and he told me about the rise and fall of a man named Adolf Hitler. I was horrified, enraptured and curious. I was told never to forget and to tell his story all my life. I made a promise to him that I would.

My parents then thought it might be worthwhile to take me to Dachau. I never made it through the front gate. My heart felt like it was going to explode and I was very upset. Since then I have met four other survivors and 30 years later as a journalist, wrote my first human interest story on a survivor for a local newspaper.

In 1971, my father was assigned to USAREUR Heidelberg, Germany. Another fairy tale began. I was able to attend both my junior and senior prom and graduated in a 12th century castle. I also met my husband there while in the 10th grade. This coming December, we will celebrate 36 years of Brat Bliss! In 1973, my father was assigned to the Pentagon, in Virginia. I cannot begin to tell you the immense culture shock I was subjected to. After a while, I was able to settle in, and eventually ran into some classmates. Whom, I might add, I thought I would never see again– because it was before the age of the World Wide Web!

Off to college I went. I spent the next 20 plus years working in newspapers, and raising my two beautiful children. Now my time is spent enjoying a quiet life in a small East Texas town and loving being a grandmother. My one wish is to return to my beloved Berlin and Heidelberg. It's on my bucket list. I never tire of telling people who will listen, of my wonderful adventure of growing up in Germany. I am truly blessed. Tschüß, my friends!

Ruchia (Roo) Eargle Moran, class of 1973
1967-1971

Nikolaikirche (St. Nicholas' Church), Berlin 1968

Duty Train Memories

I arrived in Berlin in 1967 and left in 1970. I was really into sports. I played football and soccer and wrestled at Berlin. I had the good fortune of being at Berlin for the three back to back championship years, in fact the '68 year was undefeated. Our year, the one where I was a junior, had only one loss and that was kind of questionable. We ended up at the end of the year with more points scored for us and fewest points scored against us than any other team in Europe. We had the famous Cleo Johnson '70 on our team; I got to be good friends with him. Bill Galloway '70 was another good guy, Todd Darress '70, Charlie Hipkins '70 and Pierre Bonit '70– he was our quarterback. Bunch of good guys, great memories.

CLEO JOHNSON
Halfback
Captain
All Europe

That takes me back to memories of the Duty Train. Man have I got some stories about the Duty Train. One night, the most famous trip– it was actually a soccer trip my sophomore year, Coach Hiller was our coach, unfortunately, he's no longer with us. The day started off normally, we stopped off in Frankfurt on our way back to Berlin. We picked up our half chicken (at Wienerwald) and our liter of Limonade. We'd sit down after the train got started and we'd have our meal and we'd get to talking and jawing. Telling all kinds of stories, you know how boys are; they always tell stories that make them look good.

We had just about settled down, and we were doing our thing, and the next thing I know I got whacked upside the head with a spit ball. And that started the night. We kept going and going. Finally, Coach Hiller bust in to our compartment and said, "I don't want to hear any more!" He calmed us down and we stopped fighting. The bunks were six to a room, stacked three on each side. Very tight quarters for a bunch of teenagers.

Being bored like I was– I was down on the bottom–I decided to slowly take apart the light switch. And when I took apart the light switch, the switch from the compartment next to us would come out. Stuck my straw through there and whacked a guy in the other compartment. He didn't know where it came from so they started fighting. Coach Hiller busted in there and told them to stop fighting. A few minutes later I did it again. Coach Hiller really got mad at them. These were upper classmen so I really was playing with fire. I started to do it a third time and as I got the straw in there and was about to blow, someone on the other side had wised up, put his mouth on that straw, blew and shot the wad back into my throat.

MELVIN DE VILBISS
Center

Well, that started the compartments war. Things were flying outside the train and into our compartment. Unfortunately for us, the wind was with them. We caught most of it. We'd bust into their door and if you've been on the Duty Train long enough, you knew the trick. You could open the door from outside even if it was lock. You know boys are kind of ingenious about things like that, especially when they were dastardly deeds. Anyway, we got to going, we got to fighting. Coach came down one more time and said, "I'm about to do you guys a number. That's it, no more, never again." Alright, we all got quiet. Got bored again.

Well, remember I'm on the bottom bunk. The guys in the middle bunk were getting ready to do a trick. What they'd do is the guy would push up on the bunk above him with his legs, he'd flip the lever, and the guy on the other side would flip that lever, they'd drop the bunk and the guy in the bunk above would come down. Well, we saw them conspiring to do that to the guy two above me. And my opposite bunk mate was conspiring to do it to the guy above me. The timing was perfect. Whoom, whoom!! Both guys came down on the right side. When they came down they all ended up on the opposite side. Those guys conspired to squish me against the wall. As they were squeezing me, I was losing my breath and telling them to stop.

The upperclassmen in the compartment next to me slammed the door open and in came a garbage can full of water. Whoosh! The only guys that didn't get wet was me, squeezed behind the bed and the guy up in the top left side. About that time Coach Hiller came in. He informed us that we all were going to run 20 laps around the field when we got home. And when you add the baseball field and the football field together–just 4 laps was around a mile. We had a lot of running to do and it was going to last all week. And if anyone came out of the compartment that night, they were off the team. Just when he slammed the door shut, I think it was Quesnel who said, "Oh, I gotta pee!" Well, he filled that Limonade bottle back up. We didn't want that bottle around, because it looked just like Limonade. So, we got rid of it. But, that's another story. That's the way we lived, our trips, they were great!

Melvin De Vilbiss, Class of 1971
1967-1970

When the Enemy of My Friend Became My Brother

I met Helmar Kulike my second day in Berlin while walking our new neighborhood the summer of 1967. I was full of anticipation over our new home and about beginning the ninth grade. Helmar spoke perfect English; I barely remembered any German from when I was in grade school five years earlier in Darmstadt. I remembered that German and American kids were mostly antagonistic toward one another back then. In fact, there was a group of German kids, my guess is they were about three or four years older than my group of American kids, that enjoyed finding us outside our housing area and harassing us- almost always getting the better of us- but that's another story. Never-the-less, because of this earlier experience, I was cautious in developing a friendship with Helmar.

I did slowly begin to trust this German boy, two years older than me. More and more I found myself doing things with Helmar usually every other weekend as I played sports year round. My German got better and I generally learned about Berlin life like I would never have learned it with my American high school friends. He and I had our favorite little corner restaurant where we ate all kinds of traditional German cuisine, and drank lots of German beer. That, unfortunately, was one aspect of our friendship that got Helmar on my parent's you-know-what list.

But to tell you the truth, my friendship with Helmar most likely kept me out of trouble. I didn't do the typical stupid things American teenage boys did and to this day remember my friendship with Helmar with warm regards as a gentle maturing process. We were, however, not above being teenagers. It was during my second (sophomore) year in Berlin that I invited Helmar into our teen club on a Saturday for one of the rare visits I made there. He and I got into an argument. I have no memory what it was over– he probably beat me at table foosball. What I do remember is that it was one of the few times we got physical with each other. I generally lost the rough housing events and this case was no different. I remember he had me in a headlock and was rubbing the top of my head very hard. I kept yelling for him to stop and spinning him around as I had him around the waist. I finally broke loose and ran out of the game room. But shortly, I sensed an eerie silence.

I eventually strolled back into the room to find Helmar holding his mouth with Bill Galloway '70, as big as Helmar, standing face to face with him while clinching his fist. Helmar was mumbling something like, "Wwhyyy'd yaaa dooo dat." Bill simply said, "Leave the little guy alone!" By the time I got over to the two guys, Helmar was pulling one of his front teeth out of his bloody mouth. I asked Bill why he did it and he said he thought the guy was beating me up. I said something to the effect that we were just rough-housing and that Helmar was my friend. Bill had one of those "oh, *&^%" looks on his face as Helmar and I left to go to the hospital.

I don't know why I took Helmar to the American hospital, but they did clean the wound and provide a referral for a German dentist for Helmar the following Monday. He eventually got the tooth replaced. What I do remember in our travels that night is that Helmar had very little good to say about Bill, or me for that matter.

I couldn't get the incident out of my mind the entire weekend. It affected me deeply as I thought it through moment by moment. I sought Bill out at school on Monday. He was one of the biggest black guys in our school. I was a moderate sized (little to Bill) white guy. Bill, without any request for assistance, had taken it upon himself to come to my aid. That meant a lot to me!

I remember Bill immediately started to apologize when he saw me approach and I interrupted him with, "Bill, it was a mistake, but the reason you did it means more to me than the mistake. Helmar may never like you, but you will always be my friend. If ever you need me, just let me know and I'll be there for you."

Yes, there were a few kids on either end of the race spectrum that could never come to terms with their own biases. But for the most part, in Berlin, we were all a family– and this during one of the most tumultuous times in American history. Bill, by example, taught me a wonderful lesson and this is how the enemy of my friend became my brother.

Melvin DeVilbiss, Class of 1970
1967-1970

DEPARTMENT OF THE ARMY
OFFICE OF THE U.S. COMMANDER, BERLIN
APO 09742

AEBU-AG 14 February 1968

MEMORANDUM FOR: Members of the American Community in Berlin

SUBJECT: Anti-Vietnam Demonstrations

1. As a precautionary measure against involvement in possible demonstrations against US policy and commitment in Vietnam, all dependents and their US sponsors in the American Community in Free Berlin are restricted from the general area of the Headquarters Compound, Saargemundestrasse, "Club 50", Shopping Center, Sports Center, T. A. Roberts School, Outpost Theater and adjacent streets between 1300 and 2400 hours on Sunday, 18 February 1968. Exceptions are authorized for those military and civilian personnel required to enter or leave the restricted area on official business.

2. Additionally, the following facilities will be closed on Sunday, 18 February at the times indicated. All other facilities will follow normal Sunday schedules, duplicate facilities are available at McNair and Andrews Barracks.

Shopping Center Snack Bar - 1300 hours
Shopping Center Stars and Stripes Newsstand - 1300 hours
EES Gas Station - 1300 hours
Outpost Theater - all day
Sports Center and Bowling Alley - all day
Indoor Tennis Courts - all day
Foodland (BBde Compound) - 1300 hours
AYA House - all day
"Club 50" - all day
Harnack House - 1300 hours (except for transient guests of Harnack/Dahlem Guest House)
Crump Hall Library - all day

3. The following activities are cancelled for Sunday, 18 February and will be rescheduled at a later date:

Page 1 of 2 concerning Ant- Vietnam Demonstrations on February 18, 1968

BAHS Cheerleading

If memory serves me correctly it was my freshman year at BAHS ('68-'69 school year), my second year in Berlin, having transferred from Sam Rayburn Junior High in San Antonio, TX. After having a fun filled 8th grade between the AYA and school I was all psyched to try out for the JV Cheerleading squad. Not being a limber sort of person I spent countless hours for weeks on end stretching and working on an individual routine.

We were told we would have to "try out" in front of the faculty first and then the student body. The day of try outs came. We individually had to walk out of Ms. Barlow's P.E. locker room into the gym, introduce ourselves to the faculty assembled and perform our own little cheer that we created. Wanting to come up with a cute opener my mother and I spent weeks coming up with a little jingle (now remember Barry Manilow first became famous for his jingles: State Farm, McDonalds and "I am stuck on Band-Aid, 'cause Band-Aid's stuck on me!" are just a few). We settled on the "Oscar Mayer" jingle made famous just a few short years before in that infamous 1965 commercial. "Oh, I'd love to be an Oscar Mayer Wiener ...that is what I really want to be–, 'cause if I was an Oscar Mayer Wiener, everyone would be in love with me!" My words went something like... "Oh, I'd love to be a BAHS cheerleader...that is what I'd really want to be–cause'..." Well, you get the idea.

I did my cutesy intro, did my individual cheer and all went well. Again, if memory serves me correctly, the very next day we were allowed to "try out" in front of the student body. The students then were the deciding vote on who their cheerleaders would be. The next day I learned I had not made the cut. Crushed, I then learned the purpose for trying out in front of faculty was that unlike our stateside schools, or even schools in the Zone for that matter, WE had to catch the Duty Train out on Thursday nights, be away from home for several days, to play other American schools in the Zone. Faculty didn't want any girls being on the squad they considered a "Risk." Word around campus was that Ms. Rekucki marked Jeri a "Risk." One check mark and you're out! To minimize the pain…or possibly avoid a challenge...having been so marked you were allowed to try out in front of the students….but then would be told you didn't get the votes.

Just a couple weeks before try outs, Ms. Rekucki had caught me on the senior floor– Berlin Brats will remember that the ground floor of the school was dedicated to seniors only– holding hands with a guy! She proceeded to rip me, humiliating me there in the hall for my indecent PDA (public display of affection), while everyone was changing class periods! I guess I will never know for sure, but I can tell you Ms. Rekucki scowled at me the remainder of the year! The next year I made sure no PDAs took place at the school, then tried out again my junior year. I was successful this time but I think by the '70-'71 school year the faculty try outs had been abolished.

Jeri Polansky Glass, Class of 1972
1967-1971

BAHS Varsity Cheerleaders, 1970

Life in Berlin: 1968- 1972

In November of 1968 my father returned stateside from a tour in Viet Nam and we were headed to Berlin, Germany. I was in my freshman year and I didn't want to leave the friendships behind that I had just spent two years making. Something we Brats have in common: uprooting ourselves and saying goodbye to friends and family.

I knew nothing about Berlin–not that it was a city divided between the Russian occupation in the East and the Allied Forces of the French, British and Americans in the West, nor that it was the tenth largest city in the world. I did not understand the pivotal place the city held in the Cold War or that there were spies among us. During the three years and seven months that my family lived in the city, we were constrained to travel by plane or by Duty Train at night. My father was a soldier and his duty was aligned with the mission of the Army Security Agency (ASA). His work was confidential and because of it we were forbidden to go to the East or to even ride on the S-Bahn train because we might be kidnapped and held hostage. We were too young and naïve to understand the implication of our restrictions. In spite of them we lived a good life in West Berlin among other military families.

Our apartment was on the fifth floor of military housing and faced Sundgauer Strasse. Across the street from our house was a playground and park where we spent a lot of time just hanging out mostly with other military brats– but there were some local teens that infiltrated our group. One night we threw a big party with beer in the park. The police raided the party and I left my 45 record collection behind…I never saw it again. When I arrived home my parents knew I had been drinking and my father sent me to bed and put me on restriction. I was on restriction a lot those days.

Summers also meant trips to the Wannsee to swim or rent a boat and row to the German nude beach and drink Berliner Weisse. With no age limit to consume alcohol it was always available to us and we accepted drinking as a normal part of our existence. There were evenings spent downtown at restaurants consuming pizza and beer or at clubs dancing and drinking. We had a lot of freedom and we took advantage of it.

THE AMERICAN HIGH SCHOOL Choir, under the direction of W. C. Fenstermacher (far left seated), provided an afternoon program of Christmas carols and songs for the American Women's Club Christmas tea held Dec. 4 at the Harnack House. The soloist is Cathy Gilman.

BAHS Presents 'Intimate Christmas'

The Berlin American High School Band and Chorus, directed by Wayne C. Fenstermacher, will present "An Intimate Christmas," a program of familiar and unfamiliar music on Thursday, Dec. 19, at the high school auditorium.

The show, to begin at 7:30 p.m., is in miniature, using only students as soloists and in ensemble. Music from the 12th century to today will be featured.

Admission price is 50 cents for adults and 25 cents for students. Children under school age wil be admitted free. Tickets are on sale from band and chorus members or at the door.

BAHS Choir led by Herr Fenstermacher

In my junior year of high school I fell in love and everything in the world seemed better. Academically things were going well too! I made the honor roll and I worked at the three libraries earning credit hours shelving books, repairing book spines and decorating bulletin boards.

I spent my spare time listening to vinyl records in the listening room at the McNair Barracks library. I loved that special time alone with my music. And speaking of music, I sang chorus every year. I didn't have a great voice but I loved to sing. Some of the most memorable events in Berlin for me were the trips that Herr Fenstermacher arranged for us to the Berlin Philharmonic.

We saw the Vienna Boys Choir perform as well as an opera of Hansel and Gretel. I am so appreciative to Herr Fenstermacher for that exposure to music and theatre. It is a passion that has stayed with me for a lifetime.

Prom that year was like something of a fairy tale. I had a beautiful dress, a popular boyfriend, and the evening was enchanting. Life was good. But then the breakup and everything changed around me and within me. My senior year was abysmal. I fell into some bad habits, isolated myself from most of my peers, and lost my way. I did not attend my senior prom; I didn't even buy a yearbook. I hated life, I loathed myself. But God saw me differently from how I saw me and He intervened. If it were not for the compassion of Leona Odegaard, BAHS faculty, I would not have graduated with my class. I am so thankful for her and for my experience in Berlin.

How many senior class trips are made to Amsterdam, Holland!! And how many high school alumni associations make the gatherings we Berlin Brats enjoy possible? I am much older now, wiser, and very blessed to be a part of such a wonderful group of individuals. I have made many new Brat friends in recent years. We shared an extraordinary experience. Proof of that... the Allied Museum opened a major exhibit on the military dependent education during our reunion in Berlin in 2006. What a legacy we left behind in Berlin. Be proud.

Joyce Clark Mallon, Class of 1972
1968-1972

The Friendship Connection

Deb and Gail, the Matterhorn, Swiss Alps 1972

When I look back at my childhood, growing up in a military family and moving every 2-3 years, I envied people who lived in one place all their lives, attending the same school from first grade through graduation. They would never know how it feels to be the new kid in class, wondering if you will be accepted or if you will make friends easily in yet another new location. I thought "forever" friends are possible only if you stay put in one place forever. I was wrong. As a Brat, I was fortunate to form a friendship at a very young age that still carries through to this day. My best friend is Gail, also a Brat, and this is our story.

One was chubby and shy, the other was slender, pretty and popular. I was the chubby one. The year was 1967, we were in 6th grade, and just 11 years old. For reasons I cannot explain, Gail and I became instant friends. We were inseparable, and looking back on our beginnings in Nürnberg, I remember every nook and cranny of her house, even better than my own. It was a given that every weekend I would spend it with Gail and her family (I also traveled with her family as a child and through adulthood). We lived in the military quarters in Fürth-Dambach, Nürnberg, and our streets were named after famous composers. I lived on Hayden Strasse, while Gail lived on Beethoven Strasse, just a block away. Our houses were separated by the playground where we spent hours playing tetherball, and spending time with Beth Nielsen (better known as the recording artist Beth Nielsen Chapman) listening to her latest compositions on the guitar.

I lived for the weekends to hang out with Gail and her family. We would stay up late, talking, laughing, and....drawing! We would draw funny cartoon characters, each with a story which would have us both rolling on the floor with laughter. We were quite creative! Gail still has many of those old cartoons. We sipped Coca Cola from slender, frosted glasses, probably meant for a Tom Collins, but we felt cool drinking from them. We munched on Cheetos and Fritos out of the Army-issue blue tin cans we got from the Commissary. We would play Monopoly, Life and Easy Money. The latter was my favorite. Gail's dad, whom I called "Daddy Boo" played along with us, and he had an infectious belly laugh that would make me just crack up! We tried to get Gail's mom, Sally, to play with us as well, but she usually had an exciting library book at hand and couldn't tear herself away. Little did I know forty years later I would be asking Sally for book recommendations, for I valued her opinions implicitly. She and I were crossword buffs, and we enjoyed solving crosswords together. If Sally were alive today, she would be a master at Words With Friends!

The Hatchett household was always a fun place to be, where silliness was encouraged (and discouraged in my house), so I became a permanent weekend fixture at Gail's home at 22 Beethoven Strasse. I remember one Halloween when Gail's parents turned their home into a haunted house at Halloween, complete with cold spaghetti dangling from the ceiling, giving the eerie feeling of cold worms crawling over you in the dark.

Gail and Deb celebrating their 50th birthday

Gail's family loved Germany, and they did two tours of Nürnberg, with Gail graduating from Nürnberg American High School. My family left Nürnberg in 1968, and moved to Berlin, the city where my parents met and married, and where I was born. What amazes me is that Gail and I were friends for just over a year when my family moved to Berlin, and in that one year, we formed a bond of friendship that 47 years later is still intact. We didn't have Facebook or email to keep in touch in the early years. There were times when she lived in the US and I was in Berlin, or she was in Nürnberg and I was in the U.S. So…we relied on snail mail.

And unbeknownst to me, Gail kept most of the letters I ever wrote to her over the years, and recently gave them to me. What a trip down memory lane to read these letters, and share them with my husband and daughter! In one letter I wrote about the famous moon walk, and in another, I mention President Nixon's visit to Berlin.

They say Brats form bonds, even though initial contacts are brief, they can last a lifetime. It's called, cleverly, the "Brat connection." Although I did attend some of middle school and my last year of high school in the US, I can't say I regularly keep in touch with anyone from those days. I do, however, keep in touch with my BAHS friends on a regular basis and have been known to host BAHS Gatherings, including lunch outings with folks from BAHS who live in my city. And of course, I keep in regular contact with Gail, and although we live in different states, we visit each other frequently. And when we get together, we are 11 years old all over again!

Deb Brians Clark, Class of 1974
1964-65, 1968-69, 1971-73

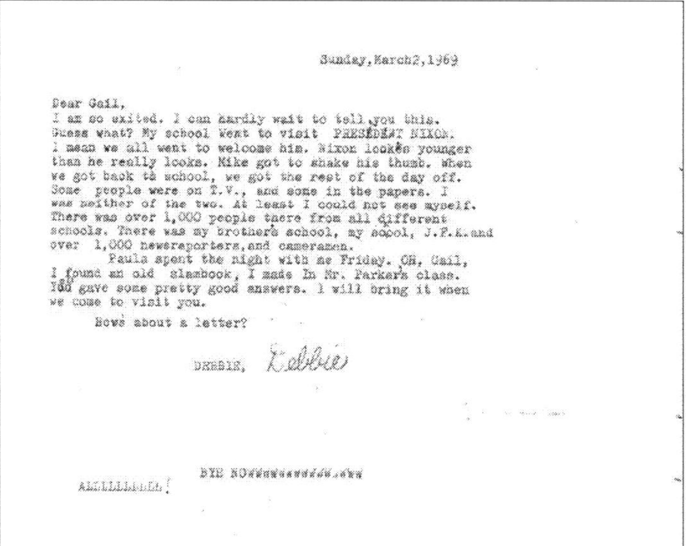

Sunday,March2,1969

Dear Gail,
I am so exited. I can hardly wait to tell you this.
Guess what? My school Went to visit PRESIDENT NIXON.
I mean we all went to welcome him. Nixon lookes younger
than he really looks. Mike got to shake his thumb. When
we got back to school, we got the rest of the day off.
Some people were on T.V., and some in the papers. I
was neither of the two. At least I could not see myself.
There was over 1,000 people there from all different
schools. There was my brothers school, my school, J.F.K.and
over 1,000 newsreporters,and cameramen.
Paula spent the night with me Friday. OH, Gail,
I found an old slambook, I made In Mr. Parker's class.
You gave some pretty good answers. I will bring it when
we come to visit you.
Hows about a letter?

DEBBIE, Debbie

ALLLLLLLLLL! BYE NOWWWWWWWWW.WWW

Debbie (My autograph)

Left: Letter from Deb about President Nixon's visit to Berlin

Below: Nixon vistits Berlin, February 26, 1969

Thousands of Berliners Cheer President Nixon

Chief Executive Lauds Berlin Brigade Troops

THE BERLIN OBSERVER

Ha, Ha, He! Berliners are o.k.

The Crabs

We had a great team back in the fall of 1969. We were about to finish the season against a non-conference foe, Bremerhaven, and knew a victory would seal at least a tie for the Division Championship. This would be the third year in a row the Berlin Cubs would be the Division Champions. We had one loss that year and were miffed we would share the top spot with one of two teams we had beaten- who were playing each other that weekend to see who would share the top spot with us! So what's this got to do with crabs? I'm getting there- hold on!

Needless to say, our spirits were high and levity was beginning to set in the night before our final game. Several of us were taking a self-guided walking tour after dinner and visited a huge bombed out gun emplacement near Bremerhaven harbor. We talked about how we'd finish the season and how great it would have been if we could have finished it as sole Division Champion like the year before. After all, two years as champion is unusual, but three makes a dynasty. What about the crabs? Geez, wait a minute!

We were running a little late but on the way back from the emplacement, there was a large rowboat on its side with water in it. And low and behold, there were a couple of little crabs. Now you're asking, is that it? I took them back to the large open bay barracks Bremerhaven stuck us in. A little more interested now? I know it's hard to believe, but my teammates thought me a little mischievous. I wanted to have a little fun, but it had to be with someone who didn't know I had the crabs. There were just a couple of guys who had returned yet- so my choices were limited.

Thurman Nash '71, one of our star running backs, a classmate and good friend, became the prime candidate. A few minutes before lights out,

Thurman was sliding into bed (yup– you guessed it). He instantly shot out of bed and ripped his covers off the bed. Then something happened I didn't count on. Thurman got mad, I mean really mad! Storming up and down the barracks, pointing fingers, proclaiming what he was going to do to the >%^&&*^ who put that crab in his bed!

I was going to tell him, believe me I was, but not after that tirade. I now thought silence was better than valor in this case. But it got worse! Bill Galloway '70, who was aware of what I was doing and bunked right next to Thurman, was laughing his head off. You should know that Bill had a booming baritone voice. He sang in the chorus and led all of our football warm-up chants. The barracks was rocking with his deep throated laughter. All this did was infuriate Thurman even more– which made everyone laugh even more. The energy was building and I really was afraid Thurman was going to lose it. He did!

Finally, Thurman had had enough of Bill's laughter and threatened him with violence, at which time Bill jumped out of bed and stood his ground– face to face with Thurman (and about six inches taller and 50 pounds heavier). Just then, Coach Pepoy came in and asked what all the commotion was about. In typical fashion, not one player said a thing. Coach firmly stated, "Get to bed," and stood by the light switch to turn out the lights. Bill got into bed, still chuckling underneath his breath, and Thurman lay on top of his covers, still mad as all get out.

But WAIT– I had two crabs! You all know the true life story of Michael Oher, in the movie *Blind Side*, right? Well, Pascal Sherrod was our true life 6' 4", 240 lb. version of the gentle giant. But why this huge football player liked sleeping on the top bunk, I'll never know. When the coach told us to

get to bed, Pascal pulled his covers back and, still in a seated position, slipped his feet slowly down his sheets. As soon as that huge foot touched the crab, his eyes got really big and he started going "OOO," while shaking his covers. I've never seen a big guy move so fast. But the top bunk?
He pushed off so hard from his bunk, with the guy still in the bottom bed, it went over almost knocking the next bunk with two guys in it over. The bunk he jumped to in the opposite direction fell over when he landed on it as did the one next to it. I could not believe NOBODY got hurt. It was also the only time I ever heard Coach Pepoy cuss as he yelled, "What the hell is going on!"

As the rest of us were picking up the bunks, Pascal stripped his bed to uncover a little crab. Coach angrily said for us to get the mess straightened up and he'd be back to turn the lights out. I swear he was holding back laughter as he was walking out of the room; he did have a big smile on his face. While waiting at the Bremerhaven train station after our 50-0 victory we heard that Wurzburg and Augsburg played to a 6-6 tie, giving us sole position as Division Champs!

Thurman would mention from time to time what he would do to the ^%$&* who put the crab in his bed– I never had the guts to tell him until I friended him on Facebook last year (he's never sent me a message since). I did tell Pascal, who slapped me in the face and said, "Boy, don't you ever do that to me again!" Then he started laughing almost as loudly as Bill Galloway!

Melvin DeVilbiss, Class of 1970
1967-1970

Berlin Cubs- 1968 Silver Division Crown Winners

Berlin Cubs to Open Season Guided by New Coach Pepoy

The Berlin Cubs will open their 1968 football season with an away game at Bad Kreuznach with the Bear Kats on Sept. 21. Following a second away game with the Baumholder Bucs on Sept. 28, the team will return to Berlin to face the Bitburg Barons on Oct. 4 at the Berlin American High School football field beginning at 3 p.m.

This year the varsity team will be spirited on by a new head coach, George Pepoy. Pepoy came from Bremerhaven High School where he coached the Bremerhaven Knights for seven years. He was named "Coach of the Year, 1966-67," by "Stars and Stripes" for defeating a powerful Berlin team.

It is interesting to note that the Cubs will close their season on Nov. 2 by playing Pepoy's ex-team, the Knights, here.

Returning lettermen for the Cubs this year are seniors Howard Ashcraft, Jet Thomas, T. J. Winter and Mike Stingel. Stingel be playing his fourth year on the Berlin squad. All are linemen. Other returning lettermen are juniors: Todd Daress, guard; Al Darden, tackle and last year's co-captain; Jerry Parker, quarterback; and Cleo Johnson halfback, who last year was the only member of the team to make all-conference.

The team roster includes 77 members, grades 9-12. Assistant varsity coach will be Tom Hiller and the coach of the junior varsity team will be Jim Rice.

In 1968, Berlin Cubs win Silver Division Crown for the second year in a row, this time with new heacd coach George Pepoy, former coach for rival Bremerhaven Blackhawks

Below: All Conference Halfback and captain, Cleo Johnson and the USDESEA Championship plaque

Cubs Win Silver Division Crown As Team Records Perfect Year

Led by new head coach George Pepoy and the sensational performances of halfback Cleo Johnson, the Berlin American High School Cubs football team swept to an undefeated season and won the Silver Division USDESEA football title.

At the end of the season the Cubs placed 11 men on the Stars and Stripes, All Silver Division football squad. Later five players were named to the All USDESEA team which includes the best high school players in Europe. Cleo Johnson, T. J. Winters, Ray Sanchez, Howard Ashcraft and Dennis Cousins were all named to the USDESEA "Dream Team".

Drive to Success

The Cubs began their drive to success in their opening ball game with Bad Kreuznach. It was a non-conference game but the Cubs were in mid-season form as they knocked off the Bear Kats 30-6. Cleo Johnson set a pace that was to carry him and the Cubs through the season as he scored five touchdowns and had two more trips to paydirt called back.

Another road trip followed the next week, with the Cubs traveling to Baumholder. Berlin quarterback Pat Black and halfback Oakie Wheeler teamed up to bomb the Bucs 16-0 for the Cubs first league win.

Taking advantage of two long runs by Cleo Johnson on the next weekend, the Berliners smashed by the Bitburg Barons 14-6. It was the Cubs first home game and Cleo Johnson put on a scoring show for the hometowners as he scored two TD's with runs of 80 and 3 yards.

Against the Wuerzburg Warriors the following week, the Cubs took over undisputed possession of first place in the Silver Division. The Cubs ran over the hapless Warriors 42-18 with Cleo Johnson and Pat Black providing the heroics.

Johnson Continues Assault

On the next Saturday Johnson continued his assault on opposing team's goal lines as he scored four touchdowns to beat Augsburg 44-20.

Two fourth period touchdowns by halfback Johnson on the next weekend gave the Cubs the Silver Division crown. It was the sixth-straight win for the Cubs as they downed Baumholder again, this time 14-0. Johnson sparked the Cubs to life with less than 10 minutes left in the game as he plowed over from three yards out. Then with less than six minutes showing on the clock, Johnson slashed off tackle and with some brilliant broken field running twisted his way to paydirt.

Cubs Claw Blackhawks

The final game of the year was homecoming against the Bremerhaven Blackhawks. The Cubs celebrated the annual occasion by shooting down the Blackhawks 26-0 to capoff their undefeated year. Again, as had been the case all year, Cleo Johnson was the star. Cleo scored 24 of the Cubs 26 points while routing the Blackhawks.

Three-peat! Berlin Cubs- 1969 Silver Division Crown Winners

Bottom row: James Wright, Rick Speer, Carl Kennedy, Leo Short, William Hamilton, James Wilcox, Charles Hipkins, Samuel McCaskey, Russell Lewis. *Second row:* Thurman Nash, Larry Garrels, Dexter Galloway, Ronald Rathnow, Herbert Black, Cleo Johnson, Jean Benit, Steve Moranci, Melvin DeVilbiss, Todd Darress. *Back row:* Mr. Pepoy, John Robinson, Matthew Schneider, Gregory Baxter, Larry Williams, David Howard, Frank Wilson, Harry Smith, Pascal Sherrod, Steve Oesterreicher, William Galloway.

Coach George Pepoy gives a few pointers to All Europe Co-Captains Todd Darress and Cleo Johnson.

Cubs End Football Season on Top of Standings

The Berlin Cubs football squad have ended their season atop the Silver Division standings again. This is, in fact, "old" news. But the making of a sound football team requires a long seasoned look backward.

About the middle of August, when the days were warm and the sun shone brightly, a group of young men, numbering roughly about 35, started practice sessions in hopes of repeating as champions. Under the helm of coach George Pepoy, the Cubs only had a few returning letterman with experience. A lot of hard work was in store before the first exhibition game on September 20 against Karlsruhe.

When opening day arrived, it was Cleo Johnson who dazzled the avid game fans with his amazing running ability. He scored the Cub's first touchdown of the season — a 70-yard jaunt — and Berlin was off and running in '69. The Cubs added an insurance score late in the game on a 35-yard run by quarterback Jean-Pierre Benit to take a 16-6 victory over the Spartans. Coach Pepoy labeled the win as "ragged", but the following week the high-schoolers were destined to improve.

Opening Silver Division play, the Cubs trounced a Baumholder eleven 38-6 to extend their win streak to eight games over the past two years. Johnson, Thurman Nash and Herbie Black led the pack with TD's while the Cub's defensive unit was beginning to gel.

The following week a slight over-confidence chilled the smiles of the Berlin gridders, but it quickly vanished when two key players were put out of action during the game, setting the stage for a 16-8 upset by Bitburg. Jim Wilcox, starting guard on the offensive squad, sustained a knee injury midway through the contest and would be lost for the season. And secondly, Cleo Johnson was knocked unconscious early in the second quarter and he sat out the remainder of the game. The loss bumped the Cubs into second place with an October 11 clash coming up against league leader Wuerzburg.

The mark of a good team can be seen after a frustrating defeat. To rally for the next game once you're down is hard, but the Cubs came up with a similar performance against the Wolves, winning 24-14. Once again it was Johnson who led the pack. He scored three six-pointers, while end Harry Smith added the other. The victory was indeed sweet and it put the Cubs back on the winning side of the ledger.

The following week Berlin exploded for their most points of the year against Augsburg, and another win. The hapless Apaches could only penetrate the Cub's tight-end defense once for a score, while Berlin racked 10 touchdowns for a 66-6 victory to cap the Homecoming theme "Emerald City."

Journeying to Baumholder once again, the Cubs matched their earlier victory by an identical 38-6 drubbing of the Bucks. Johnson had a typical prolific day — three TD's — and the shutout moved the Cubs into a three-way tie for top spot with Wuerzburg and Augsburg to close out their league play. Berlin scheduled an exhibition tilt with Bremerhaven, while the Wolves and Apaches held their last game. The Cubs bumbled the Bulls, coupled with an Apache-Wolves 8-8 tie to break the three-way tie and hand the conference crown to Berlin.

POSING for a team picture are members of the Berlin American High School's football Cubs recently. The Cubs took the Silver Division Championship for the third year in a row with a mark of four wins and one loss. Their only defeat came at the hands of the Bitburg Barons, to break a win streak going back to the 1968 season.

Melvin, Coach Smith and Coach Pepoy

The Berlin Cubs win the Championship for the third year in a row!

Team Captain, Cleo Johnson, was later drafted by the Denver Broncos in 1971

A Perspective on Berlin

An American military brat lives a special life made more exceptional if lived overseas with a serving parent(s). My family was in Darmstadt, Federal Republic of Germany (W. Germany) from '59 to '62. My father had to go alone to secure quarters (housing) before the Army would give us transportation orders. My mother, pregnant with my brother, and I were about to leave Oklahoma when I came down with the German measles. My grandmother had to care for me because of the dangers to a developing fetus (try explaining that to a six year old). When I was finally well enough and no longer contagious, my mother and I left on a train through Chicago to New York where we boarded the Troop Ship Rose. On the long two-week voyage I contracted strep throat and ran a high fever. Due to mission requirements my father was unable to meet us at Bremerhaven where the ship docked. My very pregnant mother with a very sick child had to figure out how to get to Frankfurt on her own. By the time we got into the Frankfurt train station I was really sick- but fortunately, my father had been able to break away to meet us. This was my introduction to being an Overseas Brat.

Melvin and brother, Darmstadt, 1962

Life in Darmstadt was Spartan. We lived in two different civilian quarters on the economy, fifth floor temporary quarters, and finally permanent quarters on the third floor. There were still many bombed out buildings in the city from WW II and my associations with German kids were mostly combative, where I usually received the worst of it, to say the least. In the meantime, my brother was born during my father's first of many training deployments after our arrival. It is a fact that "things" always happened when my father was deployed. As an Overseas Brat it was simply a part of our lives that you lived without your serving parent for up to half the time spent in country due to mission requirements.

My first connection with Berlin:

My father commanded a 280mm Artillery Battery (the first Atomic cannons) in Darmstadt. He had just returned home the evening before, from a six- week field trip to Grafenwoehr when the alert was sounded at about 4 a.m. It was operating procedure that the first thing a soldier did upon returning from a field trip was clean his field gear and repack it for immediate deployment. And so he left for what would be another six weeks with his battery and atomic projectiles at the ready for positions near the East/West German border. Why the alert? The construction of "the Berlin Wall" had just commenced! The families were given marching orders to stay ready for emergency deployment back to the States. The tension in the air was palpable- even us "kids" knew this was serious stuff! Stateside, Americans may have been concerned; but in Germany, American soldiers were on the front line, and their families were just behind them!

After a tour in the States, my father was deployed to Viet Nam. By now I was an adolescent flapping my wings trying to grow up, without my father. One particularly poignant event was an argument I had with my mother. I don't remember the cause; I just remember she started crying. At that moment, something clicked in my youthful brain that told me this wasn't about me, it was about something much larger, more real and terrifying- it was about a family, separated, lonely, in harm's way and desperately trying to keep things together. I apologized to my mother and told her I would be a better son; she hugged me and we both cried some more. Most military brats experience a realization similar to this at some point in their lives. I was fortunate to have it happen to me at a young age. It helped shape the rest of my life in a meaningful way.

Unfortunately, as it is in any walk of life, not all Brats are able make adjustments to the constant deployment of the serving parents, whether the deployment is a family accompanied tour, a short unaccompanied tour, or (for distinction) a short unaccompanied tour in harm's way. I attended nine different schools from K through 12. I found the transfers challenging, but also very exciting. I actually enjoyed the challenges for the most part, but I know my brother, seven years younger, did not.

My formal introduction to Berlin:

Just a year after my father returned from Viet Nam we found ourselves back in Germany, in Berlin. In his position as IG (Inspector General), we had several opportunities to accompany him through Checkpoint Charlie into E. Berlin while he conducted "official" business. There was nothing scarier for me than crossing through that border having to show identification to armed grim-faced Soviet soldiers and seeing first-hand the no-man's strip where people died trying to gain freedom. That image will be forever seared into my memory! Yet another vivid image was the nakedness of East Berlin compared to the robust and lively West Berlin. Nowhere could an American so readily observe the stark differences between totalitarianism and freedom.

But the most telling event I remember was the Soviet invasion of Czechoslovakia in 1968. It shocked all of NATO because the Soviet forces were on the ground quelling the Czech population's brave but premature bid for independence before we even knew what had happened. The Berlin Brigade was placed on alert and took up defensive positions around the city along with the French and British allies. Sitting deep behind the Iron Curtain even the military families knew there was absolutely nothing we could do if all the East German and Soviet Divisions surrounding the city attacked. We would be the first to go! It was then I realized the inescapable truth about what made being a Berlin Brat so special: for the one and only time in our lives, we were, at least symbolically, serving side-by-side with our parents in uniform! No other American dependent had that privilege!

A fond farewell to Berlin:

Six years after leaving Berlin, I found myself stationed in Giessen, FRG with nuclear weapons. My wife and I visited Coach Pepoy and his wife in 1976. This was my last time in Berlin. I also visited my life-long German friend from the old neighborhood, with whom I still communicate. Traveling the checkpoints just wasn't as scary as it had been 10 years earlier.

While still serving (stateside), Germany was reunified and the "Wall came down." The full spectrum of emotions over those three decades of living with "the Berlin Wall" is hard to put into words, but explicitly understood by Brats, especially Berlin Brats. It is this common experience that uniquely binds us! Ich bin ein Berliner– jetzt und für immer!

Melvin DeVilbiss, Class of 1971
1967-1970

Melvin getting ready to fire a 280 mm gun, Grafenwoehr 1962

When Nixon Visited Berlin

Nixon visits Berlin

On February 26, 1969, President Richard M. Nixon, with Foreign Minister and former Berlin Mayor Wilhelm Brandt and West German Chancellor Kurt Georg Kiesinger, made a visit to Berlin to show support for the occupation. It was a snow-covered day. I was in sixth grade at the time. The news reported the number of American students who met Air Force One on its arrival at Tempelhof Airport. I don't remember traveling to the airport but rather standing along Clayallee. We waved small American flags and shouted, "We want Nixon." Apparently this was a "big deal" as Nixon came to warn the Soviet bloc that the "West will never bow to pressure from any source and will keep the city free." I have a faint memory of seeing Nixon drive by. This was the first time I had ever seen a President.

Looking back on that day brings to mind an odd juxtaposition of events. On the one hand, America was mired in the fields of Vietnam in a war that we would not and could not win. While on the other hand, America was a symbol of strength, peace, and freedom in a city surrounded by a Wall that suppressed those very ideals. Berlin was always known as a city of four powers- US, British, French, and Russian. But Nixon exclaimed that a fifth power existed- Berlin. That is the power that remains in all of us who experienced the city during the Cold War.

Lisa Randle, Class of 1975
1967-70; 1972-75

Extra Credit

In my eighth grade Earth Science class during the 1969-70 school year, I offered the opportunity for extra credit. The student had to design a project, get my approval, and then present it to the class. Several students opted to do this and I was pleased with the variety of projects I was able to approve.

One snowy, cold morning, I found Charles waiting at my classroom door, looking more than a little worried. He explained that his dad had helped him make a rather elaborate volcano model. His plan was to explain how the volcano had been formed and then to have it "erupt" thereby demonstrating the resulting escaping gases and lava flow. His problem was that he needed hydrogen peroxide to make the interaction between the ingredients work and the PX was all out. I told him this was not a problem since we had an abundant supply in the lab. I filled a large glass test tube with the peroxide and, after putting a cork in the top, sent him on his way.

Later that morning, we had an urgent intercom announcement that we should immediately evacuate the building and go to the back of the parking lot to wait for further instructions. It turns out that someone had called in a bomb scare and immediate evacuation was the required procedure. After standing in the freezing cold –without coats– for more than an hour, they decided to send the students home for the rest of the day. Teachers were also told we could go home, but that we were to remain by our phones for the remainder of the school day. I had not been home very long before I received a call asking me to return to school and go directly to the conference room. So, I slogged my way all the way back to school.

When I walked into the conference room, there at the table sat the principal, Dave Twohy; the guidance counselor, Christine Aliano; three or four men in uniform; a couple more men in suits; and a very pale Charles! They explained that Charles had accused me of providing him with the "suspicious" looking liquid that was in his locker. Further, that there was now a bomb squad on its way to remove it. After listening to my full explanation and placing a call to Charles' father, they let us all go with some mumbling about wasted time and failure to use labels. Dave Twohy just shrugged and said, "At least it wasn't vodka."

Lois Vandagriff, Faculty
8th grade Earth Science, 1968-1970

At Berlin American High School

Student Wins Annual B & L Honorary Science Award

A senior student at the Berlin American High School has been awarded the annual Bausch and Lomb Honorary Science Award, BAHS Principal Paul F. LeBrun announced this week.

Howard Ashcraft, son of Mr. and Mrs. Howard W. Ashcraft, has maintained a perfect "A" average during his four years of high school science.

In announcing the 1968 winner, Mr. LeBrun said: "The award is especially significant. Howard has studied science at the Berlin American High School for the past four years and, as such, is a product of our science department."

As a winner of the Honorary Science Award, Howard is eligible to compete for a Bausch and Lomb Science Scholarship at the University of Rochester.

The combined Bausch and Lomb and University of Rochester investment in a four-year scholarship is approximately $2,000 per year for four years, allocated on a need basis.

Howard Ashcraft

A product of the BAHS Science Department: Howard Ashcraft '69 honored with the prestigious Bausch & Lomb Science Award.

Astronauts visit West Berlin- Oct. 12-14, 1969

Berliners, Allies Cheer Arrival of Apollo Trio

Vol. 25 No. 42 U. S. ARMY, BERLIN Friday, October 17, 1969

REACHING OUT TO SHAKE HANDS with the astronauts are hundreds of German and American school children who were bussed to Tempelhof for the arrival of the space travelers last Monday. Neil Armstrong (front), Michael Collins (center) and Edwin Aldrin witnessed record-breaking crowds on their motorcade through the city. photo by Marelli

Two BB Employes Cited For Their Superior Services

October 17, 1969 THE BERLIN OBSERVER Page 3

Bands, Flags and Outstretched Hands

Chapter 4: The 1970s

"Blessed are the people whose leaders can look destiny in the eye without flinching but also without attempting to play God."

- Henry Kissinger, statesman and 1973 Nobel Peace Prize laureate

Berlin: Great Life Experiences

My Dad, now Air Force retired, was assigned Mission Supervisor of Charlie Flight in Berlin from 1968 to 1972. I began my schooling in Berlin at TAR in 5th grade and ended with BAHS in 8th grade. Our family's living quarters for the first few months was "on the economy." In other words, since housing on base was not yet available, we lived in the private sector. We lived in a duplex style house located on Gutzmannstrasse which was located a short distance from the Wall. It was an older house and not in the best repair. I remember my little sisters, Carol, Linda and I watching a man mow the front yard area and when he spoke German, how funny we all thought that sounded.

Guzmannstrasse, 1968

245 Argentinische Allee

After a few months, military housing became available. We lived in an apartment complex in the BB (Berlin Brigade) Housing Area at 245 Argentinische Allee, on the third floor. The novelty of climbing three flights of stairs wore off quickly! The flat was completely furnished and amazingly enough, there were maids' quarters in the basement area. Maids were usually young, college-aged German girls living in dorm-like fashion. Our family had a maid available that was used mainly for babysitting.

Everything was within walking distance. School, PX, commissary, movie, all had to be accessed by crossing the very busy Allee. I shudder now to think how many times I, my sisters and my friends crossed that busy street by ourselves every day! Many times we walked by the site on which the German/American Volksfest came annually.

1970 German-American Volksfest, ride inspired by the Apollo 11 crew's flight and visit in 1969

Our family took two vacations during our time in Germany. One I remember was to Bavaria (Southern Germany). On the way through East Germany, Dad could only pass through each Checkpoint with proper "Flag Orders." First, we visited Garmisch, a popular mountain resort town. Next, we toured Oberammergau, location of the famous ten-yearly Passion Play. We spent time walking the streets of the city where my Dad purchased a hand carved chess set that he still has to this day. We also went to Berchtesgaden and toured Hitler's Eagle's Nest. We also toured the "Walt Disney Castle" (Neuschwanstein Castle). Finally, we went to Salzburg, Austria and saw the location where The Sound of Music was filmed.

The second trip was to the Netherlands. We traveled to Amsterdam and Rotterdam where we saw a tulip auction, towering windmills, and even a cheese shop where they made huge rounds of Edam and Gouda cheese. Most

Bavaria 1971: Linda, Dad, Carol and me (not too thrilled)

memorable to me was the Anne Frank house. I had read the book and could not have imagined how small the house and the attic area really were. Years later, I reread the book with new appreciation.

Holland 1969: The girls and Mom

During my 7th grade year, an opportunity came for a class school trip to ski in the Berchtesgaden/Bavarian Alps. Since the trip limited the number of us to go, a drawing was held. The cost was about a hundred dollars which was a lot of money for a young military family. I remember a lot of pleading and begging for permission to enter my name in the drawing. My name was entered and was drawn next to last. My first trip without my parents– to the Alps no less! I stayed in a room with three other classmates. I learned to ski and had the time of my life. I will never forget the instructors shouting over and over "Schnoe plow!"

Another memorable life experience came on another class trip. We were to take the train to an ice skating rink. While on our way, a few of us were jumping from car to car just as it would leave the station. As I jumped from one car onto the platform, the doors closed and left without me. I was stranded in a strange place, spoke very little German, had no idea the name of the place the rest of the class was headed, and scared out of my wits knowing I was in big trouble. I approached a station worker and did my best to make him understand my situation. No such luck. My only alternative was to wait or hop on and ride until I saw something or someone familiar. Thank goodness I did not choose the latter. In the meantime, a friend told a teacher what happened and she sent someone back to find me. I arrived to a round of applause and had a great time learning to skate. Later I learned that I was only two stops from the border; with my Dad's classified status, I could have created a huge mess for him.

I had three very close friends in my last year in Berlin. They were Shirley Peabody '76, Gaby Adler '76 and Laurie Pidek '76. With limited access to the pop culture of the U.S., we lived for the next issue of *Tiger Beat* magazine and stayed glued to the radio for the next pop hit. With limited TV channels, we could not watch the popular stateside shows such as the *Partridge Family*, *The Osmonds* or *The Jackson Five*. How frustrating for us all!

The one teacher I remember well was Mr. Kermit Long. While we learned to type, he would sing the 1950 hit song "Music, Music, Music." Every time I hear it: "Put another nickel in, in the nickelodeon…," I think of him. He was very upbeat and encouraged me to participate in the school newsletter, the *Bull Sheet*. He would probably be the one teacher that influenced me the most.

As I arrived in Berlin, I had already accepted that military life afforded you very few lasting friendships. They came and went with each assignment. And, although I have had many friends, two in particular have lasted to this day. Both were a result of our time in Berlin. My best friend Barbara Porras lived in the next building, as well as sisters Patti and Doris Pangelinan. I communicate with them often thanks to Facebook.

These are merely the highlights of my memories. I now appreciate the enormous life experience and enrichment I gained from my Berlin years. I am a proud Berlin Brat!

Patricia Simurra Price, Class of 1976
1968-1972

Separated by the Wall

At the end of WWII, the Allied forces divided Berlin into four sectors. In 1948, the Soviets closed the city to all traffic prompting the Allied forces to undertake "Operation Vittles," also known as the "Berlin Airlift." Prior to the Soviets closing the city, a young German girl, named Gretchen Lutzner, from the small village of Niederschona (E. Germany), was visiting relatives in Berlin by herself. When the Soviets suddenly closed the city, she wasn't allowed to go back to Niederschona and was stranded in Berlin. She was adopted by relatives there.

Across the world in Iowa, a young American airman named Raymond Ryan was about to deploy to Berlin to assist in the Airlift. Once there, he met this pretty German girl, fell in love, and they eventually married. Raymond and Gretchen are my parents. My brother Mike was born later and they embarked on a military lifestyle, traveling the world. My parents had a daughter, Renee and four more boys, Robert, Ronald, Rex and myself.

With Gretchen's ties to Berlin, my father was able to secure three tours in Europe during his career. The Soviets wouldn't allow Gretchen to see her family in E. Germany, until Dad's last tour in Berlin from 1969 to 1972. The Ryan clan invaded Berlin American High School. Mike was a senior in 1969, and the Vietnam War was gaining momentum. He received his draft notice to serve in the Army, but after some controversy, he enlisted in the Air Force and was sent stateside.

Berlin was the most memorable place that our family was ever stationed and over the years, many members of our family returned to Germany. As recently as 2011, Robert, my mother and I traveled to Niederschona, where I was able to see many relatives for the first time. We visited BAHS, which hasn't changed over the years, now being a German school. Memories of playing sports, partying at the lakes and the AYA, and intimidating the Soviets manning the machine gun towers along the Wall, will be cherished forever.

Ralph Ryan, Class of 1972
1968-1972

Active Ryan Family Honore[illegible] By Community Service Awar[illegible]

by MSgt. Robert Hoffmann

Outstanding service to the community has earned another Air Force family the coveted Berlin American Community Service Award. SMSgt. and Mrs. Raymond A. Ryan and family were presented the award in brief ceremonies at their quarters Friday evening before departing the Divided City Sunday for their new assignment at Edwards AFB, Calif.

Col. Gail S. Halvorsen, Tempelhof commander, made the presentation on behalf of Maj. Gen. William W. Cobb, U.S. commander, Berlin.

This was only the second time that the award has been presented; the first one went to AF CMSgt. and Mrs. John Freeman last month prior to their departure from the City. It is designed to honor families who have rendered outstanding service to the Berlin-American community.

The Ryan family was cited for their outstanding services to the community from February 1969 to March 1972. The citation read in part "... Throughout their stay in Berlin the entire Ryan family constantly displayed an intense and enthusiastic concern for the welfare of the community evidenced by their active involvement in community activities".

Sergeant Ryan, who was a telephone maintenance superintendent with the 1946th Communications Squadron at Tempelhof, served as a tour guide for visiting high school students groups, organized and directed the sale of refreshments for the Berlin American High School Booster Club and was also Cub Scout Webelos Leader with Pack 152 during his stay in Berlin.

Mrs. Ryan acted as a volunteer, interpreter and guide at the 1969 Volksfest, conducted weekly ceramic classes for the AYA, coordinated the Christmas Card Fund Raising campaign and held weekly adult art classes for the Berlin American Women's Club. She also worked in the Air Force Sergeant's Association chili booth during the 1971 TCA Open House, organized German-American neighborhood coffees and this past January was one of the nominees from Tempelhof for the Air Force Wife of the Year.

The six children, Michael, 21; Ralph,18; Robert, 16; Ronald, 14; Rex, 13; and Renee, 11; have all been extremely active in the community.

Michael graduated from High School here in 1969 and is now an Air Force Sergeant [illegible] Washington; Ralph has [illegible] High School soccer and [illegible] teams, sold programs at [illegible] fest and was a homecoming [illegible] tee member; Robert has [illegible] on both the soccer and [illegible] teams and was active in AYA [illegible] programs.

The other two boys — [illegible] Rex were both active in AYA [illegible] while Renee performed in the [illegible] recitals at the Harnack [illegible] past two years.

RYANS RECEIVE AWARD — Admiring their Berlin American Com[illegible] Service Award recently presented to them by Col. Gail S. Halvorsen, [illegible] pelhof commander, are front row left to right, Rex, 13, Mrs. Ryan, [illegible] and Ronald, 14. Back row left to right are Robert, 16, Ralph, 18, and [illegible] Ryan. The unidentified family member is the Ryan's dog.
(Photo by MSgt. Robert [illegible])

Berlin Observer, 1972-Ryan clan recognized with Community Service Award

Thanks for the Memories, Berlin

I remember when my dad, SFC J. Richard Phillips got orders for Berlin, I had images of a post surrounded by tanks and barbed wire, but those years turned out to be the most memorable years of my life. We flew into Tempelhof in spring of 1970 and moved into Sundgauer apartments, my first friend was Jeannette M. and she proceeded to introduce me to this wonderful, exciting city. As I was one of six children we were able to move into a large townhouse on Buchsweiler Strasse, with its own built-in bomb shelter. My brothers J. Rick- '73 and Mark-'76 and I had many parties in our basement and backyard.

I remember one year Mr. Leonard flew back to the U.S., so I decided not to attend history class while he was gone. The day he came back I attended class; he walked up to me and said, "Welcome Back Miss Phillips, hope you had a nice vacation!"

The call of the Bierstube on a nice day, a quick hike to Krumme Lanke to swim, or out to the Wannsee to rent a boat were so much more inviting than sitting in class. I remember ice skating at the Europa Center, drinking beer at the Irish Pub and wandering the streets in the shadow of Kaiser-Wilheim Memorial Church.

I played clarinet in the band under the direction of Mr. Fenstermacher; he along with Bev Lacour, our drum majorette whipped us into a marching band, and we were able to attend the football games and music festivals in West Germany. Riding the Duty Train to Frankfurt was an experience in itself, the train traveled at night and required 'Flag Orders' to navigate the Soviet Occupied Zone, at the checkpoint you were not allowed to open your shades or make eye contact with either the Soviets or East German guards.

During one Frankfurt Music Festival, I stayed with a family and we went to the movies to see "West Side Story" and I amazed them by sleeping through the whole fight scene in the movie, I wonder why?

Berlin drew a lot of big name musical artists. I went to so many concerts at Deutschlandhalle : Alice Cooper, Rod Stewart and the Faces, Uriah Heep, Deep Purple, Ten Years After, Mott the Hoople, Johnny and June Carter Cash, Chicago, Paul McCartney and Wings. I remember drinking on the U-Bahn on the way to the Ten Years After concert and sleeping through the concert in our floor seats. Rod Stewart was late and the crowd was getting nasty, he then proceeded to throw his microphone into the audience which caused a surge and the "Polizei" came in and we decided to depart.

When I turned sixteen, I went to work at the AAFES cafeteria. I have memories of making sundaes to "Schools Out," opening bottles of wine and hostessing at "Steak Night." I made friends with a diverse group. Two of my friends were Turkish political science students at the Freie Universität, Umit and Ismail introduced me to their culture and their families. Jeff was a backpacker sleeping on a cemetery bench. I invited him home and my parents took pity on him; he stayed with us until he criticized the Steelers and my dad booted him out. He sent us a postcard from Greece. Bud, Blake and Keith were three University of Georgia students backpacking their way through Europe; they worked at the cafeteria long enough for my friends and I to develop crushes on them, and then they were gone.

The AYA and bowling alley are linked together in my memories, dances, fussball, softball, huddled on the bowling alley heater, purchasing hamburgers and cigarettes. I remember an incident that took place at an AYA dance, one cold, January night. My boyfriend and I were kissing on the heater, the dance finished and the AYA closed. To my dismay, my coat was inside the AYA, and I had a long walk home. Someone said they knew a way in to get my coat, I heard the smash of glass, and I had my coat. Next day my little brother ran upstairs and says the MPs are here to put me in jail. Facing the MP's was not nearly as bad as the look on my dad's face. He got a Delinquent Report put on his record.

Volksfest was a much anticipated event; I worked at the hamburger tent one year; it was fun flirting with G.I's and Germans alike. I had free rides all evening. My mom would work and save all year to take us on vacations, we camped through Holland, Belgium, Luxembourg, Austria and down into Italy.

I made some wonderful friends: Jeannette, Astrid, Gloria, Debbie O and Debbie A, Frank D, Frank L., John, Roberto, Umie, Jack and Renate. It was the 70's, so it was a wild time with parties, concerts and nightlife: the Riverboat disco, Eierschale jazz club, clubs in the French and British Sectors. I even acted like I was married to gain entrance to the Club 50… And it was a fun time with trips to W. Germany, Pizza at Frank's Pig Pen and hanging out with friends. Thanks for the memories Berlin!

Laura Phillips Jesse, Class of 1974
1970-1973

A Light in the Window

It was Christmas Eve, my last as a child in Berlin. Admittedly, at sixteen, I no longer felt like a child, having long ago lost that magic that makes Christmas so special to the very young. After weeks of anticipation, following German tradition, we'd opened our presents as soon as it grew dark outside. The gaily wrapped parcels underneath our tree were soon replaced by empty boxes and crumpled paper, and the entire evening still loomed before us. With nothing left to look forward to but the prospect of Christmas dinner the next day, our feelings of celebration soon ebbed. We were all happy with our gifts, to be sure, or at least we said so, as we'd been taught. But they were opened. There were no more surprises. It wasn't Christmas anymore.

We decided to save what was left of the evening, and paid a visit to Barney and Fay, who lived in the apartment next door. Barney and Fay were as bohemian as it was possible for a military couple to be. Normally, that in itself would be enough for my parents not to want to have anything to do with them, but Barney and Fay were smart, funny, and vibrant; everybody liked them. They couldn't help it.

Fay was eleven years older than Barney, her fifth husband. Five husbands- imagine that. Somehow, though, it was impossible to judge her in the same harsh light that fell upon other frequent fliers on the matrimonial express, even though she spoke blithely and openly of this, that, and the other lover when Barney wasn't around. That was just Fay, so it was forgiven. She was also a Rosicrucian, and passionate about seemingly everything in the world around her. Barney, as was everyone who came into contact with her, was smitten. They drew people to themselves- the bored, the curious, and the dispossessed- and their apartment was rarely empty. And so we found a party in progress at their place.

My parents immediately gravitated to the dining room, where a discussion about politics was taking place. My father had long found favor in their circle as their beloved token conservative, and he quickly and cheerfully fell to waging the same battle that he lost every time he engaged in it. There was a group of single GIs in the living room, and so I stayed there. Like I said, I was sixteen. I met my first love, Gary C., that night. He was twenty-three, from Wyoming, and he worked with my father. That in itself was enough to ensure that he always remained the perfect gentleman. But that's another story.

Hours passed, and the apartment grew smoky enough that windows had to be opened despite the swirling snow outside. What there was to be eaten had been eaten, what there was to be imbibed had been imbibed, and no one was ready to let go of the conviviality and go home just yet. We had at least an hour and a half to go until midnight; how thus to spend it? I've tried in vain to remember over the years who came up with the original suggestion; it was as brilliant an idea as any I've ever heard in all the years since. We decided to go Christmas caroling– all of us, en masse. And not just through the German neighborhoods, where we were as likely as not to have the Polizei called on us for disturbing the decorum of a holiday held sacred. No... we were going to go caroling at the Wall.

The cars parked in front of the apartment building could only accommodate so many people, and thus we elected to take the U-Bahn, making our undertaking even more of an adventure. Reaching our destination took a good forty-five minutes, during which time we discussed what carols to sing. As all but a few of us knew only English lyrics, it was important that we chose songs that also had translations in German, so that they would at the very least be recognized as Christmas songs. Half of the younger GIs were well on the way to being drunk, so this process was laced with merriment.

Finally we arrived. The sight of the Wall immediately plunged us into a more somber mood. It was immense, imposing, forbidding, colder by far than any winter night, topped with broken glass and razor-sharp concertina wire. The harsh glare of floodlights bathed the area on either side in an eternal artificial day. It was a scar on the landscape, a nightmare given substance. Sobered, we ascended the two flights of stairs up the rickety wooden observation decks and took our positions. Snowflakes swirled in eddies in the yellow haze of the floodlights. The wind chilled us to the bone. But we'd started this madness, and it had to be carried through to its end.

Before us lay what was known as no-man's-land, a stretch of barren ground criss-crossed with more concertina wire and studded with land mines. Beyond that, Russian and East German soldiers patrolled with guard dogs. More soldiers manned the guard towers at the eastern perimeter of the border area. And just beyond that was a street in another world, with houses and apartments in which people lived and died, and rarely opened the drapes that covered the western windows of their homes.

With no cue to prompt us, we began to sing. We had decided on Silent Night, it being the quintessential Christmas song and originally German. No one bothered to consider that none of us knew more than the first verse. And so, once we'd finished, we just launched into it all over again, stronger and with more confidence the second time. The guards patrolling the perimeters slowed their pace, and relaxed their grip on their weapons. A dog began to bark. Much to our bewonderment, a gloved hand reached down to its muzzle, silencing it. And that's when the real magic began.

Across the expanse of no-man's-land, beyond the swath of the militarized zone, in the darkened shadow of an old apartment building, a pair of curtains parted, just eighteen inches or so, but enough to tell all of us that we'd found an audience, and one brave enough to risk the appearance of communication with the West. The silhouette of a human figure appeared in the light of the window. "Sylvia....sing Stille Nacht!" Fay whispered to me, taking care to properly enunciate the glottal ch, as we'd practiced together so many times. ("It's disrespectful to the spirit of the language if you don't get it exactly right!" Pure Fay.)

No one ever said no to Fay. And so I began. One young voice, alone, strong above and beyond the horror surrounding it, gave the message and the gift that is and has always been more powerful by far than the circumstances in which it finds itself. There was no sign of the stage fright that plagued me until my late thirties. I was a part of something bigger. All that existed was the song, the night, and the figure in the window. And it was perfect.

The figure disappeared when I finished, and returned with a light that it placed upon the windowsill. The curtains thereupon closed, but the light shone on, a greeting to us and a testament to hope, courage, and to triumph.

We sang together one more time, and then began to make our way home. No one said much on the trip. Gary and I held hands. And I don't think Christmas has been the same for any of us since. Every year I remember, and am touched by the wonder of it all.

God bless the watcher, if he or she still lives. God bless the guard who silenced his dog, recognizing a sacred thing in spite of his atheistic indoctrination. And God bless our ragtag group of carolers, who were given Christmas that night for all time. May we all always remember. And may you all find your own light in a faraway window, to elicit the gift of what's always been within.

Sylvia Greeney Morris, Class of 1972
1964-67; 1968-71

Winter at the Wall

Homes along the Wall

Guard tower in No-Man's-Land

Coming of Age in Berlin

I've made eight trips back to Berlin as a photojournalism professor. In cooperation with the University of Florida's International Center, I conduct a two-week study-abroad course for 12 to 15 students. Under my direction, but with much freedom, students experience not only the Berlin of my past, but the Berlin of today, one in constant flux and change. Students get to see hills in parks made from leftover war rubble. They get to photograph the thriving arts scene. They get to hear constant techno music and watch Berliners wash down beer like it's water.

Berlin has always been a city on the edge. Divided after World War II into four sectors, it tried to recover from massive destruction and rebuild. And while the American, British and French Allies worked together, the Soviet Union had other plans to achieve dominance. It tried to starve the "free" sectors with a yearlong blockade of food and supplies from West Germany. When that failed and East Berliners began an exodus into the more prosperous western sectors, the Soviet Union erected the Berlin Wall in 1961 to stop the brain drain. As a result, the American, British and French Sectors wound up being surrounded on all sides.

As high school students in Berlin, we really did live in an island city, with the 27-mile long Wall cutting through the heart of the city and 100 miles of barbed wire ringing the back boundary. As students at the only U.S. Department of Defense high school behind the "Iron Curtain," most of us shared the bond of having a parent with the U.S. Army, Air Force or State Department. The usual tour of duty overseas was three or four years. We operated much like a small-town high school. With only 55 students in my graduating class (1971), athletes participated in almost all sports year-round. It was a special treat going to away football games, because that meant an overnight trip on the Duty Train. In military sleeper cars with six bunks to a room, team members, cheerleaders and spectators would load up on a Friday night, have the game in Frankfurt the next day, then journey back on the train Saturday night. Arriving Sunday morning, there were always stories to tell about the trips. It was also spooky passing through East Germany to and from Frankfurt, because the Russian guards observed our train's every movement. They made sure no East Germans tried to jump aboard to escape to freedom in the West.

On summer days, we often took the bus to Lake Wannsee, where the military maintained a dinner club, a swimming pool, and sailboats to rent. My father enjoyed 18 holes of golf and my mother took part in craft or church activities. West Berlin was considered a plum assignment, partly because of its metropolitan flair and size (3.5 million). Our large Pontiac Star Chief had been shipped over, and as my classmates recently reminded me, I was one of the few to drive during my senior year.

Some parents had secret clearances or worked military intelligence, so could not venture into East Berlin. My family was allowed to enter with the proper paperwork and if my father was in uniform. As a 16-year-old, I acquired my first camera, a Praktica, in East Berlin after passing through the famous Checkpoint Charlie on a day trip. The Eastern Sector was so drab and plain compared to West Berlin. Our visits into the East were fairly solemn affairs. We would check in with the MPs at Checkpoint Charlie and fill out a form with our expected time back. We would slowly maneuver the Pontiac through a series of partial walls designed to prevent fast driving, and with windows rolled up, display our "East Passes" to the East German soldiers. Depending on their mood, it might be a quick nod to proceed or a long drawn-out let's-smoke-a-cigarette and make-you-wait approach.

Checkpoint Charlie, 1968

Eventually we'd proceed to the "best" stores in the East, frequented by wealthy visiting communist dignitaries or high-ranking officials. My parents shopped for leather goods and crystal, and we often bought fur-lined boots for the winter. But for the average East Berliner, there were few choices and maybe only one color or size of an item. Because there was no competition in Eastern Bloc countries, advertising signs and neon lights were missing. The people seemed sad to me, the buildings were gray, and my mother was often nervous about us getting stuck on the wrong side of the Wall. Because of an extremely favorable exchange rate, we sometimes did special dinners in the East.

On one visit over, for my 17th birthday, my father took me to the Moscow Haus. True to its name, the restaurant was full of Russian soldiers, and they stared at my dad in his uniform as we sat down. About the time the soup arrived, so did one of the Russians, who pulled out a chair and sat down. He tried to strike up a conversation with my father, who stared straight ahead. "Do you come here often?" the soldier asked in English. "What is the nature of your visit? What kind of work do you do?" He then tried to ask me questions as my dad directed a silent right-to-left shake of his head to me, meaning, "Don't answer." Finally the solider left. We finished our meal and drove back to exit through Checkpoint Charlie, looking in the rearview mirror the whole time. Evenings like this were why my mother was nervous. But that's how life was in Berlin during the 28 years the Wall separated the city into two halves.

When my twin sister and I lived in Berlin for our sophomore through senior years (1968 -1971), Dad worked at Tempelhof, former site of the Berlin Airlift, helping with radar and air traffic control as a U.S. Air Force sergeant. Mom maintained our four-bedroom, one-and-a-half bath apartment with wooden floors and Oriental rugs. It was a good life. Tempelhof closed in 2008 to make way for a giant airport on the outskirts of the city. The grounds now have become a multi-use park, where a typical day find sunbathers, roller bladders, picnickers, organic gardeners and those who want to say they rode bicycles on a former runway.

Berlin has one of the greatest public transportation systems in the world—covering major tourist sites and also far reaching into neighborhoods. All subways, buses and streetcars are integrated. Riders hop on and off observing an honor system controlled by occasional undercover ticket inspectors.

A survivor, the city has largely shaken off its Nazi connection and has risen from the ashes of World War II. It's become a city of tolerance for immigrants, gays and lesbians, businessmen and filmmakers. On a recent blog post, one of my students wrote: "Berliners do not seem to focus on the petty issues that truly don't affect them as a society. They are very accepting of everyone and seem to let each person lead his or her own life."

In weak moments I sometimes think each trip back will be my last. Should I just call it good with eight fantastic visits to revel in nostalgia? But by the end of two weeks, the spirit of Berlin enchants me again. This past May, that magic moment happened when friend, an AFP wire services photographer, sent me a late-night email inviting me to a party. "If you can break away from the students, come on by," his message read. "We'll be up late." Getting to his place at midnight I found it full of friends, family, neighbors and co-workers speaking English, German and French. As the night faded into early morning, the party became all that Berlin is— people who accept one another from all walks of life.

When I gazed from his 4th floor apartment to the busy street below, I had the goose-bump moment of remembering how, 40 years ago, I had been at high school parties in 4th floor apartments in West Berlin, never once thinking that I'd be back or that the two Berlins would become one. But now, here I was in the former communist sector of East Berlin, enjoying freedom with new friends in a unified Berlin.

John Freeman, Class of 1971
1968-1971

Homecoming 1970, John far right, twin sister Roma is Homecoming Queen (front)

BAHS Graduation 1971, John on guitar

Memories of Berlin and Berlin American High School

I arrived in Berlin in March, 1969 as an Airman's wife. My husband, Ron was stationed at Tempelhof Air Force Base. Our first apartment was on Martin Luther Strasse–just down the street from Rathaus Schöneberg where JFK spoke to the Berlin people in 1963.

The apartment had a very small refrigerator. In shopping at the commissary I had to remember not to buy so much that I couldn't carry it all home on a city bus. I shopped some in a German grocery store as well. One of my first German purchases was a tan leatherette bag to carry items home from the store. All the German women carried a reusable shopping bag.

One day Ron said a man was coming to our apartment. "Mr. Green" said the government would pay us to use our apartment periodically when there were people in Berlin they wanted to interview. They paid us $25 an hour and we just made sure we were gone at that time. They only did this about three times, then we never heard from "Mr. Green" again. He was probably from the US Mission or CIA. I saw Mr. Green in the PX one or two times. So, did we provide a place for some clandestine meetings? We were glad to have the extra money.

Our friends, the Homolkas knew a German lady whose relatives were in the East Berlin ballet. We went to "Swan Lake" in the beautiful Staatsoper (East Berlin Opera building). We arrived early and met the German lady's sister in the parking lot and gave her toothpaste, panty hose, and Juicy Fruit gum, in return she gave us tickets to the ballet. Jerry (Homolkas) and Ron had to wear their Air Force uniforms to go to East Berlin and the ballet.

I worked at the PX camera counter when I first arrived in Berlin as there weren't any teaching jobs available. In April 1970, I was working at the camera counter when the principal came by and asked me if I could substitute teach in art for six weeks as Miss Pietsch had to take medical leave. I was so excited, I received a speeding ticket on the way home from work that night. I made it through the six weeks of teaching art. I had had some art/design classes in college.

That summer I worked some in the Army Education Center teaching some GED courses. Then I was offered a teaching position for the 7th grade biological science class at BAHS. My teaching certificate specified junior high science and home economics. So, I got to teach aboys' home economics class for one semester as well. I really enjoyed that.

It was great to have a teaching job. When Mr. Twohy became principal, he decided he wanted to make sure the students were getting out into the city and learning about Berlin culture. He said the homeroom classes would have "Widening Wednesday" once a month where school was not in session and the teachers would take their homeroom on a field trip. Trips that my 7th grade homeroom: The Botanical Gardens, Berlin Zoo, Berlin Aquarium, the Reichstag and the Englischer Garten when the tulips were in bloom. We had several mothers travel with us on these Widening Wednesday trips. We traveled on the U-Bahn or the city buses.

I guess I was naive and never guessed the students would do some troublesome activities while on these trips. In the aquarium, I learned some of my students had set off a stink bomb and the class was asked to leave. Class members also damaged some decorative grasses at the Botanical Gardens. I was appalled and sad that a few students in the class were doing these activities.

Another memorable moment was looking out the classroom window and seeing the C5A transport plane leaving Berlin after being on display at Tempelhof AFB Open House. It was a huge plane and it was amazing to see it in flight.

In the 1970s [1971-1998] there was a terrorist group in Germany called the Baader-Meinhof Gang. The school had some bomb scares where all the students and faculty had to go outside the school and wait until the school was cleared. All four of the founding members of Baader Meinhof were finally killed and that relieved the school and country of some of the terrorist activities.

In 1971-72, I was cheerleader sponsor at BAHS as they didn't have a sponsor that year. I didn't know very much about cheerleading, but Byron Smith said he had to be present for basketball practice so he would help me with the cheerleading team. Mrs. Smith also gave me tips and helped sponsor the girls on some of the trips. When playing games out of town, we had to travel on the Duty Train. The train left at 7 p. m. from the RTO and stopped at the Russian checkpoints as required where they looked over all the "Flag Orders." Flag Orders were completed for each person on the Duty Train and turned into Byron Smith, the athletic director. He had a student who assisted in this paperwork to submit for the Flag Orders. The Duty Train arrived in Frankfort at 7 a. m. and from there we were bussed to the town where the basketball game was being played.

Our mascot was a white bear cub. One time Ron and I were driving back to Berlin in our car and we had the mascot. I actually thought of wearing the Berlin cub head piece while going through Checkpoint Alpha at Helmstedt. However, I heard shots fired and decided that wasn't the time to be joking with the bear head.

Byron Smith needed a coach for the JV basketball team and my husband, Ron said he would be coach. He enjoyed working with Coach Smith and coaching the JV team in 1971-72.

Werner Prigge was a German teacher at BAHS and organized many faculty social events. We played kegel (a German bowling game), visited a musical organ factory, ate at a restaurant that had Feuerzangenbowle (a mulled wine and rum beverage that is served aflame in a bowl at Christmastime) and enjoyed many other activities that Berlin had to offer.

My husband's Air Force tour was over in June 1972 and we returned to Kansas. We kept in touch with teachers Byron Smith, George Pepoy, Adam Hildenbrand and Ron Engbrecht via letters after we returned to the USA. Eventually we lost touch with all but the Smiths. When we read in the Wichita local paper about the Berlin Brats Alumni Association, my husband and I checked out the website and found out that former cheerleaders, Jeri Polansky Glass '72 and Toni Yarbrough '71 were active in the organization. We have been in touch with them ever since and we thoroughly enjoyed the Berlin Brats Reunion in Berlin, Germany in 2006. It was so meaningful to be back in Berlin and experience buildings and museums in the former Berlin Brigade area with past students, their parents and their children. Love the Berlin Brats!!

Glenna Harrison, Faculty
7th Grade Biological Science, 1970-1972

An Eagle Scout Adventure: Berlin to Mt. Fuji, Japan

Scout Troop 46 Gives Honors

Troop 46, Boy Scouts of America, held a court of honor, Tuesday evening, to award merit badges and new ranks to 14 of its members.

Following the candlelight opening and the Pledge of Alligence, Assistant Scoutmaster Bob Fairris presented eight former Tenderfoot Scouts with their new Second Class badges. Those receiving the new rank were: James Smith, Ken Allison, Duane Tiffany, Bernard Beausoleil, Briand Beausoleil, Steve Pillion, Gordon Edwards and Steve Goozdich.

The next award of the evening was the Star Scout Award and Mike Kelly was the recipient. It was presented by Major Arthur M. Wilcox, the Neighborhood Commissioner.

Tom Brennan received the second highest award in Scouting, the Life Award. Lieutenant Colonel Frederick T. Abt, Commanding Officer of the 3d Battalion, 6th Infantry, which sponsors Troop 46, presented this award to Brennan. The Life Scout ranks just below the Eagle Scout.

A number of Merit Badges were also presented at the Court of Honor. John Robinson received eight badges and Tom Brennan received five. Also receiving Merit Badges were Mike Kelly, four; Lee Kent, three; Joe Griffith, two; and Tony Brennan received one. Assistant Scoutmaster Mike Wade made the presentation of the badges, which were earned by the Scouts at their summer camp, Camp Freedom, near Dauphe, West Germany.

Troop 46 is planning a Halloween party tonight, together with the Girl Scouts of Troop 402. The festivities get underway beginning at 7 p.m., at the Andrews Barracks Chapel.

A Tenderfoot Investiture ceremony is planned by Troop 46 for Nov. 12. Details may be had by calling Scoutmaster Robert G. Snyder at 3579.

Berlin Observer article listing Troop 46 honorees, including Bernard and Briand Beausoleil

The Boy Scout program in Berlin, Germany was alive and well from 1967 - 1972. There were two troops, Troop 46, and 152. I was a Scout in Troop 46. Leonard Therrien '72, a good friend of mine was one of approximately one hundred other Scouts in 152. Leonard made Life Scout, which is almost Eagle, a significant accomplishment.

But my experiences centered around Troop 46. It would turn out to be a family affair, and four years of memorable adventure! My Dad, Air Force Tech Sergeant Joseph Beausoleil, with no Scouting experience, became the Scoutmaster by default after other leaders rotated back stateside. He excelled as a great Scoutmaster after studying the Boy Scouts Handbook, overcoming initial challenges, and charging forward with a 'can do' spirit! He was ultimately voted Scoutmaster of the Year, Transatlantic Council, Europe. Troop 46 produced many top Scouts, including Eagle Scouts Sam McCuskey '71, Bernard Beausoleil '72, Briand Beausoleil '73 , Ed Ritter '73, Mark Oliver '73, Star Scout Gerald Beausoleil '76, and many Life, Star, and First Class Scouts. The parental involvement with the majority of Scouts' parents was awesome!

Troop 46 was extremely involved in Berlin community affairs. My dad spearheaded an effort to have Troop 46 renovate Rose Range, converting it to a recreational full-service campground facility. He accomplished this by networking with Air Force and Army enlisted and senior officers, including Army Major John Thomas, Mr. Coats, Chief of Engineering and Materials Procurement, and Army Major General William Cobb. Troop 46 Scouts built a large cabin equipped with foldaway beds, fifty-five picnic tables, obstacle course, campfire and barbecue pits, and more. Berlin military personnel, their families and Scout groups enjoyed Rose Range during our tour of duty.

Troop 46 hosted the May 1971 Berlin Camporee at Rose Range. The camp was instantly busy with over 700 Boy Scouts from Troops throughout West Germany, competing in various Scouting events and ceremonies. Troop 46 made Berlin proud taking first place honors in summer camp competitions, and its Scouts earned a highly respectable amount of merit badges. For these reasons, the American military community held the Scouting programs in high regard.

Vol. 27, No. 24 U. S. Ar

SCOUTS GALORE — More than 750 American and British Boy Scouts spent three days of camping, eating and generally having a good time in Berlin recently. The occassion was the annual camporee of the North Star District of the Trans-Atlantic Council of the Boy Scouts of America.

Boy Scout Camporee- 750 American and British Scouts

In August 1971, two Eagle Scouts were selected from the troops to represent Berlin and the Transatlantic Council at the 13th World Jamboree held at Mt. Fuji, Japan. Twenty-five thousand Scouts from 100 countries were to attend, as well as over 100,000 visitors. Eagle Scouts Mark Oliver '73and Bernard Beausoleil '72, were selected to represent Berlin and the Transatlantic Council. The American Women's Club of Berlin financed the entire trip, which included round trip airfare, hotels, Bullet train travel, and bus tours of Tokyo, Nikko, Nara, Kobe, and Kyoto, Japan, plus 10 days at Mt. Fuji.

The trip:

Mark and I took the Duty Train to W. Germany. Then we took another train to Brussels to rendezvous with an international contingent of Scouts from countries throughout Europe. Two hundred and twenty-two of us boarded a Czechoslovakian IL-62 airliner with four jet engines on the tail. We joked that it had this skinny rod with a tiny wheel on it to keep it from tipping! Due to the Cold War at the time, we were not allowed to fly over the North Pole, so we went through four flight crews flying 31 hours from Brussels to Athens, Kuwait, Bombay, Manila, Singapore and finally Tokyo.

After a while, the interior of our aircraft looked like a frat house, with food, drinks, clothes, banners, draped and hanging everywhere! Several Scouts were in their underwear! One moment we were walking on a super dry, super-hot tarmac in Kuwait, then several hours later we were drenched in a monsoon in India.

On our first morning in the Olympic Village in Tokyo, we had just gotten up and went downstairs for breakfast. As I took my first bite, I was just about to eat my spoonful when everything violently shook and rattled! My breakfast bounced right off the table and hit the floor. The two foot wide cafeteria columns which reached to the ceiling supporting the huge room were doing a hula dance all around us! We were introduced to one of Japan's earthquakes! Then it was over.

After routine inspection of rail lines, we boarded trains and buses for Tokyo, Nikko, and Nara. We then boarded the Bullet trains for Kobe and Kyoto. Going 250 km per hour was an awesome experience! After kayaking, and going to Mikimoto Pearl Island, we traveled by tour bus to Mt. Fuji, Japan's famous volcano. We set up camp with a sea of Scouts from all over the world. Flags, banners, colors, and signs heavily dotted the huge Asagiri Heights World Jamboree camp. The first few days were awesome, full of pageantry, music, TV crews on the ground and in helicopters. We made new friends from around the world! Truly a once in a lifetime experience!

Then it happened! Two o'clock in the morning. I felt the ground shake, which was the volcanic rock being pounded by heavy rain! I rolled over on my sleeping bag, fell off and into water. LOTS of water! I had all of my expensive camera equipment sitting inches away from the water and I grabbed it. All hell was breaking loose outside my tent! Then we heard evacuation orders! We had to leave everything behind, except my camera bag and hike as fast as possible up a paved road. Within minutes, we were waist deep in a fast flowing river of water on the road! We were in a large typhoon, Japan's version of a hurricane!

We were then herded onto army trucks and evacuated to emergency school gymnasium makeshift shelters, located at a higher elevation. We stayed with Japanese families and finally made it back to the destroyed camp a few days later. We made the most of it, picking up the pieces, but it was a very depressing scene! Finally arriving back in Tokyo for our flight out, we were greeted with another earthquake! WOW, are you serious? They should have renumbered the Jamboree anything but 13th!

I arrived back in Berlin with a lifetime of memories, 800 color slides and twelve rolls of movie film. I still have all of the film and photos today, including the typhoon footage!

Since Ken Replogle '72 and I knew most of the guys at the AFTV television station, I had mentioned prior to leaving that I would take a lot of photos and film. They agreed to work with me to produce a TV special for the Berlin community. After editing, doing voice overs, sound on sound, and pre-recorded 'live' thank you interviews, we condensed it all into a 30 minute entertaining documentary. It was widely received and due to a high number of requests, AFTV aired the program again. For a couple of seventeen year old Eagle Scouts from Berlin, it was a trip we would always cherish! To this day, it was one of the greatest experiences of my life!

Bernard Beausoleil, Eagle Scout, Class of 1972
1967-1972

31 British, American Troops Get Together

Berlin Hosts 750 at Annual Boy Scout Camporee

Troop 46 hosts Boy Scout Camporee at Rose Range

Full Circle

As I think back over my years at Berlin American High School, a smile and a realization come to mind. I arrived in Berlin the summer of '67 headed into 8th grade. I hated being uprooted from my junior high school in San Antonio but as did so many other Brats, I readily adapted and fell in love with my new school! Fast forward to my sophomore year, I ran for class secretary and made it. I enjoyed being involved in every aspect of school life. By my junior year I wanted more. I tried out for cheerleading, made the varsity squad and then ran for President of my class. I don't think I quite realized at the time that the junior class organizes the 'Junior-Senior Prom.' What had I gotten myself into! What a daunting task for a Brat of 16!

Mr. Douglas (biology teacher) was our class sponsor. He had no experience (and dare I say any interest) in organizing something of this magnitude. I can't recall what actually transpired but someone on school staff, in their infinite wisdom, realized a change was needed. Enter Mrs. DeYoung (formerly Ms. Croom– my former math teacher). All of a sudden she and I were planning the prom.

I absolutely loved Mrs. DeYoung as a math teacher. She was hard core but she made Algebra my favorite subject. (I went on to major in Business but statistics and economics were my passion.) Sadly, as many of you will remember in 1969 Ms. Croom married Mr. DeYoung, the dashing young blond junior high science teacher. All the girls in school had a mad crush on him. I digress, but going back to my first year in Berlin, 8th grade, let's just say I was having a little too much fun and my grades started slipping from their stateside high. My mother knew I liked and respected Mr. DeYoung, so she requested a Parent-Teacher Conference with him. Would he please have a talk with her daughter...she's become 'boy-crazy' and her grades are slipping. He called me in for 'the talk.' I was mortified. I don't think I spoke to mother the balance of the school year but my grades did improve! (Okay Mom, I give you that one.) I mentioned "sadly" earlier. Mr. DeYoung passed just months after their wedding. He had a brain aneurysm at age 34. School administration announced his passing over the PA system. The whole school mourned. For most of us this was our first brush with death. It was devastating. Our 1970 Yearbook was dedicated to him (see below).

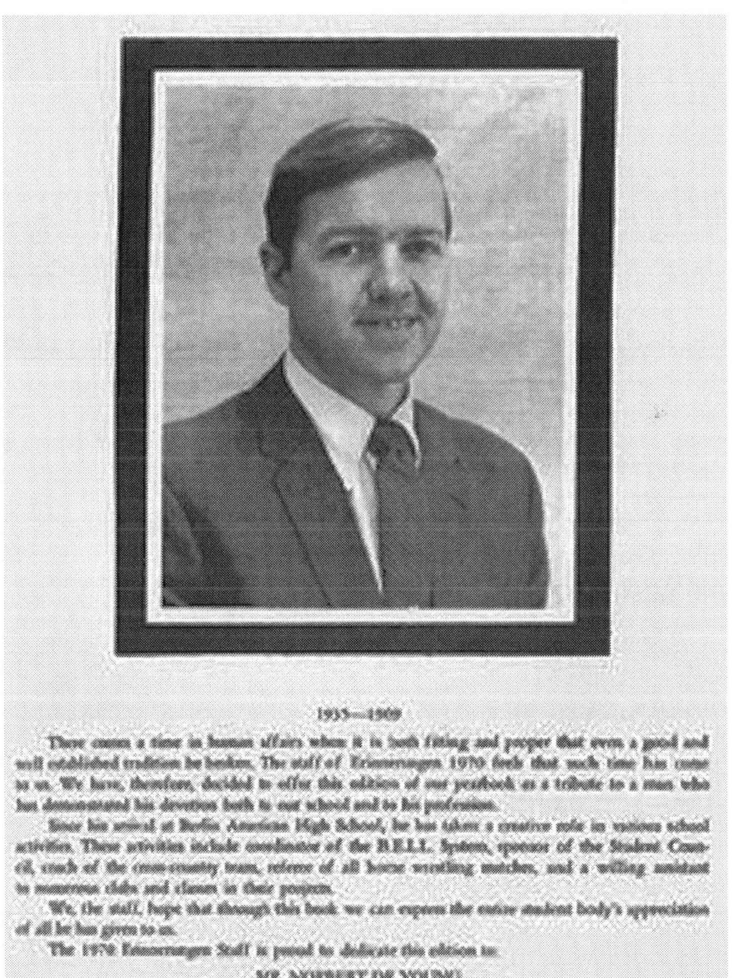

1935—1969

There comes a time in human affairs when it is both fitting and proper that even a good and well established tradition be broken. The staff of Erinnerungen 1970 feels that such time has come to us. We have, therefore, decided to offer this edition of our yearbook as a tribute to a man who has demonstrated his devotion both to our school and to his profession.

Since his arrival at Berlin American High School, he has taken a creative role in various school activities. These activities include coordinator of the B.E.L.L. System, sponsor of the Student Council, coach of the cross-country team, referee of all home wrestling matches, and a willing assistant to numerous clubs and classes in their projects.

We, the staff, hope that through this book we can express the entire student body's appreciation of all he has given to us.

The 1970 Erinnerungen Staff is proud to dedicate this edition to:

MR. NORBERT DE YOUNG

And so it was with new-found respect for Mrs. DeYoung that we sat down in the fall of 1970 and started planning the 1971 Junior-Senior Prom. As with math she was a stickler for the details. If I don't say so myself, the '71 Prom was a wonderful event that came off without a hitch.

NOW about the smile at the beginning of my story: Some 40 years later I now realize what an impact Mrs. DeYoung had on my life. I went into the accounting field ultimately becoming a financial controller of a multi-state manufacturing company and presently coordinate military and Brat reunions. Mrs. DeYoung, I think I've come full circle with you! Thank You!

Jeri Polansky Glass, Class of 1972
1967-1971

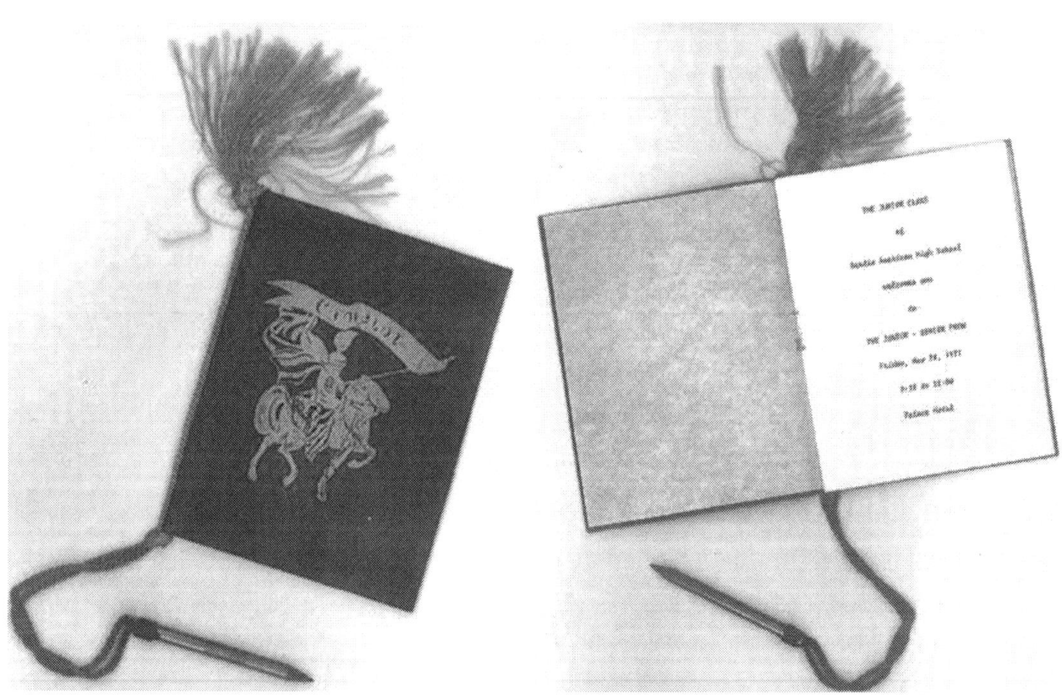

1971 "Camelot" Prom Program

Close Call at Checkpoint Alpha

I wonder how many of my classmates drove themselves through East Germany from Checkpoint Bravo (W. Berlin border) to Checkpoint Alpha at Helmstedt (W. German border)? I made this trip myself and with friends numerous times heading down to the Alps on mountaineering and skiing trips and had a few scary adventures between the years '71-'73.

There were certain procedures to be followed at each checkpoint. Leaving Berlin through Checkpoint Bravo you stopped for your briefing with the MPs. From there you went to the East German Checkpoint where they checked your paperwork. Once passed, you moved on to the Soviet Checkpoint. This is where it got tricky. At Bravo you were required to GET OUT OF YOUR CAR and carry your paperwork into the Soviet Checkpoint and hand it over to the officer in charge. At Alpha you were instructed to STAY IN YOUR CAR and the Soviet would come to take your paperwork from you. These directions were to be followed to the letter.

As the son of the Provost Marshal my parents and I occasionally attended "parties" with our Soviet, British and French counterparts. I met twice with Dad's Soviet counterpart and his family. Once in East Berlin and once in West Berlin. I was always cautioned (as were many of us) by the Old Man to be aware of Soviet spies, intelligence gatherers, etc. In my "all knowing" teenage naiveté I always thought, "Oh yeah, right. Like anybody on the Soviet side is keeping tabs on me. " Little did I know.

On one of my many trips through these two checkpoints I reported to the American Checkpoint Bravo to receive my briefing and instructions before crossing through East Germany. I then went through the East German Checkpoint and reported to the Soviet Checkpoint where I GOT

OUT OF THE CAR and took my Flag Orders and paperwork into the Soviet officer on duty. Everything was in order and I was passed through to make the trip to Checkpoint Alpha at Helmstedt-Marienborn.

It was 104 miles across East Germany and I arrived at Alpha a couple of hours later. Not thinking, when I got to the Soviet Checkpoint, I proceeded to GET OUT OF THE CAR and take my paperwork into the Soviet officer on duty. As I walked through the door I realized my error, but decided rather than trying to get back to the car I'd brazen my way through it. I walked up to the officer (a hardcore looking Soviet Major) at his desk and handed him the paperwork like this was what I was supposed to be doing.

He sat back and gave me a very cool, appraising look. He then told me to stay right where I was and left the room. At that point I broke out into a cold sweat and thought, "Oh boy, am I in deep S#!& now." After about 15 minutes he returned to his desk. He then proceeded to ask me how my Dad the PM was doing. I said he was doing fine, and did he happen to know him? His comment was, "Oh, we know your father very well." He then proceeded to question me about Mom. "Did your Mom enjoy her recent trip to Spain?"

"Why yes," I said, "she had a great time." At this point I'm sure I was visibly sweating and it was obvious he was enjoying my discomfort. He then began to question me about my current trip and asked where I was going climbing. I'm sure my eyes bugged out right about then, but I managed to respond we were heading to Berchtesgaden to do some climbing in that area. After a bit more conversation he sat back and said, "Ron, you realize you screwed up don't you?" I smiled with resignation and said, "I realized I screwed up the moment I walked through the door."

He gave me a very hard look for a few moments then said, "Good thing I'm feeling generous today. Now get your a$! back to your car and have fun on your trip." I said, "Thank you, Sir" and beat feet out the door. I was so happy to get to the American side again I d@mn near kissed the ground.

Ron Rathnow, Class of 1971
1966-67; 1969-73

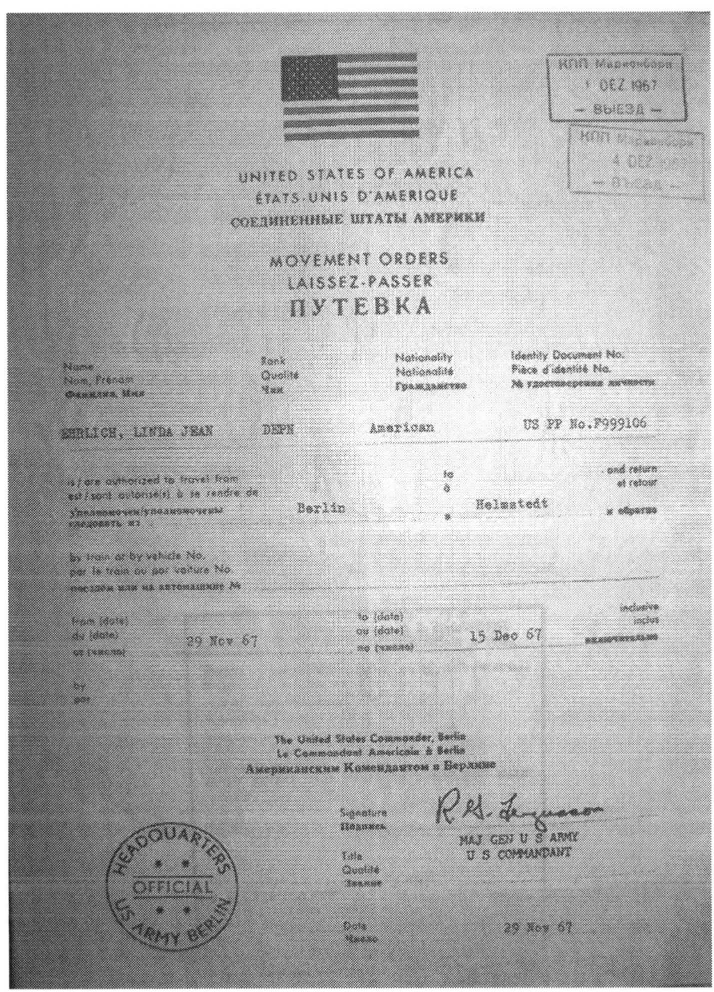

КПП Мариенборн
1 DEZ 1967
— ВЫЕЗД —

КПП Мариенборн
4 DEZ

UNITED STATES OF AMERICA
ÉTATS-UNIS D'AMERIQUE
СОЕДИНЕННЫЕ ШТАТЫ АМЕРИКИ

MOVEMENT ORDERS
LAISSEZ-PASSER
ПУТЕВКА

Name / Nom, Prénom	Rank / Qualité / Чин	Nationality / Nationalité / Гражданство	Identity Document No. / Pièce d'identité No.
EHRLICH, LINDA JEAN	DEPN	American	US PP No.F999106

is / are authorized to travel from / est / sont autorisé(s) à se rendre de: Berlin to / à: Helmstedt and return / et retour

by train or by vehicle No. / par le train ou par voiture No.

from (date) / du (date): 29 Nov 67 to (date) / au (date): 15 Dec 67 inclusive / inclus

by / par

The United States Commander, Berlin
Le Commandant Americain à Berlin
Американским Комендантом в Берлине

Signature: R. G. Ferguson

Title / Qualité: MAJ GEN U S ARMY / U S COMMANDANT

Date: 29 Nov 67

HEADQUARTERS
OFFICIAL
US ARMY BERLIN

Flag Orders- necessary for travel by train or car through East Germany

Weekend in Potsdam

One of the most interesting memories I have of our time stationed in Berlin during the early 1970s was when my father was the weekend Duty Officer at the Potsdam House in East Germany. I would like to share the logistics involved in moving a family of eight from the free West side to Potsdam, provide some impressions of East Germany, and finally, I would like to describe the Potsdam House. I know it was a chore for my mom to get us ready and extra work for the administrative staff to cut the orders but these special trips will always remain in my mind forever.

My father, Lt. Col. William A, Burhans, USAF retired, was assigned to the United States Military Liaison Mission (USMLM) in the summer of 1971. While he was based in Berlin at the mission, the Potsdam House in East Germany was the representational Headquarters and as such was manned by the US military 24/7. One of his assigned duties was to man the Potsdam house as Duty Officer on the weekends. Our family had to pack up and be over at the mission in West Berlin Friday afternoon and transfer to a military vehicle to start the journey to East Germany. The mission was using Ford Galaxy 500s to tour in the GDR those years and it took two vehicles to haul us out there. Once the head count was complete and required passes accounted for, we were able to start our journey.

The next stop was the Freedom Bridge. The Glienicke Brücke was a working military crossing point into the GDR (German Democratic Republic) that was the site of several famous prisoner exchanges between the Soviet Union and the United States during the Cold War.

There was no guard shack on the West approach and the first barriers became visible at the midpoint of the bridge. Long strands of rusty barbed wire were strung over everything in sight. Jersey barriers formed a serpentine approach to the East end of the bridge. Once we cleared the barriers we had to wait for a sliding gate to open then approach a weighted cross arm. The Soviet guard shack was on the left side of the bridge as we stopped at the barrier and an East German shack was manned on the right side. My father proceeded into the Soviet guard shack with our passes while we sat anxiously in the car like gold fish under the creepy scrutiny of armed Soviet and East German conscripts.

Glienicke Brücke-Freedom Bridge

Once we cleared the checkpoint and drove into the East it felt like we stepped back in time and it was apparent that we were in a different world. The first indication was a pall of gritty coal smoke that permeated every sense of the body. The horizon and entire landscape became grey and it immediately felt like the world was smaller. One of the sites that I clearly remember is a group of little old ladies wearing head scarves armed with brooms made from tree twigs bound to a handle sweeping the street in front of a gated house.

The grey buildings on the side of the road were scarred with bullet holes, and tangled electric wires were strung overhead for the trolleys. All of the cars seemed dilapidated and spewed diesel exhaust into the already polluted air. At the turn off of the highway there was a cobbled together shack manned 24 hours a day by the Volks Polizei who tracked the comings and goings of the mission members. We used it as a waypoint to start searching for a glimpse of the American flag. The first child to see the flag won, but we all felt a real sense of relief and pride knowing that we were soon going to be back on American held ground.

The end of the road revealed a majestic 4.5 acre complex on the Lehnitzsee. The circular driveway approached a four story white building with a red tiled roof. The grand entrance off the foyer was open to two stories and flanked by two staircases. There was a large ball room on the first floor with raised ceilings. It felt like we had stepped back in time. We really felt like royalty when we visited Potsdam. The house was staffed and I clearly remember Gudi and Dagmar, two statuesque East German women who prepared and served the meals and cleaned the house. There is a good chance they passed information to the Soviets and East German Stasi. The formal dining room's windows extended from floor to ceiling revealed a striking view of the Lehnitzsee. I loved having dinner there on Sunday afternoon. It seemed like a formal dining experience. The table was fully set and the first course was usually egg drop soup presented in a tureen.

We were served the best schnitzel along with platters of the amazing fried potatoes and purple cabbage that only the Germans know how to make. Potsdam was also the first place I ever tried goose or rabbit and for some magical reason the food was always excellent.

There was always something interesting to see or do while we were visiting Potsdam. On the 3rd floor was a grand game room filled with a full sized pool table. The enlisted drivers had papered the wall with Playboy centerfolds. All of the movies that cycled through AFN theatres in Berlin played in the ball room at Potsdam too. I remember watching such classics as *Yog: Monster from Space, My Name is Trinity* and my first R rated movie:

The Last Tango in Paris there. For some reason, the staircase to the 4th floor was blocked off, I remember lots of antennas on the roof; perhaps there were some radios up there. We found time to play soccer and hide and seek on the grounds, and one winter we even got to skate on the lake when it froze over. We always had a great family experience at Potsdam.

My family had several moves after our assignment in Berlin but that is the city I came of age in. The experiences I had in West Germany were colorful and exciting and I will always remember them fondly. The trips to the East side however were quite different; they were serious, sobering journeys that helped me realize why my father was assigned to the United States Air Forces in Europe. I, for one, am very glad the Wall came down, but I am also proud to say I got to visit an unforgettable bastion of freedom in the middle of the GDR. I recommend a visit to: **http://usmlm.us** for pictures of the house at Potsdam, the men that manned it, and the Mission.

William A. Burhans Jr., Class of 1976
1971-1975

The Potsdam House, Potsdam, East Germany

Sprechen Sie Deutsche?

Emilie Hamilton '71 was my student assistant in 1971, and due to various circumstances, I had become a friend of her family and was sort of her confidante, which is probably why one Monday– to my great delight– she came to me with this story.

Her group of friends had gone out for a camping cook out party in the Grunewald over the weekend, using some kind of Army cooking devices- kerosene cookers- whatever (I have always been a technical nitwit)... and they were happily sitting around the 'campfire' with their marshmallows and the rest of their PX goodies, most certainly engaged in deeply philosophical conversation.

I'm not sure but I believe that Emily reported that while all of this mental and verbal exchange was going on it was Steven Reisler '71, who was sitting across from her looked at her very seriously and said, "Em - there's a wild boar behind you."

"Of course it is- ha ha- sure enough," she replied and continued to laugh it off until she realized that everyone else who could see behind her had frozen. I am not sure if my memory of the rest of Emily's story is precise and if anyone actually climbed a tree. Facts are that the wild boars were definitely there and that the BAHS kids fled as soon as they felt safe enough to do so.

Now here's my German teacher's great big chuckle: After they had escaped the beasts' attack, they remembered that they had left the kerosene cookers burning in the Grunewald and, conscientious as they were, they went to the nearest house to ask for help. That, of course, was a German home, and– shame on me– their German was not good enough to explain exactly what had happened. The word 'Feuer' got across, and the German family called the fire brigade.

When Emily told me all about this I really laughed; I had no idea of what kind of trouble the German fire brigade's action might cause for the kids– never followed the law's procedure– but am pretty sure that nothing really happened.

Maybe they got bawled out by their parents. Nobody blamed me for not teaching them enough German. And I still have that image in my head of their peaceful campfire with unexpected guests which will make me laugh to the rest of my days.

Nowadays not only wild boars but foxes are all over the outskirt districts of Berlin, marauding yards and occasionally attacking cyclers at night.

Katrin Hotzel Strätz, Faculty
German Host Nation Teacher, 1965-1971

The Grunewald on a snowy day

Freedom Isn't Free

Those were magical times! We lived in the middle of history with the Berlin Wall surrounding us! The high school was situated with the Grünewald forest directly behind us. I loved looking out the back of the school and seeing the forest. I remember our mile runs through the beautiful forest as part of Miss Barlow's PE class, always keeping an eye out for the "Gruney Man." Linda Bracey '73 and I would try to break our mile run records. We even got Mr. Douglas to excuse us from biology class once so we could go run another couple of miles.

Some of my most fun memories were with the band directed by Mr. Fenstermacher. We got to travel to the away football games with the team to perform halftime shows. Riding the Duty Train from Berlin to Frankfurt was our mode of transportation with its compartments of two sets of bunk beds. Feeling the train stop in the middle of the night and hearing the East German guards talking outside was eerie. One trip we decided to bring squirt guns and we chased each other up and down the isle of the moving train until we got caught and scolded by Mr. Fenstermacher. We had lots of fun times in the band and the choir with lots of great friends! I got to go to a week-long music festival in Bacharach with my friends Judy Evans '73, Tom Webb '75, Paul Greer '72, Mike Foster '74, and Marsha Ball '73.

As part of the Senior Travel Club I was involved with, we put on a spaghetti dinner in the cafeteria after a home football game to earn money for our Senior Trip. Everyone pitched in and had an assignment and we had a successful dinner, and a successful Senior Trip to Denmark I heard (right?), as I wasn't able to go. I enjoyed working in student government and working with wonderful people like Bonnie Bates '73, Laura West '73, and Mary Firsching '73. I remember looking for prom locations throughout the city with Bonnie when she was class president. We settled on having it at the Officer's Club at Tempelhof in 1972, and if my memory is correct that was the night we had the bomb scare and had to go to the bunker for a time. Bomb scares seemed fairly frequent at that time and there was a lot of political unrest with the Communists. We were evacuated from school at least once during my school years in Berlin for a bomb scare.

A few teachers stood out: Mr. Leonard and "Minnie Motor Mouth," Herr Voigt with his correctional finger up the back of your neck if you misbehaved, and Ms. Rekucki in social studies. I finally learned to like science in Mr. Engbrecht's chemistry class. Mr. Hildenbrand was a great geometry teacher, and many more great teachers. I enjoyed field trips to Checkpoint Charlie and other sites in the city where we learned of the city's history and the importance of freedom.

The best thing about going to high school in Berlin, Germany was the amazing culture and history that surrounded us every day, and the wonderful friends and teachers that were there. Living in Berlin at such an impressionable age taught me to cherish my freedom and I learned firsthand that freedom isn't free. I learned about people every day that risked their lives to be able to be free. It was an incredible experience that I wouldn't trade! Thank you Berlin, for being a part of my life!

Marilyn Halvorsen Sorensen, Class of 1973
1970-1973

Adventures at BAHS

Future Shock

I was team teaching social studies/English with Ruth Nielson (as I recall) in one of those tiny rooms, later supply storage, beneath the administration wing. We were using Alvin Toffler's book *Future Shock* but the class wasn't getting the concept of shock. Therefore we decided to shock them. Since there had been some hostage taking in the news, we decided to use some of her upper class students to stage a hostage-taking event.

I was leading the discussion about the effects of rapid change in our society when a couple of masked gunmen burst in the door and shouted "everybody down" or words to that effect and grabbed my fellow teacher who was conveniently standing next to the door. I charged toward them to stop this event and the students were diving under desks/chairs or getting behind someone. I took a couple of shots to the chest (from my starting pistol with which I had provided them) and collapsed onto the floor in an agony of death… It was all over in a minute but it took quite a time for the class to calm down…..

We had a good discussion afterwards about how one cannot always predict reaction to stress/change. However, I shudder to think what would happen if I tried to pull such a stunt now. I also wonder that there was no reaction from faculty, administration or parents.

Visit to East/Communist Berlin

We had an activity called "Widening Wednesday" when I first taught junior high in the early 70s [BAHS was a junior and senior high school]. Due to our rotating schedule, we had a different set of students each Wednesday, for an all afternoon activity. I selected a field trip to the ice rink in Wedding in the north of Berlin. To get there, we had to make two changes of subway lines in order to get around Berlin Mitte, the "dirty Commie" part. After skating, I took them back to BAHS in the American Sector but by the simpler, one-change route which ran under Berlin Mitte, the dirty Commie part. It was safe because the West Berlin-operated subway system did not stop at any of the Communist-controlled stations, except one: Friedrichstrasse.

The next day there was a "request" that I report to the front office ASAP. Several ranking officers were awaiting me and were very "unhappy" at my risky adventure into Communist territory. Some of the students had bragged that Mr. Benson had taken them to Communist East Berlin. Travel to the East was very tightly controlled. I explained my geography lesson about the "Wall" which had preceded the field trip and its success in helping the students understand the peculiar Berlin situation.

Even if one of the students had gotten out at Friedrichstrasse, there was no way out of the station except through Communist checkpoints that were well guarded and they would have been stopped though there would have been an ugly incident… Our family, like thousands of West Berliners, often used the route. But I never took students on this route again!

Art Benson, Faculty
Social Sciences, 1970-1992

Reflections on Great Teachers at Berlin American High School

When I attended BAHS in the early 70s, I had the pleasure of being a student in Mr. Lou Moreno's typing class. He stood out as the teacher who meant business (and ironically, taught business and typing), but made it fun. I looked forward to his class. BAHS had many wonderful teachers, some of whom I admired and some I feared. Mr. Moreno cared for his students, and provided 50 minutes of learning combined with fun. When I look back on my top three teachers who had this same approach to learning, they are Mr. Leonard (history), Mr. Sullivan (English), and Mr. Moreno.

Mr. Leonard would playfully accuse us long-haired hippies of shooting up peanut butter; to which we would reply, "How about your addiction to coffee?" He always had a mug of coffee in his hand as he taught. I admired that even though he could dish out the "abuse," he could also take ours. What a good sport he was. And we learned something. I can still remember the details we had to learn about The Marshall Plan. I thought to myself, "Why do I need to know this?" The irony, of course, is that the Americans were in Germany as part of this plan to help Europe recover and to keep Soviet communism from spreading.

Mr. Sullivan was known for his jokes that would make us groan, roll our eyes, or just flat out, give him a group response of "Boo!" His jokes were so bad– but oh, how I remember them! Once, a student brought a bottle of Lambrusco to class hidden in a brown paper bag and carefully stowed underneath her desk, as she was attending a rock concert later that day. In the middle of class, we heard a crash…the bottle fell out of the bag, broke, and red wine flowed everywhere! The smell was awful (must have been really cheap wine). Mr. Sullivan didn't miss a beat, and being ever so quick-witted, said, "Well, I bet you can't cover up that cent with a dollar!" I think that was the first time we all gave him an uproarious belly laugh as we were so thankful he wasn't angry at our fellow student. Another joke I remember clearly is when we were studying Greek Mythology, and learning all of the gods and goddesses. When we got to Demeter, the goddess of corn, grain, and the harvest, Mr. Sullivan said, "You know, like the guy that comes to your home to check your electricity- he reads Demeter." I remember I groaned pretty loudly at that one. And 40 years later I still remember it!

Teachers have an important role in our society as they help shape our children, who in turn, shape our future. When famous actors accept their Oscars, some have often thanked their teachers...or, showed the teacher who doubted them, that they really could be successful. In my case, whether it was Leonard, Sullivan, or Moreno, I learned skills that I still use today. That's a sign of great teaching. Although Mr. Leonard and Mr. Sullivan are now gone, their legacy still lives in their students.

In 2010, Mr. Moreno was weighing heavily on my mind. I didn't know why he kept surfacing in my thoughts. I reached out to Berlin Brats to get his address. I wanted to let him know that so many of his former students were asking about him, and we always hoped he would show up at one of our reunions. I decided to write him a letter, to thank him for being a great teacher and positive influence on my life. Although I did not get a response, I found out that he died two months after I wrote it. Part of me hopes he read it–as it was not returned– and hope it made him smile.

Deb Brians Clark, Class of 1974
1964-65; 1968-1969; 1971-73

Mean Green

We moved to Berlin when I was 12, almost 13. That was the summer of 1968. I remember we left Munich in a caravan with my mom driving the red 1964 VW bug with my brother, and I think I was in the yellow 1958 Opel wagon with my dad. Dad had accepted a music teaching gig at BAHS. I don't remember what time of day we left, but I recall driving through the East German checkpoint in the evening. That was probably about 4-5 hours out of Munich.

Being 13ish, I didn't pay attention and don't remember the goings on at the border. I learned later that it was a big deal to drive through the East Zone. We were driving with US military license plates on the cars and I'm sure there were many rules and regulations to follow. We drove on in the dark. I remember being told that we must not stop because there was no telling what the penalty would be–jail or maybe worse. It certainly made an impression on a young man.

We drove a long time on a very dark Autobahn that probably had no maintenance since it was built it in the '30s. There were no lights on the road, no porch lights or window lights and very few other cars. I don't recall seeing any houses along the road, for that matter. At some point, I think I was asleep and the Opel broke down. We were in the middle of nowhere in the dark. I recall that eventually some East Germans saw us and upon realizing we were Americans and we spoke German they towed our car to a garage and made some repairs. The East Germans were just regular folks and not two headed monsters. I have no recollection of how long we were there, but I do remember the scary feeling of being behind the Iron Curtain. I found out later that our drive was timed and my dad probably had to report the incident to the American authorities (although we were civilians, technically).We eventually arrived safely and took our apartment on the ground floor of the building on the corner of Marshallstraße and Stewardstraße behind the commissary.

Being the son of a teacher had its ups and downs. Everybody knew me or my dad and I couldn't get away with anything. Teachers threatened to tattle and students did tattle. I was a pretty good kid anyway, so I minded my Ps and Qs. We would have teachers over to the house for dinner or sing-alongs so I got to know some of them a little better than merely from school. I had musical talent too, but it was way overshadowed by my parents (mom was an opera singer) and my brother, so I decided to be more behind the scenes at musical events. For concerts and plays I helped with the lights and scenery.

I really got into photography, however, and that gave me another purpose. At the time there was a dark room lab at Andrews Barracks and I took the bus from the PX to learn how to develop film and make prints. The instructor was an old German photographer who I recall was employed by the Nazis during the war; but because he never joined the party, he was exonerated by the Allies of doing anything wrong and got the job teaching GIs how to work in the dark room. He was a great teacher. I was on the yearbook staff my sophomore, junior and senior year at BAHS as a photographer. We (the other photographers and I) took a lot of candid shots, many of my photos ended up in the yearbooks.

I specifically remember the yearbook of 1973. Mr. Priebe was the advisor. I believe Frau Pietsch had been the advisor for the longest time and she retired. When it was time to discuss the yearbook cover, someone–could have been me– (memory is a little fuzzy), suggested a flashy neon green. That would have been a total departure from the past, but we wanted something different. I don't recall a lot of dissention from Mr. Priebe, so we went with the green. Unfortunately, it turned out that the green was more of a Canadian goose poop green instead of psychedelic neon green. Oh well!

Carl Fenstermacher, Class of 1973
1968-1973

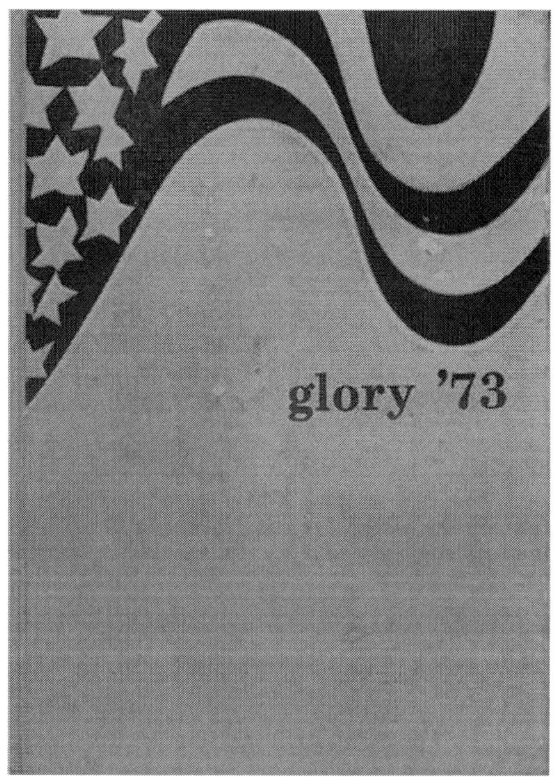

The mean green '73 yearbook--in black and white

Berlin: An Outpost of Freedom

I am the son of a U.S. Army officer. There are many unique and valuable experiences that have come from this defining reality of my life, but chief among them were the years I spent in Berlin, Germany, during the 1970s.

I attended Berlin American High School with hundreds of other American youth, nearly all the children of state department officials, diplomats, and intelligence analysts if they were not military brats like me. We lived, in many ways, the lives of typical American teenagers. Dates, sports, movies, dances, and mischief filled our lives.

Yet we were also living behind the Iron Curtain, and the Cold War ruled us. It was not uncommon for our sleep to be interrupted by the sound of tanks clanking through the city's streets or for our fathers to disappear from our lives days upon end with the sole explanation that they were "on alert." Some of my friends who lived nearer the Berlin Wall occasionally heard machine gun fire in the wee hours of the night. When our high school sports teams played against other American schools in Germany, one of the two rivals had to travel through Communist East Germany on a "Duty Train." It was routine for these trains to be stopped by heavily armed soldiers who used dogs and mirrors to search for escapees. My civilian friends back home would only know such scenes from movies about WW II.

We were isolated expatriates, and so we became dear to each other. We are dear to each other still. Our teachers naturally loomed large for us. The ones who influenced me were history teachers and had names like Beam, Ferguson, Sullivan, and Kilpatrick. That they were teaching just miles from armies eager to destroy all they held dear made their lessons about Western civilization more urgent, their craft perhaps more vital than they had imagined possible when they decided upon their profession.

I remember discussing "government of the people, by the people, for the people" with Mr. Ferguson and thinking how immediate the words seemed. Our context changed everything and made figures like Lincoln more relevant by far than the Nixons and Agnews who occupied the American stage at the time. Lincoln spoke of sacred sacrifices and the evils of slavery, of healing a nation's wounds and the better angels of our nature. Peering over the Berlin Wall into a dismal, oppressed East, we understood how the words of men like Lincoln defined an American ideal. I have never forgotten that such thoughts first came to me through the devoted teachers who elected to ply their trade among the children of the Berlin Brigade. I utter my thanks nearly every day of my life.

Today our high school building no longer houses an American school. Many of our teachers have passed from this life. There are now no American troops in Berlin. Still, in my imagination, I stop by the Post Exchange on the way home from school. I buy pommes frites at a stand near the Clayallee Strasse U-Bahn station. And I walk to football practice pondering the prophecy of my heroic teachers: "Your life in West Berlin during these Cold War Years, your experience at this high school in an outpost of freedom, will shape you all your days." They were right. Thank God.

Stephen Mansfield, Class of 1976
1971-1973

(Used with permission: from *Lincoln's Battle with God* by Stephen Mansfield)

Queen's Birthday Parade

Page 8 / The Berlin Observer / June 21, 1974

Parade on Maifeld honors the Queen

To honor the Queen's birthday here in Berlin, the British held a parade on June 15 on the Maifeld. The parade started at 11 a.m. and the salute was taken by the British Commandant, Major General D. W. Scott-Barrett.

The highlight of the parade was a 21-gun salute fired by the Chieftain battle tank. It was the first time such a salute had ever been attempted.

The three infantry battalions serving in Berlin were on parade in honour of the Queen: the 1st Battalion Coldstream Guards; 1st Battalion, The King's Own Scottish Borderers; and the 1st Battalion, The Worcestershire and Sherwood Foresters. Altogether there were 450 soldiers on parade.

Military musicians from England and West Germany combined in a display of massed bands. These included the 13th/18th Hussars from Fallingbostel, Royal Engineers from Chatham, Worcestershire, and the Worcestershires, Sherwood Foresters, and the King's Own Scottish Borderers.

In addition, the Pipers and the Corps of Drum from various Berlin units performed. (Photo by Karl Tietz)

Queen's Birthday Celebration at Olympic Stadium

Every year, the British military present their forces to the reigning monarchy. They refer to it as "Trooping the Colour." In England this celebration is not held on the official birthday of Queen Elizabeth II, but on a Saturday in June. Her actual birthday is April 21. In Berlin, this event was celebrated in May because of the weather. This was another opportunity for collaboration among the various armed forces and citizens of Berlin to celebrate freedom. I recall attending this event at least twice while in high school (between 1973 and 1975).

I have very fond memories of the event. I love parades, military music, and all the pomp and circumstance. I don't remember boarding the bus to Maifeld next to the Olympiastadion (Olympic Stadium) but I remember sitting in the bleachers and being surrounded by hundreds of people. Nobody does a parade better than the British.

The field before us seemed to go on forever. It was probably no larger than a typical football stadium in reality. In the rear, opposite the bandstand, were the Chieftain battle tanks. They fired ceremonial salutes with blanks. Next, three infantry battalions marched by while firing a salute to the attending members of royalty. They moved from left to right and back again from right to left. Not to be outdone, next was a series of military vehicles. The whole time, the band continued its medley of military music.

Finally, a helicopter flew over streaming the colors of the British flag. This was an event not to be missed. Whenever I hear military music, I'm brought back to times like this. Did I know who was in attendance? Did I know who represented the Royal family? No to both questions. It didn't matter. It was being a part of the event that mattered. Queen Elizabeth II herself attended the parade in 1965, 1978, and 1987. There are many websites by former British military personnel who either attended or participated in these historic events. I think it's odd that Americans did not record these events. Perhaps that's because it was a "British" thing. I think it was a "Berlin" thing and I will always remember it that way.

Riding the Duty Train

The trip between Berlin and Frankfurt was an overnight trip. At checkpoints we were "advised" to keep the window shades down and not make eye contact with the Soviets. Well, as teenagers, the minute you say, "Don't do this," we try to do it. At the time, I didn't realize that locomotives were changed from Communist locomotive to West German locomotive at Helmstedt. The trip from Berlin to Frankfurt required two changes- in Potsdam from a West German locomotive to an East German locomotive and in Helmstedt from an East German locomotive to a West German locomotive! And of course, we had to have Flag Orders to ride the train. I assume the school took care of all that. An American officer would take our passports and orders into a small building with the Russian officers to check our papers. This would take upwards of an hour or more. During this time is when we would try to sneak a peek. All the while, we knew there were guards walking on both sides of the train with submachine guns. We wanted to see. Unfortunately, I didn't see anything. It was so dark! They, the Russians, didn't want any escapees. The Americans didn't want any incidents.

Lisa Randle, Class of 1975
1967-70; 1972-75

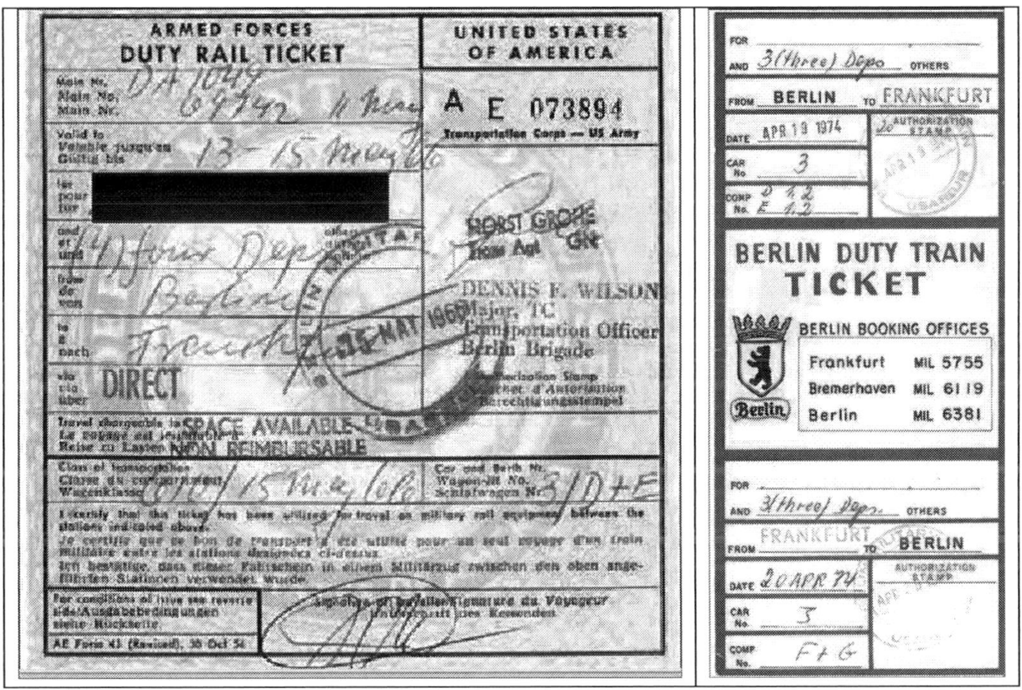

ARMED FORCES
DUTY RAIL TICKET

UNITED STATES
OF AMERICA

A E 073894
Transportation Corps — US Army

Valid to
Valable jusqu'au
Gültig bis 13-15 May 66

DIRECT

SPACE AVAILABLE
NON REIMBURSABLE

DENNIS F. WILSON
Major, TC
Transportation Officer
Berlin Brigade

For conditions of issue see reverse side/Ausgabebedingungen siehe Rückseite.

AE Form 41 (Revised), 30 Oct 56

FOR
AND 3(three) Deps OTHERS
FROM BERLIN TO FRANKFURT
DATE APR 19 1974
AUTHORIZATION STAMP
CAR No. 3
COMP No. D 4 2 E 1 2

BERLIN DUTY TRAIN
TICKET

BERLIN BOOKING OFFICES

Frankfurt	MIL 5755
Bremerhaven	MIL 6119
Berlin	MIL 6381

Berlin

FOR
AND 3(three) Deps. OTHERS
FROM FRANKFURT TO BERLIN
DATE 20 APR 74
AUTHORIZATION STAMP
CAR No. 3
COMP No. F + G

Duty Train tickets- 1966 and 1974

Reflections on My Time in Berlin

An Eagle Scout in Berlin

Inside
Swine flu vaccine is here -- pg. 3
French commando training -- pg. 4
Sailboating on the Wannsee -- pg. 6
Trimming down with Slimnastics -- pg. 8

THE BERLIN OBSERVER

U.S. Command, Berlin

500 scouts invade Berlin for Camporee

I had the privilege of being in the same troop with the Orbock family and having Lt. Col. Ed Orbock as our Scoutmaster. The year was 1976 and under his leadership we planned and executed the first-ever Berlin Camporee. Over 500 Scouts from around West Germany and Europe attended. The logistics were a challenge with the Duty Train and buses. Nonetheless, it was a tremendous success and included camping and Scout activities in the Grunewald, as well as tours of Berlin. I remember having a photo taken with the 500 Scouts on the steps of the old Reichstag Building near the Berlin Wall and Brandenburg Gate. It was bizarre to return to Berlin in 2000 and have a photo on the steps of the newly reconstructed Reichstag. It was also uncanny to be staying in the new hotels near Checkpoint Charlie in the center of former East Berlin. I recall construction going on in every block of this new vibrant, German capital.

Memories of a PK in Berlin

My father, Chaplain Chris Martin, was assigned to Tempelhof Air Base from 1973-1977. I was a PK – a "Preacher's Kid." As the son of a chaplain, I enjoyed watching my father engage people throughout the installation. Chaplain Martin was also a former Air Force pilot, so he was particularly effective at being a "flight line" chaplain. Chaplain Martin loved to associate with the aviators as they transited Tempelhof.

Flying the Berlin corridor from West Germany required a special qualification, so only very select aircrew were able to fly the Berlin missions and Chaplain Martin got to know many of them very well. In fact, many of these associations and friendships had a positive effect on me joining the Air Force and pursuing a flying career. Chaplain Martin also served with Col. Gail Halverson, the famed "Candy Bomber" of the Berlin Airlift, and subsequent Tempelhof Base Commander in the early 1970s. Interestingly, not only did Chaplain Martin serve with Col. Halverson in the early 1970s, but my wife and I flew C-9s with Col. Halvorson's son, Robert, at Scott AFB near St. Louis in the late 1980s.

Col. Halvorsen with Secretary of Defense, Robert Gates (left) and Donald Rumsfeld, retired Secretary of Defense (2009)

Our friendship with the Halvorson family has grown over the years. We've enjoyed seeing Col. Halvorson, who is 94 years young, at various military events around the world—hearing him tell great stories of the Berlin Airlift and what Berlin represented to Freedom and Allied teamwork.

These themes were highlighted in a children's book entitled "Mercedes and the Chocolate Pilot." Mercedes was a young German girl who lived in West Berlin and made a point to catch as many of the chocolate parachutes as possible. As years passed, Mercedes eventually developed a friendship with her "chocolate pilot"- Col. Gail Halverson. In the book, Mercedes said Col. Halvorson and the Allies delivered more than food and coal to the city, they delivered HOPE! Berliners' confidence in the West grew as the world united to prevent the Soviet blockade from isolating the people of Berlin.

Golfing in Berlin

I learned to golf at the American Golf Course near the Wannsee not far from Potsdam. It was not uncommon for high schoolers who were learning to golf to hit an "errant" ball off the tee box in the direction of the East German guard towers. To this day I'm surprised we didn't have more "international" incidents after provoking the guards with "errant" tee shots!

Five Characteristics That BRATs Bring to an Organization

On August 18th, 2011 I had the honor of speaking with host Dennis Campbell and associate producer and co-host Jeri Glass on BRATCON Radio- a radio station on Voice of America dedicated to connecting BRATS and celebrating military service-members and their families. During that hour interview I shared themes on why BRATs make for a strong team and are people of character- they bring many strengths to an organization:

- BRATs are adaptable. Constant moves require BRATs to develop skills to adapt in any situation...new school, new surroundings, new friends, etc. Change is a constant in the life of a BRAT. Organizations often face change and BRATs are adept in dealing with change and helping others adapt to change.

- BRATs are great teammates: BRATs learn early in their lives to work with others. The frequent moves and exposure to new communities and schools help BRATs appreciate the importance of contributions from fellow teammates. BRATs learn early that they are part of something larger than themselves.
- BRATs are a quick study. Due to many moves and demands on the life of a BRAT, they learn to prioritize well. BRATs learn quickly to focus on the objective – the task at hand.
- BRATs value freedom. Living abroad makes one appreciate the freedoms we enjoy in the United States. BRATs are exposed to extensive travel, both domestically and internationally, and that experience highlights the differences and strengths of America. BRATs are part of families who "serve" their country– that service forms the connection between freedom and responsibility.
- BRATs value diversity. Living in various regions and cultures and learning a foreign language contributes immensely to different perspectives. BRATs are exposed to other races, ethnicities, and backgrounds and their thinking is strengthened by hearing different perspectives from people around them. BRATs learn early that diversity is strength in an organization.

BRATs Rock!

Maj. Gen. Frederick H. Martin, Class of 1977
1973-1977

Berlin Was My Second Home

Berlin is my second home. My teen years were spent in this marvelous city. Mom was very good at making us comfortable in a new place. We moved every couple of years and Mom made it possible because she was a consistent source of love, friendship and encouragement.

BOB RECEIVED EAGLE SCOUT AWARD, MCNAIR BARRACKS CHAPEL, 3 AUGUST, 1973

We lived in a huge house at 50 Auf Dem Grat. It was a great place. We were a typical noisy American family in a typical quiet German neighborhood. We did make a bit of noise racing around the huge yard. One neighbor complained about us causing too much ruckus. Mom made them a cake and brought it to them to apologize and we never heard from them again.

I took piano lessons for a time; the teacher was a bit of a tyrant. We rode the bus and U-bahn everywhere. When I would go to piano lessons, Mom would give me enough money to take the bus and buy gummy bears at the candy stand. That is probably why I took lessons as long as I did.

We traveled a lot while there. We saw Europe and really enjoyed it. Mom would pack up our big station wagon with games, camping equipment and lots of food. We had Vienna Sausages, bread and cheese for snacks along the way. We camped almost everywhere. My favorite camping dinner was Spam, instant potatoes and canned peas. Mom was very busy with Dad and his job at Tempelhof, but still made Berlin feel like home.

Robert Halvorsen, Class of 1975
1970-1973

The First Burger King in Berlin

Burger King in Germany opened its first restaurant in Berlin in 1976. The establishment was located on Kurfürstendamm (Ku'damm) which was the busiest street in Berlin– very close to the Kaiser-Wilhelm-Gedächtnis-Kirche (Kaiser Wilhelm Memorial Church) that had been bombed in 1943.

One day in August my good friends Jolene Shriver 76' and Dianna Nope 76', walked over to the PX. We saw a sign stating that Burger King was looking for American students to assist in opening a restaurant downtown on the Ku'damm. We all spoke a little German and thought this would be a great after school job. We went in for the interview and were hired!

Our first day we came dressed in our fashionable red and yellow Burger King uniforms ready to learn how to make the famous "Vopper" (Whopper in English) and Pommes Frits. The second best part of our job was serving that "foamy beer on tap, " and every 30 minutes with our heads held high we proudly belted out that famous tune, "Hold The Pickle Hold The Lettuce..." to all our customers. The Germans did not know what to make of the 'singing cashiers,' as well as, being shown how to eat a hamburger with your hands instead of with a 'knife and fork.' For all us Americans it reminded us of "HOME".

Over ensuing months that the three of us worked at Burger King, we collected business cards from people visiting Berlin from the US. Many US visitors were curious to know where we were from and why we were living in Berlin. The most memorable customer to Jolene was a gentleman who had worked with her grandfather in Gary, South Dakota at a grain elevator.

When we got off work at midnight, we would take three double decker buses just to get home. To add to the nightly experience, we would run into the same 'working girls' in those glass store window fronts–something you would not see in the USA back in 1976 (ha-ha). Our times at Burger King will always be cherished.

THE EINMANNWAGEN (one-man bus) has only a driver and no conductor. Passengers enter the bus through the double doors at front and pay the driver. The sign over the front doors indicates that persons holding Sichtkarten (weekly or monthly passes) may enter at left; persons who must pay cash (Barzahler) for a ticket or who have Sammelkarten or Umsteigers (transfer tickets) enter at right. Passengers leave the bus through the center doors. When you want to get off, press a button located inside next to the exit doors. The signal tells the driver that a passenger wishes to get off at the next stop. (Photo courtesy of BVG)

Kim McLean, Class of 1977
1975-1977

Jolene Shriver, Class of 1976
1974-1977

How about a stroll down Kurfürstendamm?

[illegible]

The Ku'damm shortly before Burger King opened

Checkpoint Bravo

Checkpoint Bravo

Grey concrete watchtowers filled with armed guards were a normal day in West Berlin...every day. After some time you didn't seem to notice the Soviet soldiers peering through binoculars, AK47's slung across their backs, watching your every move, toward and near their precious Wall. We didn't care. The West was free– or so we wanted to believe– and they, the grey men, were not. They couldn't even scare us anymore. The Wall was always near and the tank traps, and the mines...the minefields stretched across "no man's land," the barbed wire, the machine guns, the ominous watchtowers, the hammer and sickle flags– THE WALL– all separated us and only kept them out of our world, our lives, our fun, our freedom…

And then, my first driver's license...no more riding below the city on the U-Bahn, waiting for the bus, or hoping to make that connection to stay out of the cold- the bitter cold of winter where the wind stings and steals your breath, punishing any piece of exposed skin with a memory of numbing so severe that hot cocoa will not cure nor thaw…

So it was set...as the newest driver in the family I would be the one to navigate the family van out of the grand old city, through the East German and Soviet checkpoints, and onward deep into and through East Germany to the final destination in the Bavarian Alps for a much anticipated ski vacation. Mom worked in the Flag Orders section at Berlin Brigade HQ so our paperwork was expedited and we were soon on our way.

The lights on the Autobahn were dim, eerie and yellow, casting an alternate form of grey onto the highway, on snow glistening trees and on side shoulders of the road. With dad as my navigator, I steered the 1972 VW camper down the Autobahn toward the first checkpoint out of safe Berlin.

"Slow down but don't stop at this one," dad said.

"Why not? They have machine guns too…"

"We don't recognize the East German government– they're puppets of the Soviet regime," dad replied.

I swallowed hard as they stared us down…machine guns at the ready...but kept on driving...ever so slowly...

As we made our way around the first set of fences and barricades, we came into another enclave where the several armed soldiers in grey uniforms stood in pairs– Soviet soldiers, two concrete guard towers watching our every move as usual- but this was different. We were in THEIR territory now. Guards held AK47's at the ready, watching us closely- there was no one else around…

One guard made his way to the front of our vehicle, raising his arm to signal "Stop." Two others circled the van inspecting everything...Dad told me to wind down the window and show our papers to the guard who had made his way to my driver's side. As I extended the papers the guard stepped back and indicated that I should get out and follow him. I looked nervously back toward my father and he nodded his head in approval.

"Don't forget to salute back," dad said as I stepped out of the van.

It was December and I should have been feeling the bite of the wind and the snow- but time and space was standing still as I nervously closed the car door wondering if this was my last moment on earth. I turned back toward the soldier to see him saluting me– ME! ...a long-haired, seventeen-year-old American kid who just got his license– "What the...?" I thought- then remembered to return the salute as dad had instructed. He motioned for me to follow him. As I tried to hurry to stay in step with the soldier, who was in a serious fast march toward the nearest building, I thought the tower guards would pepper me with lead if I even appeared to run to catch up with him.

Once inside, the smell of slightly burned scrambled eggs filled the air. A few plain wooden chairs sat against the wall in a small, otherwise empty, waiting room with a wood floor and a paint-covered customer service type window that you couldn't see through. No decorations, no propaganda posters...nothing. The guard pointed to the window, gestured that I should slide our papers into the slot- and sit down to wait. So I did and he walked out, closing the door behind him…I was alone...

Just when I thought the smell of burned eggs was going to kill me– which was about 30 seconds– the entry door opened again and the guard motioned to me to come with him. I looked back at the window slot because our papers were not there– and he shrugged and waved me to join him anyway.

He led me around the building, gesturing to get out of the view of the towers– and I thought one of two things– they were now taking me hostage in exchange for my dad's crypto-level secrets of the highly-advanced TPX-42 radar...or...

We had heard stories of the Soviet soldiers and how sometimes they would make trades with Americans once inside the East– if you met the right ones...but how would I know? How could I tell who was friendly- they all had AK47's loaded and ready!

The guard struggled with broken English… "Trade?" and opened his coat to reveal a plethora of Soviet souvenirs to exchange. I was relieved and elated…he then said "Cigarettes...playboy...dollars?" I motioned that I needed to get back to the van and he indicated by pointing and hand signs that we should not be obvious to the tower guards, and waited behind the building. I scurried back to the van.

"What are you doing?!" Dad exclaimed. "Where are the papers???"

"Relax, hand me a carton of my smokes– we're going to make a trade!" I replied. Suddenly my apprehension had subsided. If there was one thing I was comfortable with– it was business transactions...

Everyone in the van was staring in disbelief...

I rejoined the guard around the building, picked out a few things, and handed him the cigarettes– we shook hands and he pointed to the building where our papers were now ready.

As I walked back to the van, approved papers in hand, I realized that the grey men were people too, who wanted to share in the simple pleasures in life as much as anyone else. I looked back, smiled to myself, and drove into East Germany, with a new found confidence about the road ahead...

Jason Sprankle, Class of 1978
1975-1979

Showdown at Checkpoint Charlie

My diplomat father was assigned to the U.S. Mission in West Berlin in 1977. The U.S. military did not "recognize" East Berlin as the capital of the GDR, but we had an embassy there; so, with diplomatic passports, we were allowed through checkpoints to the East conversing amicably with border guards-whom we had to pretend did not exist when driving through Checkpoint Charlie in our military-licensed car, pressing our East Passes up to the window, eyes front. The paradox bemused and sometimes, amused us.

My brother Nathaniel came home from college the summer of 1978—my sophomore year at BAHS. He brought his friend, Mark. Nat, who possessed an audacity contagious and thrilling to be around, was unsettled by the walled-in city; even more than those of us so inured–who lived there year-round. The first time Nat and Mark crossed into East Berlin, they walked through Checkpoint Charlie—Nat with his diplomatic and Mark his civilian passport. Mark bought a visa and the obligatory number of East German Marks (at a fraudulent ratio of 1:1 with the West's). After exploring, shopping, and listening to families' histories of lives separated by the Wall, they befriended an elderly couple who invited them to dinner the next evening.

With my parents' permission, this time they drove. Nat checked in with the U.S. Military Police who clarified that he had 2½ hours to return. He showed his East Pass to the GDR border police—duly not "seeing" them—and drove through, picking up Mark (obliged to walk through) in the Soviet Sector.

Sometime after dinner, Nat remembered the time restriction. Two hours late, they rushed back to the checkpoint. An agitated MP detained them and confiscated the car until my parents arrived. Nathaniel was banned from the Soviet Sector for the remainder of his stay in Berlin. Mark flew home; Nat stewed. He wanted to cross over once more before he left for university. He needed a big GDR flag, a Freie Deutsche Jugend T-shirt, maybe a Soviet belt buckle....

Scheming, Nat took me, doting little sister, aside. He had a plan; I was game. I got permission to drive, and Nat jumped in with me. A few blocks from Checkpoint Charlie, I let him out. Dark sunglasses and jaunty hat pulled down low over his eyes, he started to walk. I was to meet him in the East. What was the chance that the MP on duty would be the same and recognize him?

As I pulled up alongside the MP, I glanced in my rearview mirror and saw Nat ambling along, looking straight ahead. I rolled down my window to sign in. "Chapman, eh?" the MP growled. "You related to Nathaniel?"

"He's my brother," I grimaced—thinking, "Don't look now..." He looked. Nat was about twenty feet away, his disguise suddenly lame—his character not easily subdued.

"Hey!" the MP shouted. "Chapman!" Nat did not flinch. A few more feet...he'd be beyond his jurisdiction. The MP turned to me. "What do you kids think you're up to? When he comes back through that checkpoint...!"

I blinked innocent eyes.

"My brother!? He's banned from the East!" I declared, avoiding an outright lie. He let me go, shaking his finger. I drove on, pressing my East Pass to the window for the East German guard, opening it when he nodded, then on through to find my brother in the East. Safe!...for 2½ hours.

"Technically," Nat rationalized, "I was banned from the Soviet Sector, but not from East Berlin, Haupstadt der DDR [capital of E. Germany]." His banter caused me to miss the turn to Potsdamer Platz. Impulsively, I deviated down a side road to go back. It was a dead end.

Nat and I looked up to see about five signs, all containing the same word, "Verboten!" Forbidden. Within seconds, four Volks Polizei cars surrounded us, sirens blaring. Police jumped out, pistols aimed, shouting at us to get out. I sat, frozen, my mind recalling the, "What to Do If Retained in the East" security briefing at the U.S. Mission. I reached for the door pocket where we kept the handy card with the message: "I DEMAND TO SPEAK TO A SOVIET OFFICER," written in English, French, German, and Russian.

Nat got out of the car. "I'll explain," he said, unconcerned. Alarmed—he had missed the security briefing!—I grabbed the card and rolled down my window to hand it to a policeman. Nat began explaining in his beautiful German. Obviously concluding he was an East Berliner…in my car…trying to escape...they grabbed his arms and pushed him up against the hood.
Grabbing his passport from the glove compartment, I got out of the car. Protocol or not, it was time to recognize these gents. I explained that they had to let my brother go. I showed them his passport, clutching it along with the card demanding a Soviet officer— technically a mixed message but who had time to split hairs? Amazingly, the VoPo's released him and ordered us to leave. We willingly obliged. As we drove off, Nat rolled down his window to wish them all a good day and hoped to see them one day on the other side.

We spent the next two hours shopping with cheap East Marks while I fretted about having to face that MP. Nat suddenly had a revelation. He could take the U-Bahn across—the MP would never see him! I cringed, the security officer's voice in my mind: "You may not, under any circumstances, take the U-Bahn to or from East Berlin!" The underground border not monitored by MPs, if the East Germans or Soviets wanted to pull something, no one would see to report it. It was risky, verboten.

Still…less threatening than that MP! I dropped Nat at the Friedrichstrasse U-Bahn station near Checkpoint Charlie and drove on to face my interrogator who pounced when he saw me. "Out of the car, Miss Chapman," he hissed. I stood to the side as he assiduously searched the car, delaying me. I had not hidden him; he had no reason to keep me. I kept my cool demeanor. "When you see your brother, you let him know: I'm onto him!"

My nerves frazzled, I finally drove off. A few blocks away, I parked and dashed down into the U-Bahn station where we'd agreed to meet. A train was receding into the dark tunnel. No Nat. I sat and waited for the next…and the next. I panicked. I knew it! He'd been detained. I needed a phone, had to get help.

I ran into an adjacent Kneipe [pub], found a payphone at the back and dialed home. Our mother answered.

"Hey! What took you so long?" I turned at the voice. There was Nat, grinning over a beer.

I quietly replaced the receiver. He could explain later.

Sarah Monahan, Class of 1979
1977-1979

DYA 1978 Junior All-Stars

For many Berlin Brats too young to participate in BAHS sports teams, the DYA became our avenue for friendship, sportsmanship and camaraderie. With so many military dependents living there in the late 70s, the DYA fielded four junior football teams and cheerleading squads every fall. At the end of the nine-game season, the football coaches got together to pick the best 25 players to represent Berlin in the USAREUR DYA Junior Boys Class A Football Championships.

For the cheerleaders, we individually presented a routine to a panel of coaches who chose seven girls for the junior squad and seven for the senior squad to compete in the USAREUR Cheerleading Championships. On November 18, 1978, both the junior football team and the junior cheerleading squad came in second at the championships held at Patch Barracks in Stuttgart. Tom, Phil and I reconnected via Facebook recently and wanted to share some of our fond memories with our fellow Berlin Brats about what the DYA and the trips to West Germany as All-Stars meant to us.

Initially called the AYA when we all arrived in Berlin in 1976, the DYA (Dependent Youth Activities) was more than an organization that provided sports competitions for youth; it kept us active, helped us make friends, and provided us the chance to travel to West Germany together. Phil points out that the DYA, "Gave me the opportunity to meet and work with kids that otherwise I wouldn't have even met. I was 11 when I signed up for my first season with the DYA. At that age, I only knew the kids in my class and the ones that lived around my playground in Düppel." Tom adds, "Throughout the year, every major sport was offered to us at no cost to our parents.

Not only were the majority of the kids in Berlin in great shape, but they also learned valuable lessons in life, such as teamwork, leadership and how to get back up after being knocked down. We Brats are a pretty tough bunch! We had a knack for adapting to new lifestyles, cultures, and most of all, making friends."

For me, the DYA was also a physical space where the cheerleaders would compete to make the All-Star squad, practice for the competition and have squad sleepovers, where we talked about boys, school and other young teenage girl topics well into the early morning hours. Making the All-Star team was exciting on many levels. It was a grand adventure, but I also realized it was an honor to represent Berlin.

Phil agrees, "I know now that it was a big deal to represent Berlin, but I always looked at it as a bigger deal that the DYA and the parents gave us kids an adventure that would stay with us for the rest of our lives." We knew that we were unique in that as newly created groups, we were being sent to face players and cheerleaders who had worked together all season long, while we only had one week to prepare before climbing aboard the train for the semi-finals. The trips to West Germany offered us opportunities to bond.

While other kids back home were probably sleeping in their own beds, we slept on the floors of barracks or on the top-level of apartment buildings in either Mannheim for the semi-finals one weekend or Stuttgart for the championship the next weekend. This, after having a fun night of hanging out on the Duty Train together. Phil recalls, "My fondest memories would have to be the time spent traveling. Our nights on the Duty Train were spent listening to a Richard Pryor tape someone had brought on and playing Mattel Electronic Football." Tom asks rhetorically, "Did any of us really sleep on our way to Frankfurt?"

Once we arrived in Mannheim to play the Mannheim Chiefs on November 11, 1978, the boys were all business. "I just remember the Mannheim game being a slugfest between two strong defenses on a cold drizzly day," Phil recalls. Berlin won 8-0 on a three-yard run with only 1:30 left in the game.

Phil also remembers after that game the boys were on a bus without the coaches. "So we thought it would be a good idea to see if we could rock the bus onto its side. Once the grownups noticed the bus a rockin' they put a stop to it. I wouldn't be surprised if we got that thing up on two wheels."

The next weekend, we all took the trip again to West Germany, but this time to Stuttgart for the championships. The cheerleading competitions occurred in the morning before the football game. My main memory from the previous year's cheerleading competition and the 1978 competition is that we all looked so small compared to the other girls. Our coaches, Louise Naquin and Jo Anne Miller, helped us put together a fun routine that focused more on entertainment and precision than gymnastic abilities and lifts. We seemed to impress the judges enough to come in second, a placement we were all thrilled with after only working together for two weeks and feeling so overwhelmed by the other squads!

Coached by Chuck Hassan, Bob Cummins, Fritz Prater, Tom Gruber and Frank Foster, the junior Berlin Bears hit the field for the championship game that afternoon in which we came close, but lost 22-12 to the Pattonville Jets. Phil recalls that the Pattonville contest was the exact opposite of the Mannheim game the week before. "It was a fast, high-scoring game on a warm sunny day."

"For me," Tom reflects on his time in Berlin, "the one thing that stands out in my mind was the 1978 Berlin All-Star team that played in the championship game. As in the many football movies that Hollywood has made about that championship season or that 'what if ' game, we too had one in Berlin that year. Many players of that team can still talk about that season as if it were last week."

L to R seated: Mike Short '82, David Peters '83,Phil Jaynes '84, Mike Foster'83, Alex Mills '83 (back center football player), Chris Hassan '82 (cheerleader between adults)

Being part of the DYA athletics program also meant feeling like you were part of a big family, literally and figuratively. Coach Hassan's daughter Chris Hassan '82 and I were on the junior squad together. Coach Naquin's daughter, Nicole Naquin Branson '83 cheered on the senior squad, and Phil's dad Chuck traveled with the team, taking the photo about the championship game that appeared in the *Berlin Observer*.

Even though neither the team nor the squad won in the truest sports sense, we all feel that this All-Star experience at the ages of 13 and 14 positively affects us 35 years later. Tom sums it up best, "Yes, many details and accounts have been forgotten or exaggerated over the years, but one thing that remains is, we belonged to something special. Special to us, if to no one else. I hold my former coaches, teammates and cheerleaders dear to my heart to this day. We remain ever thankful that this great city gave us the opportunity to bring this group of kids together and to remain in contact with one another. Yes, this truly was special."

Liese Hutchison, Class of 1983
1976-1979

with Tom Dietz, Class of 1982
1964-72, 1976-79

and Phil Jaynes , Class of 1984
1975-1979

Berlin All-Stars win: Go to 'A' finals

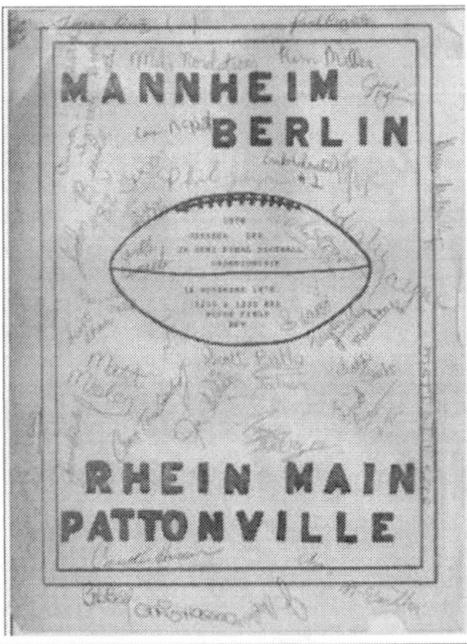

The 1978 DYA Junior All- Stars

'You Are Leaving the American Sector'

Late one evening in the winter of 1978, the very distinctive ring of the Bundespost phone echoed throughout the fourth story apartment at 73 Lindenthaler Allee, Düppel Housing Area in W. Berlin, Germany. A call this late usually meant my stepfather's unit was conducting an 'Alert' exercise or due to the time difference with the States it was news about a family crisis or tragedy. Tonight, it was neither. Instead, this phone call informed my mother that a defection from Communist East Berlin– commonly called 'The East'– had taken place that night. Little did anyone know, this phone call would significantly affect our family's worldview and serve as a catalyst for my mother's insurgency campaign against the Communist regime.

The Berlin Experience (East vs. West)

Our family arrived in Berlin in April of 1977. My stepfather was assigned to Field Station Berlin (Teufelsburg), where he served as a Military Intelligence Cryptologist. Since this was our first overseas experience, our family decided to embrace the host nation and join a German/American cultural exchange program called 'Kontakt.' This program paired German and American families with the intention of developing cross-cultural relationships. In the autumn of 1977, my family was introduced to our Kontakt family: Doris and Herman Schmidt.*

After the obligatory visits and dinners, we began to learn some very interesting facts about Herman and his family. When the Wall was erected, Herman's family was trapped in East Berlin. In the late 1960s, Herman escaped to the West in the wheel well of a diplomat's car, but his mother, father, brother (Michael) and sister (Dorothy) still resided in the East Berlin.

As military dependents of a WWII Occupying Power our family (not my stepfather, due to the sensitive nature of his military duties) had special privileges that enabled us to cross the East/West border at Checkpoint Charlie with diplomat-like immunity. Most dependents used these cross-border privileges for shopping trips, but for our family these trips would represent something much more significant.

In 1978, the East German government allowed Herman's father and mother to immigrate to West Berlin. Since Herman's father and mother were of retirement age and his father's occupation was a clergyman, the East Germany government deemed the couple not useful to the 'state' and allowed the couple to immigrate to the West, where the West German government would be financially responsible for the couple's pension and health care. Three months after the couple immigrated, Herman's father became seriously ill.

Once word reached Dorothy and Michael that their father was seriously ill, they requested a three-day visitation pass from the East German government. Since Dorothy was a respected medical doctor married to a government agriculturist (Hans) and Michael was married with children, they were determined to be a low risk for defection and were granted a three-day visitation pass to West Berlin. No one knew that Dorothy and Hans had previously pledged that given the opportunity, either would defect to the West with the intent to pursue all options available to get the other out of the Communist state.

When Dorothy and Michael crossed the border checkpoint, they could only take two changes of clothing, their East German passport, and ten West German Marks. After visiting with her father and consulting with her brother, Dorothy declared her intentions to defect to the West. That evening, Dorothy was flown to France and her brother Michael returned to East Berlin one day before his visitation pass expired, to discuss his sister's defection with Hans. During this consultation, Michael secured all of Dorothy's academic records, medical accreditations and personal documents in anticipation of East German officials visiting their tiny apartment once it was determined that Dorothy had not returned from the West.

Operation Liberty

After that late evening phone call, my parents discussed the possibility of being actively involved with assisting our Kontakt family. There were a number of risks ranging from adverse implications on my stepfather's Army career to our family being shipped home in disgrace for violating Berlin Brigade's policies and regulations to serious violations in international agreements and treaties. Even though they understood the danger, my mother, an American history teacher, who fully embraces the principles of freedom, convinced my stepfather that this effort was worth the risks.

Meanwhile, in East Berlin, East German officials were subjecting Dorothy's co-workers, friends, and husband to intense questioning concerning her defection. This questioning effort would culminate with a gathering of the individuals mentioned above. During this meeting, each would have to declare (verbally or by writing on a black board) that Dorothy was a bad person for defecting. Dorothy had first-hand experience with these proceedings (having had to participate in them at the hospital where she'd worked) and informed us of this practice after she returned from France.

A few weeks after Dorothy's defection, when it was believed that East German officials were no longer watching her husband, my mother met Hans at an Hungarian restaurant. Like a scene from the pages of a Cold War spy novel, my mother slid a sealed envelope under the table to Hans. This envelope contained 10,000 East German Marks, the exact amount that East German officials fined Hans for his wife's defection. If Hans were unable to pay this fine, he would be jailed in an East German prison. About a month later, my mother arranged for another meeting in East Germany. This time, she met Dorothy's brother Michael in the parking lot of the East Berlin Opera House. During this exchange, my mother secured all of Dorothy's documents certifying that she was a doctor. Without these critical documents, Dorothy would have been unable to substantiate her medical credentials in the West.

Business as Usual

Over the next 18 months, my mother successfully transported important documents, family photos, and numerous personal items without incident. Due to the routine nature of these trips, my mother would sometimes bring my brother or myself along for the ride. On many of her trips, she delivered letters, small gifts, instant coffee, and other items Dorothy sent to Hans. During one trip, we delivered a new car battery for Hans' car (there was a shortage of 6-volt car batteries in the East). For his part, Hans volunteered to be my mother's personal shopper and East Berlin guide.

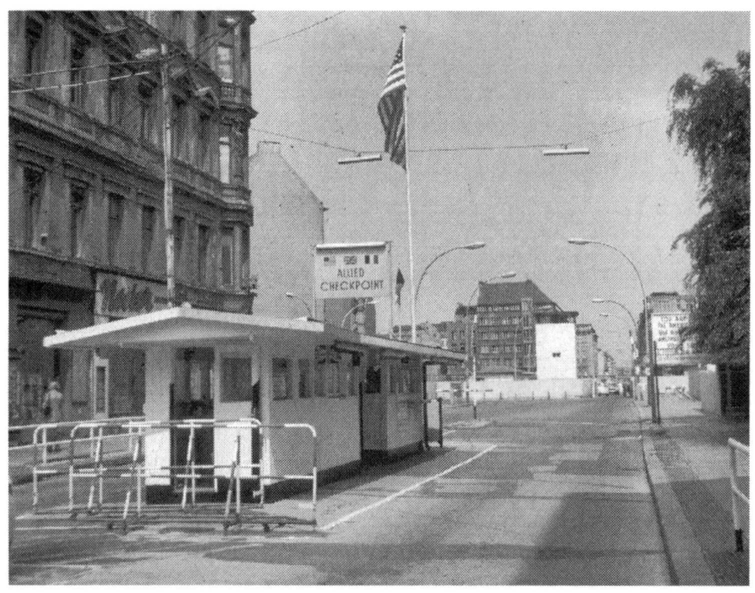

Checkpoint Charlie looking towards the East

Trouble at Checkpoint Charlie

During one visit to the East, I accompanied my mother. After meeting with Hans to secure some of Dorothy's clothing and personal documents, we finished Christmas shopping in Karl-Marx-Platz and returned to the border checkpoint. On the East German side of the border, the border guards inspected our border passes and conducted a visual inspection of our car (under the occupation agreement, they were not allowed to touch our car). Once through the East German border, a female MP in the rank of Specialist greeted us. On previous trips, the American MPs normally asked if we needed to declare any items and conducted a cursory search of our car. We would always provide a negative response and after a few minutes, they would waive us through Checkpoint Charlie. Today was different; the MP informed us that she would be conducting a search of our VW Bug. After conducting a thorough search, she inquired about the clothing inside the bonnet (which belonged to Dorothy). Without hesitation, my mother explained that these items were going to the Thrift Shop (and prayed that the MP did not inquire further concerning the origin of this clothing). Satisfied with her inspection and my mother's response to her inquiry, the MP asked my mother to sign the standard documentation and waived us through the checkpoint. This incident served as a reminder to the seriousness and the risks involved with our actions.

What Happened to Hans

In the summer of 1980, our tour ended and my family was transferred to San Antonio, Texas. Over time, our Berlin experience became a distant memory as we successfully adjusted to normal life without border walls and checkpoints. Late in 1981, we received a short letter explaining that a few months after Dorothy's defection, Hans had quit his job as an agricultural specialist–a highly regarded position in the East– to take a position as a hotel night clerk. With his personal worth to the Communist state declining, the family was able to bribe a number of East German officials and in mid-1981, Hans successfully immigrated to the West and was reunited with Dorothy.

The Conner family consisted of SFC Gwen & Peggy Conner and their two sons Tom and Jon Washer. Peggy Conner was a teacher at the Berlin American High School from 1978 to 1980.

** Names changed to protect privacy.*

Tom Washer, Class of 1982
1977-1980

Spying on the Soviets

In the 1970's, after I finished university in the US, I joined the Special Services working for the U.S. Army and was posted as a civilian to a town near the border in West Germany. I did a four year civilian tour there. Our military post's job was to monitor the border. My job was to go in and take pictures and come out...obviously undetected. I was detected a couple of times–everybody was– but the arrangement between the Powers was soft and lax and we were only ever held 24 hours, then 'exchanged' in the mornings... Not at all like in the movies: foggy nights on a bridge somewhere. We just got put on a train that went between Erfurt and Frankfurt and were met at the western end.

Border Guard Tower

We took many pictures of the towers. There were two guards in each tower, one Russian and one East German. They were (supposedly) not allowed to speak to each other on their shift in case one tried to talk the other one into 'jumping.' As seen in the picture, atop one in every ten posts or so there is a small extension to the height of that post. That extension had a radio activated projectile that could be shot along the fence line in case anyone tried to go over the fence.

The villages pictured are empty. They were inside the 1K Zone and were used to host troops and to create the appearance to the West as working villages. But they weren't working villages... no people, no civilian cars, no farm animals, no smoke from the chimneys, no activity at all.

Fake East German villages

Our job was to determine what activities were actually going on in these villages. We flew over them, strafed them with fuel and on some occasions, landed inside the region and took on-the-ground photos. I shot with a Leica M3 film camera because it was silent and looked like a tourist camera. I also shot with a Fed-S camera which was a Russian copy of the Leica, in the event I had to offer an explanation as to why... very good camera, by the way. I still have those cameras.

Helicopter patrolling the Inner German Border (left) and helicopter surveying a artificial East Germany town

We had dozens of Mi24 Hind East German helicopters land at our post. Our side would keep the helicopters and send the pilots back. I recall one incident when the Soviets put bags of flour into a small gun and shot them at the helicopters. The flour that hit would stick and the Soviets would photograph the white splotches as evidence [of incursions] for the Berlin monthly Soviet/Allied meetings where border issues were discussed.

These incursions were marked as demerit points which limited the travel of East and West diplomats by car through the East/West Zones. These were games both sides played. It was our normal back then. We were young and unbreakable and it was only a 'Cold' War so it didn't really matter except it was a job we all felt had to be done.

Daniel Jenkins, Class of 1965
Wiesbaden High School Alumnus

East German Border markers (upper left and lower right) and East German Guards watching their watchers

I Met Muhammad Ali

During my senior year, Berlin American High School heard that the man who "floats like a butterfly and stings like a bee"–none other than Muhammad Ali–would be visiting our school while on a world exhibition tour. I cannot remember exactly how I managed to be right next to him as he walked from the school to the football field where the entire student population was gathered to hear him talk. It may have been to interview him (though I don't remember ever writing it up).

In any case, it was a warm, spring day–it must have been because I was wearing sandals–and I was right next to him, thrilled to be in the presence of a living legend. He wore black creased pants and a white shirt, and black, leather shoes. He was surprisingly overweight, and I think there was the lingering question of whether or not he would fight again. All of a sudden, he stumbled over something, and, in regaining his balance, the edge of his hard heel came crunching down on my baby toe. As I cried out, he stopped still, confused, and his foot remained on top of mine–my toe on fire, trapped under all that weight. The pain left me speechless and so, instead of finding the words to tell him to get off my foot, I reacted by punching him in his fleshy belly, in an attempt to shove him off. He caught on and moved aside, saying, in that distinctive rasp, "OH! And I am heavy."

So, that is how I came to punch Muhammad Ali.

Sarah Chapman Monahan, Class of 1979
1977-1979

A Wall Too High

Brandenburger Tor (Brandenburg Gate) and its short Wall

Berlin is awash with impressionistic memories for me: new city, senior year, collision of history, walled city, sporting events, museums, music clubs, night clubs, U-Bahns, ubiquitous Schultheiss beer signs, wandering around at 4 am on the Kurfürstendamm, looking for Greek food and Retsina, or currywurst and beer. And the constant for all military brats: a new set of friends.

I moved to Berlin in the summer of 1978, and immediately became friends with Tom D. and Ed P., while volunteering to work for the Senior Trip Club to raise money for our planned trip to Mallorca. But that's another story. We went, but not without combatting the school.

Many of the pictures in the BAHS 1979 yearbook were taken by one of us, as we were a de facto photography staff; I think because Ed sort of appointed us as such. We traveled far and wide around West and East Berlin, taking pictures of the Brandenburger Tor, the Reichstag, the Russian War Memorial in East Berlin, the Grunewald and Charlottenburg. Not to mention the various sporting events, clubs, and random school pictures. We were always stopping somewhere to soak up the culture and have a beer. We walked a lot. We laughed a lot. You get the picture.

East Berlin was always an adventure. We– I was always driving– found ourselves breaking traffic rules in East Berlin often, being chased by whistle blowing policemen and gleefully ignoring them– because we could. We once caused a Russian military base to scramble and shut their gates. This was followed by some testy conversation and the exchange of cigarettes, and several laughs, and an admonishment to watch where we were driving.

We usually ended these East side journeys with cheap six course dinners purchased with black market Ostmarks (East German currency). Somewhere in our wanderings, the idea was hatched– I don't remember who had the initial idea– that we were going to paint "The Class of '79" on the short wall surrounding the Brandenburger Tor. A lot of planning went into this. Paint purchased. Logistics worked out. A trial run on some obscure portion of the wall. Quick whispered meetings. A few others recruited (can't remember who exactly).

The night arrived of our planned foray. We packed up the VW van, and set out for the Brandenburger Tor. But it was early, so we decided to stop at the house of one of our classmates, to hang out a little and let it get late. This classmate and her best friend were known as the best sources for hash in our class, and, as expected, we were offered some. As none of us had indulged at all over the course of the year, we decided, what the hell? I still remember the smoky dimly lit living room… A lot of laughter and the ever slowing flow of time. Time, in fact, became immovable. I was wandering around trying to remember how we were getting there, if we were still going, and knowing there was NO way I was going to drive. Some discussion– with long contemplative, wandering silences punctuated by giggles– was had about getting the stuff onto the U-Bahn. Tom wandered off and started examining trees with great intensity. Looking for highways, I think. And Ed? Well, Ed couldn't move. He was stuck in the grass.

We never made it.

In retrospect, it is good that we never made it. We were eighteen, and though we were bright, we were still too stupid to know that this was a plan that had no way of succeeding. We would've gotten caught. Or shot at. Or caused some sort of international incident. Or gotten thrown out of Berlin on the eve of our graduation. Who knows?

It was a great fantasy, and I'm sure we weren't the first group to have it. I still laugh when I think of that evening and the visual tableaux of us in the yard, higher than a gaggle of kites, and about the nights and days that followed. The increasing restlessness about the impending scattering across the globe of our classmates. A scattering that all Brats experience at some point in their lives. But this, this was the ending of our lives as children of military or state personnel, and we were all about to step out into worlds of our own making, taking that heritage with us.

William Charlton, Class of 1979
1978-1979

Hail, Berlin!

Moving from one military post or base to another is usually a hard transition for any military dependent. Packing all of your household goods is a large undertaking for military families; often you have to get rid of accumulated items from one move to the next, because the military only ships up to a certain amount of weight per move. Any amount over that threshold you have to pay for.

Leaving friends is the hardest part of rotating to another post or base. Moving, but staying in the lower 48 is easier, things are familiar, schools are more uniform, and communicating with people from your last move is possible. But when the new orders say you are moving overseas, things take on another dimension.

We had a whirlwind move from Kirtland A.F.B, Albuquerque, New Mexico to Tempelhof A.F.B., West Berlin, West Germany in the summer of 1979. My older sister Carolyn was miserable. We were leaving Highland High School, one of the premier high schools in Albuquerque with graduating classes that averaged over a thousand students, to come to Berlin American High, where her graduating class would now have 79 students. Needless to say, between the long flights, getting settled into temporary housing, and then showing up for school that first morning, she was NOT a happy camper!

But God always seems to do something that, at the time doesn't seem that significant, but years later you realize how necessary that one thing was. Then one small thing occurs… that starts a thaw in the block of misery-your heart, caused by another rotation.

And that small thing was our encounter with John Cleary. His friends knew him as "J.C." and if you ever met him, you would never forget him. We were sitting in the Principal's Office as they were going over our paperwork, after coming into the front of the school, which was WAY smaller than the façade of our last school! Highland looked like a college campus. BAHS looked like an elementary school.

Suddenly, this guy pops his head into the door of the office, and shouts, "Hey! Are you all new?" We just stared at him for a moment, taking in his droopy smile, his 60's Beatles Bowl haircut, and the fact that he was WAY too happy for it to be 8 am! Finally, Carolyn answered, "Yes." And he disappeared, slamming the door behind him! We looked at each other, shrugged, and went back to our silent musings of despair!

A moment later, the door opened again, and sure enough, it was the same guy, this time he squawked, "What grades are you in?"

I couldn't help but smile back at him, and answer, "10th." My Sister told him, "I'm a senior" (seniors always have to let you know; '12th grade' is NEVER their answer!).

Well, he whooped out loud, shouted, "ALRIIIGHT!" pumped his fist in the air and disappeared again! After a moment, we both turned to each other and smiled, shaking our heads in wonder. Just WHO was that?

Well, we came to know over the next few years who that guy was. J.C. was the BAHS Welcoming Committee, Social Conscience, Pep Band leader, Track Team Manager, and behind the scenes impetus for many spontaneous fun times with his boom box on his shoulder. It was a rare day when you saw John Cleary sad. If he was in your corner, he had your back. You could depend on him.

At one track meet we had in Wiesbaden, W. Germany it was a

miserable day! It was wet, cold, raining, and mud was everywhere! J.C. was our track team manager. He was everywhere that day, encouraging runners, helping the officials, helping Coach Perry Jones. Coach Jones was a Pan Am Pilot and former Olympian who came to Berlin for track season, just to help our team out.

Coach Jones always brought us breakfast bags from the Pan Am flights before our meets! J.C. spent a lot of his day making sure that any needs Coach Jones had were immediately taken care of. I remember one conversation they had that has always stuck in my mind. J.C. came up to Coach Jones with the equipment box, and began to spatter him with questions, "Do you need anybody taped? I have the box right here, Coach! Anybody need their cleats cleaned off? I'm here to help, you KNOW you can count on me Coach! Anything you need, you know I'm your man!" This back and forth conversation went on for several moments, as we all began to smile and laugh quietly, before Coach Jones finally found an errand for J.C. to run!

Coach Jones turned to us as J.C. ran off on his new mission, and smiled, shaking his head, laughing, "That J.C. is something else, isn't he?" As we all laughed with him and nodded! J.C. made that trip and many others more fun than you can imagine!

Our sports opponents came to HATE coming to any Berlin Bears games where he was present with his drum, and his "Hail, BERLIN!" Chant! Many times, he took over the cheering section, whipping the crowd into a frenzy! The only time I saw him settled down, was when he got a girlfriend!

Years later, at our reunion in Greenbelt, Maryland, J.C. came up to stay with my family. Our families had stayed in touch over the years, and he blew into the house, making us all smile and laugh! J.C. was driving a Trans Am, and we were all game to pile into it! When he did the "Hail, BERLIN!" cheer at the reunion, the classes that came before us wondered, "What is THAT?!?" But we all knew it was just John 'J.C.' Cleary bringing us all back home.

Any time you are in a new place, just remember that sometimes the smallest gesture of welcome on your part might be the very thing a stranger needs to start the thaw around their hurting heart. J.C. taught me that.

I will always be thankful to God, that the first student I met at Berlin American High School was someone who was glad to see me even though he didn't know me yet, someone like John 'J.C.' Cleary. May he never be forgotten.

"Hail BERLIN!
Hail BERLIN!
HAIL BERLIN!
HAIL Zweibrucken.
HELL NO!"

In Memorium: John 'J.C.' Cleary, *d. March 4, 2007*

Trisha A. Lindsey, Class of 1982
1979-1983

Chapter 5: The 1980s

"Mr. Gorbachev, open this gate. Mr. Gorbachev, tear down this wall."

- President Ronald Wilson Reagan, at the Brandenburg Gate

What Did Living in Berlin Mean to Me?

Although I consider myself an articulate person, explaining to my friends what it was like to grow up in Berlin, under the shadow of the Iron Curtain, surrounded by THE WALL, is still very difficult. The fact that Berlin was potentially a political powder keg was lost on us children. We saw it as just another location, another base, American children in a foreign country, living on their own little island. But Berlin was so much more.

Berlin was a beautiful city, with incredible history. Everyone knew of Hitler and WWII, but the city's origins date back to the 12th Century. Though Bonn was the capital when we lived in Germany, to see Berlin restored as the German capital is even more special. And though it is Germany's largest city, I don't think we ever felt crowded.

In the summer of 1975, on home leave from our previous CIA assignment in Hong Kong, I remember being excited to finally be able to remain in the United States, where I had never really lived. We were driving across the US, from California to New England, to see the country that I hadn't visited, growing up in Frankfurt, Berlin, Taipei, Bangkok and Hong Kong. The last thing I wanted was another overseas assignment for my family. I wanted to go to an American high school, to be able to understand everyone, to have American food and candy! I was crushed when my father told me, on that trip, that we were going to Berlin for a second time, even though I was too young to remember our first assignment there.

We returned on October 2nd, and the next day I was pretty sick. In fact, that second day in Berlin in 8th grade remains the last time I threw up—

though not because I didn't want to live in Germany! I still tell people of my streak, which is now 36 years and counting! We moved into a house on Thanner Pfad, a huge place with a bomb shelter, two living rooms, and a sink in my bedroom. We then changed housing, going to Ripley Strasse, across the street from the Oskar-Helene-Heim U-Bahn station. We were a street away from the Duck Pond, where I had many happy memories of camping, playing basketball, and finding my 8 year old sister sampling my mother's Viceroy cigarettes.

The 'Duck Pond' in winter and spring

We went to Berlin American High School, grades 6-12; a school that I understood was barely accredited. One principal was arrested for some drug offense. I loved most of my teachers, many of whom had much better pedigrees than I knew. Who knew that Mr. Sullivan had studied at Oxford? Our yearbooks never said anything about the teachers' education when I was there. Sometimes, they even used the same photo as the previous year!

We had plenty of sports to keep everyone busy. Although our football wasn't great, there were good basketball teams, and I think my boys' tennis team beat almost everyone we played during our last three years. We had Model United Nations, where we represented countries smaller than some states, but going to The Hague as a junior and senior was indescribable.

Model United Nations in The Hague, Holland, Jan. 1980

I got conned into joining Boy Scouts in ninth grade by my brother and my good friend Mike Linnane '86, and it turned out to be the greatest thing my brother ever did for me. I became an Eagle Scout in 12th grade. And what opportunities we had! Who else saw the Leaning Tower of Pisa while at Boy Scout summer camp in Italy, or went skiing with their scout troop to Garmisch for two weeks, funded largely by our sales of corn on the cob to the Germans at the Tempelhof Air Show? You couldn't write this stuff! It was a city with great opportunities.

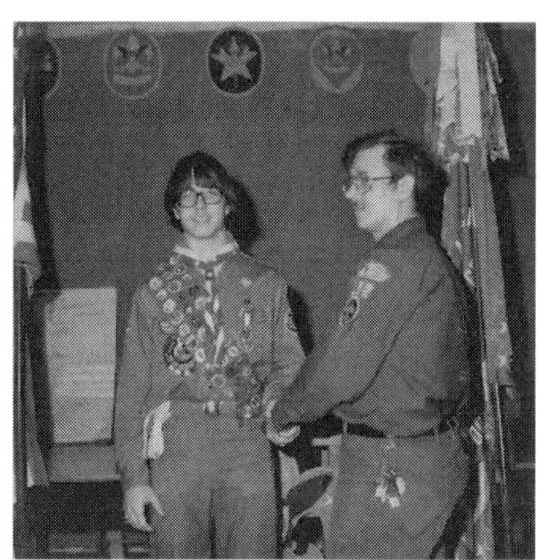

Peter's Eagle Scout Ceremony

Due to an arrangement the Americans had with the Germans, and because of an agreement that we would turn over our facilities to the Germans if and when the American troops left Berlin, the Germans built the best facilities of any station in Europe. We had a great gym, pool, tennis bubble, recreation center, fields, and so forth. Berlin was a small contingent of Americans, having only two generals (as compared to 30+ in Heidelberg, for instance), but was known to have the best of everything. Although we were set apart from the rest of West Germany, we didn't seem to mind the overnight travel on the infamous Duty Train, from Berlin to Frankfurt, and back again, complete with "Coffee, tea, and Marble cake!" Stopping at every little town in East

Germany got a little old, but we slept through it. A few of my friends even had show and tell with the Soviet guards!

I'm sure there were those who stayed mostly around the American complex, but my family and I ventured out into the city. Although I think I only made it to East Berlin once or twice (the Agency didn't really encourage us to be over there), we got to explore a marvelous town. There were some buildings in the city with war damage. You could still find houses in ruins, never repaired since the war, with unused bullets and other WWII trinkets. There were forests, lakes, and even a nude beach or two!

We were able to travel anywhere the subway went, as long as we stayed on the U-Bahn, and didn't mistakenly take the S-Bahn, which traveled through the East. We had bikes (I was never old enough to drive there—you had to be 18), and Berlin has a very well-developed system of bike lanes. Everyone could go anywhere on their bikes. Even though I rode mine to school for five years, in rain, snow or shine, I remember having to go to some Colonel's office and explain that, "No, it wasn't me whose name the bus driver reported as misbehaving, someone must have given my name!" But between the buses and subway, we could get to any section of West Berlin, and to almost any street. The public transportation was amazing, and something I have missed tremendously in the years since.

Being in Berlin affected every facet of our lives, in such a positive way. We could drive to Italy, Spain, England, Switzerland, France, and so on. To say that we were afforded tremendous opportunity, in so many areas, wouldn't begin to explain how lucky we were. We were witnessing history, living in a friendly foreign country, in a time when it was still safe enough to do so. What more could we have wanted?

USING THE U-BAHN system is really quite simple. First, make sure that you've paid for your ride, as free-loaders pay an on-the-spot DM 20 fine if caught. To go from Oskar-Helene-Heim to the British FX at Theodor-Heuss-Platz, for example, ride the U-Bahn to Wittenbergplatz and transfer to the Line 1 train heading to Ruhleben (the destination and color-coded line number are on the front of each train and posted prominently elsewhere), getting off at Theodor-Heuss-Platz.

For another example, say you want to go to Tempelhof Airport. Getting on at Oskar-Helene-Heim, get off at Fehrbelliner Platz, transfer to Line 7 heading to Zwickauer Damm, get off at Mehringdamm and transfer to Line 6 heading to Alt-Mariendorf, riding one stop to Flughafen (Airport).

There are maps of the U-Bahn system in all trains and U-Bahn stations, and free small ones that you can ask for at ticket booths.

The doors on U-Bahn cars close automatically as in the States, but you must open them manually at U-Bahn stations. Please observe the "Raucher" (Smoking) and "Nichtraucher" (No Smoking) signs on the cars.

Warning: U. S. personnel and their dependents are forbidden from riding the U-Bahn (Lines 6 and 8) into or through East Berlin. (Stations marked with an X are located in East Berlin.) Also off-limits are the dull-red S-Bahn trains operated by the Communist government in East Berlin.

Berlin U-bahn route map

In my adult life, I don't have local friends I grew up with, whom I've known my entire life. What I do have, though, is a world that I have experienced, in which I feel completely comfortable traveling. I can't explain what we had, but I wouldn't have had it any other way. And I am so grateful to my family and government, for having given us this marvelous opportunity.

Finally, my friends from Berlin will always be the closest friends I have in my life. We just had something special. We can't explain it, but it's there. Ask any Berlin Brat!

Peter Stein Class of 1980
1965-66; 1975-80

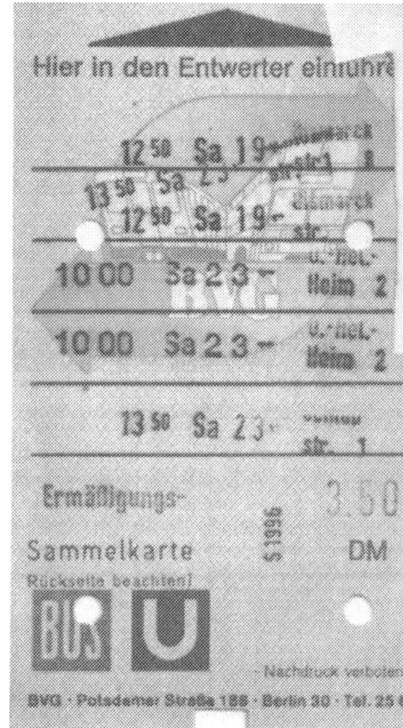

Sammelkarte- U-bahn/bus multi-ride ticket had to be punched for each ride. The U-bahns operate on an honor system with only occasional inspection of tickets.

Growing up a Berliner

The Wall Experience

I grew up in Berlin. I was actually born there, in 1962– six months after the Berlin Wall was built. I had a lot of brothers and sisters– there were ten of us. When the Wall went up my parents had 7 children in the city. One of the many stories our father told us was about the early days of the Wall. We had really tall trees in our back yard, and when the Wall was going up the Soviets were flying their MIG jets at tree top level, they were just skimming over the top of the city, and actually skimmed over the tops of the trees in our backyard. We also had a bomb shelter in our home, obviously families were thinking of contingent plans at that time.

My dad went down to the Wall with a neighbor friend of his and saw firsthand the Soviet and American tanks facing each other off. The soldiers were up in the buildings locked and loaded. That experience was very real for them. Growing up in Berlin we were always conscious that we were in a free city in the middle of a Communist country. If you got on your bike, and drove far enough you were going to hit the wall. You just couldn't move freely in and out of the city, you had to make arrangements. Anyone who rode on the Duty Train with sports teams remembers the train stopping all night and the Soviet and East German troops surrounding the train and coming on board creating an eerie environment.

So, when the Wall came down in '89, it was almost miraculous. It happened so suddenly. Having grown up there, we never knew if that was truly going to happen. Just the whole concept of Germany even being reunified after the fall of the Wall, was incredible. We saw the Soviets as this big bear. They were this huge empire. When it fell, it all moved so quickly. I remember picking up the phone and calling my mom, and saying to her, "You're not going to believe this, you've got to turn on the TV!"

She responded, "We're watching it right now, we know what's going on!" It was a huge deal for our family, it was very personal.

Sports at BAHS

We were a very sports-oriented family, we all played sports while we were there. Not only did we play high school sports, but we also played AYA -American Youth Association- which later came to be called the DYA, Dependent Youth Activities. So when I went on to high school at Berlin American High School, I played on the football team, I played varsity three years, I was team captain my senior year. I also wrestled; I wrestled all four years, two or three years on varsity. I was team captain my senior year there. Those were the two main sports that I played.

The school's athletic programs were first class, well equipped and we had good coaches. One of the cool things was that a lot of the coaches were students' fathers, who were in the military. A lot of them had played in college, or competitively at the high school level. They were able to come out and assist the faculty coaches. So we had some really unique perspective from a lot of people from all over the United States. It was a great opportunity. I think that anyone who played sports in Germany or at Berlin American High School has to have pretty fond memories.

It was also a unique experience, because we were in a closed-in city with American, French and British troops there, as well as the German population. There was a very large Turkish population who were there helping to rebuild Germany after the war. It was kind of the crossroads of freedom being in Berlin. We all knew that we were in this thing together. I think the Americans and the Germans had a great respect for each other.

There were some great cultural opportunities there. Every year each Sector had Volksfest. You had the German-American Volksfest, the British and German Volksfest...the French also had a Volksfest. It was an opportunity to bring the different cultures together in a festival type atmosphere. Each culture had an opportunity to showcase- the French would have things that were unique to France, and the Germans would have their part. Having the opportunity to be able to go out and eat in different restaurants and meet people from all over the world was amazing.

I think the real benefit of living in Berlin was that it gave us a much broader view of the world. I think we're much more culturally sensitive people from that experience; we were a minority in another country. And we had to learn, not only to stick together, but also even within the American community we were from all different parts of the country, we weren't from one town or from one place, so we had to learn how to get along. People came and went, so you also had to learn to say goodbye a lot; and to say hello to new people and get to know them.

This account is a transcription of the video interview with Mr. Dan Short

Danny Short, Class of 1981
1962-1981

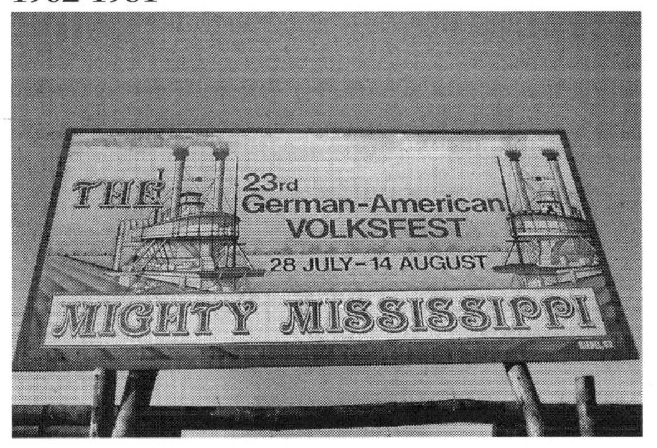

Each German-American Volksfest had/has an American geographical theme and was hosted in the American Sector next to Truman Plaza- the main base shopping area.

The Iran Hostage Crisis

I worked at Tempelhof in the Officer's Club as a waitress my senior year of high school. We Air Force Brats didn't have the luxury of being close to the American compound like my friends who worked at the Harnack Haus. I had a 45 minute U-bahn ride to and from work.

One evening when I was working at Tempelhof, my mother called me. This rarely happened, because due to security issues, phone usage was at a minimum in Berlin. We even had an egg timer by the phone to remind us of our time limit. When I answered the call at work, my mother asked me if I had my letter jacket on. Of course I did, because I wore it proudly everywhere I went. That day, she asked me to wear it inside out when I returned from work because I didn't need Berlin American High School broadcasted everywhere. As you might imagine, letter jackets screamed, "American." I asked her why and she only responded with, "Just do it." I could tell by the tone of her voice that she was serious.

I think that was the quietest U-bahn ride I ever had. I found a seat in the corner with my back up against the wall and tried not to make eye contact with anyone. After I got home, my mother told me it was because of the Iran hostage crisis and we were possible "targets." For a brief time during the Iran hostage crisis, Americans were even given a curfew of 10:00 pm.

Besides this incident, I never really felt threatened in Berlin. We would often joke about, "Here come the Russians," when we would hear a sonic boom—but there was a brief time I didn't know if I really was safe or not.

Karen Paige Seller, Class of 1980
1976-1980

Do You Hear What I Hear?

I've often thought about why we Berlin Brats are such a close group of friends. I believe one of the reasons is because of our many weekend "slumber parties" on the Duty Train. We took the Duty Train whenever we travelled from West Berlin to West Germany. It would take us all night to travel through East Germany. Since all the other American schools were in the West, we travelled on the Duty Train quite often. We spent so much time together bunked up in 6-bed cabins we became the best of friends. We would leave on Thursday evening, travel all night through the East and arrive in Frankfurt Friday morning. We would travel to our destination via bus on Friday, play our sporting events, spend the night in the gym on cots or in "sponsor" homes, head back to the train station on Saturday afternoon, ride all night again and arrive back in Berlin Sunday morning.

10
BERLIN
12
GOOD FOR TWO — Karen Sellers pops in two points for the Lady Bears during their first game to add to the winning score of 43 to 33. (U.S. Army Photo by Jim Joerger)

Karen shoots two for the Lady Bears

After traveling all night and arriving in Frankfurt in the morning, there was always a bus waiting to transport us to whichever military installation we were traveling to for our sporting event. The busses we rode on were usually pretty nice. Even our school busses were Mercedes, since we lived in Germany. Although the busses did vary, they usually always had an intercom system on them. We would use the intercom on the bus to entertain each other. I used to like to pretend I could sing by singing backup for the others who actually could. Sometimes we even had requests.

It still amazes me that since we would get to Frankfurt hours before the train was scheduled to leave, our coaches would give us free reign of the city. Most of us would head for McDonald's first because we didn't have one in Berlin. Then we would head out in groups on our own adventures after our bellies were full. As far as I know, none of us ever missed the train. I did hear a story of some of the football players having to run and catch the train as it was already pulling out, but they made it.

One night on the train, several of us decided to sing a song to one of the Russian guards as the train was stopped and being "checked" on our trek through the East. The train would stop periodically as we passed through East Germany to be inspected by the Russian and East German guards to make sure no one was trying to defect. This evening, we had the window of our compartment down and sang our hearts out to the guard with all our heads hanging out the window. I think we sang, "Fire," by the Pointer Sisters.

After we finished singing, the others went on their way and I was at the window alone. I remember looking out into the darkness with my arms resting on the window sill wondering what was out there. Then in the quiet, I thought I heard something. I lifted my head and looked around. I heard it again, "What is your name?" I realized it was the Russian guard we had been singing to, talking to me. I looked at him and said, "What? Are you talking to me?" He was trying to whisper when he said, "Yes, what is your name?" At that point I went into panic mode.

I was raised to fear anything to do with communism and this was something that scared me. I jumped up, ran out of the compartment and down the corridor to the lounge car where the coaches and parent sponsors were sitting. All I could say was, "He talked to me! He talked to me!" I remember Mr. Conway, my coach, telling me they thought it looked like the guard was talking, but they weren't sure. Then he looked at me and said, "Well, did you tell him your name?" When I told him I hadn't, I think all he said was, "Good." The adults all had a good laugh out of it. Probably a big part of it was from the look on my face.

Sometimes, I wonder what kind of impression I left on that guard. I was frightened at the time, because I never really saw someone who was a Communist as someone who could possibly have a heart and care about others. Truth is, he was probably about the same age as us. I have wondered over the years if he wished he could defect, and if so, did he?

Karen Paige Seller, Class of 1980
1976-1980

"Everybody knows taking pictures from the Duty Train window is strictly 'Verboten.'"
View of the Wall taken from the Duty Train window

"US Army Berlin Duty Train Entering Berlin through the Wall, 1982" courtesy of Ret. USAR Col. Thomas Millen, former LTC, Transportation Chief, Berlin Brigade

One Year in Berlin

Usually when our parents received their orders they were either concurrent (travel together as a family/sponsored) or deferred (non-sponsored and no quarters/housing available). Most of our trips were concurrent except two. The second one being Berlin! My sister Melissa and I just happened to be off age to travel by ourselves. My Dad was assigned to Berlin, Germany during my junior year in high school. But since he got deferred travel, my sister and I got stuck finishing out our second school of the year in rural Alabama with our grandparents.

Dad had to be on base in March. Mom and the dog travelled in April. As soon as school was done in May, my sister Melissa (age 14) and I (age 16) flew to Berlin without our parents (two teenage girls and eight pieces of luggage). We had to travel from Montgomery to Atlanta via Eastern Airlines, change planes in Atlanta, then fly to New York's JFK Airport.

Once there, we had to taxi (before AirTrain) from the Eastern Airlines terminal to the Pan Am terminal. The taxi driver could fit only seven bags in his trunk with one bag in the front seat. He drove us to Pan Am terminal, got our bags out, and then left. When I counted bags, I discovered that my red suitcase was missing! It donned on me that it was still in the front seat. I told Melissa to stay with the seven bags while I ran toward the direction of the taxi– as I'm running, I see a guy (our taxi driver) jogging towards me with my red suitcase flopping off his leg. I thanked him for bringing it back. Once I got that bag back, I made my way back to my sister.

We then got a porter to take our bags in. He took us to the first available agent. When we got to the counter to check in, we discovered that we had to go to the military line, which looked to be about 60 counters away. I asked the agent if she wouldn't mind watching two of the bags--she snarled and I snapped…Long story short, we got our bags to the military counter. Now mind you we were only allowed to check 100 pounds each. The agent looked at the bags, the scales, Melissa and me three times! She wrote down 200 pound. Saved us from having to pay!! Once we got to our gate we of course were early.

Once our plane arrived, we boarded and flew to Frankfurt. Then we had to find gate 41 for our flight to Berlin. We didn't see it, so I stopped a German policeman. I asked if he spoke English. Thankfully he did. I asked where to find gate 41. He turned and started looking and didn't see it either. Then something caught the corner of my eye…a glass window that said "Passport Control" so I bent over and there was gate 41, enclosed. I thanked the policeman and we went on our way to our next flight. We boarded and took our seats. After take-off I asked the flight attendant when we were going to land, she said 55 mins. So we decided to take a nap; well 5 minutes later the captain comes over the speaker to say we were landing. Melissa and I look at each other, not knowing what was going on!

As we came in for the landing we could see The Wall! Once in the airport only my dad with his credentials could get us out of the gate area that was once again enclosed. His driver got a luggage cart and ran to get to our bags. Mom was waiting on the other side, crying! She was excited to see us, and gave us official Berlin Bears stuffed animals.

Nothing would compare to the culture shock of Berlin! This was now my senior year and fourth high school in two years. Not knowing anyone I decided to play sports (volleyball and tennis). I thought the culture shock was done until the weekend rides on the "Duty Train!" The Duty Train would leave promptly at 7 pm. We would board to our assigned sleepers, 2 to 6 beds per cabin. Some were lucky to get in the cattle car (6 person sleeper). Hated that top bunk! When the train would stop hard you sometime fell off that top bunk.

As my parents would say, we travelled "under the cloak of darkness!" We had to travel with the curtains closed. I remember peeking out of my curtains anytime we would stop. Only to see the Soviet guards standing there with their AK47 rifles. We had to stop so many times during the night because the American train played third fiddle to all the Soviet and East German trains– they took precedence over the Americans. Once we got used to the Duty Train it became part of a normal routine.

On one of my last Duty Train trips back to Berlin, both my sister and I got placed in the General's car. We decided to stay awake and sit out in the lounge of this car with the MPs. It wasn't till that point (a year of riding the train) that I discovered that the Soviets would board our train to inspect our papers! When they saw Melissa and I sitting there, they spoke in Russian to the MPs. We started laughing! Melissa and I caught the gist of what they were saying. They told the MPs we were supposed to be asleep in our assigned sleepers. Nothing more was said and they got off at the next stop! Of course after the Russians got off we all had a good laugh!!

The Duty Train itself is that– a Duty. We had to obey the laws set forth. When traveling with our sports team we were assigned sleepers with the same sex in one car. Boys in one and girls in another. We weren't allowed to mingle with the opposite sex (however a classmate and I broke that rule on one train trip)! When we had to go use the lavatory that in itself was another story: the water was non-potable, so we could brush our teeth, but we could not swallow. When the toilet was flushed we could see the tracks going by inside the toilet. Yep our waste went out on the tracks into the fields. And then in the morning an hour before pulling in, the conductor would come and knock/tap on the window on everyone's cabin, to make sure we were all awake. Then the waiter would come through selling orange juice, coffee, tea and snacks.

Living in Berlin went from culture shock to one of the greatest experiences of my life, and I would never ever trade it for the world.

Theresa Ledbetter, Class of 1980
1979-1980

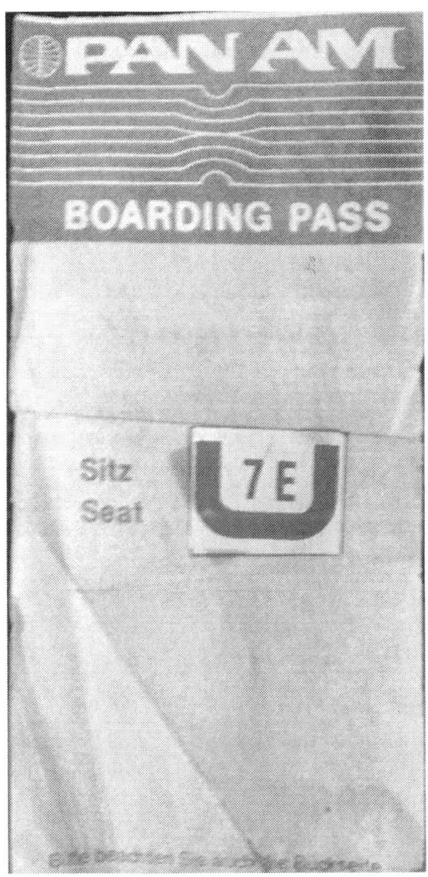

Pan American World Airways boarding pass, 1983. Pan Am first began providing military transport of US troops overseas during WWII.

Remembering Berlin

East Berlin

My mother was a travel agent when we lived in Berlin. She used to take tour groups to East Germany, and I would go on her tours quite a lot because I like to shop. She knew all the great shopping places and all of the places to get the things that I wanted. I really love clothes and shoes, so I could get all of the latest leather shoes. They were behind in fashion--they weren't as updated as West Berlin– however they had a lot of great leather goods. I still have shoes from East Berlin, and purses and a couple of belts.

I used to think that East Berlin was cold– but Germany was cold period. But it seems like the climate would change when you go to East Berlin, and everybody would be standing around watching us and looking at us because it was a Communist city. They were really under a different regime than West Berlin was. I had a lot of good experiences there, a lot of good experiences. A lot of good shopping, seeing people.

The Ishtar Gate at the Pergamom Museum— one of five internationally significant museums on Museum Island in former E. Berlin. The Ishtar Gate gets its name from the goddess Ishtar to whom it was dedicated. The gate is 46 feet tall made with glazed brick with rows of bas-relief animals.

One time my parents took us on a trip to see the wall of Babylon at a museum. I can't remember where that was, I just know it was in East Berlin. I saw a documentary on TV about five or six years ago, and was reminded of that museum where we saw that wall [Ishtar Gate].

Shortly after arriving in Maryland after leaving Berlin, I met a lady from Berlin, which was unusual. She told me she married an American and moved here. She said her brother was killed in East Berlin. Her family lived there when the Wall went up– she was a little girl. Her brother was trying to get out and he jumped from their apartment building to try to jump over the Wall, but was shot in the hip. He lay there for an hour screaming for help, because the East German Police would not let the West German Police, or Americans, or the British who were there as well, get him. So he lay there and bled to death. And that was in the days before they had CNN and satellites and all that.

I will always remember that story. Half her family was in East Berlin and the other half was in West Berlin. Her family was divided all those years. When that Wall came down I thought about that and thought about her brother. I can't remember his last name, but I remember his first name was Peter ...I'll always remember that story.[Peter Fechter, d. Aug. 17, 1962]

The Fall of the Wall

When I think back on how I felt about the day the Wall came down—I consider it to be one of the greatest things to happen in our lifetime. Because that Wall being up and the way the East Germans were oppressed, it was like a form of slavery. They were told where they had to work, how they had to work, how much money they could earn. Unless you were one of the select few, and most of the selected few were like the athletes who were on the East German Olympic teams, you were really oppressed.

I remember when the Wall came down, being at home and seeing something on TV about the Berlin Wall. Anytime that I saw anything on TV about Berlin, it would immediately get my attention. And [that day] they were saying the Wall was coming down. And that, to me, was one of the greatest days that I could remember. I was crying, I was calling people that I knew that had been in Germany saying, "The Wall is coming down, the Wall is coming down! Turn on CNN, the Wall is coming down!"

Military Life

The thing I hated most about military life was moving– you were always leaving your friends. I went to four different high schools, with Germany being the last one. I came from a really big high school in the States called Highland High in Albuquerque, NM where there were thousands of students, to Berlin where there were 300 students including the middle schoolers. So that was really what you all call it these days a 'downgrade,' a really big downgrade. I was miserable, I hated it. I remember crying the first night we got there and saw the high school. "I don't want to go to school here, I want to be back at Highland, being a cheerleader, being a part of everything. I don't want to go to school here!"

The first day I got there, one of the first people I met, and he's dead now, bless his heart, was JC Cleary. Just thinking about JC brings a tear to my eye. JC Cleary came in to the office and he said, "Hey how you doing, I'm JC where you from?" and I told him. "What grade are you in?" I said, I'm a senior and Trisha said, "I'm a junior" and he said "OK, great, you're gonna love it here." I remember thinking, I don't see how that's possible.

A few minutes later Cletis Smith '80 and Charles Henry '80 ran down and said the same thing, "You're gonna like it here!" I thought, these people are really friendly. Overall, I didn't want to leave when we left Germany. I met so many people, made so many friends, and had great, great times. My family travelled all over Germany, we travelled all over Europe– we were always going someplace.

Yoshika and Carolyn either headed to the Kudamm to go shopping, or returning from the Kudamm.

Speaking of going out, Yoshika Lowe '83 had a strict mother, but she would let her go out with me. And I used to go and get her and my sister Trisha and take them to do all the things they weren't supposed to be doing, which was partying. It was all sweet innocent fun, but they were partying with me.

But looking back on it, it's been about 30 years since we left Germany. I think of all the people that we are still in touch with and the people we've had fun with, and all the things we did, I realize I wouldn't trade being a military brat for anything in the world.

That is why I work for an airline, so I can take my kids different places and show them the world. The military community is a big melting pot. If you want to, really I would think, stamp out prejudice this is the way to do it, because there's no black or white in the military. We're all military and that's that.

This account is a transcription of the video interview with Ms. Carolyn Lindsey Grobes.

Carolyn Lindsey Grobes, Class of 1980
1979-1983

Sightseeing in East Berlin

Socialist workers near Alexanderplatz

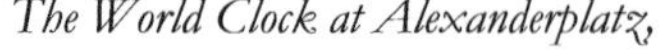

The World Clock at Alexanderplatz,

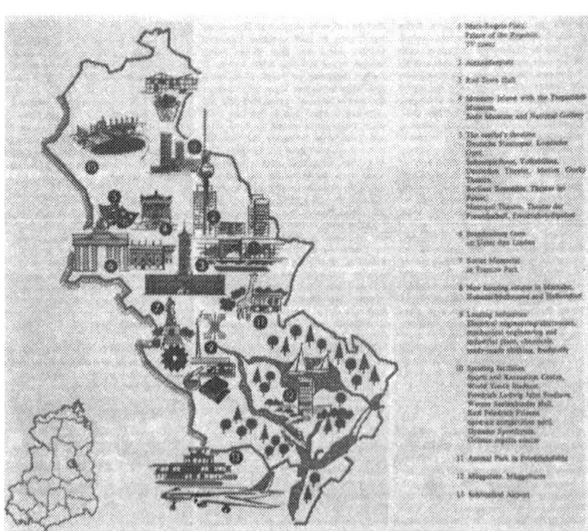

Left: Alte Nationalgalerie (Old National Gallery); Above: Berliner Dom (Berlin Cathedral)

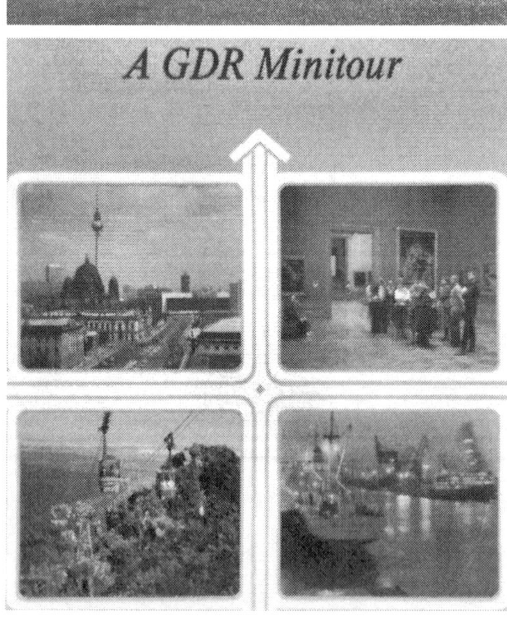

Left: GDR tour book with pictures of things to do and see in E. Berlin. Above: Tourist map of sites in E. Berlin.

Working in the City

We arrived in Berlin in November of 1979; it was a cold and dark day. We had five children in our family so we were to be issued a large house, but the house wasn't ready when we arrived. So, we moved into temporary quarters at Pückler, in the Dahlem district. While there, we would take our dog on long walks in the Grünewald. What an adventure that was! The woods were thick and got darker as the paths went deeper into the woods. Some days you could hear the dog training school that was located further into the woods.

One day when I was thirteen, I was walking alone with my dog. It was chilly and the leaves were on the ground. I was getting a creepy feeling that I wasn't alone, so I quickened my pace. At one point it was clear that I was not alone. I stopped in my tracks and looked into the woods, just off the path. There, just about 20 feet from me was the notorious Gruney Man. He was tracking along with me and making obscene gestures. I called my dog and took off. If it hadn't happened to me, I wouldn't have believed that story if someone told it to me. However, I saw him several more times over the years, and it always freaked me out.

We eventually moved into larger quarters the following summer over by Thielalle, which was and is an affluent part of Dahlem. Mr. Schmoll and Mr. Sullivan (two well-liked teachers at BAHS) also lived there for a time. It was a great neighborhood. Because of the size of the houses, all of the Mormons and the Catholics lived there with their big families. These homes, part of the affluent borough of Dahlem, had been requisitioned after the war when the American Forces occupied the Steglitz-Zehlendorf district. We could walk to the Duck Pond (a popular local pond and sometimes hangout, in nearby Dreipfuhl Housing Area) and to the Harnack.

I started working at the Harnack House when I was sixteen. The Harnack House, originally built as a 'centre for intellectual and scientific life,' had been turned into the Officers Mess by the American Forces. It was a beautiful place, frequently used for affairs of state and diplomatic events. It was even the locale for many of Berlin American High School's special events such as junior-senior proms, homecoming dances, and athletic banquets/dances. It was a great place to work.

All the American students who were employed there would work Sunday Brunch and all the big Dining In ceremonies (also known as formal mess dinners or regimental nights) and parties. We got an unexpected view of some old Army traditions that are normally reserved only for active duty members. We ran all over that building in all kinds of hiding places behind the kitchen, in the basement, behind the stage and all the secret passages. That building was a giant playground for the high school students working there.

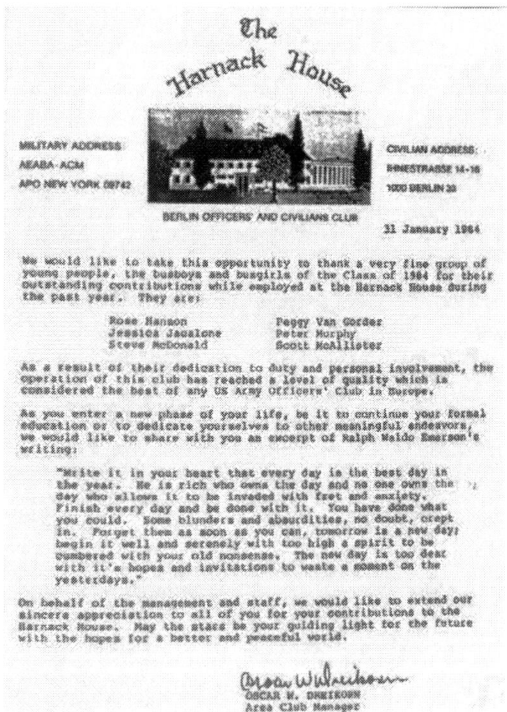

The Harnack House

MILITARY ADDRESS:
AEABA-ACM
APO NEW YORK 09742

CIVILIAN ADDRESS:
IHNESTRASSE 14-16
1000 BERLIN 33

BERLIN OFFICERS' AND CIVILIANS CLUB

31 January 1984

We would like to take this opportunity to thank a very fine group of young people, the busboys and busgirls of the Class of 1984 for their outstanding contributions while employed at the Harnack House during the past year. They are:

Rose Hanson — Peggy Van Gorder
Jessica Jacalone — Peter Murphy
Steve McDonald — Scott McAllister

As a result of their dedication to duty and personal involvement, the operation of this club has reached a level of quality which is considered the best of any US Army Officers' Club in Europe.

As you enter a new phase of your life, be it to continue your formal education or to dedicate yourselves to other meaningful endeavors, we would like to share with you an excerpt of Ralph Waldo Emerson's writing:

"Write it in your heart that every day is the best day in the year. He is rich who owns the day and no one owns the day who allows it to be invaded with fret and anxiety. Finish every day and be done with it. You have done what you could. Some blunders and absurdities, no doubt, crept in. Forget them as soon as you can, tomorrow is a new day; begin it well and serenely with too high a spirit to be cumbered with your old nonsense. The new day is too dear with it's hopes and invitations to waste a moment on the yesterdays."

On behalf of the management and staff, we would like to extend our sincere appreciation to all of you for your contributions to the Harnack House. May the stars be your guiding light for the future with the hopes for a better and peaceful world.

OSCAR W. DREIKORN
Area Club Manager

Harnack House full page yearbook ad for the class of '84

When we worked special events at the Harnack House, we might get off work around 11pm. If we hurried we could get on the U-Bahn and go downtown by midnight, before the trains shut down until 4am. I remember being downtown at dance clubs and bar hopping. I am sure many of my classmates remember the *Klo* with its clothes lines and bed pan beer and toilet paper rolls on the tables. A long-running tradition was to go to the Hofbrauhaus on graduation night for huge steins of traditional German bier. The Ku'damm was full of adventure, both day and night: shopping at KaDeWe, the second largest department store in the world (Harrods of London is bigger), eating Spaghettieis by the peep shows and meeting folks at the Athena Grill.

Later, I had the pleasure of working at the golf course bar and restaurant, too. It was managed by the Harnack House. In my senior year they trained me to be the bartender and as soon as I turned 18 (February) they made me a bartender. I got to meet a slew of people: the US and British military of every rank, the wealthy Germans that could afford the guest membership and the odd string of civilians that worked with the military.

As the bartender, I heard all kinds of stories. I heard firsthand how Major Arthur Nicholson (famously known as the last casualty of the Cold War) was shot on March 24, 1985 by a Russian sentry. I heard the details about the difficulty in getting his body back from the Russians. I was told about the care of Rudolf Hess (former leader of the Nazi Party under the Third Reich) at Spandau Prison and what it was like to be around him.

Another customer, a German man, told me about his children being stuck in the East. He would visit them regularly, but he couldn't help them because he wasn't allowed to bring anything over the border. Yes, I heard a lot of great stories working as a bartender in West Berlin.

Rose Hanson, Class of 1984
1979-1985

Partners in Crime

We had the greatest adventures traveling around Germany! I met Yoshika Lowe '83 through sports, a friendship over these many years that has led to us writing this book together. School days when I first got to Berlin were spent just learning about the city itself. I don't think I hung out with just one group, I was everywhere. I rarely met a schoolmate I didn't like. I had a habit of sticking myself into bullying situations; nobody was too small or too big that I didn't stand up for them. Charlotte Redd (Wood) '82, Orlando Rivera '81, Christie Schleifer (Przywojski) '83, and I had the most fun, dancing at DYA dances and having a great time exploring Berlin.

Trisha, Charlotte, Orlando and Christie

Tracey Turner '82 was the best partner in crime over my stay in Berlin! Most of our adventures began when Tracey would wonder what there was to do wherever we were. On one sports trip, we got matching hats and T-shirts printed up with our nicknames on them. One DYA trip, we bought toy cap guns, and fired them at people on the Autobahn, making cars swerve and their occupants curse at us profusely! I remember skipping school to go to the Wannsee one cold winter day. We got there and the lake was frozen over. The ice had peeled away from the retaining wall about 6 inches, so we had to jump over the rails to the ice, where we spent time skating in our tennis shoes, bothering two old men who were ice fishing.

On a trip to Karlsruhe with the DYA, one of our favorite destinations, we missed the DYA event bus back to Frankfurt and had to take the military bus there! I remember dancing in the Frankfurt RTO one time surrounded by a crowd of German people, as we thought we were going to be famous!

My older sister Carolyn was always with us on our outings and we were able to go out to adult places in Berlin as long as Yoshika's mother knew we were with her! One time, Carolyn snuck us into the club at McNair Barracks (US Army base in Berlin), the Starlight Grove, through the kitchen. Renault, brother of Loren Washington '83, was working in the kitchen, so we came through the back gate fence and through the kitchen. We slid out the kitchen door along the wall and she met us to give us our marching orders, which we promptly forgot, just excited to be out at an adult club!

She told us, "Don't do anything to make yourselves stand out, if you need something come find me." Well, pretty soon, she had to get Yoshika, who was complaining loudly because the Pac Man machine had taken her quarters!

I was in Candy land! My dad didn't allow us to date the young GI's, but he didn't say ANYTHING about the German men and I have a thing for Dolph Lundgren lookalikes, which Stefan Mueller was close enough to! Well after placing myself strategically in his space, "Mister Magic" came on and he smiled and asked me to dance (I was SO obvious) and we were off to the races! The dance called the Smurf was out then and we began to do the Smurf in a square around the outside of the floor, knocking people left and right! Talk about being conspicuous!

I was just about to round a corner at the breakdown part, when Carolyn grabbed my arm and pulled me off the floor better than Sandman on *Showtime at the Apollo*! She screamed at me, "Have you lost your d@#*

mind? What did I tell you and Yoshika?" By then Yoshika was at her side, giggling maniacally! "You all act like you've never been OUT before!" At that screamed judgment, Yoshika and I both began to laugh until we cried. Needless to say it was a very short night after that and it took some convincing for her to take us anywhere else but the Riverboat or the Talk of the Town nightclubs after that.

Yoshika and Trisha, 1982

And then there are the stories that we can't write about, but that bring a smile to our faces, all Berlin Brats have a shared heritage of scrapes that they got into that we KNOW better than to write down.

The best part about being in Berlin was its isolation. We learned to only depend on each other, because if we were ever attacked, we knew we would be on our own until or even if help came. It didn't matter what color you were, what music you liked, how you dressed, how smart or how dumb you were, we stuck together.

I only remember one incident of racial negativity the entire time I was there. We were all at the base gym, our regular gathering point and a guy called someone a racial slur. He was sitting on a brick wall that was about mid waist height. Out of nowhere, all we saw was a red haired blur in a blue polyester shirt that rippled in the wind, launch itself through the air, and with one tennis shoe to the face, Bryan Frazier '82 knocked that guy off the wall! We erupted in laughter, clapping and yelling out praise for him! Bears stick together.

With the coming of the Internet and Facebook, we have been privileged to get in touch with Berliners we lost touch with and share our stories. Growing up in Berlin was a time of magic, and even though Brats can boast of having lived in multiple duty stations around the world, being stationed in Berlin was a perfect place for me to understand that being an American wasn't about race, culture, language, rank, ability, education or any number of small things that we hide behind when we are uncomfortable with ourselves or others. It's about having the backs of our fellow brothers and sisters and reaching a hand out to bring others into the tribe whenever they wish to join us.

Trisha A. Lindsey, Class of 1982
1979-1984

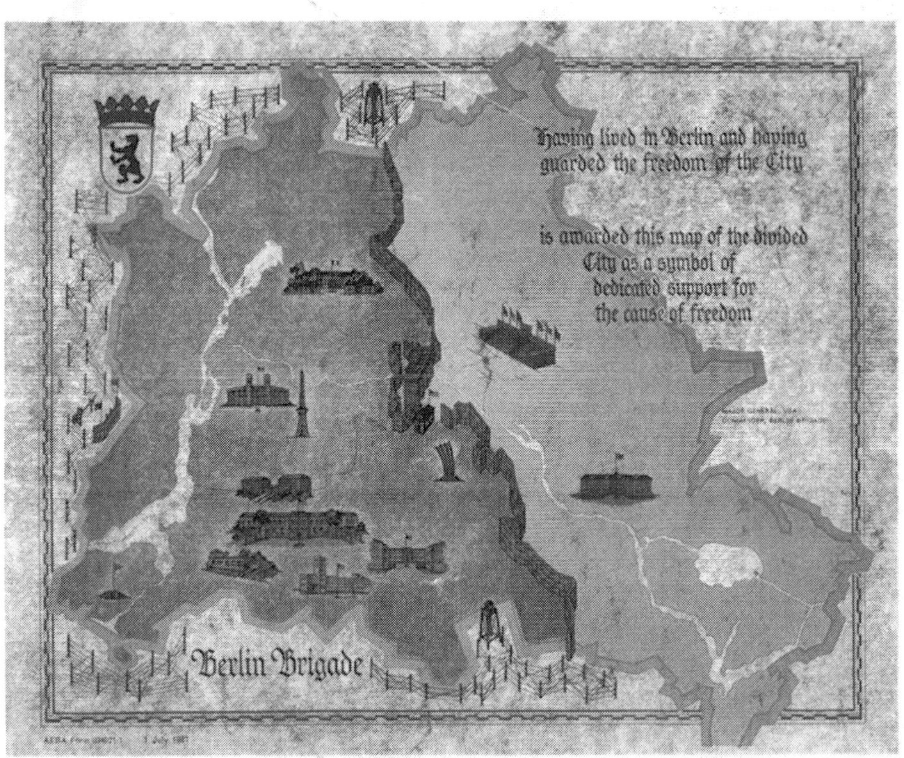

A map of the Divided City showing the Wall that separates East from West Berlin and the boundary between West Berlin and East Germany on all other sides.

Destined for Berlin

I was fifteen, a freshman in high school and my younger sister was fourteen in the eighth grade. It was 1979 when we traveled to Berlin– our first tour overseas as military brats. We were from Chicago and had no idea that our mother had eloped and taken a honeymoon trip to Puerto Rico. When our Mother returned from what we thought was a mini-vacation, she sat us down and shared the exciting news that we would be moving to Berlin!

My response was one of ecstatic joy. I always knew in my heart that we would travel to far away countries. In fact I had recurring dreams of traveling to unknown places. My thoughts of moving became a well-kept secret dream and hope of a better future and adventurous life! With the surprise announcement of my mother's new status as a military wife, I suddenly realized my dreams would soon become reality.

My sister's response was quite the opposite, she was not happy to say the least, but Berlin was a city of intrigue, fun and so much to do! Berlin's diversity, culture and great food could turn around the most stubborn of critics. How could she not help but fall in love with such a beautiful city, rich with so much history!

My mother was now a married woman! After all she had been through she deserved to be happy! Our step-father had already previously served ten years in the Army. He was my mother's childhood friend, next door neighbor and now my mother's lifetime love and mate! We looked him over as if to say with our eyes, "You better treat our mother right!" He certainly had the look of a man in love! Well of course– our mother was a gorgeous woman! What man wouldn't marry her! He would have to be blind not to notice her beauty from the inside out!

However, ten years earlier my mother was engaged to be married to another man who she believed was truly her soul mate, he was handsome, taller than the average man, standing at a height of six feet-five inches. Mother's fiancé was a Marine. One of The Few and Proud, he had an uncompromising sense of purpose. He was a loyal and faithful man with a strong belief in God and family values. He had such a great love for my mother.

I have just a few vague memories of him, but there were also some special moments that left a loving imprint on my heart when I would witness his loving expressions! Like the day he carried my mother in his arms as she laughed and as he gently spun her around in a circle. There were a few times he was Daddy and he would read us fairy tale books before bed. My mother's time of engagement was quickly interrupted. He had to go off to war. He fought in the Vietnam War and he promised her when he returned they would fly to Hawaii and get married.

He never made it back, he died a Hero! He was my step-father's older brother! It's strange how life takes its twist and turns and somehow fate always prevails. It was as if his promise to marry Mother was finally fulfilled ten years later through his younger brother. God had pre-destined us to be a military family!

Life in Berlin would be the beginning of our military life and an experience that would impact our lives forever! I remember how different Berlin was compared to Chicago. Daily living was at a much slower pace than I was accustomed to. The people seemed to enjoy life much more. The only fast pace motion I saw were the cars on the Autobahn. There was no speed limit, which horrified my mother. I couldn't wait to get behind the wheel, unfortunately for me that did not come until several years later!

The legal drinking age in Berlin was 16. In Chicago I never considered drinking as a teenager, but drinking in Berlin became a lifestyle. It was fun at the time, but later taught me some tough lessons when I overindulged–now that is another story.

I remember our first dance at the DYA. Stepping into a new environment for the first time for my sister and I was not scary, but sheer pleasure! We knew that we were wearing the latest fashions that screamed Chi town: "The Windy City!" I don't know if anyone cared, but it sure looked to us that they could use some help with their wardrobes!

Now when we saw all eyes were on us, we were not shy! Like true Puerto Ricans we hit the dance floor and showed off our dancing skills straight off the streets of Chicago! Oh yes, it didn't take us long to adapt! This military life was going to be one adventure after another! My sister's attitude actually changed when she realized, not only are we the new girls in town, but we could actually become the new trend setters! Ok ...maybe that's a bit of an exaggeration, let's just say we became very popular and we made a lot of friends! Berlin had impacted our lives in such a great way that it became home! Even decades later we still call Berlin our home!

Evelin Cruz Collins, Class of 1982
1979-1982

Athlete of the Year

I was a very good athlete in three sports when I was in high school, but when we moved at the end of my freshman year to Berlin, Germany, I was crushed. We were stationed at Kirtland Air Force Base in Albuquerque, New Mexico. I was going into 10th grade, and my older sister was entering her senior year. We were shell shocked coming from a school that had almost a thousand students in the senior class to one that had less than one hundred. It was cold, wet and rained continually, a real change from the year round warm weather of New Mexico.

I decided to try out for cheerleading, accepting finally that some miracle wasn't going to happen and we would not be reassigned back to Kirtland. I had to wait for seniors to rotate out of the basketball and volleyball teams to try out the next year. I made one lifelong friend who was only at BAHS for a few months, before her family was reassigned to Kaiserslautern, W. Germany, Charlotte Redd (Wood) '82. We wrote and called when we could and when track and field season came, I knew I had to run track because we had a track meet in Kaiserslautern! I had run track at previous schools and was no stranger to the 100m hurdles.

BAHS Cheerleading: Trisha and Mina on top left and right

I worked really hard that season. We were blessed to have a coach who had been an Olympic athlete himself, Perry Jones. He was a Pan Am pilot, the first African-American pilot that I had ever met. Pan Am was my favorite airline; one of my earliest memories was flying Pan Am to Madrid, Spain for my Dad's assignment at Torrejón Air Force Base in the 1960s.

We had track meets in Berlin, but also got to travel on the Duty Train overnight to Frankfurt, where we would then take a bus to reach our destination: one of the DoD's schools in the 'Zone' or what was then the Federal Republic of Germany. Before every away meet Mr. Jones would meet us at the bus at the Frankfort RTO and he would bring breakfast for us! They were Pan Am bags that had a brotchen roll with salami and cheese, a strawberry yogurt, an apple and a napkin and spoon. Those sandwiches were the best!

I ran with a lot of people over the years, but Christie Schleifer '83 ran the middle distances, the 800 and 1500 meter races, she was unstoppable! Carrie Huml '82 ran the long 3000 meters and Tena Steiner '82 ran the 400 meters. I ran the 100 meters, 100 meter hurdles and did the high jump and the long jump. It was soon a normal thing for our combined first place points to beat women's teams that had upwards of 20 members or more.

We would come back to Frankfurt Saturday night, and arrive back in Berlin early Sunday morning. I would get a couple hours of sleep, and then jog over to the small Snack Store. It opened earlier than the PX on Sunday morning and it would have the Sunday copy of the *Stars and Stripes*– the Armed Forces newspaper that circulated worldwide on military posts and bases.

It was May 18, 1980, and I went to pick up my papers to see the times that were posted at other meets around Germany, only to stare at the front page in shock! The extra work I put in resulted in my name being in Armed Forces Europe's *Stars and Stripes* the morning after our first meet, with a picture on the Sports page! I was so happy, I screamed, shocking the worker behind the register and the few souls in the store at that time of the morning. I grabbed a handful, paid for them and ran all the way home to show my dad!

And life changed from that moment on, Robert Lindsey (my dad) went out of his way to make sure I was the best athlete I could be. I had the best equipment– he found me a German track team, Sud Berlin, to work out with in addition to the BAHS track team. Thanks to them, I lived one of my dreams– I got to run hurdles in the Berlin Olympic Stadium! The same field that Jesse Owens ran on in the 1936 Olympics; I also have a picture of my favorite modern era runner, hurdler Renaldo 'Skeets' Nehemiah, the first man to break the 13 second barrier in the Men's 110m high hurdles running in that same stadium.

Trisha winning the qualifying meet in Frankfurt, Spring 1980

RS AND STRIPES ★ ★ Page 25

Clearing barriers

Scoring victories in the finals of the DODDS Germany track and field championships at Schwetzingen Friday are Larry Reiman of Stuttgart (left) and Trisha Lindsey of Berlin (above). Reiman uses the Dick Fosbury technique known as the Fosbury Flop to clear 6-feet-6 to win the high-jump competition. Lindsey shows fine hurdling form on her way to the 100-meter low hurdles victory. She was clocked in 15.3. —S&S photos by Didio

Trisha at All-Germany Finals

It was a pretty big deal to get mentioned in the article notes for the meets around Germany for high school sports, but it was a REALLY big deal to be on the Sports page for the opening of the season. I was blessed to be pictured one more time while I was at BAHS in the *Stars and Stripes* and still fondly remember running to get that paper to see what they said about us that weekend.

I went to the All-Germany Finals that year for the first time, for the women's team. Tena, Carrie,

Christie, and I all went. We did so well, we placed 3rd overall out of over 30 teams! Cletis Smith '80, James Triplett '82, Orlando Rivera '81 and David Bryant '83 were standouts on the men's team. Mr. Jones was instrumental in getting Cletis back to Berlin on Pan Am in time for his senior prom.

I got to play volleyball and basketball in subsequent years, receiving All-Conference and All-Tournament honors in both sports over the next few years. I was awarded the 1982 Outstanding All-Around Female Athlete Award at a school assembly.

GERMANY TRACK & FIELD
REGIONAL FINALS
PARTICIPANT
23 - 24 MAY 1980

Trisha's ticket to the All-Germany Finals

Ms. Barlow was my P.E. Teacher for all the time I was at BAHS, and a great blessing to me. She was a constant source of encouragement. She would put together assemblies for us–I had the best time doing gymnastics with Mina Buenviaje '83. Ms. Barlow taught us to play badminton and let us do every kind of stunt we wanted to on the trampoline. She taught us to play field hockey and one of my best memories is listening to Wardi Ibrahim '83 yelling at us because we were not taking it seriously! Wardi came to our school from East Germany every day, his father was assigned to their Ambassador Service; a lot of kids had parents who paid for them to come to BAHS.

Trisha's powerful jump serve

Trisha A. Lindsey, Class of 1982
1979-1984

Once in a Lifetime Experiences

My family arrived in Berlin the summer of 1980. When my dad got his PCS orders for Berlin, I was devastated. As an Army Brat, I had already moved schools and homes multiple times. For once in my short life, I finally had friends and stability. For, I had actually been at the same school for two whole years! Both 7th and 8th grade were spent at the same middle school, and I had been ecstatic to transition to our local high school without a change of duty station. However, my dad was telling us that my brother, sister and I would again be uprooted. We would be returning to Germany.

We had lived in Hanau in the late 60's and early 70's; my sister was born in Frankfurt. But that was eons ago! Although I was never one to give my parents attitude– I could not hide my disdain and even told my dad he was ruining my life. I was so depressed, I tried to think of some way to stay behind– but there was no way. We had no close family members, both of my parents were from small country towns, and I would sooner die than live in the small Texas town. So, it was off to Berlin. When we left Fort Hood, Texas by car to New York, it was during the worst heat wave in decades. Our car broke down many times, but we somehow made it cross country. When we arrived in Berlin, on July 17th, it was actually very cold, we needed coats! Talk about culture shock!

Although we arrived in mid-July, I was able to secure a summer job for the second half of the summer. The Summer Hire program was open to all dependent youth and it was luck of the draw to work at one of a myriad of places each summer. I worked child care at the Kinder Keller that first summer, but subsequent summers I worked at the hospital as an assistant to an EENT (Eye, Ear, Nose and Throat) doctor, then at Berlin Command

HQ as an office assistant and again at Berlin Command HQ as a keypunch operator (!), and finally during my last summer I worked at the East Pass Office (making ID cards to enter East Berlin). The great thing was we were paid 8 DM per hour, which was about $4.00 - $4.50 an hour when minimum wage in the US was $3.10. Over the years I've queried other Brats about where they worked Summer Hire, and they included: the golf course, US Post Office, Rod & Gun club, Tempelhof Airport, various administrative offices in various parts of the US military command, the Harnack House, the Wannsee, the DYA, the Sports Center, the swimming pool, and the list goes on!

What do you plan to do this summer?

Four of the above Berlin Brats said they planned to take advantage of the Summer Hire Program, 1983

Besides the chance to make good money and buy my own clothes, I enjoyed the opportunities we were afforded to travel. I loved traveling on the Duty Train for school trips! One of my first school trips on the Duty Train was for a band exchange program. We went to Osterholz and spent the weekend in various band members' homes. The family that hosted me had a VCR!! This was 1980, and we were overseas, so nothing feels like home like watching movies from the States. But for those of us without a VCR, one was relegated to watching AFN or German TV, both of which were excruciatingly boring. AFN mostly played propaganda commercials: "your unguarded words on the phone could be the missing link… (cue visual of an atomic bomb blast)." It was the 'loose lips sink ships' warning. Plus, the VCR had just come out, so they ran close to $1000! We stayed up so late watching movies that I almost passed out the next day at joint band rehearsals.

I took two more band trips, which were equally enriching. The second one was the District Band Festival in Bonn. Bonn was the capital of Germany at that time. We were really surprised at how poorly funded the military community was there compared to Berlin. They had only a two lane bowling alley, while we had a full-service, multi-lane facility, with a great snack bar. Their DYA building was old, small and run-down. Ours was in a brand new building with amenities such as enrichment classes, pool tables, lounge areas, a full kitchen (for cooking classes), a full gym, a dance floor, etc.

But, the students were fun and friendly. I felt I was the luckiest of all-my host home was that of Mr. and Mrs. Lin—the Chinese Ambassador to Germany! I don't find it easy to make friends, despite being an Army Brat, but I hit it off right away with Maggie, the Chinese Ambassador's daughter. What the base lacked in accommodations (and overall size), the Ambassador's home made up for in luxury and amenities. The Ambassador's family had a flat that seemed to be comprised of two adjoining large apartments.

Unlike most of our trips I got my own bed! Usually, we slept on floors in sleeping bags Maggie and I had a room to ourselves, with our own kitchen! Maggie's dad had filled the freezer with frozen confectionaries and even more goodies were in the fridge! My only regret was that the band program kept us out attending so many events and practices that I never got to eat my fill of yummy goodies (mostly goodies not available in the Armed Forces Commissary).

I was surprised at how 'Americanized' Maggie and her very sweet family were. I also thought that, being Communists, they were required to live in the kind of austere surroundings we saw whenever we visited East Berlin. I always wondered what prevented them from defecting to the West. I had expected them to behave more like the East Germans and Soviets we had encountered over the years– guarded, secretive and paranoid. They allowed me in their home! Maggie and I talked and laughed all night like regular 'free' teenage girls.

On each of these band exchange trips we were expected to bring a gift for our host family. I brought Maggie a souvenir plate from Berlin with illustrations of various famed places in the Walled City (I thought it was fancy at the time!).

My last band trip was to an event called SOPA (I cannot remember what the acronym stood for, but it was an All-Germany competition band event). I was first chair flute, so I tried out and made it into this very special band comprised of band members from every American school in Germany. I long ago lost the poster and keepsakes that I'd tucked away, which were destroyed in a flood, but I do remember that it took place in Baden-Baden. It was a great way to meet other musically gifted students and it was a wonderful learning opportunity.

Though I had dreaded moving overseas, and especially to the scary city-behind-the-Iron Curtain, I grew to love Berlin and the opportunities the US government so graciously provided us military dependents.

Yoshika (Yhoshekia) Loftin Lowe, Class of 1983
1980-1983

Spring Break Memories

There are a lot of memories I have of Berlin but probably one of the things I remember most and really appreciate about attending Berlin American High School was spring break. Every spring, like just about every other American school, we closed for spring break. What I enjoyed about BAHS was the school sponsored trips. I lived in Berlin from 1980-1985. I went on two ski trips and a 10-day trip to the Soviet Union.

These trips are very special to me. On the first ski trip we took to Austria my most vivid memory was the fact that we were served rice…a lot. The first evening apparently we didn't eat as much as the cook expected so we were served the leftover rice the next day. When we still didn't eat it all, it appeared at breakfast (I believe in some sort of pancake). The next day it showed up in soup. It became the big joke after the ski trip with us asking each other if anyone wanted rice.

The next ski trip I took I remember the talent show at the end of the week. It was so much fun and we all laughed and it just seemed like we were all one big happy family. It didn't matter if you were in the popular group, or a jock, or a punker (emo), or a brain. We were all "Brats" even back then. This also brings about another special thing about Berlin and maybe the reason why we are so connected. In Berlin you didn't feel like an outsider. You didn't feel like you were intruding or out of place. Everyone was new at some point; everyone was going to leave at some point; and everyone understood so it didn't take but a matter of moments to be welcomed and feel like you belonged.

I have another memory from this ski trip and I guess I should start first by saying I had the pleasure of both my parents chaperoning EVERY school trip, sports or fun event (yeah, as a teenager I LOVED them doing this especially since they were sticklers for the rules). On this particular ski trip we were told not to ski down the face of the mountain until we were cleared to do so. Well, John Miller '87 and I got a little brave and a lot bored so we decided to amp up the excitement and ski the face before we recieved clearance. We did great! Not one fall, not one tumble, not one broken bone.

We were so proud and as we came to a stop at the bottom of the hill who should be standing there, hands on hips and a scowl on her face but one of the strictest chaperones. I suppose you have guessed at this point it was dear old mom and there was no getting around punishment. We were both kicked off the hill for the rest of the day. John and I couldn't believe it. But again, it was a memory I hold dear to this day and for some time after, I got teased about getting kicked off the mountain by my own mother.

I have many good memories of the trip to the Soviet Union. How many kids can say they had this opportunity? I remember staying in a different hotel each night except in Moscow and one other place. It was very cold and by the time the heat started working, we were ready to move on to the next place. I remember visiting the tomb of Stalin and the bus picking the best routes through Moscow so we didn't see the slums. I also know now that I did not appreciate all the things we were able to see and will probably never have the money or opportunity to revisit.

I was ten years old when we moved to Berlin and fifteen when we moved back to the states. I believe the teenage years play a big part in a person's life, shaping their habits and who they will become. I loved being a Brat, still do. I am proud to say "My mamma (and daddy) wore combat boots!" I wouldn't trade my time in Berlin for anything and often wish we could have stayed my remaining two years of high school. Life was so much different back in the States. But my parents returned several years later and I was able to visit again two summers during my college years.

To this day I cannot hear the words, "Coffee? Tea…?" without adding "MARBLE CAKE." Ah, the memories of the Duty Train. Several things stand out. One is having to shut the shades through the "corridor" so that we couldn't see what was going on outside of the train. The other is waking up the morning we returned to Berlin to a half-day-old room temperature McDonald's hamburger. The first McDonald's didn't arrive in Berlin until I believe late 1983 or 1984 so for the first three or so years I was there, the only McDonald's you could get was in Frankfurt. I think that's why I joined so many sports teams.

Before getting back on the Duty Train it was my routine to get a Big Mac, fries and drink plus an extra single hamburger. The hamburger always was placed just above my head where I slept that way it wouldn't get lost. When we woke in the morning I ate it before doing most anything else. To this day if we go to McDonalds and there's an extra burger I put it in the fridge so I can have it in the morning. I also don't mind drinking a warm Diet Coke straight out of the can. My American friends don't understand either of these habits, but my Brat friends do!

Dawn Hayes, Class of 1987
1980-1985

Triple Whammy

Sometimes military brats have trouble answering the question "Where are you from?" As a 17 year old freshman at the US Air Force Academy, I never had trouble with it. "Berlin" was always my quick answer. Of course the explanation took a little longer, but it was obvious after I explained I lived in Berlin three separate times growing up. I spent my last three years at Berlin American High School as a member of the class of 1983. Even then we were all aware enough to realize our years spent in the Divided City were unique and our experiences made us just a bit more worldly than the average bear. Being a military brat didn't really set me apart at a military academy, but I quickly learned that most kids didn't have any idea what it was like to have lived overseas. As an example, many entering 18 year old cadets were newly legal to drink 3.2 beer according to Colorado law back then. I realized I had a head start in the beer department.

The second part of my triple whammy was being a zoomie. Zoomie is a term for a cadet or a graduate of USAFA. Being a zoomie is a strong identity trait and provides for great rivalries with our brothers and sisters from West Point and Annapolis. Being a zoomie and a military brat certainly was not a unique circumstance at the academy or out in the real AF. I soon realized I had a third trait that I thought made me one of a kind.

I'm also a PK, a preacher's kid. My Dad was the brigade chaplain at McNair Barracks (one of the US Army bases in Berlin) from 1969-1972. The stereotypical PK is precocious and perhaps wayward. I never thought of myself as that, but being a PK isn't very common. It wasn't until 1998 that I met another triple whammy.

The 2001 Berlin Brat Reunion was in Wichita that year. We were all on buses after attending a dedication ceremony for the upcoming American Overseas Schools Historical Society museum. I was discussing my triple whammy status with Jeri Glass '72 (head of our alumni association) in the back of the bus. After I explained what I meant, she pointed to the gentleman sitting right next to me. It was then Colonel Frederick H. "Rick" Martin '77. It turns out that Rick is also a PK, is also a Berlin Brat and a zoomie! Up until that moment I had never met another triple whammy and I haven't met another one since. As Berlin Brats we are honored to claim anyone among our own, but Major General Rick Martin is one who has met with more success than most. It was a great privilege to share the stage with him at a pinning on ceremony for Lt. Col. Michelle Estes '90 at the 2012 Berlin Brat Reunion in Washington DC.

Surprisingly, I also paired up with General Martin (his first name will always have to be General to me) on a shuttle ride from the hotel to the airport after the reunion in Phoenix in 2009. It seems we are somehow drawn together by forces greater than ourselves all around the world. The fact that we are also both pilots could make for a quadruple whammy, but I'll leave it at triple for now.

Larry Speer, Class of 1983
1969-72, 1976-77, 1980-83

Gen. Martin, Lt. Col. Estes and Ret. Major Speer

Midnight Train to Frankfurt

Because of West Berlin's unique geographical location– 110 miles behind the Iron Curtain– we had to travel quite a bit to participate in extra-curricular activities. The sole means of transportation for our trips was the Duty Train—the US Duty Train was Army green, emblazoned with the Berlin Brigade insignia.

When I first began riding the Duty Train with my family on trips to the West to see my orthodontist, I hated it. We were in a car that had 6 bed births– two on either side at the bottom, which we all sat on like couches, and four more that let down from the wall. These cars we referred to as cattle cars, because it was very uncomfortable to sleep 6 to a room when the beds were so narrow and thin. My dad said that the accommodations depended on how far in advance you scheduled your trip. On all subsequent trips with my sports teams, we still slept 6 to a room, but the beds were thicker and wider. Since we traveled almost every weekend of any given sports season, we spent a lot of time on the Duty Train.

The Soviets allowed 16 to 19 trains to travel to and from Berlin. They traveled from Frankfurt and Bremerhaven to Berlin and vice versa. Because the Soviets only allowed night travel through East Germany, the train left the RTO (military train station) each night at 8:30 pm and arrived in Bremerhaven at 6:30 am or Frankfurt at 7:30 am. Shortly after we left the station, a German man would come by with a food cart selling snacks and drinks: "Coffee…tea…marble cake!" My family was of modest means, so we never purchased any food, and always brought our own snacks.

One of the really cool things about being on a sports team at Berlin American High School, was that we got to miss school on Fridays– it was an excused absence! I loved this so much that my primary motivation for joining the basketball team was to miss school on Fridays and travel away from home every weekend. We left on Thursday night and arrived in the West on Friday morning. When we played any team other than Bremerhaven or Osterholz, we took the train to Frankfurt. From there we would take an Army bus, which was waiting for us at the train station. The bus would drive us to eat breakfast at the mess hall at Rhein-Main Air Base or Ramstein Air Base, depending on which was closer to the town where we would be playing ball. When we played Bremerhaven or Osterholz, which were north, we typically took the bus to one of their mess halls.

Yoshika Loftin Lowe '83 spikes the ball

I played basketball and volleyball. My junior year I was on the JV volleyball team, and on the varsity basketball team. To be honest, the only reason I made the team (I had tried out in the States and not made the cut) was because Berlin was a small school, with few options. I happened to be tall for a girl, so despite the fact that I was awkward and uncoordinated, I made the cut! It was on our first volleyball trip that Trisha and I became friends. Despite being über popular, and a star varsity volleyball player, she was very friendly and accepting of newbies like me.

On our train trips we would leave Berlin on Thursday evening, stay up all night raising cane and arrive blurry eyed in Frankfurt. Then we took the bus to our rival city, where we played a game on Friday night, then another game on Saturday morning/afternoon. The crazy thing is, because we were Americans overseas, the military community was so tight-knit that our games, especially on Friday nights, were attended by the whole community.

The order was thus: JV girls played first, then JV boys, then Varsity girls, and finally Varsity boys (because they were the 'main event').

During my time there we had a phenomenal varsity boys' team. After we finished playing on Friday nights, we would watch the varsity boys play, then be bussed to a local school gym (the games were usually played at the main military base gym), where we would sleep on hard wood floors. Early Saturday morning, we'd be bussed to the local mess hall for breakfast. Then we'd be dropped back off at the local base gym. We were free to do whatever we wanted--but we better not miss our assigned game time!

Varsity girls' basketball team, 1982
From bottom: Antoinette B. '85, Evelin C.'82, Yoshika L.'83, Cheryl F. '85,Trisha L.'82, Jessica J.'85 I still have this jersey!

After our Saturday games, we'd ride the bus back to Frankfurt and be dropped off at the RTO. We were then told by our coaches and sponsors to meet back at the RTO in time for the train to leave. We typically had a good three or more hours to hang out in Frankfurt. The only limit to what you could do was the depth of your pocketbook. As athletes, we were always ravenous and headed straight to McDonald's because we didn't have one in Berlin at the time. The crazy part, well, crazier than being totally unsupervised for much of the weekend, was the location of the McDonald's in Frankfurt. It was on the edge of the Red Light District. That is because the main Hauptbahnhof is near the Red Light District. I don't know why more people didn't go check it out, but unlike the drinking and partying, I don't recall that being a thing.

When we ate at McDonald's (or anywhere) Trisha and I ate A LOT! I mean, we ate as much or more than the boys, who would tease us because we were both rail thin girls. We didn't care. Without a full bench to relieve us, we had the dubious honor of being required to play all four quarters of every game, every Friday and Saturday– so we were burning serious calories. After a hearty meal, we would walk to the nearest Weinerwald rotisserie restaurant. They made the BEST Grillhähnchen (grilled chicken). We would buy a whole chicken and have them cut it in two and wrap them separately. As a math person, I hit on the idea that if Trisha and I pooled our money every trip we could afford to buy more food.

At the Weinerwald it cost more to buy two half chickens than one whole one, so we ordered a whole and asked them to cut it in half! We would put them in our bags for a late night snack on the Duty Train (remember I said my family could not afford to buy snacks on the train—plus this was way better!). I always baked a batch of peanut butter cookies before each trip, placing them in a large oatmeal canister to keep them intact. Around midnight we would take out the cookies and open our packs of chicken. The wonderful aroma would waft down the hall of the Duty Train, and the guys, who were not allowed in our car, would try to sneak down and beg us for some. Of course we did not share, and they were always incredulous that two skinny little girls could each eat a half chicken! Why they never thought to plan ahead like we did, I'll never know!

Yoshika (Yhoshekia) Loftin Lowe, Class of 1983
1980-1983

A Duty Train Life: This is Our Normal

Part of living in Berlin was traveling on the Duty Train for sports trips. The Duty Train really became part of your life because you were on an island in the middle of East Germany and the only way to compete against the other teams that were in West Germany was via the Duty Train. I probably was on the Duty Train a dozen times a year going back and forth as a member of the cross country team, as well as the wrestling team to go to wrestling matches.

Living in Berlin it was easy for us to process Flag Orders and such that to get to Frankfurt– of course the Duty Train only went to Frankfurt or Bremerhaven. You'd usually get on a bus to travel to whatever school you were having that meet with that weekend, and we'd be hosted by other military families.

Typically you'd arrive in Frankfurt early in the morning, get on a bus, go compete, and then turn right around and go on the Duty Train and go back to Berlin (for a one day event). That amounts to a lot of traveling, especially, if you're trying to rest up for some kind of sporting event. But the experiences on the Duty Train really are what stand out. It was all timed and you had to hit all the right spots at all the right times so that the Russian guards and the East German guards would process everything correctly– all the paper work.

If you were awake at that time of night you'd be stuck in a train station somewhere in East Germany and see the guards with German Shepherds walking up and down the platform. All the East German guards would be trying to look all important with their hats and their uniform– glaring at you as if to make sure you didn't do anything wrong– which we never did of course.

I'm kidding about never doing anything wrong– but that was a totally unique experience. You can't think of another situation where that was your normal everyday routine for going to a meet against another team; and all the Berlin teams did that from football and golf to volleyball. Even the swim team which wasn't affiliated with the school, it was more of an independent activity, they went through the same thing and we traveled all over Europe for that type of stuff. Amazing experiences.

This account is a transcription of the video interview with Mr. Larry Speer.

Larry Speer, Class of 1983
1969-72, 1976-77, 1980-83

Typical day in the life of a Berlin Brat: On the Duty Train (left) and on a bus to the next school event (right). Tom Jones '85 (far left in first picture), Angela Ott '80(striped shirt), Mark Britton '84 (upside down), Tom Britton '83 (next to Mark), Toni Moore-Hutcherson '87 (front center in bus picture) and Ron Moffett '85 (far right in both pictures)

Behind the Iron Curtain—No Americans Live There!

I was in Berlin for the years of 1980 - 1983. What stands out in my mind most, is how little people truly know about Cold War West Berlin. When my dad told us we would be going to West Berlin I was in middle school– 6th grade. I remember telling a teacher that I would be moving to West Berlin. He told me that I must be mistaken because Berlin is behind the Iron Curtain, and no Americans live there. He was very wrong.

I entered school in the 7th grade. It was frightening, because at Berlin American High School, 7th grade was in high school. I skipped the preparation that middle school or junior high affords with the issues of first kiss, liking boys, first dances, and the like and was dumped into the cesspool of high school. When our family arrived, we were greeted at the central military bus depot by an interesting and elusive guy who said he was in high school. Among many things, he told us that half the school was sent back Stateside the previous year for drug possession in school. This type of revelation of my new life made me realize that I would have to grow up quickly.

Once I was over the initial shocks and fears, I learned to enjoy my time in Berlin and at BAHS. I even started a school club– The Bear Adventure Club. I was the first president. It was a club for adventure sports, which afforded me an opportunity to do the activities I'd always wanted to try. We learned to scuba, sail, rock climb, repel and so much more. To fund the activities of the club, I started BAHS' school store. We sold paper, pencils and pens (branded for the school), gum, candy, and other school supplies. To this day my sister mocks the club because we were underclassman, but I had fun and got to experience Berlin in a different way.

There were also a few events in Berlin that I particularly liked:

The German-American Volksfest was the first time I went to a festival with just my friends– no parents. There were rides, activities, food, and gambling– well slot machines. It was the first time I played the slots, it made me realize I didn't like losing money. I also didn't like the taste of beer, so there was no fear of my drinking with my friends. The biggest thrill for me was the bumper cars.

Then there was *Christmas,* which is great every year. However, Christmastime in Germany is almost magical, with the Christmas markets and festivals. The wood crafted gifts like nutcrackers, ornaments, and other items. I still have a hand carved house bank that I bought at one of those markets.

And *Green Week*– this was a festival of agriculture and horticulture with crafts, food, and activities celebrating countries around the world and natural products from those countries. The school would take a day off each year to load us all on buses, and off we went to the Green Week conference. Half the students and teachers did not make it back on the bus thanks to the free beer given out by the beer exhibitors. Each year I would collect posters at Green Week from the various countries that I wanted to visit.

My room was plastered with those posters. I had them on the walls, ceiling, and the door. I fell asleep dreaming about going to those countries. Those posters sparked something in me– the desire to be a world traveler. As an adult I have been blessed to visit 28 countries on six continents (and counting!). The one country I recall wanting to visit the most was the Dominican Republic. One day I'll get there too.

Another unique part of life as a military brat in Berlin was the summer work program. Each year, we would be paid the equivalent of $4 per hour (this was when the federal minimum was about $3.35 per hour). Each summer I had a different interesting job. The one I remember the most was working at the Dependent Youth Activities (DYA) Summer Camp. I got to see and experience some of the best and sometimes lesser known jewels of Berlin, like the Wannsee, Peacock Island, and the Grünewald.

There are so many more stories and events I could tell, but these are some of the highlights. The experience of living behind the Iron Curtain was beyond anything I could have ever imagined.

Pleshetta Loftin, Class of 1986
1980-1983

DYA membership card—these membership cards were bright yellow with blue lettering

Remembering a Hamster Named Max

You will have to forgive my fuzziness/rusty memory but the specific date is lost to me, although I believe it all happened some time in 1982. However the event is an amusing story that I have shared with only a few people. I will share it now in a sort of confession to those who were unwittingly duped by two high schoolers with good intentions and a twisted bit of humorous luck.

The tale happens like this. My little sister had a hamster named Max, a golden hamster that she was very attached to. It died and she was really crushed. I buried it for her in our backyard. At the time, my father was a civilian working for the Army/Air Force as a job classifier. He was a GS-12, but as a government contracted civilian he was not entitled to government housing. We lived on the economy down the street from General Boatner. His son Pete used to ride our bus. Directly behind the house we lived in was Andy Yoon '83, the Korean Consul General's son.

But my favorite bud at the time who also hung out with me and rode the same bus was Markus Fischler '84. Markus's mother was American but had remarried a German man and he attended the school as a local national. Markus was an interesting character and among many other fascinating aspects, he served on "flag duty" and wound up pulling some strings to get me on as well. We had to raise the American flag for the school and being on flag duty meant that I got to be five minutes late to first period. It was a nice perk. I also got to leave sixth period fifteen minutes before everyone else because we had to take down and fold up and secure the flag. This meant not being crushed against the lockers when leaving the crowded hallways. We'd be waiting for everyone on the bus when the bell rang.

What was not to like, right? So, back to my sister and her dead hamster Max. My sister attended an elementary school down the road from BAHS. Her bus would pass by our school in the morning a while after we were already in class. So to make her feel better I promised her that we would fly the flag at half-mast in memory of Max (I didn't expect that it would stay there too long, and I certainly had no idea of what was about to come).

I had an old harmonica, which I played fairly well and at Markus's suggestion when I shared with him what I wanted to do, I grabbed the harmonica and brought it along to play Taps for Max.

When we arrived we solemnly raised the flag (or rather, Markus did, as I played Taps) all the way up to the top of the flagpole and then lowered it to half-mast and tied it off. We went inside and started to go to our lockers and the vice principal came rushing out of the office having spotted the flag and being perplexed, asked us why the flag was flying at half- mast. Who had died?

In trepidation I prepared myself for having to raise it to full mast and suffer the consequences for our decision. But Markus was sharp and fast on his toes. Before I could say anything he shook his head and looked shocked and disgusted at the man. His little speech was powerful and effective. It went roughly like this:

"Are you kidding me sir? You are the VICE PRINCIPAL of an American Armed Forces School, serving our troops and our great nation and YOU don't know who died? SHAME on you sir!"

Not wanting to look like he didn't know, the man immediately lit up as if recalling who it was and said: "OHHHHHHHHH of course. I'm glad you guys remembered. Sorry about that. Carry on!"

We were dismissed trying hard to bite back our laughter knowing that he had bought it. As he started back down the hall the principle, Dr. Jack stopped him and we overheard him ask, "So who was it that died?" And Mr. Chavies shook his head and used our line on him.

"We're here in Berlin serving the US military and YOU don't remember who died? Shame on you!"

Funnier still Dr. Jack immediately nodded going, "OH yeah. Okay," and then vanished back into the office.

Markus and I were about to pee our pants laughing. So the flag remained even though we had to lower it back once at second period and gave the attendance office person who did it the riot act. It just so happened that I worked at the attendance office during fourth period and it was during that time that an Air Force Colonel came by to pick his daughter up for a medical appointment. As part of my duties I went to the classroom to pull the girl from class and make sure she went to the attendance office to meet up with her father.

Upon my return the man asked us if we were aware that our flag was flying at half-mast. I figured it had worked with two senior school staff members; why not try it on this guy, right? So I hammed it up. Head shaking and eyes looking at him in surprise.

"You're an Army officer sir! I cannot believe that you don't know who died! You should be ashamed of yourself!"

He had the EXACT same reaction as the others had, but on top of this he called Tempelhof Air Base in a panic and insisted that they get on the horn and lower all the flags to half-mast immediately. This soon spread to the Army base and HQ. Flags everywhere were dropped to half-mast. But everyone was confused and asking who in the hell had died?

My mother worked at ITT Tours and Travel. Now I knew that the Air Force folks had dropped the flags. But I was not aware that this had spread everywhere. So when I got home my sister who had seen the flags everywhere flying at half-mast for Max the Hamster was elated. My mother, however, got home and was very confused. Talking about how they were at work and suddenly there was a phone call and the GI's went outside and lowered the flag to half-mast. But nobody could figure out who had died?

I was in hysterics laughing. I literally fell to the floor and laughed until it hurt in my gut and I was coughing. My mom thought I had gone nuts. I finally regained my composure and explained that, "It was Max the Hamster mom!"

She was not at all happy about that, worrying that we were going to get kicked out of Berlin if anyone figured out the stunt that we had pulled. Nothing ever came of it. But I will always remember the day that Max the Hamster was honored.

Erik Brush, Class of 1983
1981-1983

Four Friends Reminisce About Life in Berlin (1981-1983)

Sports Trips

Marcia: We had so much fun on sports trips. We had our little Walkmans that had two different holes that we could plug our earphones in. That was fun, we'd get on the Duty Train and travel all night and go to all these different places in Germany to compete.

Yoshika: You got to miss school on Fridays.

Sam: Yeah, But like with football you had to take a historical field trip.

Yoshika: Really? There was nothing historical about what we were doing. They would just drop us off downtown, and said "See ya later!"

Sam: Yeah, we went to Dachau, no not Dachau, the one in uh....good Lord I can't remember. We went to a concentration camp. We went to the VW assembly line, a few museums.

Yoshika: Wow, football?

Sam: Yeah.

Yoshika: They never did anything like that with us.

Marcia: No, we weren't doing the historical thing.

Yoshika: Naw, nothing historical. I mean we were living history. I think the only thing we did was the Rhine River Cruise. Was that volleyball? Were you on that trip?

Sam: We did that together.

Pleshetta: I was there, you were there, 'cause I remember that.

Yoshika: Ok, Rhine River Cruise, but I don't know why we did that that time?

Sam: The Laurali, that's the boat.

Yoshika: Yes, the Laurali. That's right!

Pleshetta: It was a last minute thing.

Yoshika: Yes, it was a last minute thing, and they told us that the Sirens would lure the uh...

Sam: Sailors!

Yoshika: Yes, the sailors into the rocks. Yes, Yes!

Sam: Yeah, we were on the same boat.

Marcia: I don't remember that at all.

Pleshetta: I was there, but nobody remembers I was there.

Yoshika: You were an underclassman.

Pleshetta: See that's what they always say, I was the baby. Nobody remembers I was there.

Yoshika: You're class of '86, no one cared that class of '86 was there when class of '83 was in the house!

Sam: Hey, I was trying to make my own way up.

Yoshika: He couldn't be waiting for you.

Marcia: I was trying to date someone that was older.

Sam: Yeah, I was trying to upsell. I would have brought you with me.

Yoshika: But, it was the Pirate Code. [Any man falls behind is left behind.]

Sam: Yeah, I remember doing that boat trip together, because that was the only time that...we really didn't travel [together] that much.

Yoshika: Yeah, yeah, we always travelled with track guys and they would get dropped off somewhere and we kept on going and we always had the bus to ourselves. Like when we first got to the RTO in Frankfurt. I had forgotten about that until Vince Lingner '82 reminded me at a reunion.

Marcia: I don't remember that either. Was it soccer that traveled with us for volleyball?

Pleshetta: Cross country.

Marcia: Soccer must have traveled with us when I played tennis, then. Because I do remember traveling with Steve McDonald '84 and those guys that were in soccer.

Sam: OK, wait, now was cross country together with volleyball when they had the big "somebody threw up on the bus" incident? And we lost our class president?

Marcia: I don't remember that.

Yoshika: Who was the class president?

Marcia: Your class president?

Sam: No, it was..er, not class president, student body president.

Marcia: Who was it?

Sam: I don't know, but whoever it was... he lost his position over it…

Pleshetta: That happened at Green Week, I don't remember that happening on the bus...

Marcia: Yeah, someone throwing up on the bus…

Sam: —–threw up on Dr. Jack.

Pleshetta: I remember that!

Yoshika: Oh yeah, on Green Week!

Pleshetta: Yes, Green Week!

Green Week opens today

Green Week, Europe's largest indoor visit to the country, begins today in the Funkturm and will run through Feb. 3. It offers thousands of people the chance to enjoy food and wine festivals, horse shows, livestock exhibits, flower shows and much, much more. Don't miss it!
(U. S. Army Photo)

International Green Week takes place in Berlin every January. The first Green Week was in 1926.

Teen Shenanigans

Marcia: Here's what I do remember: William Pollard at Laura Morgan's Graduation party.

Marcia: He gets hammered. My stepdad decides he's going to drive him and...

Yoshika: Wait a minute, who's your stepdad– what's his name?

Marcia: Gary Spohn.

Yoshika: And he was a..?

Marcia: Colonel; and he had his Mercedes Staff Car.

Yoshika: Oh no!

Marcia: And so he's going to drive William POLLARD '83 and Tyrone Worlds '84 home. And, William pukes all over the back seat of the staff car. And then he has to go home and tell his dad the next morning that he threw up in Cololnel Spohn's staff car.

Yoshika: His dad was an officer, too. His dad was a captain I think. Sir, your son threw up in the staff car of a Colonel!

Sam: Both Air Force, if he had been Army that would have been ok.

Marcia: I remind him of that every time I talk to him.

Yoshika: My kids know. Underage drinking, that was part, unfortunately, part of our story.

Marcia: [To Yoshika] You know what though, I don't remember you being that involved in it.

Pleshetta: I do.

Marcia: You remember her or you remember you?

Pleshetta: I remember her [Yoshika] being involved!

Yoshika: Children, no I wasn't. [Directed to two of her kids sitting there.]

Pleshetta: I wasn't involved in underage drinking.

Yoshika: She wasn't.

Marcia: But you know, things were very different for us. Hardly anybody had a car, because you couldn't get a driver's license until you were 18. There was no driver's ed. I didn't know how to drive until I got back.

Yoshika: Me either. You didn't have to worry about driving drunk.

Marcia: We all took the subway everywhere you went and you went in big groups. It was just very different...

Yoshika: And you were in a Walled city, and had so much security, where were you going to go?

Marcia: The only thing that I remember that did happen and in today's world this would be really serious but at the time it was very funny… Barbara Petullo '83 and I were at— remember that little Italian restaurant?

Everyone: Fra Diavolo's!

Marcia: We were at Fra Diavolo's by the Outpost Theater and, I don't know, they wanted us to leave or something. Barbara was totally being a smart aleck and she's always laughing and she did a thing like [makes her hand like a gun] "Bang, Bang" at the guy who owns Fra Diavolo's. [He said] "You get out of here, you get out of here right now! You get out of here, you not ever come back!"

Yoshika: Yeah, nowadays, that would be an incident. Oh, my gosh, me and Trisha got in trouble with the staff at Fra Diavolo's, too. Because we brought our own Dr. Peppers in!

Sam: Once again with the Dr. Peppers.

Yoshika: Yes! Trisha and I loved Dr. Pepper. There was a machine by the PX, by the AAFES, sodas cost 25 cents. Actually we didn't pay for the sodas.

Pleshetta: Now, tell the truth, that's what I'm talking about...

Yoshika: Even though the sodas were only 25 cents, we figured out that if you bumped it the right way it fell out!

Marcia: Very nice!

Yoshika: And we didn't want to pay for the overpriced sodas at Fra Diavolo's...We brought them in my purse because Trisha would never carry a purse. We set them on the table after we ordered our pizzas and they told us to get out. "But we already ordered our pizzas!" [But, they said] "Get out, get out." [We said] "We're not leaving without our pizzas."

Marcia: Well, I'm happy to hear that somebody else had a run-in there. Glad I wasn't alone...

Yoshika: They were yelling at us, they were very mad.

Marcia: They were yelling at us, too. "You get out, you get out right now!"

Yoshika: Germans were very mad at us, Germans did not like us already. Whenever you'd do those American things...

Pleshetta: They're so nice now when you go back to Berlin, totally different.

Yoshika: Oh well, now, yeah, everyone in Germany is nice now. They stop and help you...

Marcia: I thought, for the most part, I thought everybody was nice then.

Yoshika: I didn't think so. The thing is, by the time we were there, they were tired of being occupied. When we had the reunion in 2006, we had a panel of alumni from each decade. The people from the 40's and 50's said the Germans were really nice and thankful to them because they could remember being liberated. The 60's was kind of a transition. The 70's and 80's they were pretty much done with us.

Sam: Well, it did have something to do with us, though. Cuz...

Marcia: We were obnoxious teenagers!

Yoshika: Yeah, we were obnoxious.

Marcia: Well, we probably weren't, as teenagers, overly friendly.

Yoshika: Yes, we didn't speak German. And a lot of us had the attitude that if you didn't speak English…

Marcia: I could order beer and french fries...

Yoshika: I knew enough German to shop, go to restaurants, because that was important...

Pleshetta: I could shop.

Sam: Speaking of sports and underage drinking, I ordered my first beer by accident at the McDonald's in Frankfurt.

Yoshika: And see, McDonald's has beer in Germany.

Marcia: You could order beer at McDonald's?

Sam: You didn't know that?

Marcia: I didn't know that!

Yoshika: I don't know how we didn't know that. They never had chaperones with us, they just let us go down there.

Sam: You'd come out of the basement and come back into the... you know where it was?

Marcia: Yeah.

Yoshika: It was right on the edge of the Red Light District.

Sam: So, it was me, Loren Washington '83, John Wilburn '83...and Jurgen, I can't remember Jurgen's last name.

Sam: So, everybody is ordering, and I try to order a strawberry shake. "Erdbeere," and the person behind the counter heard "Ein Bier." And so I get it, and I'm like "What is this?" I'm like 14 I think.

Yoshika: 'This is not strawberry.'

Marcia: You're sticking to your story.

Yoshika: 'I did not say Ein Bier.'

Sam: And I think it is Loren who says, "That's what you ordered." I was like, "I said Erdbeere." He was like, "You're going to drink it."

Yoshika: I forgot that strawberry is Erdbeere in German.

Sam: So I sat down at 14, ate my hamburger and drank my beer. I then went downstairs to the U-bahn and drank another one. And that's the story. Haven't looked back yet.

Bier is a very important part of German culture, so much so that there are laws governing its production and purity. Germany ranks 2nd in per-capita beer consumption (behind the Czech Republic). There are 5000 brands of beer sold in Germany. Berliner Kindl is the official sponsor of the city of Berlin; therefore it is served at all major public events.

Fear and Loathing in Berlin

Marcia: I tell you what I remember, on a more serious note, is I can remember having it being really surreal as I was in my bathroom getting ready in the morning, to go to school every morning, as Yoshika can attest my hair had to be perfect. I mean I spent like two hours on my hair.

Yoshika: Oh yes, it was always perfectly feathered.

Sam: It was a nice helmet.

Yoshika: You're right, it was like a helmet, perfectly feathered.

Marcia: It was! I'd have the radio on while I was doing it. You'd hear the news reports about somebody trying to escape, somebody from the Eastern side– somebody made it, somebody didn't. I clearly remember looking in the mirror, while I'm still doing my hair mind you, because you have to have your priorities straight. Still doing my hair and thinking, "Wow, that's weird. Here I'm free, I am in high school, I can do for the most part what I want. There's somebody not too far from me who...didn't make it."

Yoshika: Someone who wanted freedom so bad.

Sam: When I first got there that used to freak me out; the first couple of months.

Yoshika: Me, too. Listening to the radio every morning...

Sam: And hearing that. But, after the first couple of months, I was fine. I mean, I understood what was going on. And being in Düppel, it was like...

Pleshetta: Oh yes, you were right there.

Yoshika: Oh yes, you were right next to the Wall. The Wall was right behind...the Düppel Housing area.

Sam: It was behind James Miller's house– because there is that picture of Miller throwing his cap over the Wall.

Yoshika: That's right, he threw his cap, that's right!

Sam: But, it just became like a way of life.

Marcia: It did. But still, I can remember thinking that is was weird. But, it was a way of life.

Yoshika: Like you said at first it was just scary. I remember spending the whole first year being scared all the time. Hearing these reports and thinking, "They're going to come over the Wall after us." I was just really freaked out. You know how they prepared us, told us most likely you won't get out ...if the Cold War...

Sam: If the balloon goes up...[military language for notification of an attack]

Yoshika: Yes, if it goes up, we're all dead. After that it became a fascination. Every morning I wanted to know if anyone tried to get over, or if they'd been shot, did they live. If anyone made it we'd cheer, "Yes, they made it!"

Pleshetta: Somebody snuck across by someone else, that was crazy.

Yoshika: It was like this game of cat and mouse. Who was going to make it? It was sad when they didn't.

Marcia: Did you guys have a, um, bunker in your house?

Yoshika: No, that was for officers only, we were NCOs.

Pleshetta: I know, "Did we have a bunker?" Really? We had to fend for ourselves!

Sam: Come on, come on, really? We were just like fodder. As the tanks roll across we were there to slow them down before they got to your house.

Marcia: Well, our house had a bunker and that place creeped me out. It was off of the bathroom in the basement. And nobody ever went into the basement. And out of the bathroom there was this window and you could crawl through this hole and it freaked me out. Yeah, that freaked me out.

Yoshika: Yes, because you lived in that mansion.

Marcia: We lived in an unbelievably, crazy house.

Yoshika: It really was a mansion. Remember, we had that volleyball team sleepover… We explored the house for a good part of the night.

Marcia: I remember before we moved there, we lived in a duplex in Italy. When we were going to move to Berlin, they told Gary that they had a 29-room house for him. And it's like, "29 rooms?" There are three of us– mom, stepdad and me.

Yoshika: Those were some crazy times…

This account is a transcription of a video interview with Sam Anderson '86, Pleshetta Loftin '86, Yoshika Loftin Lowe '83 and Marcia Spohn Welch '83

Sam Anderson, Class of 1986
1980-1983

Marcia Spohn Welch, Class of 1983
1981-1983

The iconic image of James Miller '83 flinging his hat over the Berlin Wall on Graduation Day- June 11, 1983

Misadventures at BAHS

I was supposed to graduate in 1982, but due to my lack of intellectual abilities, I had the pleasure to attend classes at BAHS another year. My first year there, I felt lonely because of my background. I didn't quite mesh with anyone. I dressed and talked differently. I wore trucker caps, cowboy boots and Western shirts. I worked on cars, chewed tobacco and listened to country music.

One morning in home room, Bob Krasnican '82 came runnin' 'n hollerin,' "Moose! Come quick! There's a guy upstairs that's just like you! He's got on a big cowboy hat, boots, and has a 'snuff can ring' in his jeans pocket! And he is big!" Well, I about busted my desk trying to get upstairs. Enter: William David "Tiny" Crawley '84.

Tiny and I became like brothers that day. He came to Berlin with his father. His dad worked nights and a lot of holidays too, so my family sort of adopted him. My mom always got him presents for his birthday and Christmas. She was a great country cook, so he loved visiting over holidays and any other time there was food. At Thanksgiving that year (1982), my mother, knowing that Tiny's mom and dad were divorced, invited him to our Thanksgiving Supper. Tiny's dad worked all night and wanted to stay home and rest up. That day was great! We watched *Miracle On 34th Street* and relaxed while Tiny told us all about Del Rio, Texas. Mom and Tiny became instant friends and that was a blessing to me because I loved him like a brother and he really did become like an adopted son to my mom.

Mom bought us each a pocket watch and gave them to us on that Thanksgiving Day. She told us that we better never be late getting home or to school. And she meant it! Tiny made Mom a cutting board for her kitchen and gave it to her that Christmas. Mom didn't 'put it up' as she did with many of her treasured gifts. Heck no. She used that board for nearly every meal until her death in 2004. For 21 years my mom used that simple gift that was made with care and love from someone she cared deeply for. Yes, that Thanksgiving was probably my favorite one and for sure will be the one that I will never forget.

Before I continue with "The Mis-Adventures of Moose and Tiny," two quick pre-Tiny stories are in order. English teacher Mrs. Bair gave her class a written/verbal assignment. We were to come up with a product and try to sell it to the class. It was assigned Friday and due Monday. Easy grade. Turn in Monday: A, Tuesday: B, etc. Most everyone had theirs Monday. Except me. Mrs. Bair explained to me Thursday that if I didn't have my presentation ready by Friday, it would mean an F.

Thursday night, fuming about having to stand in front of the class, a product came to me: "Teacher Terminator." I explained how a few drops in a teacher's coffee cup would eliminate them. Some in the coffee pot in the lounge would get rid of most of them. I gave a three minute spiel on the benefits of the product; gave the price plus shipping and handling, an address and 800 number. When the laughter ended, Mrs. Bair gave me a C!

When I was a senior the first time in the 81-82 school year, we wanted to use a VW Beetle for our senior prank. I was trying to think of how to get it on the roof, but had to settle on the cafeteria. We all gathered, and some of us painted '82 and our names/nicknames on it. Then we pushed it inside, removed the wheels and left. In his haste to leave the scene, Vince Lingner ‘82 tripped and all the wheel lug bolts went flying all over the ground. It was just getting dark when we put it in there. Later, we decided to go back and see our handiwork, like an artist leaving a work to get another perspective. Much to our amazement and horror, when we returned, the lights were ON! There was a P.T.A. meeting in progress! There were teachers, parents and students sitting around it in a big circle. Like an Indian Pow-Wow around the fire. The next morning, Dr. Jack and Mr. Chavies were there. They wanted to know who was behind it and they wanted it moved...NOW! Well, after we rounded up all the scattered lug bolts, we got it back outside. The yearbook crew wanted a photo, so all of us that participated, stood on and around it for a shot that made the "Involvement '82" yearbook.

The '82-Mobile Senior Prank tricksters

Back to Moose and Tiny: occasionally Tiny and I would have a self-proclaimed 'Suit Day.' We would show up at school wearing our three-piece suits. People would snicker at us. Tiny would leer at them and they would go away.

During the summer of 1982, the theme for Volksfest was "Northwest Wilderness." The planners must have seen the two of us, because the next thing we knew, we were given green suspenders and red stocking caps. We became 'lumberjacks.' For free food and rides, we just walked around and people talked to us and took our picture. I wish I had one of those pictures.

During the '82-'83 school year, a group of us guys put an engineless VW Beetle on one of the new concrete tables outside the cafeteria. The next morning, Assistant Principal, Mr. Chavies saw me and said, "I want to see

YOU and YOUR FRIEND in MY OFFICE...RIGHT NOW!" I found Tiny and returned. Mr. Chavies was mad and wanted to know who helped us. We wouldn't tell. We knew that lifting down was easier than lifting up. We claimed full responsibility. Mr. Chavies said, "You put it up there, you take it down. If you do, no suspension." Mr. Chavies stood in awe as we removed the car from the table and set it on the ground.

On another occasion, Tiny and I enlisted some buddies. Each was given some chain and a padlock. Their assignment: wait until everyone was in the cafeteria for lunch, then chain all the doors closed. Dr. Jack (the principal) was not amused. He was worried there could be a fire. We were warned without suspension.

One day, Tiny and I stepped into the cafeteria from the outer doors dressed in sheets with pillow cases on our heads. Pandemonium broke out as everyone jammed the hallway, running away. Suddenly, someone noticed our cowboy boots. A shout rang out, "It's Moose and Tiny! Get 'em!" Now it was us trying to get away!

I remember one time when the cosmetology teacher, Mrs. Beech was having trouble with someone parking in her space by the Cosmetology building. Tiny and I painted two white lines on the cobbles and erected a sign: "Reserved for 'Ma' Beech. Enforced by Moose and Tiny."

Ms. Beech on a Duty Train trip

One morning, the Auto Shop teacher Mr. Eichner left the class for a few minutes. Tiny decided to go out in the shop to oil the doors and machinery. When Mr. Eichner returned he said, "If anyone wants my old blue shop coat, it's yours. I just got my new one." It was WHITE. He told us to study for a quiz while he finished something in the shop. A moment later, there was a shout and the classroom door flew open. There stood 'Ike' with a black stripe up his new white coat, all over his face and glasses. He didn't have to look far to find out what happened. Tiny had 'oiled' the wire wheel on the bench grinder!

Whenever we rode the Duty Train, Tiny and I would share a berth with two other guys. Tiny’s feet smelled so bad that we would tie his boot straps together and hang them out the window. When we arrived at Frankfurt or Berlin, the boots were always still there. We figured that the guards at the checkpoints either didn't have feet that big, or just couldn't get close to them for the smell!

One morning, Tiny and I turned English teacher Mr. Sullivan's room completely around. Everyone was confused as to where to sit. After we did take our seats, Mr. Sullivan announced: “I haven't the 'Tiniest' idea who did this. A wild 'Moose' couldn't drag it from me. However, the perpetrators left a note. It reads ‘Moose + Tiny wuz heer’ and the spelling proves it!”

Tiny and I would still be in prison today if we pulled these pranks anywhere else. A great student body and a faculty staff with a sense of humor allowed us to be creative. Luckily for Tiny and me, no one was ever hurt or offended by our actions.

Due to my career as a long distance tractor-trailer driver, I had a load to Tiny’s hometown of Del Rio, Texas. We were reunited after ten years apart. The last time I was there, a few years ago, I couldn't find him. Probably got rid of his home phone and got a cell. I hadn't seen him for a few years and forgot what road he lived on. He may have moved too; I sure miss him!

Mark Haines, Class of 1983
1981-1984

The Infamous Senior Trip of 1983

One of the great things about living in Germany was the proximity to so many other European countries. During my time in Berlin, our high school had a yearly tradition of going to Spain for our senior trip. When I heard– oddly enough, by word of mouth– that there was to be an after school meeting for all interested juniors and seniors I was terribly excited.

At the meeting, run by– also oddly enough– another student, we were given the necessary paperwork and information. We would be traveling via motor coach service, with lodging at a fine hotel which included a continental breakfast– and we would be fully chaperoned. All of this for only $200 for a whole week! Surprisingly, my mother decided to give me this trip as a graduation gift! I had never been allowed to go on a trip this far away without my parents! And my family had never been the type to take vacations– ever! I could not believe it.

As all trips from Berlin began for us teens, our parents took us to the RTO station to ride the Duty Train to Frankfurt where we boarded a bus to Spain. We had booked our trip through the now defunct Bartl Tours International. Part of our package was to go on some excursions to Barcelona. Unfortunately, my fellow classmates had no interest in culture. I was pretty disappointed when the tour guide came back and reprimanded us for not signing up for any tours– it turned out I was the only one who signed the clipboard. Being who I am/was– I stood up and chided my classmates for their lack of class and culture and for cheating me out of the opportunity to visit Barcelona. They of course booed me down and threw things at me like the classless clods I accused them of being.

Since there was a toilet onboard, we were only scheduled to make one stop on the way to Spain– Lyon, France. I remember very vividly that the whole place was automated and unmanned. I'd never seen nor heard of an Automat before! The food dispensing machines all had little glass front doors and they reached from floor to ceiling and covered the whole length of the wall. You could just choose what you wanted and then self-checkout. On our way back, I remember stopping in Lyon again, but this time my memory was that of the worst toilet paper I have ever had the displeasure to use. It was a thin brown corrugated paper-- folded like paper napkins. I also remember there being a playground at this stop, where my classmates Marcia, Barbara and I decided to take a picture on the top of the slide.

Marcia Spohn Welch '83, Barbara Petullo Grodhaus '83 and me in France

Although we had a toilet onboard, it became filled before we reached our destination, because many of the students had brought bottles of liquor. Strangely, although I am by no means innocent as far as some of the shenanigans of the week were concerned, I guess I missed the memo that we were to BYOB it. Since drinking is legal in Germany at age 16, American youth often and cheerfully took advantage of their legal status. This often led to excessive drinking. Because of the excessive drinking, the tour guide and bus driver became very upset and refused to allow any bathroom stops. At one point, the toilet began to overflow. It was pretty miserable at the back of the bus.

Add to this, one of our classmates burst the skylight on the top of the bus with his head. I don't know exactly why–though I do remember who did it–

but I believe he and some of the other guys at the back of the bus were betting how high they could jump straight up in a moving bus. By night fall, it became very cold– adding further to my, if not anyone else's misery.

We arrived in Lloret de Mar, Costa Brava, Spain in the morning, so we headed to our rooms to settle in. As I recall, we had a brief meeting with our 'chaperones' but I don't remember seeing much of them again until we got back on the bus. As it turns out, our chaperones were a newlywed couple. I learned later that in exchange for a free hotel room, we would not bother the couple and they would not interfere with us.

On the first day, we all hung out at the hotel and enjoyed the pool. Some of the rooms looked out over the pool. For some, 'enjoying the pool' meant jumping from the second story balconied rooms into it. Though a few of us warned these crazies that they could kill themselves, no one actually did. I still cannot believe that no one got hurt.

The next morning, we discovered, to our horror, what a continental breakfast was. I laugh now, but we all hurried downstairs hungry and ready to eat our free breakfast. We were stunned when they brought us a dry roll and some bitter coffee. This led to a shouting match and one or two of my guy friends 'threatening' to beat up the server (names have been left out to protect the guilty).

Disappointed, we headed into town to buy a real breakfast. My best friend William Pollard III '83 and I really wanted some scrambled eggs, toast and sausage or ham. At the first restaurant, we ordered scrambled eggs, but they arrived sunny-side up. We were not happy, but we did our best to eat the runny things which had been fried in quite a lot of grease. I tried in vain to dab off the extra grease with the napkins that were only slightly more absorbent than that French toilet paper.

William Pollard III '83

Later, William and I tried to lay out on the beach (fully wrapped like mummies in jackets, pants and hats) with our fairer skinned friends, but realized it was futile and down-right boring. So we decided to go shopping instead. The dollar was strong against the Peseta at 136 Pesetas per dollar. I actually purchased a Lladró figurine for my mother for only 20 dollars!

We tried every single morning to find a restaurant that would scramble our eggs, and even though we asked before ordering, and they said yes, something seemed to be lost in translation. Every single restaurant gave us two sunny side-up eggs. We gave up on day five. However, every shop in town had the most wonderful ice cream desserts. They were mostly parfaits with huge sweet red strawberries.

Probably the best part of Lloret de Mar for all of us was the night life. Which is unusual really, since we all enjoyed the incredible night life in Berlin– which boasted in its travel brochures that there were enough night clubs in the Walled City to visit a different one every night of the year. What set our favorite club—The Revolution—apart from all the rest was the nightly laser light show. In 1983 none of us had ever seen such a thing.

Handbill for The Revolution Discotheque

We had so much fun that week. Too much fun, in fact– for about three weeks after we arrived home, our school principal as well as all of our parents received a four page letter from the tour company and a one page letter from the Department of the Army HQ, US Command– namely Brigadier General Leroy Suddath himself. This may not mean much to the average civilian, but when the US Commander of the whole American Sector sends your parents a letter, in which he mentions your child by name, you take serious and fearful note. I can only imagine the fear it struck in my dad's heart. He was certain they were going to call all of the fathers in to account for their stupid kids' actions.

I still do not know why we did not get in more trouble. We had known of fathers being busted (demoted) and the whole family sent back to the States due to an international incident or other impropriety; that was the way the military worked in Berlin. But to send a busload of families back to the States would be a logistical nightmare. Marcia's dad was the highest ranking officer of the US Air Force Command in Berlin, maybe that bought us some mercy. I guess we'll never know.

The day the letter arrived, my parents were waiting for me in the living room. I nearly froze when they said they had gotten a letter from the General. I had not been forewarned that this letter was coming, nor that any of my friends had received one, so I was not prepared to defend myself. Not only did we not have cell phones, but we were not allowed to use the phones in Berlin at all since they were all tapped by the Soviets and the American intelligence agencies. I somehow was able to think quickly on my feet. Because one thing I knew, even though my dad would have let me go with a warning, my mother was a strict disciplinarian. My dad was not actually upset about the drinking, because he drank and all of us teens were of legal drinking age in Germany, France and Spain. However, he knew my mother did not approve of any kind of shenanigans.

As I read the letter, I tried to emote total shock and stall as I planned my defense. My parents then asked if I had stolen the blanket that I brought home from Spain. As I read the damages and missing items list I noticed that the blanket was miraculously not listed. But instead of lying, I reminded my parents that the letter attested to my prior claim that the roof hatch was broken by my classmate. I then told them that I was so cold on the way up, I thought I would catch pneumonia on the way back without a blanket. I also claimed that since dad always 'collected' the beautiful monogrammed blankets from the Duty Train, I didn't think it was a big deal at the time. The discussion ended right there, with my mom cutting a stern look to my dad and me walking away without repercussion. I think it was the only time I ever got away with doing something wrong without being grounded. And I still have the four page letter!

On the bus ride to Spain: George Moffett '84, Janice Diego '84 and Yoshika Loftin Lowe '83

Because of this infamous trip, the BAHS class of 1983 had the dubious honor of being responsible for all American youth being banned from Spain indefinitely. As it turns out all the things that I thought were 'odd' about this trip were due to the fact that it was not actually a school sanctioned event at all!

Yoshika (Yhoshekia) Loftin Lowe, Class of 1983
1980-1983

Class of 1983: My Senior Memories

The city of Berlin was important both politically and strategically. It allowed the US to have a presence in the middle of a Communist nation. As such it became famous as a city of spies. My father, like many other military personnel stationed in Berlin, had to have a secret clearance. Actually, he had a Top Secret Security Clearance. I never understood why he needed such a high level of security access when he was just a Mess Sergeant (a restaurant manager). Supposedly, it was because he managed the restaurant at the top secret hilltop base called Teufelsberg. Teufelsberg (German for Devil's Mountain) was located in the Grunewald forest, 260 feet above the surrounding area– built upon tons of WWII war debris. It was an NSA listening station, one of the largest ever built. It was a well-known fact that if the Soviets attacked, it would be destroyed, taking most of Berlin with it.

Teufelsberg, 1974 photo: Dr. Karl-Heinz Hochhaus

I discovered only recently, that my dad was meeting daily at 7 am with the President of the United States via comsat technology (communications satellite conferencing). At that time, this technology was not even close to being available commercially. He teleconferenced with Presidents Carter (1980-81) and Reagan (1981-83)! There was a special meeting room and when a certain color light lit up on the wall, everyone below the Top Secret Clearance level had to leave the room. Super cool spy stuff!

I remember one year our family was allowed entrance to the 'Hill' for Thanksgiving, when my dad would be serving an extravagant Thanksgiving feast to the top brass. No POVs (privately owned vehicles) were allowed on the hill, so we had to park in a special parking area and be taken by a military bus to the Hill. I remember it was extremely cold in the building– so cold we had to remain bundled up throughout dinner, our teeth chattering. The heating systems had broken. That was not a very enjoyable meal, but we smiled and sat politely at the table with some important men whose names I don't remember ever being given.

Security was tight, with guards in every hallway and at the elevator. There was a light on the wall that signaled when it you were cleared to go from one room to another. The color indicated whether the room had been 'declassified' and safe for none security pass holders to proceed. We were not allowed to talk about Teufelsberg: not that our father worked there, nor that we had been there, nor that it even existed (because no one noticed that huge listening station on the top of the hill in the middle of the forest).

Berlin was so vital politically, that it was common for top brass and government officials to visit. On June 11, 1982, the summer before my senior year, President Ronald Reagan visited Berlin and spoke at Tempelhof Airport. It was a huge deal, and was featured in all the local papers.

berlin observer

Welcome President Reagan

We in the U.S. Command, Berlin, welcome you on your visit to the divided city. We are proud to serve our country as defenders of Berlin's freedom and are honored to join with you today in reaffirming our commitment to this great city.

berlin observer

The Presidential Visit — story and photos on pages 4 and 5

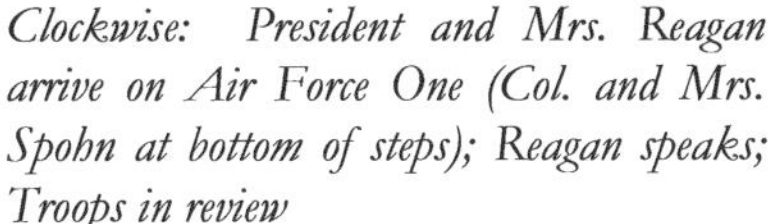

Clockwise: President and Mrs. Reagan arrive on Air Force One (Col. and Mrs. Spohn at bottom of steps); Reagan speaks; Troops in review

Later that school year, on February 1st, then Vice President George Bush also visited. He spoke to our community at the Sports Center gym. Of course school was let out for this auspicious occasion, and the gym was packed. I remember being impressed that VP Bush went through the crowd shaking hands with anyone who wanted to greet him. Two members of my class, Mark Millen and Laura Morgan, even got to present the Vice President and Mrs. Bush with a Berlin Bear and a sweater.

berlin observer

'A front line of freedom'

Vice President Bush visits Berlin

My senior year I decided to help with homecoming. We decided to have our homecoming dance at the Wannsee. The Wannsee is a posh lakeside community in the west of Berlin, with facilities for boating, yachting, fishing and swimming, a shooting range (Rose Range) and a golf course. This area is dotted with mansions that look out upon the beautiful Wannsee lakes: Grosser Wannsee and Kleiner Wannsee (Greater Wannsee and Lesser Wannsee). After the war, Berlin Command took possession of many of these homes which the Nazis had re-appropriated from wealthy Jews. Those familiar with history know that the Wannsee Conference was held in one of the lakeside villas to determine "The Final Solution." It is now a museum.

One of the officers' kids got permission from Berlin Command to use a Wannsee mansion for our dance. Upon entering the villa, our committee was a bit disappointed to discover that this house had not been inhabited in quite some time. But, Laura Morgan (senior class president and the girl who would meet VP Bush a few months later), made a decision– she would talk to her daddy, Colonel Morgan about getting some help with clean up. Colonel Morgan dispatched a team of soldiers to 'help' us with clean up.

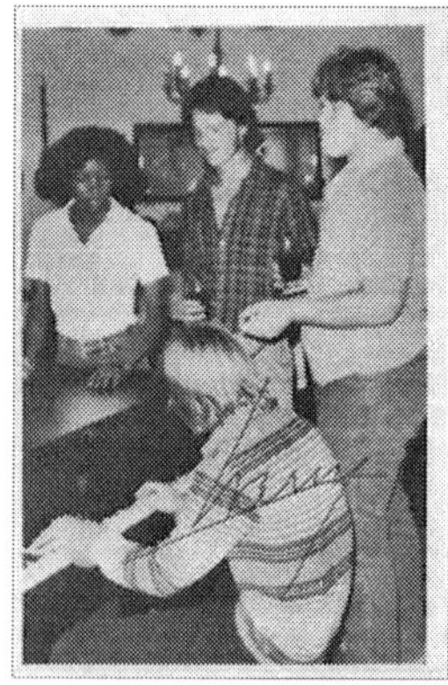

Class of 1983 Homecoming Planning Committee-Working hard and hardly working…

When we came back the next day (or it may have been a few days later) to clean and decorate, we found the place was totally spotless! And it was completely decorated! The soldiers had hung fishing nets from the ceiling adorned with star fish. Everything was decorated with the nautical motif. Appropriately, our homecoming theme was 'Sailing'– whose prom or homecoming didn't have that theme in the early 80s? The 1980 Grammy winning song by Christopher Cross fit our location and purpose perfectly.

Homecoming '82- Tyrone Worlds '84, Yoshika Loftn '83, Kevin Greene '84

Prom was a memorable event as well. I attended prom with one of my best friends, Kevin Greene '84, with whom I had attended Homecoming. As luck would have it, I started dating a guy I met on Senior Trip in April. Well, before that trip, my new guy had asked one of my best friends, Marcia Spohn Welch '83 to prom and I had already agreed to go with Kevin. By April, it was too late to change dates for prom. Marcia had a serious boyfriend in college in the States, so essentially, we both were attending prom with our close guy friends.

Prom was at the beautiful Harnack House and I really cannot remember much about prom. However, I do remember the drama after prom. The tradition was to go to the Talk of the Town disco after prom– which was a famous nightclub owned by the parents of Bobby Harrell '83 (another close friend). However, at the club, Marcia's date and I got tired of being apart all night, and after dancing together, went outside (we couldn't *bear* being apart for another moment). Some of our friends became upset with the two of us, because they felt that Marcia's date had ditched her, and that I was conspiring to help him. If I remember correctly, by the time we came back inside, our friends and dates had left. I knew Marcia was not upset (annoyed maybe); she was in love with her stateside beau and prom was over. When we arrived at the official After-Prom party at Colonel Morgan's beautiful mansion, no one wanted to talk to us. Since Marcia was not upset– I didn't care about the others. Kevin was not happy with me either, so I never got to see the picture the two of us took at prom. Thankfully, my mother had asked me to take a picture by myself. The things teens do when they *think* they're in love! Thankfully all our friends eventually forgave us!

Yoshika Loftin '83, Prom 1983

When I graduated from BAHS, I had the audacity to send an invitation to President Reagan, and he replied! His congratulatory note was signed in ink! I was astonished; although I never cared about politics before Berlin, I really admired President Reagan– he cared about the troops and freedom and that was all I cared about living in the middle of East Germany.

Talk of the Town handbill, 1983

Yoshika (Yhoshekia) Loftin Lowe, Class of 1983
1980-1983

On the occasion of your graduation, Nancy and I send you our warmest greetings and congratulations. We hope your future plans meet with every success, and we send you our best wishes.

Ronald Reagan

The hand signed note card that Yoshika received from President Reagan

Baccalaureate
Saturday, June fourth, at four p.m.
at the Kaiser Wilhelm Memorial Church

Commencement
Saturday, June eleventh, at four p.m.
at the Reichstag

Yoshika sent President Reagan a BAHS graduation invitation, not expecting an actual response

Life is a Rose: 1983-1986

In 1983 my brother-in-law Ian (then just a friend), went to East Berlin for a night on the town with his brother. He met an East German in a bar. He said that he'd be back the next day and that he had a Porsche 914(?) which he'd leave unlocked. Sure enough, Ian found the car the next night just as the man had said. After taking it through Checkpoint Charlie, he got around the corner, opened the trunk and the guy was in there. Unfortunately, Ian neglected to tell the guy to keep his mouth shut about the details of his defection. The Army actively gathered intel at the refugee houses and the guy talked about his great escape. Ian was put under house arrest and needless to say, he wasn't in the Army for long.

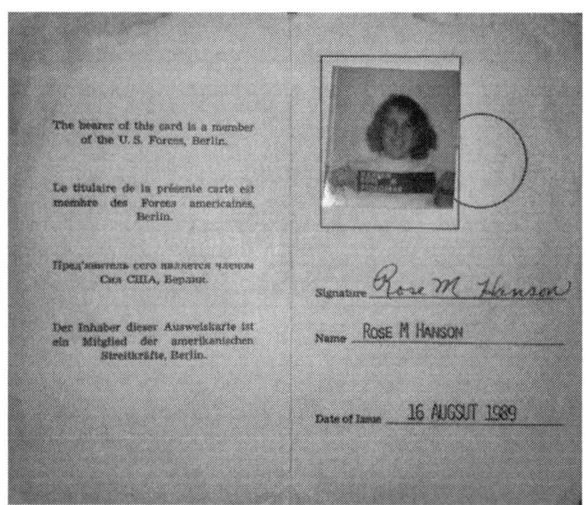
The bearer of this card is a member of the U.S. Forces, Berlin.

Le titulaire de la présente carte est membre des Forces americaines, Berlin.

Предъявитель сего является членом Сил США, Берлин.

Der Inhaber dieser Ausweiskarte ist ein Mitglied der amerikanischen Streitkräfte, Berlin.

Signature Rose M Hanson

Name ROSE M HANSON

Date of Issue 16 AUGSUT 1989

East Pass- needed at Checkpoint Charlie to enter East Berlin

As I got older, I got braver about driving over to East Berlin. My friend Kim Berg '84 and I had lots of fun shopping and going out together. Once my sister Rita, Kim and I were stopped by an East German soldier who spoke perfect English. We used to smuggle food to him and not long before the Berlin Wall came down, we smuggled out 20,000 in East Marks for him. He sent me letters when I went to college using an alias. After I graduated, I moved to Heidelberg with my parents.

On October 10th, 1989 he decided that he would escape. He went to Czechoslovakia with his family and then he ran off. He swam over the

Danube River and went to Austria. I was living in Heidelberg at the time and he came to live with my parents. We helped him find his uncle who gave him some money for an apartment. On November 10th, I went to his apartment and told him to watch the news. He absolutely couldn't believe it. He said that it was not true and that it was just propaganda. I told him that we do have some propaganda in the West-- that he might not want to believe every commercial--but the news is 90% correct.

Some of my fondest memories of Berlin were of leaving Berlin. Arriving at the RTO (the Duty Train station) two hours before we had to board-- we would go to the pizza place around the corner and eat, or just hang around on the platform and act silly. The thrill of getting on the train and getting your bunk-- once the train started moving, the mayhem would begin. No one slept. I actually kept a journal and wrote about a few rides. The stops at the border seemed tense and it was a thrill to wave or flash the guards as we went by. Once in Frankfurt, we were half dead. The trips were exhausting, but no one was too tired to stop at McDonald's in Frankfurt before the train ride home.

As I got older, I drove to and from Berlin more often. Going through Checkpoint Bravo and Checkpoint Alpha was a completely different experience. We had to have our papers in perfect order. You had to get out of your car, stop and salute the Soviet Solider and show him your papers. Then you had to go in the shack and put your papers in a slot. While

Duty Train Fun- Mike B.'84, Rene B. '83, Vince Lingner '82, Alan R. '84, Lissa A. '82

you waited for the papers to pop back through the hole, you could amuse yourself with the Soviet propaganda pamphlets that there were written in English (I still have them). Once you got your papers back, you had to go back out, salute the soldier again and get in your car. You had to drive no more than 100 kpm. If you got to the other side of Germany too fast, you could get a speeding ticket. It took about 2 hours to get from Berlin to Helmstedt. I was always too nervous to stop.

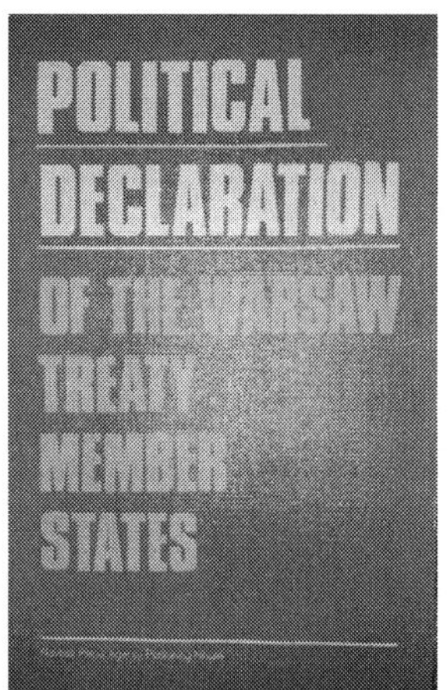

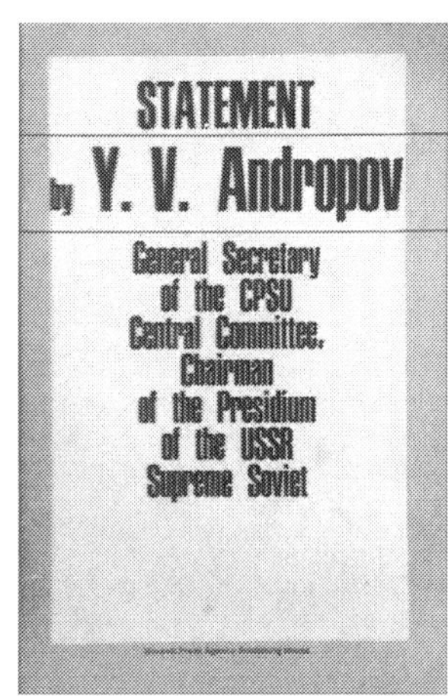

Soviet propaganda pamphlets from Soviet Checkpoint

One warm summer day, my sister Rita and I were leaving Berlin. We got all the way to Checkpoint Alpha in Marienborn (the Soviet checkpoint). We were just a few miles from the American side of the checkpoint (in Helmstedt). When I got back in my car to leave, it wouldn't start. No one knew what to do. We just needed to push the car to start it. Thankfully, the young Soviet soldiers took pity on us and pushed us. It was hilarious. A very tense moment became quite a show for the guys in the tower. We drove away honking and waving to them.

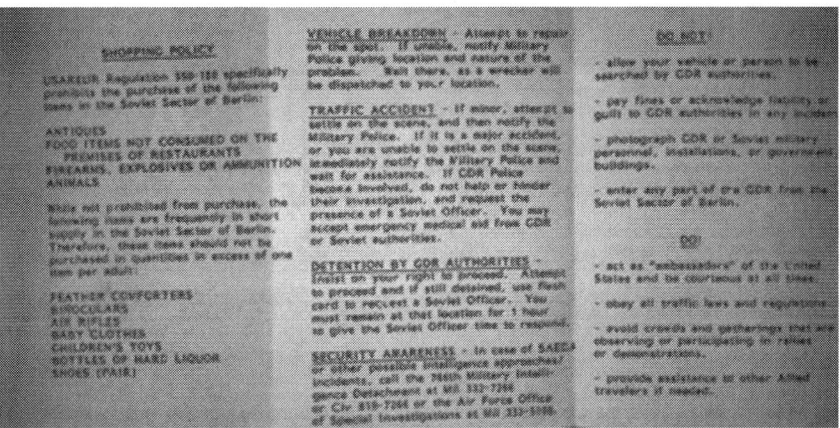

SHOPPING POLICY

USAREUR Regulation 550-180 specifically prohibits the purchase of the following items in the Soviet Sector of Berlin:

ANTIQUES
FOOD ITEMS NOT CONSUMED ON THE PREMISES OF RESTAURANTS
FIREARMS, EXPLOSIVES OR AMMUNITION
ANIMALS

While not prohibited from purchase, the following items are frequently in short supply in the Soviet Sector of Berlin. Therefore, these items should not be purchased in quantities in excess of one item per adult:

FEATHER COMFORTERS
BINOCULARS
AIR RIFLES
BABY CLOTHES
CHILDREN'S TOYS
BOTTLES OF HARD LIQUOR
SHOES (PAIR)

VEHICLE BREAKDOWN - Attempt to repair on the spot. If unable, notify Military Police giving location and nature of the problem. Wait there, as a wrecker will be dispatched to your location.

TRAFFIC ACCIDENT - If minor, attempt to settle on the scene, and then notify the Military Police. If it is a major accident, or you are unable to settle on the scene, immediately notify the Military Police and wait for assistance. If GDR Police become involved, do not help or hinder their investigation, and request the presence of a Soviet Officer. You may accept emergency medical aid from GDR or Soviet authorities.

DETENTION BY GDR AUTHORITIES - Insist on your right to proceed. Attempt to proceed and if still detained, use flash card to request a Soviet Officer. You must remain at that location for 1 hour to give the Soviet Officer time to respond.

SECURITY AWARENESS - In case of SAEDA or other possible intelligence approaches/incidents, call the 766th Military Intelligence Detachment at Mil [illegible] or Civ [illegible] or the Air Force Office of Special Investigations at Mil [illegible].

DO NOT:

- allow your vehicle or person to be searched by GDR authorities.

- pay fines or acknowledge liability or guilt to GDR authorities in any incident.

- photograph GDR or Soviet military personnel, installations, or government buildings.

- enter any part of the GDR from the Soviet Sector of Berlin.

DO:

- act as "ambassadors" of the United States and be courteous at all times.

- obey all traffic laws and regulations.

- avoid crowds and gatherings that are observing or participating in rallies or demonstrations.

- provide assistance to other Allied travelers if needed.

Rules and Guidelines for visiting East Berlin— includes instructions for vehicular breakdown

In the fall of 1983, BAHS instituted a new idea to encourage students and families to broaden their horizons, it was called Activity Week. There were excursions planned by the school that were chaperoned by teachers, or your parents could sign you out of school to go on a trip (presumably with your family). Fourteen of us got our parents to sign us out of school for three Duty Train trips that week. We went to Braunschweig, West Germany and Strasbourg, France. In the end, only three of our group took the third and final trip to Frankfurt…the rest of us were too tired!

Fourteen Seniors Adventure To . .

Left: 1984 Yearbook featured Rose and friends for Activity Week. Above: Braunschweig-Sylvia A., Kim B., Robin M., Jessica J., Al F. and Andrea D.

Left: Rose on the French Duty Train. Right: The British Duty Train headed to Braunschweig

The Duty Train trip on our way to our senior trip to Greece was a memorable experience. We couldn't go to Spain as previous senior classes had done, because the class of '83 got in too much trouble the year before! Our bus broke down for ten hours in Yugoslavia on the way. It was way too cold in Greece in March, but we still went topless on the rocky beach.

Greece trip: broken down in Yugoslavia for ten hours!

Prom '84 was held at the Kempinski Hotel Berlin, the oldest five-star hotel in Europe. Afterwards, we all wondered around the Ku'damm in our fancy clothes.

I could write a book about my exploits in Berlin, but instead I'll list some highlights: Simon and Garfunkel, The Police, and Supertramp concerts at Waldbühne (an amphitheatre built for the 1936 Olympics). VIP Visits on base: Muhammad Ali visited our high school and Vice President George Bush spoke at the base gym. Green Week [Berlin International Green Week– an important international trade fair], where the teachers got drunk on free beer in one exhibit hall, and the students got drunk in another! The school trip to the Soviet Union in February 1984. The Hungarian rock band that told us we smelled good and wanted us to take their tape to AFN (American Forces Network radio)!

Berlin will ever live in my memory and my heart!

Rose Hanson Neel, Class of 1984
1979-1985

Prom 1984 at the Kempinski:
Kim Berg '84 and Sylvia Alexander '84

Rose wearing a Russian guard's hat marching down the Duty Train hallway

Left: AFN handbill
Right: Elton John concert ticket

Embassy Secrets

My husband was assigned to the U. S. Embassy to the DDR (Deutsche Demokratische Republic) from 1983 to 1985. The U.S. government did recognize and have relations with the DDR but we did not recognize Berlin as the capital. Berlin was an occupied city and as such, could not be the capital. I don't know what we did recognize as the capital but whenever documents came to us stating "Berlin, Hauptstadt der DDR [Berlin, Capital of the DDR]," they were returned and had to be corrected before being accepted.

I had come to Berlin earlier than my husband who was the accredited diplomat because I wanted to enroll our children in school on the first day. It took several weeks and much back and forth between the Embassy and the DDR to finally get my Ausweis (pass) so that I could travel with the children by means of Bornholmer Strasse, which was closer to our home than Checkpoint Charlie. Most Americans crossed into East Berlin via Checkpoint Charlie but as diplomats in the DDR we could cross through any of the checkpoints.

My children attended the John F. Kennedy Schule and were transported daily by embassy van to the school in West Berlin. On one occasion I was bringing the children home from an evening Lantern Parade at the JFK Schule and had agreed to bring home a little boy who lived near Checkpoint Charlie. His mother was German born and often crossed back and forth between the sectors on foot with her three small children. As we approached the checkpoint the little boy began to cry as he had left his Ausweis hanging on a hook back at the school. I didn't think it would be a problem since he was often seen by the guards with his mother but they would not let him through. I used the U. S. MP's phone to call her and she had to call a colleague of her husband to go the embassy and get his diplomatic passport from the safe in the office and bring it to us at the checkpoint. I had to wonder who they thought would try to smuggle a child INTO the DDR when people literally died trying to get out.

On another occasion, my daughter had a friend come after school to have dinner with us and go to the opera. Afterwards, my daughter told me she had forgotten her Ausweis at home so I had her lie down on the floor of our VW bus while I took her friend to Pizza Rita on Friedrichstrasse in the West, where we had agreed to meet her parents. She stayed on the floor until we returned through the checkpoint and were nearly home so that another silhouette would not be seen.

There were separate checkpoints to enter East Berlin depending on your status as a German. If you were born in Berlin you were a Berliner and had to go through one crossing. If you were born in West Germany you went through another. If you were foreign born you went through Checkpoint Charlie. Many of our children's friends' parents wanted to come visit us just to get into East Berlin, so if we had a birthday party, we had to obtain permits for all the different "classes" of guests. And if only children were coming we had to carefully plan who had to go through which checkpoint and have parents stationed nearby for pickup. It became quite a production so that I think each child had one party at home and the next time we went to the Zoo or McDonalds in West Berlin!

I never had to worry about where my children were playing since we had a Stasi (Ministry for State Security-aka East German secret police) stationed at the front of our house watching our every move. My husband loved to play games with the guard. He would go on the porch and the guard would come out of his shack. My husband would pretend to use a ballpoint pen to take a photo and the guard would turn and go into his shack. We would drive out of the garage and the guard would leave his shack. My husband would pull back into the garage, the guard would return to his shack, and then my husband would pull out of the garage again. Or he would drive around the block and come back so that the guard on the other end of the street would have to report we were coming back and our guard would be standing outside whereby my husband would drive off again. I often had to scold him that we would be late for an event if he kept this up. We would then arrive at the checkpoint where there was a white line for cars to wait behind before being motioned to the guard on duty. My husband would then either stop short of the guard or roll past him so that the guard always had to walk to him. It was his own little "cold war" with the Stasi.

I would love to have access to the tapes which they must have collected in our house. We knew we were bugged and years later my boys asked why their father hadn't taken out the bugs. He didn't because they would only install new ones. We were careful about what we spoke of in our house or car. It was a very interesting time to be living in Berlin.

Mary Beth Collins, Diplomat's Spouse
US Embassy in East Berlin, 1983-1985

Memories and "Currywurst mit Pommes Frites"

I can remember arriving in Berlin in the heat of the summer of 1983. I was 11 years old and very defiant to the idea of living in an old German city. I cried every day. I missed my family and friends in the United States and was adamant about letting my parents know it every other day or so…much to their delight.

Everything was new to me and experiencing the new German lifestyle was at first very awkward. Looking back on it now, I disliked everything my parents tried to show me about Berlin…I thought that if I started to like the small things, that my parents had "won" and I now somehow approved of being plucked from my nice, little life in the States and being transported to Germany without my vote.

Over the next few months, I made many new friends in the Berlin Brigade (BB) Housing area and the surrounding housing areas. As we gained the freedom to explore the city, our rally point was the Oscar-Helena-Heim U-Bahn station. While waiting for all our friends to arrive, we always seemed to venture over to the Imbiss stand and order up currywurst and pommes frites. The first time I had them, I was not impressed with the mayonnaise served with the pommes frites, but fell in the love with the currywurst! I remember giving my dad a hard time about the mayonnaise and told him that it just wasn't normal to eat french fries with anything but ketchup. After much complaining, he clearly was not amused.

Eventually, as I got more settled into a somewhat normal life, I realized that all of those things I tried to dislike about Berlin, I absolutely came to love…including my fries with mayonnaise. After leaving Berlin in 1987 and finally returning in 2011 for a short visit, one of the first things I wanted to do was hit the old neighborhood. The excitement I felt as I left my hotel in the former East Berlin was nerve-racking. First of all, who would have imagined that I would be staying in former East Berlin! The transformation of the city from the 1980s to 2011 was amazing.

I explored the old BB area, BAHS, TAR and the Italian restaurant formerly called Fra Diavolo's. The memories flooded my mind…all the way back to that rebellious child who tried to snub everything about Berlin. As I walked down Taylorstrasse, I imagined all of my old friends and the great laughs we shared. I could see that German ice cream truck coming down the street as all of us scurried to meet it. As I looked up at the 4th floor of the building we lived in, #12 Taylorstrasse, I remembered that first night we stayed in our new place. My brother David, sister Jamie and I all huddled together not quite sure what to think of it all…my parents tried to reassure us that everything was going to be just fine and we would soon make friends. They were right, we did. I also remembered some great moments as we grew accustomed to our new home and filled it with laughter.

I can still recall the excitement we experienced when we woke up to see the first snowfall of the winter. We would quickly rush to eat breakfast, get our moonboots on and head to "Killer Hill" for some sledding adventures. The first time we went, we quickly learned the routine of having to stop before accidently heading over the cliff at the bottom of the hill. The "cliff" was only about a ten foot drop, but significant enough to get us some cackling if we messed up.

As I walked back towards the old Truman Plaza area, which essentially no longer existed at this time, my mind wondered back to the many German-American Volksfests we enjoyed during our summers in Berlin. The rides were fun and the food was even better! Each year that I spent in Berlin just kept getting better and better.

I tried out for almost every sports team I could…I learned that soccer, softball and volleyball were my favorite sports and that I was really horrible at basketball and track. I looked forward to weekends we traveled on the Duty Train to West Germany to play the other teams/schools. My confidence grew as I excelled in sports. One of my favorite soccer memories was of us playing in the snow, freezing my tail off and scoring two goals. With a few minutes left in the game, I was covered in cold mud and was pulled out of the game early so I could head to the locker room. The boys' team coach, Mr. Schmoll, met me at the sidelines and told someone to grab a camera so he could take a picture with me. He could care less that I was covered head to foot in mud. Although you couldn't tell it from the look on my face, that moment made me so proud.

Michelle and Mr. Schmoll

I mentioned earlier about the transformation of the city of Berlin, but it was not only the city that changed…the city had also changed me. I am a better person today because of the things I got to experience during my four years there. I learned that it didn't matter how diverse we were as kids…the fact that we were all different didn't seem to cross my mind at all. It actually made us stronger. All that was important to me was having a great group of friends that I could count on anytime of the day.

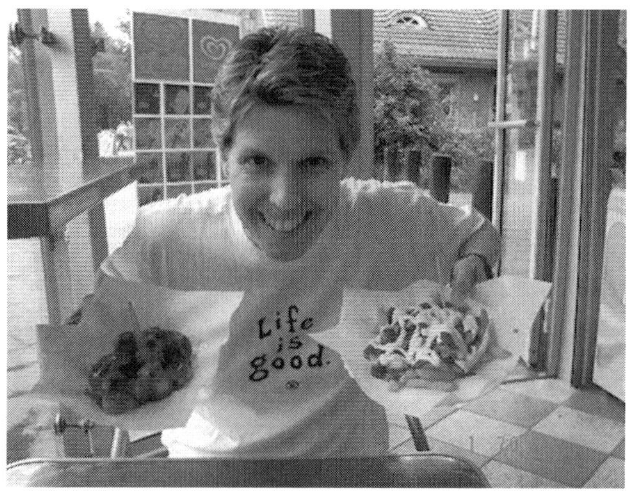

Currywurst mit pommes frites! Yum!

As I was ending my day of reminiscing, I had one more place to visit before heading back to the hotel. The 'Imbiss stand at Oscar.' I ordered my usual: currywurst mit pommes frites (and mayonnaise), along with some more memories!

Michelle Estes, Class of 1990
1983-1987

Michelle with the Allied Museum's section of the Wall

Close Call at the Disco

My family and I moved to Berlin when I was thirteen years old. By the time I was twenty I had fallen in love with and had adjusted to living in the occupied city. For most of my teen years I enjoyed doing the kinds of things that I probably would not have been able to do in the States. April 1986 was my last month in Berlin. I was not looking forward to leaving but I had planned on enjoying my last few weeks to the fullest. We were scheduled to fly out on May 1.

Berlin was a dynamic city with museums, art galleries, theaters, a symphony orchestra, botanical gardens, two zoos, restaurants, and a variety of festivals. The city's architecture was eclectic and intriguing having been influenced by the national governments that had been based there during the 19th and 20th centuries. Berlin also had a nightlife that was one of the most vibrant and diverse in Europe. It would be difficult not to find something of interest for every member of the family. It was a wonderful place to spend my teen years!

With one month left I was looking forward to having a great time doing things I knew I wouldn't be able to do once I got back to the States. The legal drinking age had recently changed in most states from eighteen to twenty-one. The things I'd been able to do since my mid-teens involved mostly going to clubs and enjoying an adult beverage without being harassed about age. With nine months to go before my 21st birthday, going to clubs and partying like the rock star I was, would be out of the question once I was stateside.

For the last year and a half that I was in Berlin I worked at the Burger Bar (yes, the Burger Bar) at Andrews Barracks. I had made friends with my coworkers and we would get together outside of work for the occasional girls' night out. We were all in our late teens or early twenties. Some were married and some were single. Clubbing was usually at the top of our list of things to do for our outings. My coworkers had decided they wanted to go to a club I had never been to before. It was a club that I wouldn't normally go to. I preferred other clubs popular at the time like the Ecstasy, the Riverboat and the 25.

My coworkers were making all the plans for this particular outing. There were a lot of clubs that were frequented by American service members and dependents. La Belle's was a particular favorite. Like I said, it wasn't a club I would normally go to but since I was leaving Berlin soon I thought it would be a great time. Why not go?

I was scheduled to work until 9:30 pm the night we planned on going out so I brought my party clothes with me. I would change clothes at a coworker's house before heading out for the evening. Since nightlife in Berlin didn't really get started until well after midnight we had plenty of time to get the party started somewhere else before heading downtown. As luck would have it our plans fell through and we ended up not going out. It turned out to be a blessing for my friends and me.

Friday April 4, 1986 was the night my coworkers and I had planned our girls' night out. In the early morning hours of April 5th, La Belle's– the club we were planning to go to– was bombed. Of the 230 people injured, two of the three killed were American soldiers. After we got back to the States I remember reading an article in *People* magazine about Sgt. Kenneth Ford, 21, one of the American soldiers killed in the attack.

At twenty it was impossible for me to grasp the implications of that terrorist attack. Life in Berlin most certainly changed for us Americans and, I'm sure, for the other occupying forces in the city. The changes that took place were strange for us at the time– we no longer had certain freedoms. In light of the events of 911, the changes in our day to day lives in Berlin wouldn't be unheard of to most Americans today.

Our ID cards were checked more closely, bags were searched upon entry to any American facility, we were told to report suspicious looking packages and, generally, be more aware of our surroundings and people who looked out of place. The most troubling change to everyday life was that American school buses had armed escorts to and from school every day. Americans also had a curfew of midnight every night.

Even today, almost three decades later, it's hard for me to wrap my brain around events of that night and how different life really could have been had things gone as we had planned.

Kerry Lastra, Class of 1984
1979-1986

AMERICAN ATTACK ON LIBYA. Governing Mayor Diepgen stated last week that Berlin's Senat has been informed by American authorities about the attack on Libya already early in the morning. Berlin police immediately had then initiated additional measures to protect the city. Diepgen asked the Berliners to show understanding for the measures. *(all papers)*

RAINING ON THE PARADE. Turnout was lighter than expected for the demonstration Saturday against American actions in Libya. The anti-American march began at the Luftbrücke Memorial, a monument dedicated to the memory of the American fliers who were killed in the Berlin airlift. The march concluded peacefully downtown near the Ku'damm. *(Morgenpost)*

Sgt. Kenneth Ford- His death at La Belle led to President Reagan ordering strikes against Libya on April 15th;although Mayor Diepgen asked Berliners to show understanding (top clipping), a demonstration was held the following Saturday.

The La Belle Disco Bombing

By April of 1986, I was already married and transferred from being a juvenile dependent to a spouse of a soldier. We were waiting for housing for quite a time and happened onto a neat little efficiency apartment on a street lined with pre-World War I apartments. Once we locked in on the apartment, we had to line up furnishings. It took the better part of a month to get everything. My husband had gone to the field and I had a newborn. My parents would not let me stay at the apartment alone, with it mostly unfurnished.

My friends and I spent a lot of time at the apartment, cleaning it and hanging out at it. On the night of April 4th, 1986, a couple of us ended up at the apartment. I can't really even recall what we did there. My son was at my parents' house, and I was sitting in what was becoming my new apartment– a place I was "not allowed" to sleep over at. Somewhere after 0100 hrs, we joked that the wallpaper was taking a whole new dimension and it was time to call it a night.

We bundled up and headed out the door to the taxi stand at the end of the street. I lived a little over a block from a busy taxi stand– frequented by the patrons of several bars, the main one being the La Belle discotheque, which was a little over a city block in another direction from my apartment. We shared a cab, and as the cab was leaving the stand, it was halted by two or three US Military gun trucks racing past. As they went by, we made the joke that, "Uh-ho, someone is lost again." (On an occasion the summer prior, we'd helped a couple of lost vehicles find their unit.)

Up until then, unless they were on maneuvers, we rarely saw the formation of two soldiers in the front and one soldier standing with a mounted rifle. It was a detail that stuck in my head for some time.

Another detail that did not add up right away: as we drove down the street, we experienced a sonic boom. As my 3 year old niece always said, we presumed it was "Jus de Wushians" (Russians) with their fly-over sonic booms. We giggled as we proclaimed, "Jus' de Wushians."

The ride to my parent's house was just under a mile. I exited the cab, crawled up the stairs to the guestroom and passed out, almost instantly. As the world was swirling away, I heard the phone ring and a sudden flurry of activity. Then a lot of foot traffic. Middle of the night phone calls generally represent family emergencies. In our house, it was not terribly uncommon, because my dad was always getting calls from the Communications Center– those calls where he suddenly seemed to speak in code and hushed tones.

There were no hushed tones that night. The guestroom had two doors on it. One entered through an ante room and one was the main door to the room. Both doors flew open simultaneously. Teenage guilt told me I'd done something wrong. My mom looked crazed for those first few seconds.

Demanding to know where I'd been, where my friends were, if I knew where they all were? She was desperate that I account for my friends. I think my sister or my father was standing in the other doorway. My brain was hardly processing any of it. I really could not figure out why I was in trouble or why my friends were. We were adults.

A moment later, after she conferred with my father, they came back in and told us that a bombing had occurred– at a discotheque frequented by Americans and they thought my friends and I might have gone there– since it was so close to my new place.

The following days were muddled. I got my furniture, and I wanted to stay at my apartment. My father and I fought tooth and nail, because I would not listen to him. He could not tell me why, but he wanted me to follow him unquestioningly. The day of April 15, I was in my apartment and he came over and would not leave. He hung all my pictures, unpacked, fixed and arranged until there was nothing more to do. Then insisted we go home and eat dinner. When we turned on the radio for the news and heard what America had done in retaliation, I realized why my dad was so bothered about leaving me alone.

There was so much that happened in Berlin that my dad knew– but could never talk about. Looking back, there were so many things that happened in front of my face that I was clueless about.

Some years later my (current) husband, who is Army, was writing a report for a class on terrorism. This was in the very early days following 911. He had printed off a lot of different sources and citations about different terrorist events over the years. I was going through his papers reading different events and came to one about the La Belle bombing. The report showed that the (US) General had been at an event and had received information about chatter of an attack on a bar/discotheque frequented by Americans. He had dispatched several sets of gun trucks out to the different clubs that were known hangouts. Additionally, in the days following, there were many reports of threats made to American school children and American families– hurting us where we lived.

Reading the reports, it all came back about seeing those soldiers in the mounted gun trucks racing towards La Belles. It never occurred to me they were going there to investigate. Following the bombing and retaliation, the Outpost Theater was closed for a time for repairs. Actually, it was closed to keep us all away from it, to avoid further harm.

It seemed that one day in Berlin we were the city of romance and intrigue, enclosed by the wall, living eye to eye in a spy-vs-spy atmosphere. I don't think we really took it seriously what we were living so close to. Then La Belle's took a hit and our school buses were suddenly led and followed by armed MPs in gun trucks. The schools were surrounded in chain link and guarded by soldiers. The innocence, or perhaps perceived innocence, faded into an entirely different reality. I'd been a high schooler and then a military spouse there. It was surreal to see my friends at the high school being guarded by my (then) husband and his fellow soldiers.

From the point of the bombing, life in Berlin became very fractured.

Juli-Jay Hamilton Wollam, Class of 1986
1981-1986

Maj. Gen. John H. Mitchell awards the Purple Heart to Pvt. 2 Timothy Henderson, one of 37 awarded medals Memorial Day.

Wounded earn medals

37 awarded Purple Heart in Memorial Day ceremony

Thirty-seven soldiers injured in the April 5 La Belle bombing were awarded the Purple Heart by U.S. Commander of Berlin Maj. Gen. John H. Mitchell in a Memorial Day Ceremony at Clay Headquarters here.

The group joined two other soldiers who have received the medal for being injured in the bombing. SSgt. James E. Goins had his Purple Heart pinned onto his bed pillow here April 30 by the Commander in Chief, U.S. Army Europe, Gen. Glenn K. Otis. Goins is still listed as very seriously ill by the Klinikum Steglitz here.

On May 2 SP4 Marvin Ragin was awarded his Purple Heart by Secretary of the Army John O. Marsh, Jr. at Fort Gordon, Ga.

The soldiers were among the 230 people injured in the terrorist bombing which killed Sgt. Kenneth T. Ford and a Turkish woman.

Marsh decided April 30 that those who medically qualified should be awarded the Purple Heart. The decision is in line with the Feb. 23 1984 Executive Order signed by President Ronald Reagan which authorized the award of the Purple Heart to victims of terrorist action.

Elaborating on that point, Mitchell noted that, "Some are confused by the awarding of a traditionally combat-oriented medal for acts of state-sponsored terrorism. I am here to tell you those people have their eyes closed and live in the past. State terrorism is not only an act of cowardice and immorality. It is an act as deadly and as war-like to Americans as any declared conflict we have had in over 200 years as a nation.

"I can assure you that I feel the same sense of pride in presenting these awards today as I felt 15 years ago when

continued on page 12

BOMBING SUSPECT ARRESTED. Most papers reported the arrest of a Palestinian man, Ahmad Hasi, in West Berlin last Saturday in connection with the bombing of the La Belle disco. Reports say that he is possibly the brother of Nezar Hindawi, who was arrested in London last Friday on charges that he had used his girlfriend in a failed attempt to smuggle a bomb on board an EL AL airliner.

LIBYAN DIPLOMAT MOHAMMED ASHOUR was a CIA agent who knew the people behind the bomb attack on the La Belle discotheque, according to Bonn intelligence. Agents of the Libyan intelligence service in the night of May 2-3 lured him to a park in East Berlin where they shot him dead. West Berlin's authorities have not yet been officially informed about the death of Ashour, but were asked to secure the estate of the deceased, Justice Administration spokesman Neuhaus said. Ashour lived in the "Salvador Allende" student dormitory at Clayallee. *(Berliner Morgenpost, Bild)*

Left: Pres. Reagan signed an Executive Order in 1984 authorizing the award of the Purple Heart to victims of terrorist attacks. Right: Political intrigue surrounds the death of the Libyan diplomat/CIA agent Mohammed Ashour who was lured to a park in East Berlin and murdered.

The Human Side of the Wall

It was December 1986 and although it was freezing cold in addition to just recovering from being sick as a dog, I was in the mood and had enough energy to hop on my 10 speed bike and go for a ride. I remember not really knowing where I was headed or what I wanted to see. I had cabin fever and just wanted to get out of my room. I arrived at the corner of Taylorstrasse, right near the church and decided to take a right. Small snowflakes began to fall and I even considered turning around…but I kept on pedaling. Something told me that I needed to just be outside. Although I could feel the tears roll down my face from the cold, I enjoyed the wind in my face. It really felt great to finally be out of the house and exploring Berlin.

I experimented with my speed, accelerating and decelerating often…loving my freedom. I rode and rode until I could ride no more…the road suddenly came to an end and I encountered an unexpected Berlin Wall. I looked up to see a guard tower and a plump old man in an East German uniform looking down on me as I peered up at him in curiosity. I wondered what his life was like…wondered if he had any family in West Berlin. I remember thinking that he didn't look very happy and must have been cold. I wondered if he was thinking that I was some crazy American or if he thought I was German.

Here I was enjoying my freedom and being able to go anywhere I wanted to (within West Berlin, of course) and he was limited. We stared at each other for a few moments before I realized that the only thing I could offer him to hopefully cheer him up was a friendly smile and a wave. He stared back for a few seconds before ever so slightly returning the smile. I turned my bike around and headed back to the comfort of my warm home.

As I entered the house, my mom was preparing dinner. I wondered if I should share my story of the encounter with my family or just keep it to myself. As simple as it seemed, I felt as though during that moment I had changed the world and contributed something to mankind. Growing up, I had always watched my parents have their own moments of kindness and now I had my very own. It made me feel very proud, even more importantly, it awakened my humanity.

After spending nearly 3 ½ years in Berlin and witnessing several incidents of frightened East Germans, it all came together at that moment. Maybe it's because I felt that the experience was just mine...my mom or dad wasn't right behind me making me use my manners and extend a pleasantry…I did it all on my own, out of the goodness of my heart. Maybe I was turning into a responsible, young adult and it felt great. Even though I wanted their approval, I decided to keep that day to myself.

A few years later, in 1989, I was living in Del Rio, Texas where my Dad was assigned to Laughlin AFB as an Air Traffic Controller. I had just walked into the house and had turned on the television. The volume was turned down but I could clearly see that tons of people were standing on the Berlin Wall and appeared to be either really defiant or celebrating. Some of the people were helping others by extending a hand and pulling others up onto the Wall. I was shocked…I didn't understand what they were doing up there.

I think I even said out loud, "Oh my goodness, if they don't get down, they are going to get shot." I quickly turned up the volume in time to hear the newscaster state that the Berlin Wall was coming down. Wow!…did I just hear that right? The Berlin Wall was coming down? Forever? Was this a trick? I couldn't wrap my mind around it but was ecstatic!!!

I ran into my parents' room to tell my Dad. He had just arrived from work a few minutes earlier. I was trying to tell him what I had seen and remember him saying that I must be incorrect because the Wall is not coming down. Out of frustration and anxiousness, I told him to hurry up and turn on the television. He couldn't believe it. Moments later my Mom walked into the room and asked us what the matter was…we just pointed to the TV and said "The Berlin Wall is coming down." We all just sat there in disbelief and watched the events unfold.

My thoughts traveled back to my trip to the Wall, the guard and our small moment of kindness. I imagined him again, smiling.

Michelle Estes, Class of 1990
1983-1987

There were approximately 300 observation towers which varied in height and style, usually manned by two guards— one Soviet and one East German.

Teaching at BAHS

To visit a foreign country was a dream of mine since 7th grade and then, coincidentally, in my senior year I wrote my term paper about Berlin and the Wall. Resigning from my teaching position, I left for Europe with a backpack, one-way ticket and the paperwork necessary to find a job. I became a local hire and left BAHS after two years to teach at the JFK Schule.

My experience with the military was very limited albeit my family has served in every war beginning with the Crusades and ending with my son's service in the Gulf War as a Warthog pilot. I respected military rules, regulations and the mission in Berlin.

Teaching the Berlin Brats was incredible, interesting and helpful. The students, experiences and missteps left a profound impact on me. I was speaking to a student in the shop class about the beat up VW bug I was driving with no radio, although I did not listen to a car radio very often. He told me he could get me a cheap radio for ten dollars, 'no problem.' Well, sometime after I got that radio installed, I received a call from the CID (Criminal Investigation Division) asking me to come in to see them.

Berlin American High School, 1984

I did not know what the CID was; I told him I was teaching and could not come. Another phone call later, and they arrived at the school questioning me about the radio; they told me they thought I was the ring leader of several incident of stolen radios. They did not have a good impression of some of the educators, telling me another faculty member had been under investigation for other crimes; I never heard how that incident was resolved.

In addition to teaching English, I was the cross country coach. Traveling on the Duty Train was required for a coach. On one of our trips with the team it came to my attention that one of my runners was missing his paperwork and we had already left West Berlin! I do not, to this day, know how that happened. This was a serious duty of mine and I was derelict. I told the student to hide and I knew that if he was taken off the train I was going with him. This incident haunts me to this day.

During my time there, the La Belle disco bombing took place and the students were deeply affected. An armed guard trolled the hallways, and the buses were escorted by a jeep with mounted weaponry. I remember a student telling me that he had not joined the military– his father had.

The spring before I left, I biked the Berlin Wall, never giving a thought that the Wall would disappear in the following year. Those were special times. I remember telling someone later that I had taught in Berlin during the Cold War years and felt safe; there was so much military presence. He looked at me and said, "Berlin was a very dangerous place during that time."

I have nothing but the deepest regard and respect for all the students who enriched my life during my time in Berlin.

Louise Edwards Bakken, Faculty
English, Publications, Boys and Girls Cross Country Coach, 1983-1986

Mr. Leonard

I first met Mr. Alan Leonard at BAHS in the 1982-83 time frame. He was a skinny little man with big black rimmed glasses and a toupee that looked like a hair helmet. He wore collared shirts tucked into his slacks every day and had a very proper appearance. He definitely had a sort of Woody Allen vibe. He was sarcastic and witty, but not in an overt way, his jokes were subtle so that only the kids who read history lessons actually understood. In other words, most of his jokes went over my head.

I never really got to know Mr. Leonard when I was in his class, mostly because I tried to avoid going to any classes. It was pretty easy to skip school in those days. The first time I really got a glimpse into who Mr. Leonard was and how much he valued his privacy and dignity, was when he chaperoned the trip to the Soviet Union in February to 1984. We all went to East Berlin to fly on Aeroflot to Moscow. Then we traveled around the Soviet Union which included taking additional flights to other regions.

For some reason the customs inspectors at the airport decided to target Mr. Leonard. I am not sure why they felt he looked more suspicious than our resident stoner classmate, W.H. They pulled Mr. Leonard aside and searched every inch of his bags. They pulled out his underwear and rifled through his personal items. He was clearly shaken and seemed humiliated by the experience. I felt pretty bad for him, but it also endeared

Aeroflot Soviet Airlines baggage tag

me to him a bit. I started to see him as a person and less like a mysterious teacher that leaves the school campus to some unknown life.

Allan Leonard
History

After I graduated from BAHS, I stayed in Berlin and worked at the golf course. I dated a guy who lived down the hall from Mr. Leonard. One day (like an idiot), I decided to stop by and say hello to Mr. Leonard unannounced. I knocked on the door; he opened and stood there in his bathrobe. I smiled, kind of embarrassed, and uttered something kind of giddy like, "Oh, I'm sorry. I just stopped by to say hi." He promptly slammed the door in my face. That was my last interaction with Mr. Leonard in Berlin. It was not a good manner to part ways.

Then in 2005, I was living at Fort Belvoir, VA when tragedy struck NOLA. A call went out to Brats to check on Mr. Leonard and keep his spirits up. I called him as requested and so began our new relationship. He was desperate to go home when he was displaced by Katrina and living in a hotel in Alabama. I tried to find him housing for several weeks and had lined up a place just when Hurricane Rita hit, so that place fell through.

Finally, I decided to call a real estate office. I talked to Randi __. After hearing of Mr. Leonard's plight, she was moved that this retired teacher had students that were trying to get him resettled. Thank goodness for Randi. Over the next few years she became an advocate for Mr. Leonard. She helped him get his property sold, found a house for him and then when that became too much to manage, she helped find a retirement community.

During the years following Katrina and up until his death, I called Mr. Leonard regularly. I called once a week at first, until he was settled, but I never let more than a month go by without calling. He was amazed that I could go online and find his favorite old movies and have them shipped to him in less than a week. I bought a lot of old movies. He loved musicals.

He told me many stories about his life. He told of his 'ratter' of a cat in NOLA and how he got on the transport boats to Europe. He went to Japan and was quite the entrepreneur. I was advised by my good friend Pete Murphy '84 not to share too many of the details. It was post-war craziness with shortages of lots of staples...you can imagine what he was up to.

He would recommend movies made in Berlin so we could talk about them. He was funny telling me about his shot in a movie with Paul Newman (I can't remember the title). He said it wasn't a very good movie, but he has a funny scene where he watches a pretty woman walk by him in a bar. The best part is that he is going bald in that shot. We only ever saw him with a toupee. We spent many hours getting to know each other. He loved hearing my son, Jack in the background and always asked me what he was doing. I sent him photos of my family and boxes of $100,000 dollar bars. He hated unsolicited gifts, but the man loved candy bars.

As he started to deteriorate, I could hear his frustration with people that cared for him. He stopped being able to leave the home after falling too many times. He hated it when I called his brother to go check on him. I got very frustrated trying to engage him in conversation. Then I had a very sweet conversation with Mr. Bluem (a much-liked teacher at BAHS). I called him to relay a message from Mr. Leonard. I told him that it wasn't always easy to get Mr. Leonard to open up and just talk anymore. Mr. Bluem told me that he knew that Mr. Leonard could be a bit difficult, but that I was doing a good thing and not to let his demeanor stop me– that Mr. Leonard needed me to care. He told me I was a good person for keeping up the effort. It made me feel so proud to have kept my conversations going with Mr. Leonard. I always adored Mr. Bluem and his kind words and pat on the back meant everything to me.

I knew Mr. Leonard's health was degrading in the early part of 2011. He was in constant need of care and often nurses would answer his phone. He would always want to take my call even when he could barely speak. I wasn't really surprised when I got the call that Mr. Leonard had passed away. His niece called me and said that she was with Mr. Leonard at the end. She said while Mr. Leonard was in hospice care and just before he died, he asked her to call the love of his life, a teacher that he once loved many years ago and me, to let us know of his situation and his passing.

I intentionally put my name and phone number on almost every card I sent, in case anyone was trying to reach me. He died shortly after his birthday and had many unopened cards in his room. His niece said that she was genuinely touched to read them and found my card with my number.

Mr. Leonard remembered a lot of students' names and some of their antics, but he did not remember me from his Berlin days. I wasn't a good student, or a bad student, so I just blended in with the many kids that passed through his life. He didn't remember slamming the door in my face and I never reminded him. I never could have imagined that he would be worried about me hearing of his passing on his deathbed. I am just so thankful that the efforts by the Berlin Brats, and Jeri in particular, to reach out to our teacher in a time of need, brought Mr. Leonard back into my life.

Rose Hanson Neel, Class of 1984
1979-1985

President Reagan and the Class of '87

I was lucky enough to get to see Ronald Reagan during both of his presidential visits to Berlin. Although it was during his 1982 visit that I got to shake his hand, it's the second time I saw him that is more special to me.

Originally, the Berlin American High School Class of 1987 graduation was to be held on June 12th, 1987. At some point during the school year, we heard that Reagan would be visiting Berlin on that very day. We of course had the audacity to write a formal request to the White House via the U.S. Embassy in East Berlin (probably through someone's parent) inviting him to speak at our graduation ceremony at the Olympic Stadium. Being the arrogant kids we were, we actually thought he would accept.

He didn't.

But the White House did offer a compromise. If we would be open to moving our graduation to another day, the State Department would insure we had access to a private function and be recognized by the President.

Yeah, hmm, I don't know, let us think about it...

...arrangements were immediately made to push our graduation to the following day.

The year 1987 was Berlin's 750th anniversary– and the official reason for Presidents Reagan's visit was to mark the occasion and celebrate. While most people are familiar with Reagan's speech at the Brandenburg Gate, with his immortal line "Mr. Gorbachev, open this gate. Mr. Gorbachev, tear down this wall!" many are unaware there was a second speech, more intimate, at the invitation-only "American Birthday Party for Berlin," held at the B Halle of Tempelhof Central Airport. It was at this event that the American President would address the BAHS Class of '87.

On June 12th, 1987, while the rest of BAHS took advantage of the day off from school and gathered– along with the rest of Berlin– on Straße des 17. Juni in front of the Brandenburg Gate, the senior class arrived at B Halle, serial numbered invitations in hand, bedecked in caps and gowns (God, I hope I used the word bedecked correctly). Befitting a birthday party, there was free food and drinks (God, I hope I used the term befitting correctly). We milled about and enjoyed the refreshments.

Sidebar: I would like to state for the record it would have been entirely inappropriate for me and my classmates to have partaken in alcohol at an official American government (and, I suppose, school) function.

The event had a full schedule of entertainment, with speeches and music, including a singing performance by the Class of 87's very own Jasper Kump. (Yeah, WE Sang for the PRESIDENT. What did YOUR CLASS do??? And by we, I mean Jasper of course.) The speech at the Brandenburg Gate was broadcast on a giant television, with a big cheer for the President's "Tear down this Wall" challenge ringing through the hall. Our anticipation grew as the speech concluded, and President Reagan left for TCA.

We were herded to a particular area of B Halle to stand as a group, along with the senior class of John F. Kennedy Schule. (In a fit of unwarranted fairness, the State Department invited JFK as well, despite the idea and work being ours.) Before long, the President arrived. I don't remember much of the speech itself, although I do remember one of the balloons along the ceiling– to be dropped at the speeches conclusion– popping, causing the president to say, without missing a beat, "you missed me." This drew a big laugh.

Then, during his speech, this moment arrived: "...I am happy to see so many young people here this afternoon. There are two groups of local teenagers I would like to greet in a special way– the graduating classes of Berlin American High School and (some other school… the transcript gets tough to understand here). Congratulations on a job well done!"

I consider it a great honor to have been present for that moment, and for my small group to be singularly recognized. I didn't do anything special to be there. The timing of it was because of the randomness of my birth year, and the location was due to my Dad having been selected to be stationed in Berlin, and then having retired there. And others in my class (and faculty I presume) did the heavy lifting of making it happen– apologies for not giving credit to those who did that work, I am simply not completely sure who it was >cough< Homer >cough<.

But to have such a man take even a moment to speak specifically to me and my classmates is something in which I feel immense pride. Sure, I wasn't there for the big, historic speech. Thousands and thousands of other people were. At the Brandenburg Gate, the president was speaking to Berlin, Gorbachev, and the World. But a little bit later, for just a moment, in front of a much smaller crowd, President Ronald Reagan spoke to me and my friends. And I think that's pretty awesome.

(A quick shout out to Jennifer Mandel, an archivist at the Reagan Library– she was kind enough to email me the transcript of the speech, saying "Somehow we missed getting this speech up on our website– thanks for alerting us to the problem!" I'm expecting some kind of presidential medal any day now.)

Rob Ahrens, Class of 1987
1982-1987

Berlin Observer

Vol. 43, No. 24 · U.S. Command, Berlin · June 19, 1987

Gala bash President Ronald Reagan at Tempelhof Central Airport's B-Halle. Accompanying Reagan at the 750th Berlin birthday celebration are first Lady Nancy Reagan, Governing Mayor Eberhard Diepgen and Ambassador to Germany Richard Burt. For the story, see page 2.

Tempelhof Airport, B-Halle, after the balloon drop

Tempelhof Airport
Presidential arrival (left) and Mormon Children's Choir perform at the gala (right)

I Sang for President Ronald Reagan

I am the son of a US Air Force officer and lived in Germany for six years from 1981 through 1987. The last 3 years of that time, my father was stationed at Tempelhof and we lived just a short walk from what is now the site of the Allied Museum. My father was the Director of Public Relations for the Air Force in West Berlin, so he was very involved in arranging the logistics and press for President Regan's visit in the summer of 1987.

My sister and I were both very excited to hear the news of our President visiting to celebrate Berlin's 750th Anniversary. There would be a special event at Tempelhof to honor Berlin's Anniversary that was to be hosted by President and Mrs. Reagan. My father mentioned to me that they were looking for some local talent to perform at the gala. As a singer, I jumped at the chance to audition! I was among hundreds who showed up, and one of a handful of singers selected to perform. I was elated. At that moment, I had no idea how memorable that entire day would be.

President Reagan gave his speech to a packed crowd of Germans and Americans right at the Wall near the Brandenburg Gate. I was not able to go, as I was at a sound check with Horst Jankowski and the RIAS Orchestra at Tempelhof, but my sister Linda was near the very front. She said that Nancy Reagan waved at her and that many on the East side of the Wall were hanging out of windows trying to hear and see. Once the President's speech began, the hall at Tempelhof where we were rehearsing went quiet and some televisions near the press rooms were on. All of the performers and musicians nearby stopped to hear what he had to say. I was so excited that he was actually in BERLIN and proud that he spoke so eloquently. His voice was strong and filled with hope. I could see my sister on the television as they panned across the crowd– I wished that I could be there with her.

When he spoke the words "Mr. Gorbachev, tear down this wall!" my heart jumped with a strange mixture of excitement, joy and fear. I loved Berlin and considered it my hometown. How wonderful would it be to have a free Berlin where everyone could enjoy all that the city was and is? Wouldn't it be great if everyone could travel wherever they wanted, whenever they wanted? I thought of families reunited after years apart. But were these words that could start a conflict? Was tearing down the Wall even really possible? These thoughts continued to ring in my head as I listened to the roar of the crowd clapping and cheering for the President's now famous words.

After his speech, President and Mrs. Reagan made a couple of stops to greet people elsewhere in the city, and then made their way to Tempelhof for the celebration. I was so nervous! Not only was my graduating class, the Class of 1987 going to be recognized by our President, but I was going to actually get to sing for him and all of his guests with Horst Jankowski and the RIAS Orchestra! I was afraid I might not be able to do it. But I did. I stood on stage with the orchestra as the President and Mrs. Reagan arrived and welcomed their guests. I sang "Summertime" from Porgy & Bess as well as "The Greatest Love of All" originally sung by Whitney Houston. That's when the President recognized our class and I watched as my classmates stood together across the hall on another stage as he addressed them. To be honest, I was so excited that I don't even remember what he said.

At the end, just as President and Mrs. Reagan were leaving, I sang "Wochenends und Sonnenschein" ("Happy Days are Here Again"). Little did I know how appropriate that song selection was. Later that night, my friends and I celebrated and talked a lot about everything that had happened. We seemed to keep coming back to one question. Could the Wall really come down during our lifetime? This was the question that President Regan's speech put on everyone's' minds. Our answer: probably not. We didn't believe that it would happen until much, much later– and that we may never see it in our lifetime. Just two years later– Gorbachev did exactly as our President had asked. We were overjoyed and amazed.

President Reagan speaks at the Brandenburg Gate

Years later, on the day that President Reagan died, I was remembering the summer of 1987 in Berlin and his famous words. I saw footage of his speech on CNN and there was my sister, right up front! At the time we knew it was something special to be there and be part of it all in our own way. What an impact Reagan's words and his life have had on me, my family and friends, and millions of others throughout the world. But nowhere more than BERLIN!

Jasper Kump, Class of 1987
1981-1987

Remarks on the 750th Anniversary of the Founding of Berlin

"Well, Chancellor Kohl and Mayor Diepgen, Ambassador Burt, ladies and gentlemen: It's an honor for me to be able to join you today at this 750th birthday party for the city of Berlin. I'm especially pleased to be here today because—well, it's not often that I get to go to a birthday party for something that's older than I am. [Laughter]

But to subject you to a second speech here—[laughter]—you know, I keep thinking of a story of ancient Rome, where, on a Saturday afternoon, the hungry lions were turned loose on the little group of people there on the floor of the Coliseum, and they came charging toward them. And one individual stepped out of the group, said something very quietly, and the lions all laid down.

Well, the crowd was enraged and horrified that they're going to be denied the show. And Caesar sent for the man who had spoken to the lions. And they brought him, and he said, 'What did you say to them that made them act like that?' And he said, 'I just told them that after they ate, there'd be speeches.'[Laughter]

Well, let me begin by conveying the warmest greetings of the American people to all of you here today. While only a small fraction of the Berlin community can be here in this hall, our good wishes go to all the residents of this marvelous city, wherever they may live. And I am happy to see so many young people here this afternoon. ***There are two groups of local teenagers I would like to greet in a special way- the graduating classes of the Berlin-American High School and of the city's John F. Kennedy School. Congratulations on a job well done!"***

"America— Missed me! [referring to balloon popping][Laughter] America has a special relationship with Berlin that extends beyond formal political or economic ties. Like America, Berlin is a place of great energy. We see our own hopes and ideals mirrored in the energy and courage of Berliners and draw strength from our joint efforts here.

This sense is symbolized by the nearly 14,000 American soldiers, airmen, and their families who live and work in close cooperation with Berliners to ensure the defense of our common goals. And let me make one point clear: Our troops will remain here as long as they are wanted and needed by Berliners to demonstrate to the other side that force and coercion cannot succeed. Several thousand other Americans from all walks of life make an important contribution to the business and cultural life of this city. We've joined the centuries-old tradition of Berlin and, in a real sense, we have become Berliners.

A few moments ago here at Tempelhof, I shook hands with three men who testify to the way you Berliners and we Americans play such a proud role in each other's lives: Three former U.S. Air Force pilots, veterans of one of the most remarkable operations in modern history, the Berlin Airlift. On his flights, Colonel Gale Halvorsen tossed small, candy-filled parachutes to the children of Berlin as his plane approached the Tempelhof runway. Yes, Colonel Halvorsen was one of the famous Rosinenbombers or bomber priors who every Berliner of that generation still remembers with warmth and affection."

--Ronald Wilson Reagan- June 12, 1987 Tempelhof Air Base

Excerpts from Pres. Reagan's Speech at the Brandenburg Gate:

"Twenty-four years ago, President John F. Kennedy visited Berlin, speaking to the people of this city and the world at the City Hall. Well, since then two other presidents have come, each in his turn, to Berlin. And today I, myself, make my second visit to your city."

"In the Reichstag a few moments ago, I saw a display commemorating this 40th anniversary of the Marshall Plan. I was struck by the sign on a burnt-out, gutted structure that was being rebuilt. I understand that Berliners of my own generation can remember seeing signs like it dotted throughout the western sectors of the city. The sign read simply: "The Marshall Plan is helping here to strengthen the free world." A strong, free world in the West, that dream became real. Japan rose from ruin to become an economic giant. Italy, France, Belgium--virtually every nation in Western Europe saw political and economic rebirth; the European Community was founded."

"General Secretary Gorbachev, if you seek peace, if you seek prosperity for the Soviet Union and Eastern Europe, if you seek liberalization, come here to this gate. Mr. Gorbachev, open this gate. ***Mr. Gorbachev, tear down this wall****!"*

The Fernsehturm (TV Tower) aka the Pope's Revenge

"As I looked out a moment ago from the Reichstag, that embodiment of German unity, I noticed words crudely spray-painted upon the wall, perhaps by a young Berliner, 'This wall will fall. Beliefs become reality.' Yes, across Europe, this wall will fall. For it cannot withstand faith; it cannot withstand truth. The wall cannot withstand freedom."

"Perhaps this gets to the root of the matter, to the most fundamental distinction of all between East and West. The totalitarian world produces backwardness because it does such violence to the spirit, thwarting the human impulse to create, to enjoy, to worship. The totalitarian world finds even symbols of love and of worship an affront. Years ago, before the East Germans began rebuilding their churches, they erected a secular structure: the television tower at Alexander Platz. Virtually ever since, the authorities have been working to correct what they view as the tower's one major flaw, treating the glass sphere at the top with paints and chemicals of every kind. Yet even today when the sun strikes that sphere--that sphere that towers over all Berlin--the light makes the sign of the Cross. There in Berlin, like the city itself, symbols of love, symbols of worship, cannot be suppressed."

"And I would like, before I close, to say one word. I have read, and I have been questioned since I've been here about certain demonstrations against my coming. And I would like to say just one thing, and to those who demonstrate so. I wonder if they have ever asked themselves that if they should have the kind of government they apparently seek, no one would ever be able to do what they're doing again.

Thank you and God bless you all." --President Ronald Reagan - June 12, 1987

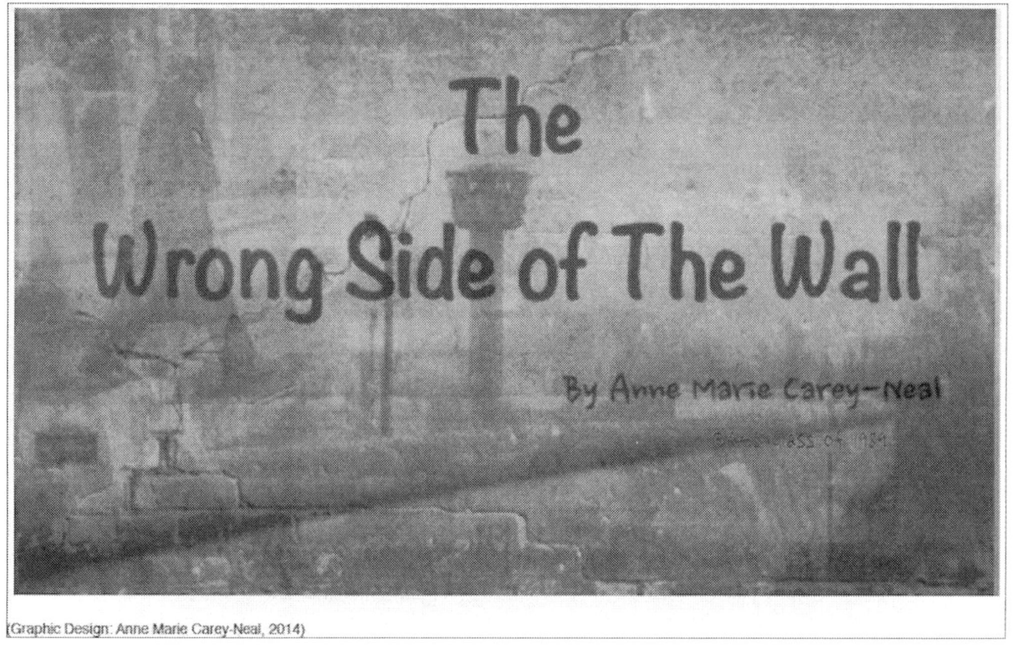

The
Wrong Side of The Wall
By Anne Marie Carey-Neal

(Graphic Design: Anne Marie Carey-Neal, 2014)

My family was fortunate enough to spend 14 years in Berlin, Germany over two tours during the 70s and 80s. My father was Air Force, assigned to the 6912th ESG, and was quite the history buff; me, not so much. Ask Mr. Bluem. God love him, he tried. When grades came out, he always told me he "liked my personality" and graciously gave me a C! My parents wanted my brothers, sister and I to understand what a rare opportunity we had living in such a history rich country and took us out and about every chance they had. I remember following them like a slow little duckling dragging behind the others as we visited numerous historical sites in Berlin. We went to the Brandenburg Gate, the Victory Column, Check Point Charlie (yawn)... just to name a few, listening to my father go on and on about the historical importance of each site. At the time, I was more interested in my shoes, or shopping, or spending time with my friends. I was not very excited or impressed. I was too young to appreciate the amazing opportunity I had.

While I really didn't have anything to compare my "normal" to at the time, growing up in Berlin seemed pretty ordinary and routine. I went to school, played a variety of sports, did my homework, went to the occasional school dance, loved going to the Volksfest and spent a lot of time with my friends! It was on an outing with friends that I came upon an observation platform overlooking the Berlin Wall. We were in Düppel. I was in my mid-teens by that point, so as you can imagine, we were not there to appreciate the historical nature of the site. We were goofing off and having a good time. The platform just happened to be near where we were hanging out.

Looking over the Wall

For some unknown reason, I was drawn to climb the metal stairs and look over the Wall. I could see the guarded zone between the two walls. Some called that area The Dead Zone, others referred to it as The Death Strip. No matter what it was called, it was a place one didn't want to be. There was an imposing guard tower a few hundred yards away. I could see the guards in the top of the tower, binoculars pointed at us, guns on their backs. It was frightening, even on the free side of the barrier. The distance between the Wall where I stood behind, and the Wall on the other side of the "death zone," was not great at all.

There were old brick buildings on the East side. They appeared to be apartments or offices of some kind. I could see curtains in the windows and tiny, boxy cars in the street just a few hundred yards away. I was studying the landscape, thinking about how impossible it seemed for a wall to separate my way of life from that of someone living in the East, when movement caught my eye. A man was walking, hunched over a bit, wearing dark clothes, a long wool coat and a brown scarf tied around his neck. I couldn't really see what he looked like from that distance, nor did I know where he was going, but I was suddenly intrigued. I wondered what his life was like. I wondered: how was it possible and acceptable in the world's eyes to trap people in a city with a wall, any escape attempt being punishable by death?

If I turned right and walked three to four hundred yards I could hop on a bus that would take me home. If he turned right and walked the same distance, he would be arrested, shot or possibly blown up by one of the many land mines that were scattered along the East side of the Wall. My heart ached at the injustice of it all. I felt powerless and helpless, but I could still go home, a home that rested in a free city. He too, was powerless and helpless, and would go home a prisoner.

My family returned to the United States in June of 1989. It was a different world from what I was used to in Berlin and most of my time was spent working and getting used to the American way of life. I was still young, 18, and didn't follow the news or world events as much as I should have, but I will never forget the 9th day of November, 1989 when it was announced that The Berlin Wall would finally fall. I was disappointed that we were no longer there to witness history in the making, but was overcome with emotion by the freeing of the city. Tears rose from an aching heart and trailed the distance of my cheeks. I was beside myself with joy and excitement. The injustice was coming to an end. A city of people would now be free.

And I thought of that man, walking hunched over that day. His image was fresh in my mind as if I had seen him only yesterday. He, too, would be free. He could walk to the West side of the Wall without fear of imprisonment or death. He was free to stand where I stood just a few years before and look back over his shoulder, see what I saw from that old iron platform, and he could now face forward and continue to walk West– a free man. I was overjoyed for him and the others who had spent so many years living as prisoners in East Berlin. An entire city of people were released from their concrete confines and were now able to appreciate and understand what it felt like to be free.

Anne Marie Carey Neal, Class of 1989
1971-76; 1981-89

The Death Strip on the other side of the Wall

A Storm is Brewing…

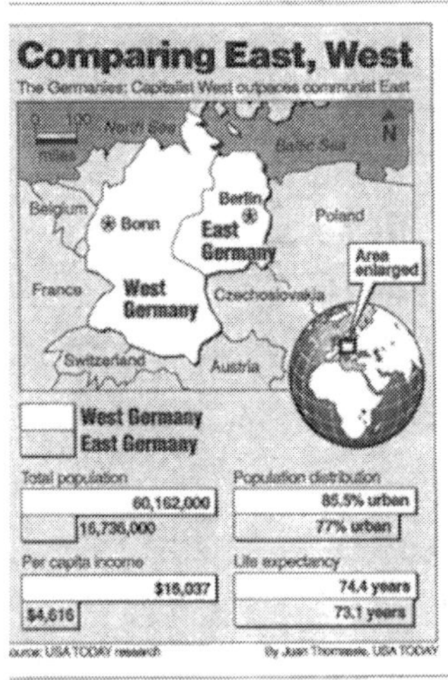

E.Germany: Silent opposition becomes a chorus for change

By Timothy Kenny
USA TODAY

WEST BERLIN — East Germans aren't afraid anymore. They're angry.

After Soviet leader Mikhail Gorbachev's weekend visit here, their demand for change has turned from hope to grim determination.

And the East German state is taking no chances.

At Checkpoint Charlie — famous allied-run crossing from West to East Berlin — would-be crossers to the East were turned back with a firm response by a green-uniformed East German soldier: "It is not possible."

Charles Bluem, history teacher at Berlin-American High School in West Berlin, was in East Berlin when troops dispersed 2,000 Gorbachev-inspired East Berliners.

He watched demonstrators as they linked arms, shouting "Gorby come out, Gorby help us." Said Bluem: "People who were watching broke into applause. There was a lot of crowd support."

It was a remarkable scene because East Berliners — unlike other East Bloc citizens — haven't witnessed such public protest since June 1953, when thousands of demonstrating workers were beaten, some killed, by police.

In early evening hours, "I didn't see anybody getting beaten up; nobody was pointing guns," said Bluem.

No one expects protest to disappear.

"There is something in the air," said Klaus Boelling, former head of West Berlin's mission in East Berlin. "The feeling there now is there's a chance to press for more rights. The number of people willing to participate in the opposition will increase."

For a people used to marching in socialist lockstep, this mood swing is stunning. Don't believe, however, that a majority is taking to the streets.

East Germany is not Poland or Hungary, where the march of social change has turned into a sprint. Change here is more cautious, timid.

Clearly, the once-silent opposition — called the New Forum — is making its presence finally felt.

New Forum says its membership, though banned by the government, grew from 30 members to 11,000.

But East German leader Erich Honecker is "hanging tough," said 17-year West Berlin resident Paul Roberts, a U.S. citizen who teaches English at the Free University.

"There is no compromise. And the young people are really fed up. They have seen what it's like on the other side" of the Berlin Wall.

ELSEWHERE IN THE WORLD . . .

HUNGARIAN CHANGES: The ruling Hungarian Socialist Party, formerly the Communist Party, adopted documents Monday condemning past policy mistakes and outlining remedies for the future. Included: a multi-party political system in which the ruling party cedes power if it loses free elections.

New Brunswick.

ELEPHANT IVORY: Delegates from more than 100 countries are meeting in Switzerland, debating how to preserve Africa's dwindling elephant population in the face of international demand for ivory.

SPANNING THE GLOBE: Seven people were killed by a bomb blast on a bus in Bogota, Co-

permanent wilderness reserve, an idea the United States opposes. … A bomb wrecked a Manila bistro owned by a former spokesman of former Philippine president Ferdinand Marcos, wounding at least five people.

AND IN THE SOVIET UNION: The official Tass news agency said scientists have con-

A Jakarta hello

Mr. Charles Bluem taught history at BAHS from 1970 to 1994, and was a favorite of many students [including author Yoshika Lowe]. Mr. Bluem was quoted in the article above, which he submitted for this book. It is dated almost exactly a month before the Wall came down. Mr. Bluem's handwritten note on the side says:

Hello Yoshika,

This article appeared in USA TODAY International Edition, Oct. 10, 1989. The demonstrators were all psyched up over Gorbachev's Perestroika and Glasnost policies as you know…So maybe [continues on back] this can be of some value in your book project??? Alles Gute to you and your family Yoshika!

Charles Bluem

Chapter 6: Fall of the Wall to 1994

"Without perestroika, the cold war simply would not have ended. But the world could not continue developing as it had, with the stark menace of nuclear war ever present."

- Mikhail Gorbachev, President of the Soviet Union

The Fall of the Berlin Wall – The Reunification of Germany: The Reunification of Family

"ABC New Special Report: We interrupt this program to bring you this special news bulletin." I thought to myself, "This better be good," as once again, ABC was interrupting my favorite soap opera during my lunch hour. The date was November 9, 1989, and I was living in Ocala, Florida. As I was taking the first bite of my turkey sandwich– made with Miracle Whip and sprinkled with extra salt, I heard the announcer say, "Today, the Berlin Wall has come down." For me, time stood still for that moment, and as I burst into tears I said, "I want to remember every detail of this moment." I remember what I had for lunch. I remember exactly what I did that morning, and I remember what I was wearing. Unfortunately, spandex was in, and so were shoulder pads and big earrings. So although I remember the outfit, I'd rather not elaborate on it!

Deb's cousins collecting pieces of the Wall, November 1989

I knew that my cousin, Frank, a native Berliner, would be one of the first people on the scene at the Wall to celebrate– to sip champagne and to take part in tearing it down. Thinking of me and my family in the US, Frank took a nice chunk of the wall and sent it to me. This piece of the wall is not just a piece of art hanging in my foyer– it's a symbol of freedom and a reunification not only of a country but of a family. My family.

My father, a captain in the U.S. Army, was stationed in Berlin in the early 1950's when he met my mother, a native Berliner, and they married at Andrews Chapel in the American Sector of Berlin in June 1955.

I was born in the American hospital in Berlin the following year. As is typical with a military family, we moved around every 2-3 years, so when the Wall was erected in 1961, we were living in Anchorage, Alaska. (We had several tours of duty in Berlin in the 60's and 70's as well.) And when the Wall went up, my mother was separated from grandparents, aunts, uncles and cousins who were living in Klötze-Altmark (where ironically my mom's family sought refuge from the Berlin bombings for a short time during WWII). There are many adjectives to describe the emotions of this Wall to our family and others: frustration, anger, loneliness, confusion, and helplessness.

The only means of communicating with each other at that time was via letters, which we knew would be read by authorities. So as the years wore on, and West Berlin became a thriving, modern "hip" city, its slogan for years being "Berlin ist eine Reise Wert" ("Berlin is the trip worth taking"), the East became a forgotten sibling, with renovations and modern conveniences practically coming to a standstill. As a matter of fact, the Trabant was one of the few cars available to the residents of the East, and they were smelly, noise polluters (more on this later).

Life in the West at that time was by far better than life in the East. Many East Berliners attempted to escape to the West in search of the good life. My mother's cousin, whom I will call "Otto" (to protect his identity), was one of them. After trying for several months to make a go of it in the West, Otto desperately missed his family. When he anonymously asked authorities if there would be any repercussions should he return to the East, he was assured he would be left alone. He was excited to finally be reunited with his family, but upon his return, he was apprehended and sent to prison for three years– one year of which was spent in solitary confinement.

Ironically, his father, during WWII, had been sent to a concentration camp for five years for belonging to a faction that did not support Hitler. Concentration camps were not just for Jewish people! There were several members of my mother's family who spent time in concentration camps, and the Wall was a reminder that Germany was still not a "free" country. You were not free to express your opinion– if you did, you might be tagged as a spy and your every movement watched. This led to constant paranoia and a true lack of freedom–sort of hitting a wall, if you pardon the pun.

The Wall meant many things to my family, but what about the "family" of Americans stationed in Berlin who had no native ties to the area? What did living in a walled city mean to them? Well, living in a walled city presented a few challenges. You could only travel so far, as in any corner of Berlin you reached a barrier, with armed guards and warning signs of "Achtung!"("Warning!"), against trespassing. Think about it: as Americans living in the US, we take simple freedoms for granted. We can jump in our cars or grab our bikes and drive or ride as far as we wish. In Berlin, we were restricted to the West; armed guards were positioned at checkpoints. They were even located at certain U-Bahn stations in the East sector where the train would slow down but not stop to let anyone on or off.

As teenagers from military families who lived all over the US and abroad, we adapted well. That's not to say there weren't those that felt uncomfortable in a walled or restricted city. Day-passes to tour the East were available to military dependents, but our family, due to its past history never took advantage of it. Ironically, despite living in a walled city as a teenager in the 1970's, whether we were white, black or Asian, we were all "minorities" living in a foreign country. We bonded well, while we heard reports of riots and forced school busing in some of the US states "back home," we all shared the same bus, the same school, and participated in sports together.

We didn't care about the color of our skin, we were just glad to be with fellow Americans! In an odd twist of fate, we found our own sense of freedom in a city that struggled for so long to find its own. Speaking of freedom...those pesky Trabant automobiles, with the fall of the Wall, invaded West Berlin– much to the ire of many. They were noisy and polluted the air. I remember my Aunt telling me, "The only bad thing about the Wall coming down is those darn Trabants. They are everywhere, and they're a pain!"

On November 7, 2009, the Berlin Brats Alumni Association had a mini-reunion in Washington, DC to tour the International Spy Museum where twenty Trabants were on display in commemoration of the 20th Anniversary of the Fall of the Wall. I couldn't wait to tell my aunt! As for my mother's family, we all gathered together in 2010, in Germany, for a family reunion over the 4th of July holiday, to celebrate Independence Day. And for our family, that day is also celebrated on November 9th.

Deb Brians Clark, Class of 1974
1964-65, 1968-69, 1971-73

Epilogue to Deb's Family Story-

I was five when the Wall went up, and it would be another 50 years before I would see some of my family members again. As an American and an Army Brat, Berlin was not only my birthplace– it was my "rock"...a place I called home when asked where I was from. Growing up a Brat and moving frequently, the one constant was my grandparents' homestead in Berlin. Though often far away, we tried to visit Berlin as often as we could, but then two things happened: The Wall went up, and I grew up.

My dad put in for orders for Germany often and was given four tours– one in Nürnberg, and three in Berlin. In 1964 while my Dad was in Korea, we lived with my grandparents for a year. My mother enrolled me in JFK Schule, but I didn't like it, so she transferred me to TAR. Thus began my preparation for BAHS on a later assignment to Berlin! And as luck would have it, in 1971 my family made the decision to retire in Berlin! I was in 10th grade at BAHS, and all was right with the world. But, in 1973 the value of the Deutsche Mark dropped drastically. We could no longer afford to live in Berlin, so we moved back to the U.S. after my junior year. I was devastated! But as Kelly Clarkson says, "What doesn't kill you makes you stronger," I grew up, finished college, married and became a working mother.

Deb and her cousins together again!

I didn't reconnect with the family members who lived in the East until 2013. Because of the Wall I had no real relationship with these cousins. Just as it is with us Brats, the connection was instant the moment we met again after all those years!

Four Days in November

The Wall comes down! Chipping out keepsakes

Thursday, November 9th, 1989

It was a Thursday night as I sat in my living room on Jänickestrasse 89a in Berlin, Germany. My parents were gone for the evening at a farewell party in the Berlin district of Wedding. My intention as I sat there in the living room was to study for a German test being given the following day. You know, one of those essay tests regarding German literature which was just way over my head?!? So, there I sat "studying" and watching *Murphy Brown* on AFN Berlin. The show was returning from commercial break when it was suddenly interrupted and the words TO BE ANNOUNCED flashed on the screen.

I don't recall all the exact words spoken by the unseen announcer, but basically the message was that the Wall was open and East Germans were now allowed to travel freely. My eyes went wide, my mouth dropped open. I may have even stopped breathing. And as quickly as *Murphy Brown* was interrupted it returned. And as strange as it may sound I continued watching it and studying for my test. It's apparent the information had not really processed. And in my usual fashion I had to ask lots of questions and get more facts before believing what was being told to me. But there was no Internet, no Facebook and no texting to go find the answers to these questions. Then again, perhaps no one would have had any answers.

Yes, things had been stirring in the days, weeks and months prior to this date. The brave and determined people of the Eastern Bloc countries risked their lives and those of their families to demonstrate and demand their freedom. There had been embassies in those countries that had been swarmed with those who wanted freedom. The freedom of movement, speech, thought. Some governments simply told the Soviet Union they were opening their borders. I may be wrong, but as far as I know the Soviets did not resist. East Germany remained the stubborn country. Erich Honecker simply did not want to give in to the people's demands. And then suddenly the Wall opened. There was nothing the border guards could do. There was nothing I could do at that moment except to allow my mind time to process this information.

After a while I decided it was time to take my dog out for a quick walk around the corner to the edge of the park. There are many times my dog became stubborn and did not want to walk, especially if there were others at home. She wanted at least someone else to go with us. There wasn't anyone home though. What was her problem? This was a St. Bernard and there wasn't a chance that I was going to be able to get her to move an inch! So, as I begged and pleaded for her to walk, my oldest brother, Tom, came strolling down the street. Funny, because my first thought was, "Thank God, now this dog will walk." Not, "Can you believe what's happening?"

Tom, on the other hand, was very excited and it helped bring me to reality. This was actually happening. We walked and discussed the events that were unfolding. I wondered out loud if this was how people felt during the first moon landing. The feeling of something happening that would forever live in history. The feeling of something happening that you never really bothered to think about happening because it was never going to happen… How long did their excitement last after the moon landing? Even in 1989 I felt exciting news events were short-lived by the media. They reported it, interviewed some people, showed some pictures and life moved on. How long would this news story last? (As I wrote this, Tom reminded me that we got back from our walk and then watched the infamous interview of the East German politician announcing the borders were open and people were free to travel–right now. I do not remember watching that, but I like that story so I will include this portion). My brother tried to convince me we should go down to Checkpoint Charlie and see what was happening in the city. Foolish me, I had to stay home and study for that test. It was a school night after all! Yeah, I know, I know.

Friday, November 10th, 1989

One of my first memories the following day was standing outside my first class of the morning at John F. Kennedy German American School waiting for the dreaded bell to signify the beginning of class. Looking back, should they not have closed school?? And here comes my good friend, the ever jubilant, Toni Gaffron running towards me screaming, "Can you believe it?" And she gave me a great big hug. We went into biology class, everyone excited about the events. Our teacher, Mrs. Nicholson, even took time out of her lecture to talk about everything. That alone was a monumental event!! After 15-20 minutes into class time a classmate, Sa'ad Shah came into class. He was late and normally Mrs. Nicholson would have had some words for someone who walked in late. However, Sa'ad lived in East Berlin at the time and I believe his father worked with the Pakistani embassy in East Berlin. He simply said the border crossings were packed with people and it took that much longer to cross over into the West. How's that for an excuse????

That evening my brother asked if I wanted to go with him to pick up a friend of his who was flying in from Munich. We went to Tegel Airport full of excitement. His friend behaved very nonchalant about things. Figures she would, being from Munich and all... For those of you who don't know, Berlin and Munich have an ongoing rivalry, and rightfully so, with us Berliners feeling a bit above them...HA, HA!!! Her reaction to this unprecedented event helped me to forever partake in this silly rivalry. We continued downtown as Tom had yet another friend arriving, only this time by train.

The trip downtown was amazing. Naturally, we rode public transportation and went down to Kurfürstendamm (otherwise known to my mom and me as "our shopping boulevard"). It was the bustling business, shopping, eating, drinking, people watching area for us at the time. The area was packed. Thousands of people were walking, hugging each other, popping open bottles of champagne, beer or wine. Drivers were honking their horns while passengers screamed with excitement as they hung out the windows. German bus drivers were being friendly and honking their horns– not the least bit upset that traffic was basically at a standstill and that their punctuality was thrown right out the window!?!

Could it possibly be that thousands of Germans were simultaneously happy, in a good mood AND being friendly??? (Of course, I say this with affectionate humor.) We went into a café to get something warm to drink and wait for my brother's friend to arrive at Bahnhof Zoo [Zoologischer Garten Station]. That is all I remember from this evening. What was in that warm drink I consumed?

Saturday, November 11th, 1989

My mom and I and the now 'willing to walk' St. Bernard dog, whose name was "Bienchen"[bees], walked the 15-20 minutes to Zehlendorf-Mitte to do some shopping. We were likely picking up freshly baked goods from the bakery and I'm sure getting Bienchen a fresh Brotchen. The lines to the banks were unbelievable. As many know, the West German government gave visiting East Germans 100 Marks. And that day they were lined up!! I'm pretty sure German banks were never open on Saturdays. No choice this Saturday! The area was much more crowded than usual and no one cared. The infamous East German cars [Trabants] rumbled through the streets. It all seemed so surreal and we just kept enjoying the moment.

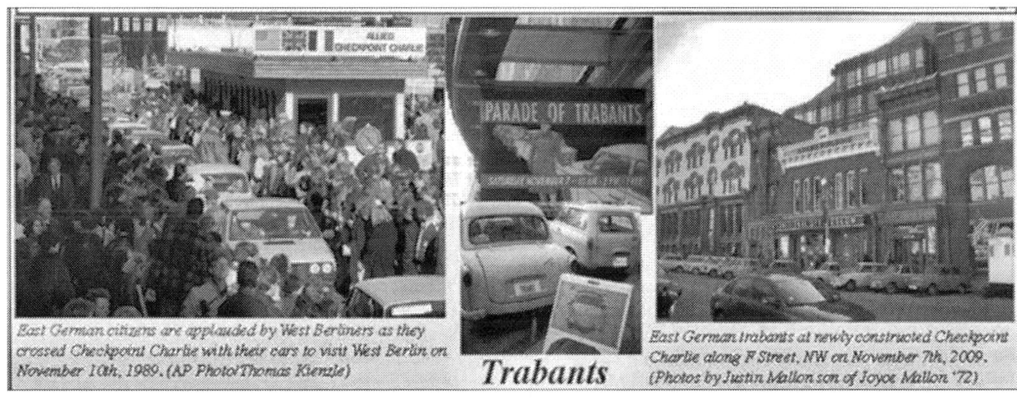

East German citizens are applauded by West Berliners as they crossed Checkpoint Charlie with their cars to visit West Berlin on November 10th, 1989. (AP Photo/Thomas Kienzle)

Trabants

East German trabants at newly constructed Checkpoint Charlie along F Street, NW on November 7th, 2009. (Photos by Justin Mallon son of Joyce Mallon '72)

The Trabant or 'Trabi' was a poorly made car produced by the East German government

Later that evening I joined some friends and we went to one border crossing and watched as people came over on foot or drove their cars over that little line painted on the street. We joined others in greeting them with hugs and slamming our hands on their cars. It's hard to explain what it was like watching someone walk over a border crossing, with their home just minutes behind them, to freedom.

We then headed on foot down to the Brandenburg Gate. Can I just mention at this point how cold it was becoming? And yet how easy it was to ignore the frost bite that was certainly attacking my toes and fingers? The area in front of the Brandenburg Gate was filled with thousands of excited and happy people and certainly the flowing of and consumption of alcohol had no part in the feeling of euphoria that was shown on their faces….

By this time the West side of the Wall was lined with West German police trucks to prevent people from climbing atop the Wall. This was part of the Wall in which the top was a wide flat surface as opposed to the cylindrical shaped top seen on the majority of the Wall. A couple of my friends and I climbed up into a tree so we could see over the Wall. In front of the Brandenburg Gate stood a long row of East German soldiers at attention. I did not see one of them make any sort of movement. And then suddenly someone on our side of the Wall decided that the police vehicles were not going to prevent him from climbing atop the Wall. There he was on top of the Wall, beer in hand, and dancing with joy. Despite the lack of dancing skills, we encouraged him with hoots and hollers.

I watched the guards on the other side. Still no movement. And then I heard a quick noise or perhaps someone shouting an abrupt order. Suddenly, two or three soldiers from different parts of their line darted forward toward the Wall. They had ladders and began to climb up to the top of the Wall. We tried to scream to our entertainer on the Wall but between the crowd and the music he couldn't hear.

A soldier appeared on the Wall and as luck would have it the man turned in time to see him and there was just enough distance between them that he was able to begin running to get away. The chase covered most of the length of this part of the Wall with our guy finally jumping down on to the top of a police van. The Polizei grinned. It was great. The revelry continued and I can't tell you exactly what we did the rest of the evening. It just was not a time to be at home.

I knew my parents wanted to get up early and witness the border opening at Potsdamer Platz complete with portions of the Wall being lifted out of their place. I knew, as I finally got home and lay my head on my pillow at 3 am that they would come knocking on my door in just 3 hours. I knew I would want to sleep. I knew that I would likely just be thawing out by that time. I knew I would regret not getting up and going out with them.

So, as promised, the knock on my door arrived with my mom likely singing her infamous, "Getty uppie time." For a moment I pondered and struggled with the decision to stay in a warm bed or continue participating in this historical event. Silly me for even pondering. I got out of bed.

Sunday, Nov. 12th

The first amazing sight, although witnessed the day before, was the line of people outside the bank at 6 am. It was more amazing than the day before because this was Sunday! No way were banks going to open on Sunday! Restaurants and flower shops were open on Sundays. Stores and banks– no way!! [German stores are closed on Sundays, then or now.]

My parents and I made our way to Potsdamer Platz where a good crowd was gathered. The mayor arrived. My eyes drifted to those sitting on top of the Wall. As previously mentioned, most of the Wall was topped by a cylindrical structure and this was the case here. So at this point, to sit atop the Wall one had to straddle it. I made up my mind that I had to at least get up on this thing one time!

Having already lost my parents in the crowd I made my way over to figure out how these people had made it up there. There was part of a barricade leaned up against the Wall that provided a boost. And despite being the fourth day of, well partying and celebrating, everyone was still being nice and providing assistance for those who would like to climb up to the top. In a short time I was up there straddling the Wall. It was quickly obvious that I had not dressed appropriately for straddling cold cement structures…

No longer illegal: Chipping away at the Wall

Again, I ignored the cold which was probably easy after a few minutes as I'm sure everything had gone numb. So, there I sat full of giddiness because I made it up there and began to search the crowd for my parents. Dad had the camera and I'm sure they would see me up there and rush over to take a picture. I waited a long time. Thinking about it now, my dad was most likely more mesmerized by the machines and tools being used to grind and drill into the slabs of the Wall as well as the crane used to lift those slabs. Silly me for thinking I could compete with that! Never got that picture of me on the Wall. I gave up on them getting my picture and climbed down. How the heck did I get down? Hmm.

I never found my parents in the crowd. I figured they made their way to Oma's house (my mom's mom). I wasn't worried about it. I found the #48 bus and I could've exited the bus at the stop near Oma's house but the bus was so nice and warm. I remained on the bus. This bus could take me back to Zehlendorf-Mitte and I could catch another bus for a few stops or walk from that point. I knew the #48 bus ride would be a long one and that was perfectly fine with me.

Monday, Nov. 13th

Monday. Apparently we were to all go back to reality. As I walked to school my surroundings suddenly seemed so quiet. Where were all the people and all the traffic? Did I dream all this? What just happened? Is our party over? Now what do we do? Life continued on as usual and yet not quite the same.

Sunday, Nov 8th, 2009

Above are my immediate memories of four days in November over twenty years ago. It is a little painful to have to say, 'twenty years ago,' because like most wonderful memories it feels like, 'just yesterday.' There is so much more of a personal story here: My dad had been a young enlisted soldier stationed in Berlin as the Wall was built, marrying my mom in Berlin (who was born and raised in Berlin amongst the rubble of WWII). We had family in both West and East Berlin, and our family returned to Berlin in the 1980's with my dad as a Department of Defense civilian. My parents witnessed the rise and fall of the Wall.

My brother has often mentioned he is (or will be) writing our entire family story. It may make the above story sound more meaningful. I know there are a couple of blurred memories stirring in my mind and maybe some memories of those few days that have vanished. I will need to seek the help of family and friends to get them straightened out. To all my friends and classmates (both at John F. Kennedy Schule and Berlin American High School) I am so glad we have the memories of Berlin. We often hear of how rough military family life can be. I am certain that those who lived in Berlin as American dependents would do it again in a heartbeat. And thanks to my parents who provided us with the opportunities to see many wonderful places and to have many wonderful memories. PROST!

Tamara Dunham, Class of 1990
1982-1990

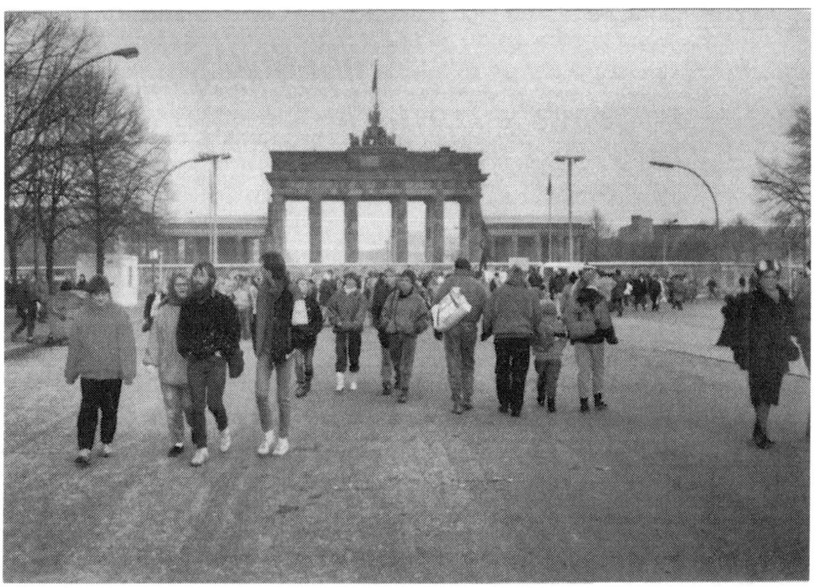

November 1989: Berlin free again! No one was allowed to walk in front of or behind the Brandenburg Gate before the Fall of the Wall.

The Fall of the Berlin Wall – Too Weird to Believe!

Gary on the Wall, Nov. 10, 1989

November 9, 1989 was very much a normal day in the life of West Berliners and their Allied friends. I was hosting a Music Boosters meeting at my house in Nikolaussee. Among the attendees was Colonel Maddox. In the middle of the meeting, I received a phone call from my BAHS colleague, Sandy Riggins; she was calling to tell me that the Wall was open. Oddly enough, I said thank you, turned to the others present and delivered the same message and then we continued with our meeting. The enormity of this event was simply too hard for us to comprehend– just too weird to believe. There was no TV to turn on at my house and certainly no internet to access. We concluded our meeting and everyone went home, none the wiser of the great event of 9 November 1989.

As planning would have it, I left for Hamburg, Germany, the next morning at 4:00 a.m. I was on my way to do some family research at the State Archives. That Friday, 10 November, was free due to our Veteran's Day Holiday. I was barely finished saluting the first group of Soviet guards at Checkpoint Bravo when I began to realize that things were no longer normal. Driving through the drab and eventless East German transit route to Checkpoint Alpha had become a party. There was honking and waving to no end. I processed through Alpha and it finally dawned on me, The Wall Was Open! I stopped at the first Raststätte (aka Rasthaus or roadside eatery) in West Germany to converse with some East Germans. There were three guys there and they were incredibly jubilant. "Our wives have no idea where we are. We heard the news on the evening shift at work and we just had to go and see if it was true." I gave them DM 20 and asked them to enjoy cake and coffee on me.

For some reason, I stupidly drove on to Hamburg. I arrived at the Staatsarchiv (state archives) and there were the pre-ordered microfilms waiting for me at a table. I sat down and said to myself, "What are you doing here?" I immediately got up and drove back towards Berlin. I got to Checkpoint Alpha. The TV crews were there filming those leaving East Germany and going into West Germany. Westerners had lined the streets and were throwing money and candy and fruit into the cars. Tears of joy were to be seen on so many faces. The line of cars getting ready to cross the border was over 40 miles long!

After celebrating on the border for a good thirty minutes, I continued my journey back to West Berlin. Arriving first at home; I got myself organized for joining the party and took the S-Bahn down to JFK Platz at Rathaus Schöneberg. The chancellor of West Germany, Helmut Kohl, was expected there in a few minutes. I listened proudly to his speech which was concluded by the singing of the German National Hymn. The assembled crowd strongly disagreed with him on the timing of this hymn [a song symbolic of national unity]. Whistling, a sign of dissatisfaction was the overwhelming sound at this time. [Some were not ready for national unity.]

My ultimate destiny was next, Brandenburger Tor– the Brandenburg Gate. I think I must have arrived around 2000 hrs and up I went and sat on top of the Brandenburg Gate section of the Wall into the wee hours of the morning. I remember very distinctly a film crew taking pictures at about

0200 hrs and I was diligent to hide my face. I explained to my neighbor that, as a part of the U.S. military in West Berlin, I wasn't supposed to be up there. He responded that he was East German and he wasn't supposed to be up there either.

The greatest impression of the evening was that, every once in a while, someone would jump over the Wall into the East Berlin side of the Wall. Fortunately, the VoPos (Volkspolizei) would catch them and put them back on the Wall. I so wanted to do this. No, I would reason with myself, they will know you are American and lock you away. On the other hand, maybe I would be the only American ever that could say, "I jumped over the Wall." Enough was enough, I mustered up enough courage to overcome the fears and over the Wall I went! Ecstatic! Yes, they caught me and then they placed me right back on top of the Wall from whence I had just jumped into East Berlin!

Gary Kelb, Faculty
Music Teacher 1986-1992

Berliners and people from around the world swarm to Berlin to claim a piece of history for themselves.

Chipping off a piece of the Wall

East Meets West

Growing up as an Air Force Brat in Berlin Germany was a unique and special time in history– not only for me but also for my siblings Kim Nix Reid '92, Duane Nix '95 and Kristina Nix '97. The best part about living in Berlin was experiencing the reality of the Communist regime and what freedom really meant to us as Americans.

My high school German teacher Herr Prigge felt it was very important for us to learn more about life in East Berlin. He made contact and started an East German Pen pal group for our German class with an English class at a school in East Berlin. My pen pal and I started writing when I was in the 10th grade, I believe. We talked about her family and mine and how they were limited to so little in East Berlin.

This gave me the idea to start sending packages with letters, peanut butter, stuffed animals and Teen Magazines. Her name was Grit Buller; but the best part was, once the Wall fell we were able to meet face to face my senior year in 1991. She was able to come and visit and watch one of our BAHS Fußball (soccer) games. I will never forget her. I learned that two high school girls from two different countries and governments have the same common high school obstacles and interests.

As I recall, the night that the Berlin Wall fell, there was an announcement made and my Dad was actually the one that told our family. There was a quick rush of East Berliners trying to pass through Checkpoint Charlie. Quickly, the East German government enacted a law that required all East Berliners to register for a Visa to cross into West Berlin in order to control the mass exodus of people. The thought of freedom after a few generations of Communist rule understandably caused major excitement to leave East Berlin/East Germany. That night going to the Berlin Wall and chipping away at it was against the law, punishable by a huge fine of more than ten thousand Deutsch Mark. Dad and I were able to go down to the Wall behind the Düppel military housing area and chip chunks of the Wall later, once it was legal. Those are memories I will cherish forever.

Another highlight of my Berlin high school years, was riding the Duty Train with my high school sports teams (soccer, cross country, basketball and softball) to Frankfurt to continue on by bus to other DoD schools for games and tournaments. I remember we could look out the Duty Train windows as we entered East Berlin and see the East German border guards inspecting the Duty Train with dogs. Once in a while, we would see the East German Border Guards walk through the Duty Train inside the corridors which would require us to stay in our cabins. We always knew not to open the windows as the border guards were very strict about the rules.

To this day I still look at the American flag with such pride, and will for the rest of my life. We have so much to be proud of as Americans and the freedom we enjoy every day. I will never ever forget those precious and priceless years I attended BAHS from 7th grade to my graduation in 1991. All Berlin Brats have an unspoken bond that is hard to explain to non-Brats. Our memories, though different, are oftentimes understood jointly. I am sure I'm not alone in saying that my Berlin years helped shape who I am today.

Wendy Nix, Class of 1991
1985-1991

Those Hallowed Halls of BAHS

I have to say the best years of being a counselor were those I spent at BAHS. I came in the fall of 1984 as Ms. Nelson and married my teacher husband, Thomas Amend, who joined me on staff in 1989– the year the Berlin Wall fell. We stayed until the school closed in spring 1994. We were fortunate enough to live in three different homes while there… one on Dunkelbergsteig, another on Koenigsallee and the last one at Sophie-Charlotte-Strasse.

Berlin was always special to me! I loved having a special pass to get into the inner city of East Berlin and enjoyed exploring the Kurfürstendamm and the city of West Berlin. We enjoyed many meals at the Europa Center and ice cream at Mövenpick.

I remember the weeks after the La Belle Disco was bombed. We were buttoned down in the community with vehicles escorting our school buses (front and back), as well as soldiers patrolling our school grounds and car checks at every entry area. We also had heaps of bricks to defend the entrances of BAHS. One day I was enrolling a new student and we were talking about courses he had taken at his old school and what we had available at BAHS. I was taking it as a routine event, when the student finally asked why we had armed soldiers and brick defenses and it reminded me how quickly one gets used to a crisis.

Of course the next crisis following this was the Chernobyl nuclear plant explosion. We were all worried about the radiation and fallout, so on advice from one of the science teachers, I wore a heavy coat to absorb the radiation despite a warm spring. One day some soldiers, who continued to patrol our school, took a break on a very beautiful day– they laid out on the embankment between the two driveways into the school, with their shirts open taking in the sun and radiation fallout from Chernobyl.

Our students were always so nonchalant about taking the Duty Train to sports events. "Coffee, Tea, Marble Cake," were offered on the night rides. We shared a four bunk-bed cubicle, with everyone talking and sharing music as we rolled through the DDR's dreary outside with little or no house lights or activities occurring. After being up all night, we arrived in Frankfurt to the bustle of the big city and moved onto buses. While there were also British and French Duty Trains, it required much more effort to get travel arrangements made for those trains.

The Duty Train allowed us the opportunity to travel out of Berlin and to have friends come visit– with special orders, of course. While routine, it never lost its charm and adventure for me as I peered outside the windows and wondered about the lives of those who were trapped in the DDR.

Driving through the corridor was also an exciting event for us! Having the Flag Orders being examined by the Russian guards at the checkpoints made me a wee bit nervous, as apparently the only way he could determine if our passage was genuine was to compare our orders letter by letter. We received a briefing before we left the checkpoint with a notebook declaring the Russians our allies and friends. I grew up during the Cold War threat where the Russians were not our "friends" except, then, in Berlin. We were told if we went too fast or too slow we'd be in "trouble" as drivers were instructed to go only at a certain speed and never pull off anywhere. We had heard many stories of people who got "caught" in different spots of the DDR between West Berlin and West Germany.

When the Berlin Wall came down, no one could believe it. Mr. Bluem, history teacher, said he never thought the Wall would ever come down and it was probably the only thing his kids would remember that he was wrong about. We went to Checkpoint Charlie the first night to watch and welcome a long line of Trabant cars carrying East Germans across the checkpoint in droves. Their excited, scared and wondering eyes underscored the enormous meaning of this event. We even saw a new bride and groom coming across the checkpoint. We then went to Brandenburg Gate, where the East Germans had tanks and guns pointed across the Wall to the West, while people in the West were shouting and cheering on bleachers looking eastward with the German police packed against the Wall on our side.

We finally went to Potsdam and watched people, after that wonderful weekend, walking back into East Berlin. The people said they had to go back as they had no place to stay in the West. For many weeks, BAHS students brought chunks of the wall to sell to teachers and other students.

Left: Kaiser Wilhelm Memorial Church; Right: the Tiergarten (originally the royal hunting grounds)

Berlin was always so beautiful with its many magnificent and historic places to visit and admire. Brandenburg Gate, the Reichstag, the Ku-Damm, the Kaiser Wilhelm-Gedächtniskirche, the Tiergarten, the Berlin Zoo; our experiences colored always with the constant awareness of the Wall and barbed wire surrounding the city. We truly enjoyed every opportunity to explore the wonders of Berlin while we were there.

Olympic Stadium, 1980s

We were often privileged to have our BAHS graduations held at the Olympic Stadium that was built for the 1936 Olympics where Jessie Owens ran to win for the United States. It was with great anticipation that our– usually famous– speaker/guest of honor helicoptered in for the great event of our student graduations. Our students proudly ran the track after the ceremony was over. The commencement ceremony for our final class was held at the Shöneberger Rathaus, the same place, where on June 26, 1963, President John F. Kennedy gave his famous "Ich bin ein Berliner" speech to an audience of 450,000. After his assassination, that square was renamed John F. Kennedy Platz. We had come full circle, and the class of 1994 represented the culmination of Kennedy's dream for a unified Germany.

Berlin American High School would become a German school, so for that I was comforted. It was with great sadness and a profound sense of history when BAHS finally closed in 1994, knowing that our last classes and steps in the hallowed halls of BAHS would no longer go forth.

Jan Amend, Faculty
School Counselor, 1984-1994

German Reunification Day- October 3, 1990

4

Unification brings changes to command

What Goes Around

In 1987 I was assigned with my wife and two children to the US Occupation Forces in Berlin. As a matter of fact, I was assigned to the same government quarters that I left in 1965 as a high school junior. I served as the US Management Officer to the US Berlin Brigade; so much of what I experienced was shaped by my experience 30 years before.

Let me start at the beginning. I arrived in Berlin as a high school freshman, going to Thomas A. Roberts School (TAR). Almost from the first day I realized this was a special experience. In my basic science class I ran across Coach Fitzpatrick. He sized me up and I spent the next three years playing on sports teams for him and his successors. There was soccer with Fitz and then Herr Longolius. Remember that name.

I shared a very special period of my life visiting Italy, Austria, France, England and other parts of Germany with the Boy Scouts, and later as a tourist on a student pass. I joined the choir and got a place in the class play my sophomore year and later in the school musical *Brigadoon*. We all knew we were living history. We saw John F. Kennedy and then experienced the very unique emotion of mourning his death with "his" fellow Berliners.

In the summer of 1965, with laughter, love and loss, I left Berlin for West Point to finish up my high school years. It was a traumatic departure and I can assure you it marked me for years to come. So much so that when my own son was in his senior year and I was asked to come back to the US to take a very coveted position, I didn't hesitate to decline the honor. I had lived this before and knew the sacrifice should be mine, not his. I had left behind so many friends in Berlin and was sure I would never have an opportunity to see them again.

Fast forward to 1987 and as I get off the plane with my family at Tegel Airport, I am met by Beth Jones, a fellow foreign service officer and one of my classmates from BAHS. We had the opportunity to serve two years in Berlin side by side in the Allied Government and went on to serve in two more posts together as colleagues and confidants. TAR was now the lower grade school and there was now a high school. In addition, the US and German communities had formed an international school– JFK Schule in Zehlendorf as well. Beth and I served on that school board together. I also served on the Deputy Commandant's school advisory committee for the Berlin DoD (Dept. of Defense) high school.

My daughter went to the DoD school while my son went to the JFK Schule. The three years in Berlin were marked with deepening memories and a true affection for the city and its people. In 1989, when Alex Longolius (the soccer coach and German instructor) lost his city council election I hired him to direct a German American foundation we founded to sponsor educational efforts. We reconnected then and later.

Sitting in on the Commandant's meetings, as my father had before me, was a unique and surreal experience. Dealing with the Bezirk (administrative district), the city and with a host of city problems gave me an in-depth understanding and perspective. All of this would come in handy when I was chosen by the Department of State to develop a plan to move the US Embassy from Bonn to Berlin.

I left Berlin in early 1990 on a directed assignment to assist our embassy in Pakistan. But three years later I was again back in Germany, this time in Bonn as the Management Counselor for all of the US civilian government presence in Germany. During this period we not only planned the move, we negotiated the property agreements, decided on the site for the future embassy, designed it and helped to create a truly bi-national school in Berlin.

One of my functions was to ensure that excess US military property was properly utilized, the military was in the process of drawing down over two hundred thousand personnel assigned in the region and bases were closing everywhere. We shipped equipment to Haiti, the Levant, Russia and everywhere in between. But we also turned entire schools– equipment and all– over to authorities in the newly incorporated eastern states of the former GDR. School books, libraries, band equipment, sports equipment, classroom furniture– you name it, was trucked across Germany.

The new US Embassy, on the left, adjoins the Brandenburg guard house

In Berlin our presence was coming to an end, military units were folding their guidons, while barracks, PXs and movie theaters were being handed back after forty years. The US State Department was involved in extremely delicate negotiations with the German government in Bonn over property we needed in Berlin if we were to relocate to that city once the German capital was transferred. We reclaimed our site at Pariser Platz for the future Embassy. The new US Embassy building opened in 2008 right next to the Brandenburg Gate, a site we left in 1939 which spent the next forty plus years in the no man's land dividing Berlin.

We acquired magnificent homes in Dahlem and other residences throughout Zehlendorf. One of those was the beautiful residence near Mexico Platz on Kleist St, where my father and later I resided. Today it is the official residence for the US Defense Attaché.

The schools closed and the military left in 1994, once the Russians departed. I was contacted about the US Army's Nicholson library and TAR School. Did I have any interest in those facilities and if not, could the city of Berlin have the facilities? I agreed to turn over the library, no problem– but was then asked if we could transfer the books– of no use to the city government– to the JFK Schule? After haggling over bureaucratic regulations it was agreed that the books would be shipped to "their" German school– JFK Schule.

The next week TAR was on the block and that required special consideration. It was full of memories. The German government wanted it for a special needs school for the region, a region that now included former East German Länder (East German states). I walked slowly through the facility, filled with desks, books, and memories and signed the papers.

Later the same day I went over to the high school. I had never really walked through it in detail. The trophy case still held the trophies of long-departed adolescent athletes– the two undefeated seasons '67 and '68. I thought about taking them with me, but the DoD's folks assured me they were going to Stuttgart for safe keeping. But what about the labs, the library, the musical instruments, etc. The Germans wanted to know if we would leave these. I checked quickly and found that the military had no need for them, since they already had mounds of unneeded school facilities and equipment in various depots throughout Germany. So, acting as the agent of the US Government I graciously transferred these to the city for use by the German children who were to occupy these halls, these classrooms, and these fields after we departed.

The military is gone now from Berlin. Only memories remain of the heroic stand they made against the Soviet threat for almost 50 years. There is little to remind anyone of their service except in the minds of the German people. The US Embassy has moved to Berlin and it now resides in many of the same houses we occupied during our long watch on the Spree (river). But it isn't the same.

I haven't been back since 1995 when I left to take my next assignment in Washington. Since then I have served at the UN in New York as Ambassador and in Bosnia as Deputy High Representative. But my heart and soul has never left Berlin. The moment of youth, the pride of adulthood and the experience of standing against a mortal threat to our democracy–standing and overcoming. It comes but once and then passes all too quickly.

Donald Hays, Class of 1966
1962-65, 1987-90, 1992-95

Berlin OBSERVER

The 1993 and last U.S. Army Berlin

Winter Formal

American military community kicks off its farewell to Berlin with three nights of dining, dancing and entertainment at the ICC

Winter Formal

Berlin OBSERVER

The Last US Army Winter Ball featured The Pointer Sisters at the fabulous ICC (Internationales Congress Centrum), one of the largest conference centers in the world.

The Last BAHS Parent Newsletter, February 1994

High School

American Parent Newsletter

February, 1994

Science Fair Winners

The recent PTSA Student Showcase spotlighted the creative works of students in the arts and sciences. The BAHS Student Union was transformed into a mini-art gallery displaying the talented renderings of Ron Hosie's art students. Science projects, reports and posters covered walls and tables as the six Science Fair finalists were announced.

7th grade: Rene Linsay
8th grade: Holly Stephenson
9th grade: Helen Sa and Marlene Medina-Cruz
10th grade: Tomomi Katsu
11th grade: Fatma Bashouni
12th grade: Shannon Nichols

Each of the finalists delivered a five minute presentation of their science project as a panel of three judges tabulated scores. The students were rated in six areas: statement of the question, research design, research process, technique of analysis, statement of conclusion, and delivery of the presentation. Eight-grader Holly Stephenson was declared the winner of the annual all-school Science Fair and was presented with a special "Brain Storm" t-shirt from the PTSA. Congratulations to Holly and all the other finalists who each received a $20.00 gift certificate from the Stars & Stripes Bookstore.

The next PTSA Student Showcase will be February 16 at 7:00 p.m. in the Student Union. The topic will be: "TEENS in TURMOIL" (How the drawdown affects teenagers). Students of the HIV Peer Counseling Team will be joined by the community health nurse, the school psychologist, and a drug and alcohol abuse counselor to address issues of concern to parents and teenagers.

COURAGE
NURSES' NOTES
DRAWDOWN
ASBESTOS
CALENDARS

SENIORS

COLLEGE APPLICATIONS: Seniors who plan to attend college the fall of 1994, should be completing their applications. Most colleges and universities have application deadlines of February and early March. The counselors at BAHS can provide addresses and information about all colleges in the United States and many in Europe.

SCHOLARSHIPS: The following scholarship applications are currently available: AWC-Berlin, deadline March 1; USO, deadline postmark March 1; ECAPTS, received by Scholarship Committee, March 1; Delta Sigma Theta Sorority, received in Heidelberg, February 26. Students may get the applications from the counselors at BAHS and should return them at least 7 days prior to the deadline.

GRADUATION: Graduation is scheduled for Saturday, May 28, 2 p.m. at the Schoneberger Rathaus. The Senior Breakfast for seniors and their parents will be Friday, May 27, 8:30 a.m. Practice for graduation will follow Senior Breakfast. The Class of 1994 needs to raise $2,500. to cover the cost of graduation. Seniors are bagging at the PX and

Continued pg.2

Berlin American High School
Parent Newsletter February, 1994

THE CHALLENGE OF DRAWDOWN

Why are we losing teachers at semester?

There are two forces at work that caused the re-alignment of staff. The population at Berlin High school has dropped in relation to the number of teachers that we have. We are extremely well staffed even after the teachers leave.

The other consideration in allowing teachers to transfer is that several of the teachers who are leaving are dual teaching couples who will have difficulty in being placed in the same location or they are new to the system and have little seniority. We are helping to keep quality teachers in DoDDS. Many of our families may see these teachers again next year.

What impact will the new schedule cause?

The majority of teachers that are leaving are from the middle school: Simone & Merrill Bryner, Ken Burland, and Dennis Osborne. The core classes will remain the same. There will be no consolidation in English, math, social studies or science. To minimize the effect of the change the students will remain with the same schedule and classes. The teachers will change.

Ms. Smith, a teacher at BAHS the past two years, will teach three of Ms. Bryner's history classes and Mr. Brown will pick up the fourth class. Mr. Burland's classes will be taught by Mrs. Muehlener a highly qualified substitute teacher. Mr. Bryner's classes will be taught by Mr. Ellis, Mr. Mason and Mr. Baum and Mr. Wall. Ms. Nobbemeyer, Ms. Greer, Ms. Norris and Mr. Lyon will teach 7th grade English. The majority of the new teachers have middle school experience and will be able to meet at the regularly scheduled 6th period teaming times. We intend to carry on the successful middle school program. Therefore, there will be a change, but the impact of the change should be as minimal as possible.

What impact will the changes have on the high school?

The high school will lose Ms. Schiffers, Mr. Lewandowski, and Ms Sanchez. Mr. Roach, Mr. Bertot and Mr. Torres are taking over Ms. Schiffers classes. Mr. Lewandowski's classes are being taken by Mr. Schmoll, Ms. Smith, and Mr. Iacketti. There will be some consolidation of classes in the high school. Drama, Chemistry, World History and Auto will all lose one section.

We are dropping speech and journalism. There was a combined enrollment of three students for second semester in these two classes. We are dropping electronics. There was one student signed up for electronics. Ms. Sanchez reading classes will be taught by other middle school teachers. Her power reading class had one student and will be dropped.

There will be more shifting of student's schedules due to the consolidation, but high school students normally make semester schedule changes and course changes and teacher changes will not be unexpected to them.

Douglas McEnery

ASBESTOS: Continued

asbestos was found in the vinyl floor tiles, the walls leading from the main building to the gym, the roof, some counter tops, and in much of the exterior panels and weatherstripping. It was noted that each of these materials is in good condition, pose no health hazard and do not require removal at this time. Results also indicated that some materials contained moderate to low level of friable asbestos. These included insulation, heat shields, and gaskets in the boiler room, as well as vents to some overhead hoods. Air samples were taken periodically which indicated that no health hazard existed.

Removal of these friable materials has been completed utilizing methods ensured that no asbestos was released In conclusion, there is no current asbestos health hazard at Berlin American High School. Copies of the school's Asbestos Management Plan are kept in the school office and are available for review.

If you have any questions or concerns regarding the information presented in this letter, please feel free to contact me at 819-6392.

Dr. Davenport
Principal

3

3rd Quarter Ends March 31, 1994

Spring Break
April 4-8, 1994

First Day to PCS & Receive Credit
May 20, 1994

Senior Breakfast
May 28, 1994

Graduation
May 28, 1994

Last Day of School June 1, 1994

The Class of 1994 Salutatorian Speech

General Yates, Col. Banks, Lt. Col. Hendrix, Lt. Col. Telencio, Dr. Davenport, Teachers, Distinguished Guests, Honored Parents of the class of '94 , and fellow graduates:

Welcome to the last graduation from Berlin American High School here at the Shöneberger Rathaus, an historic site suitable for this historic event.

We welcome your participation in rite of passage from childhood into adulthood of the finest young people the world has to offer. Not only do we represent American students, but some of the finest students from five continents are represented here today.

Being that our school is as international as it is, many students from all over the world have been introduced, through this school, to a system and culture very different to the one they have been used to from their part of the world. But also the American students at Berlin American High School have learned something about cultures different from their own, a very valuable and useful knowledge that will help them through the future.

These past twelve years have been years of learning. Twelve years that have culminated in this year. A year during which we have enjoyed the privileges that follow a senior class, but also a year where we have worked very hard to be worthy of the honor it is to be the last class ever to graduate from Berlin American High School.

One 'privilege' that we will never forget was the journals we had to write for Mr. Schmoll's English class. As Wesley McKeown '94 describes it: "Journals, journals fun to write, tend to keep you up at night." So many Wednesday nights were spent writing those seven journals [entries] that were due the following day. But we all pulled through and looking through those journals, some interesting ones appear. For example some from early on, in which expectations are expressed. The following journal entry was written by Christie King '94: "It was a new sensation, starting a new school year knowing all of my teachers and classmates. Having moved around so much, I never got the chance to become familiar with my school before. I like it. Now that I have been here two years, I almost know everybody's name [in the school], and they know mine. You feel as if you belong, when you're in a small school.

Excepting fourth and sixth period, I had already been taught by all of my teachers. That's an advantage because I know how my teachers work. There was so much less anxiety in the beginning of the school year, only anticipation of what the year would bring. Turns out I correctly forecasted lots of homework and intense studying. Hopefully, this will teach me to be more organized because I won't be able to indulge in the luxury of procrastinating and stressing out.

There are a couple of new faces, but there are too many old ones missing. The seniors all left. I can't possibly fill their shoes. I don't feel like a senior or look like one, neither do the rest of my classmates. I've always looked up to the upperclassmen and considered them to be bigger and better, almost larger than life. This new crop of freshmen certainly looks little. But the sophomores and juniors aren't making me feel like a "big senior," but that's probably because they <u>are</u> bigger than I, at least in stature.

It's fun to look at the new faces because by the end of the year, relationships will have been formed that I had never expected to happen. Not only with new people, but also with people that I have known for one or two years already. On the flip side, it's sad to look at familiar faces I no longer have a relationship with. Significant others who won't talk to me now, the people I have never gotten along with, and never will. But anything can happen, and everything probably will!"

At the beginning of this year, I would probably have disagreed with Christie's last observation; however, during the course of this year, my mind has changes. Things do happen, sometimes whether we want them to or not.

Attendance at Berlin American High School has been an unusual experience for me. I had only attended Danish schools before I came here in January of 1993. My experiences here have provided me with knowledge and understanding of Americans and the American Educational System. While at BAHS, I have participated in activities unique to American schools such as various clubs, athletic activities, and even being the Salutatorian of the graduating class.

All of the students in the class of 1994 have learned from each other and from their teachers. Our knowledge and perceptions of others have broadened. The experiences we have had as a truly international class can only help us be better citizens in a global society.

Joachim Kundert Jensen, Class of 1994
Senior Class Salutatorian; 1993-1994

Class of 1994 Commencement Program

Berlin American High School

Class of 1994

Schöneberger Rathaus 1400 hours Saturday May 28, 1994

COMMENCEMENT

GRADUATING CLASS - 1994

Tunde Femi Akindulureni
◆❖ Sarita Arya
La Toya Fanchia Bennett
◆☆ Nicole Marie Bertot
Melanie Daniela Bomhardt
◆❖ Patrizio Cavaliere
❖ Tara Chaidez
Shonna Latresa Chavis
◆❖ Shane William Clayton
Chanda Shanita Coppage
Amanda H. Diaz
Ira Dotan-Bochner
Sáez Alexis Echevarria
Jerry Thomas Hardy, Jr.
Tarek Helmy
Kristine F. Hendrix
Constantin Markus von Hoffmeister
Juanita Dian Holton
Jesse Will Howington III
Jorge Julio Inglés, Jr.
◆❖ Sherin Janey
○◆❖ Joachim Kundert Jensen
★ Troy Johnson
Joanna Marie Jones
Jovan J. Jones
Mathew David Jordan
◆❖ Nobumi Katsu
Ha Yeon Kim
●◆❖☆ Christie Ann King
Yelda Kirci
Kei Kobara
Byron William Lindsay, Jr.
☆ Winifred Michelé Marshall
Connie Ann Martin
★ Morris Martinez
Charjuana Rachelle McClain
◆ Wesley Allen McKeown
Shawn Michael Miller
Diane N. Moore
Rick Machewicz
Shannon Ella-Reneé Nichols
Christer A. Nilssen
❖ John Chad Nimmann
Markus Werner Gustav Oergel
Keith Otey
Justin Lee Penney
Stanley Dennis Perkins III
❖ Stephan Ulrich Rippelbeck
Alfred Caesar Rojas
◆ Ivettza Milagros Sánchez
☆ Anna Marie Smith
Dexter Lamond Smith
Ruben Arroyo Solis
◆ Nathan Victor Stieler
Takahiko Sugiyama
Michelle Marie Voyles
Melita Rena Walker
Wayne Williams
Melvin Williamson II
Fatima Yusuf

◆ National Honor Society Member
❖ 3.5 or above Grade Point Adverage
★ January Graduate
☆ Class Officer
● Valedictorian
○ Salutatorian

The Class of 1994 wishes to thank the following individuals and groups who have contributed special effort, time and money to make this Graduation successful:

Jacob Lodge #86
Family Support Group 6/502nd Infantry
Kobara Family
Katsu Family
Directorate of Engineering and Housing
Kristine Hendrix, Berlin H.S. Graphics Department
Ms. Gabrielle Oergel

COMMENCEMENT

PROCESSIONAL Pomp and Circumstance	Berlin American High School Band arr: Clare Grundman
STAR SPANGLED BANNER	F. Scott Key / J.S. Smith arr: Mike Story
SALUTATORY	Joachim Jensen
MUSICAL INTERLUDE	Berlin American High School Band Wind River Overture arr: Bruce Pearson
INTRODUCTION OF SPEAKER	Dr. Davenport Principal Berlin American High School
COMMENCEMENT ADDRESS	Charles Bluem History Teacher Berlin American High School
OFFICERS' ADDRESS	Winifred Marshall, Vice President
VALEDICTORY	Christie Ann King
PRESENTATION OF CLASS	Dr. Davenport Principal Berlin American High School
AWARDING OF DIPLOMAS Names Read By:	Dr. Davenport Phillipp Schmoll
RECESSIONAL	Berlin American High School Band March for a Festive Occasion Eric Osterling

Ushers: Fatma Bassiouni, Brian Brathwaite, Christine Eilers, Kelli Kirkland, Carissa Morales, Katya Schmoll and Tiffany Sellers are members of the National Honor Society.

Berlin American High School Faculty

Charles E. Alldrodge
Jan Amend
Lynn Anderson
Marie Barnes
Patricia Bassel
Dale Baum
Donna Bertot
Douglas Bertot
Beth Bishline
Charles Bluem
Francis Brown
Merrill Bryner
Simone Bryner
Kenneth Burland
Steve Butler
Chris Eichner
Micheal Ellis
Mechthild Flohr
Linda Greer
Adam Hildenbrand
Jon H. Hodge
Ronald Hosie
Gerald Hubbell
Gary Jacketti
Robert Jenkins
Susan Lambert
Ogden Lazenby
Frank Lewandowski
Jack Lyon
Edgar Mason
Barbara Molina
Allene Mueldener
Peg Myatt
Jayme Norris
Marjorie Nubbemeyer
Deanna Oleson
Dennis Osborne
George Pepoy
Werner Prigge
Jerry Roach
Jean Sanchez
Kimberly Schiffers
Phillipp Schmoll
Nita Smith
Betty Snyder
* Gloria South
Marina Stiegler
Irving Torres-Rivera
Randy Wall
Wendy Wall
Russell Walton
Jack Wayne
* Class Sponsor

Administration

Dr. Allen Davenport	Principal
Doug McEnery	Assistant Principal
Doris Brodie	Assistant Principal

SCHÖNEBERGER RATHAUS

The cornerstone for the Schöneberger Rathaus was placed at 12 noon on May 26, 1911. The building was occupied in 1914 as the Rathaus for the city of Schöneberg and this use continued until World War II.

During World War II, parts of the Rathaus were destroyed. In April, 1945, the Red Army occupied the Rathaus and by the summer of 1946, the reconstruction was finished. This room, the Plenarsaal, was used for theater, operattas and concerts. Before the division of the city of Berlin, it was also used for the meetings of the Commandantura.

At the time of the division of Berlin, it was decided by Professor Doctor Otto Suhr and the governing mayor of Berlin, Ernst Reuter, that the Rathaus would be used for meetings of the Berlin City Parliament. The first meeting was January, 1949, and in June, 1949, liaison officers of the Allied Forces moved into the Rathaus. The Allied Forces were tenants for the next forty years. In 1950, the Freedom Bell, donated by the people of America, rang for the first time.

The Schöneberger Rathaus, always a center of politics, was the site in 1961 where 500,000 Berliners protested the construction of the Berlin Wall. On June 26, 1963, John F. Kennedy made his famous "Ich bin ein Berliner" speech to a crowd gathered outside the Rathaus. After Kennedy's assassination the square was renamed John F. Kennedy Platz.

Since the opening of the Berlin Wall and the reunification of the city and nation, the Rathaus is used for special occasions, such as the exhibition in honor of Willy Brandt, art exhibitions and Graduation of the Berlin American High School, Class of 1994.

Berlin OBSERVER

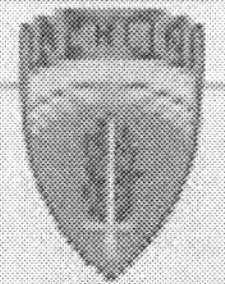

Graduation 1994

BAHS students, faculty save best event for last

by Michael [illegible]
Assistant Editor

May 28 students of the class of '94 at Berlin American High School turned their tassels and celebrated the fact that theirs was the last class to graduate. The graduation, at the Rathaus Schöneberg, culminated a remarkable year for these [illegible] new alumni, who watched not only the end of their high school career, but the end of their high school.

Class president Christi King had written in her journal at the beginning of the year, that "After being here two years I almost know everybody's name and they know mine. It feels that you belong in a small school." King's graduation speech as valedictorian cited survivors who are "able to keep their heads while others around you lose theirs," as Rudyard Kipling wrote in "If".

The graduation was held at the historic Rathaus Shöneberg, site of President John F. Kennedy's "Ich bin ein Berliner" speech in June, 1963.

Charles [illegible], the students' choice as commencement speaker, urged the young adults to start the next phase of their lives now. "For those of you who don't get accepted to college right away or don't join the military, get a job fast. Being at a job helps form your life... You will soon become another person and hardly recognize yourself in three to five years."

Joachim Jensen gave the salutatory, the BAHS band played several selections, and Winifred Marshall, class vice president, gave the officers' address. School principal Dr. Allen Davenport congratulated the class for a 100 percent graduation rate, awarded the diplomas and thus ended the last BAHS graduation.

For a story on the high school's history and the spirit that made BAHS special, see page four.

4 June 3, 1994 Berlin Observer

Beyond Iron Curtain, education shone through at BAHS

Candy Bomber drops in on Berlin American High School.

Colonel Gail Halvorsen returned a final time to Berlin American High School. His children attended this school while he was the commander of Tempelhof Airbase. He is known as the famous Candy Bomber of the Berlin Airlift. He returned to make a final appearance to the students, faculty, and administration, giving a few words of inspiring advice. The school held an assembly during which he told his famous story of charity and generosity to the children of post war Germany.

After World War II ended, the people of Berlin were isolated and blockaded from the rest of the democratic world by the Soviet Union. All land and water routes into Berlin were cut off, but the airways were left open. Only the basic essentials were flown in by the Allies. Thus the German children could not enjoy such items as chocolate, gum, and candy. Col. Halvorsen saw these poor children waiting by the runways, and wished he could do something to make them happier. He came up with a plan to drop small bundles of candy to the children waiting below. To make sure they knew which plane he was flying, he would wiggle his wings as he approached. They began to refer to him as "Uncle Wiggly Wings" and other such nicknames.

They have candy at least.

Student Body President Katya Schmoll presents Col. Halvorsen with an honorary gold card.

So Many Reasons to Celebrate!

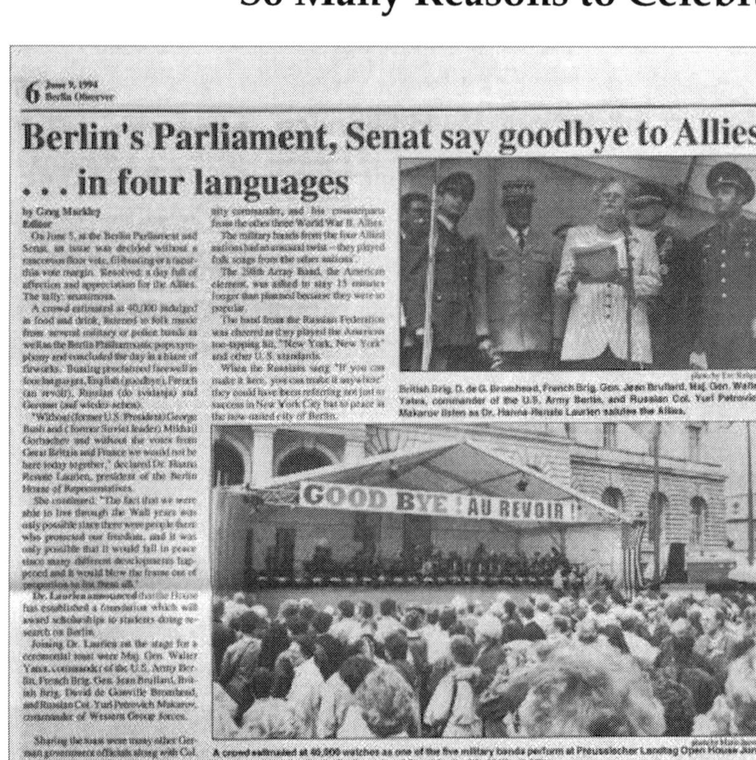

6 June 9, 1994 Berlin Observer

Berlin's Parliament, Senat say goodbye to Allies . . . in four languages

by Greg Markley
Editor

British Brig. D. de G. Bromhead, French Brig. Gen. Jean Brullard, Maj. Gen. Walter Yates, commander of the U.S. Army Berlin, and Russian Col. Yuri Petrovich Makarov listen as Dr. Hanna-Renate Laurien salutes the Allies.

A crowd estimated at 40,000 watches as one of the five military bands perform at Preussischer Landtag Open House June 5, sponsored by the Berlin Parliament and Senat for the World War II Allies.

On June 5th, Berlin Parliament and Senate put forth a proclamation, which was passed unanimously. "Resolved: A day full of affection and appreciation for the Allies." They thanked former President Bush, and former Soviet leader Mikhail Gorbachev, Great Britain, and France for the votes necessary for German reunification.

The day's event, hosted by the German people, drew a crowd of 40,000 for food, drinks, music, dancing and fireworks.

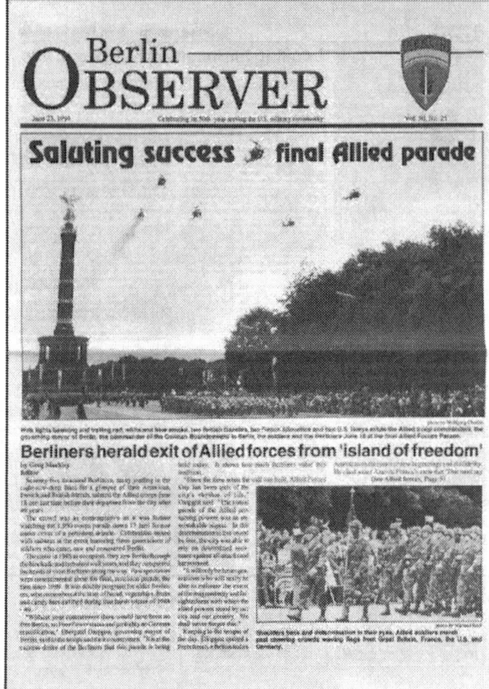

Berlin OBSERVER

Saluting success final Allied parade

Berliners herald exit of Allied forces from 'island of freedom'

Berlin OBSERVER

Parade salutes mission born on 4th of July

Commander-in-chief visits July 11 - 12

Left: June 18, 1994, Celebrating Allied Forces Day- An annual parade of Allied protecting powers— a show of determination to protect the freedom of Berlin. Right: Final 4th of July Parade in Berlin. Mission Accomplished.

Berlin OBSERVER

July 15, 1994 — Celebrating its 50th year serving the U.S. military community — Vol. 50, No. 28

Gone, but never to be forgotten

President Clinton cases colors of brigade that changed world

BERLIN BRIGADE

by Greg Markley
Editor

President Clinton, minutes after casing the Berlin Brigade colors and a few hours after passing through the Brandenburg Gate into a side of Berlin made free by that brigade, said to all the soldiers and airmen who ever served in Berlin: "America salutes you; mission accomplished."

Clinton, who began July 12 by jogging near the Tiergarten with seven Berlin soldiers, ended the 49 year life of the brigade early that evening in an honors ceremony at a bunting-bedecked 4th of July Platz. He also presented the unit a superior service award in the ceremony witnessed by 1,000 assembled soldiers, stands teeming with dignitaries and other well-wishers, and by a live television audience estimated at tens of thousands.

"From Checkpoint Charlie to Doughboy City to Tempelhof Airport and beyond, more than 100,000 men and women have served in Berlin," the president said. "More than anyone, they showed the patience it took to win the Cold War. More than anyone, they knew the dangers of a world on edge. They would have been the first casualties in the world's final war, yet they never flinched.

"In the long struggle to free Berlin, no one ever knew

(See Honors, Page 4)

Col. Jimmy Banks and Command Sgt. Maj. James Toney, the Berlin Brigade's top officer and noncommissioned officer, case the brigade colors as President Bill Clinton, German Chancellor Dr. Helmut Kohl, USAREUR Commander-in-Chief Gen David Maddox and U.S. Army Berlin Commander Maj. Gen. Walter Yates look on.

The 287 Military Police Company, commanded by Capt. Bill Loudon, passes in review for President Clinton July 12.

First Lady Hillary Rodham-Clinton and wife of German Chancellor Kohl, Hannelore, wave to the crowd at the deactivation ceremony July 12. They are accompanied by soldiers from the U.S. Army, Berlin. The two women also spent some time together at John F. Kennedy High School, where they gave diplomas to the graduating class of 1994.

Observer stops presses, AFN Berlin shuts down today at 10 a.m.

On July 12th, 1994, President Clinton cases the colors, ending the 49 year life of the Berlin Brigade.

4 July 15, 1994
Berlin Observer

Gone, but never to be forgotten

photos by Gregory Markley

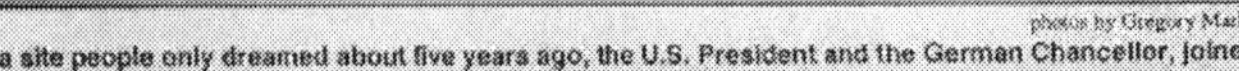

In a site people only dreamed about five years ago, the U.S. President and the German Chancellor, joined by their wives, walk through the Brandenburg Gate into eastern Berlin.

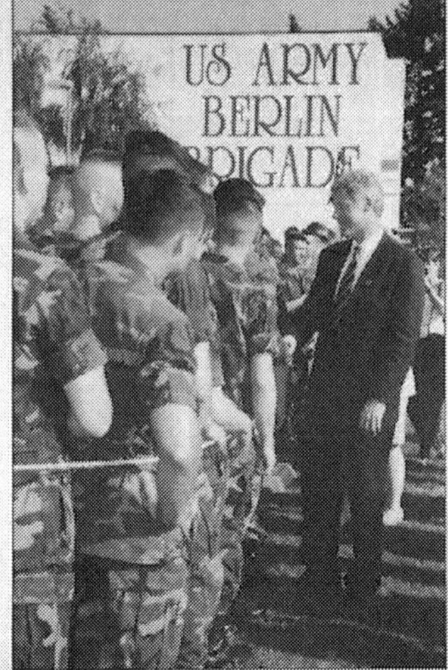

After the deactivation ceremony, President Bill Clinton greets two companies of soldiers from the Berlin Brigade. The soldiers were from A Company, 5-502nd Infantry and C Company, 6-

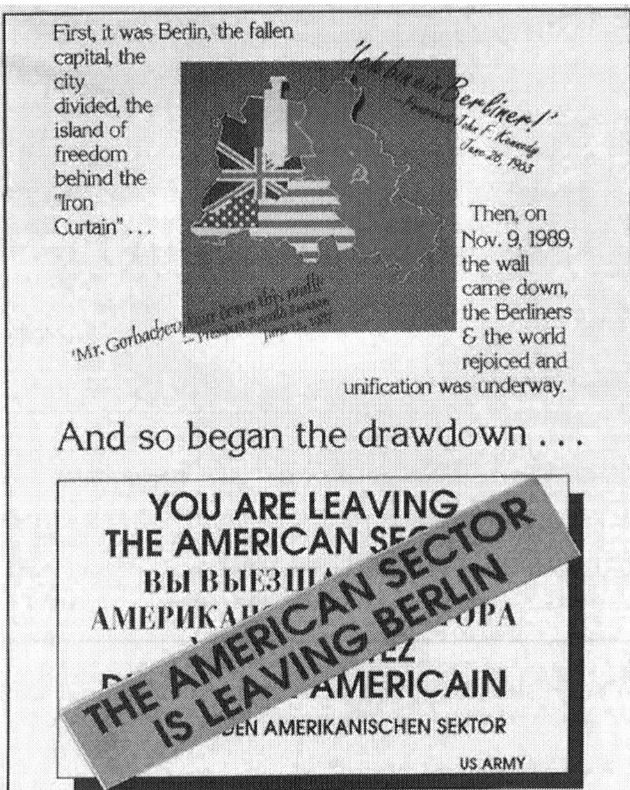

First, it was Berlin, the fallen capital, the city divided, the island of freedom behind the "Iron Curtain"...
Then, on Nov. 9, 1989, the wall came down, the Berliners & the world rejoiced and unification was underway.
And so began the drawdown . . .
YOU ARE LEAVING
THE AMERICAN SE
ВЫ ВЫЕЗЩА
АМЕРИКА
ОРА
EZ
AMERICAIN
DEN AMERIKANISCHEN SEKTOR
US ARMY
THE AMERICAN SECTOR
IS LEAVING BERLIN

Top left to right:
*An historic moment- The US President and German Chancellor, joined by their wives walk **through** Brandenburg Gate.*

Soldiers wait to meet President Clinton after the deactivation ceremony.

Left: The American Sector Has Left Berlin!

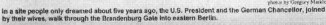

Auf Wiedersehen, Berlin!

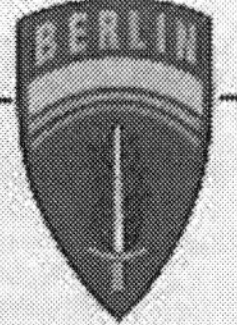

Final issue

Berlin OBSERVER

July 15, 1994 — Celebrating its 50th year serving the U.S. military community — Vol. 50, No. 28

Tschüß Berlin! Future belongs to you

an open letter to Berliners by Michael Ertel
Editor, Commemorative Edition

The last year here in Berlin for the U.S forces has revolved around two things -- drawing down and reaping the rewards of our stay. We have been the special guests of dinners, parades, concerts and other functions hosted by Berliners to show their appreciation for our efforts; and to say thank you. Yet we haven't returned the favor. With our ground-breaking efforts in trying to close a combat unit and a community, we have been quite busy. I sat in the woods of the Grunewald last weekend to write a letter of thanks, a letter that recounts the changes that have occurred in the understanding of one soldier, and a letter that challenges you to face your future.

It is the summer of 1984, George Orwell's fateful year; I am 14; the Olympics are in America this year. Born in the USA by Springsteen is playing on a new machine called a Walkman; I am riding my bicycle through my neighborhood; this is America.

I pass by a friend who is still trying to figure out the Rubik's Cube; I stop and try to help -- to no avail. I ride on.

Around the corner there is a group of girls having a tea party with Cabbage Patch Dolls, nearby their brothers play with G.I. Joe dolls, the new, smaller ones. This is America. I pedal faster, just for fun.

It is the summer of 1994; fate has brought me here; I am 24; the World Cup is in America this year. Streets of Philadelphia by Springsteen in my car's CD player; I am driving through the former East Berlin; this is not America.

I pass by a young boy stacking boxes and having trouble. Another boy tries to help -- to no avail. I drive on.

Around the corner young girls unpack boxes of cabbage, nearby their brothers sell cigarettes, the new low tar ones. This is Berlin. I hit the pedal to go faster, I am about to be hit from behind.

This is definitely not America. But the time we have spent here will certainly go down as a significant chapter in our personal histories. You, the Berliners, have left an indelible impression on us. Your customs, your bravery and your people have given us the opportunity to see a world that no longer exists -- a world behind a wall.

The U.S. military presence in this city is almost over. We have been here nearly 50 years not just to defend your city, but we also tried to show you that there is a better life to be led. Not as Americans, but as free Germans.

We weren't trying to bring you into an American neighborhood complete with baseball, apple pie and buzz-cut lawns. We just wanted you to have access to the balls, apples and lawnmowers; what you do with them is up to you.

'Let the wall serve not only as a backdrop in old snapshots in your photo album, but a constant reminder of the Iron Curtain, shut to keep the sun out and the darkness in.'

Although life does vary from our country to yours, the differences are not as colossal as before. Today the diversity has less to do with politics and more to do with toys, less to do with war games and more to do with football games; and we all know that's much ado about nothing.

This duty for we, the U.S. forces, has been both invigorating and disheartening. Invigorating because we have been able to do our jobs at a location that is at the crossroads of history; disheartening because we have been so far removed from our families and our own way of life.

Maybe that's what we need though. Whenever we forget or abuse the freedom that we were born with, we can look here to Berlin. We can witness the Berliners who struggle to recapture a lost freedom of youth or those who are taking their first glimpse at freedom never known.

Berliners rejoice as the wall opens. The crumbling of the wall was not only a significant time for Berliners, but as the focal point of the cold war, the fall of the wall symbolized the ending of hostilities between U.S.S.R. and its satellites and the United States and other democracies throughout the world. The battle for the next generation of Berliners is to ensure that freedom and peace reign.

You should not be ashamed of this fight, or your roots of oppression; take pride in growing out of them so you could see the sun and grow more; it is a natural progression.

We, the soldiers that have served here, have no recent painful memories of oppression and isolation equal to yours in our country's history. In the birth of our nation our forefathers were separated from their friends, families and foes by an ocean gap. During your isolation, you were separated only by a wall; which was far worse than a gap. It was a chain keeping you from a better life that was within eyeshot. Until your rebirth.

We borrow your memories with the hope that the experiences we learn will lead us down a path whose end reveals that our children too, have no painful memories.

You, on the other hand, are at the crossroads and must take a path where the footprints of freedom have been covered with time. Let the winds of change blow away the red sand of captivity to expose those footprints. The legacy of Lenin is gone with the wind, so let these footprints guide you to an era of equality and prosperity.

Yes, it is a long and arduous journey, and there will be difficulties. But remain focused, a better life is just around the corner; it will come. A poet once said happiness is like a cat; if you chase it, it will run away; but if you are patient, that cat will come to you and snuggle at your feet and purr.

You have waited so long for this chance at a better life and a brighter future, and now you have it, yet don't forget your past.

Let the wall serve not only as a backdrop in old snapshots in your photo album, but a constant reminder of the Iron Curtain, shut to keep the sun out and the darkness in.

Our departure can be credited not only to the strength of our forces but your desire for us to succeed. Together we formed an indestructible body. We were the muscles and bone that defended you; you were the heart and soul that defined you; communism was the enemy that repressed you, but now, because of our body armor of resistance, it must cede to you.

It was an impressive victory. Hang on to the battle's medals, remember the scars of the cold war and proudly wear your experiences like a badge over your heart. It is a symbol that there is a new sheriff in town and his name is democracy and unity.

Pray that you may be able to deputize your children into this posse of pride.

Your parents sacrificed for your future, whether they sacrificed as victims of the holocaust, burning in the stoves of bigotry or if their sacrifice was contained within a wall, shivering in the box of the cold war, they did it for you. What will you do in return? What will you do for your children?

Hopefully you can lay the foundation of a democracy that will give them the opportunity to succeed no matter what their race, religion, sex or ideology.

Embrace your former enemies, and show them the strengths of unity and democracy. They were just foot soldiers fearful of repercussions if they disobeyed. Let them make their own decisions and accept them. Utopia won't happen overnight, but it will happen.

And maybe... *It is 2044, 50 years after Orwell's fateful year, and you are with your grandchildren who have come to visit. The log in the fireplace is burning brightly and provides the room's only light and heat; you feel the warmth of the room. The young ones are laughing and playing. You call them over and begin to tell them about the wall years. They haven't got a clue about the tyranny and oppression. They think you have lost your mind and exaggerate a bit too much. You sit them on your lap, the fire crackles; you begin the story; they roll their eyes and all you can do is you smile and snuggle in happiness.*

Final Edition of the Berlin Observer, July 15th, 1994

Looking back: The Wall Years

Berlin, 1961. The shadow of two West Berliners waving to friends across the border falls symbolically on the newly erected Berlin Wall.

Shadows of two W. Berliners waving to friends across the border. 1961

Risky Business: Scott '81 and Bill '79 Charlton straddle the Wall, 1975

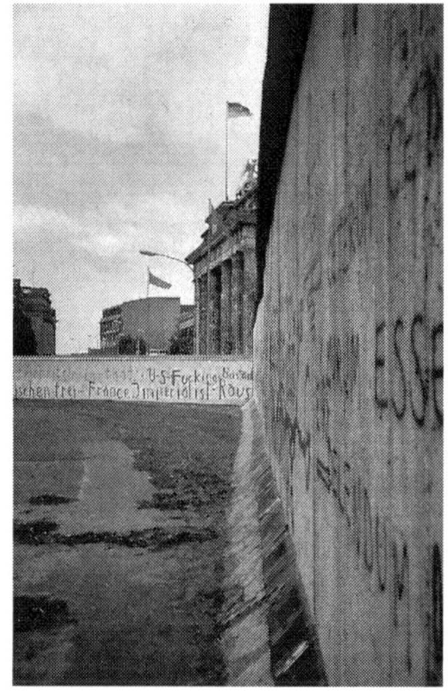

The Wall and Brandenburg Gate, 1984

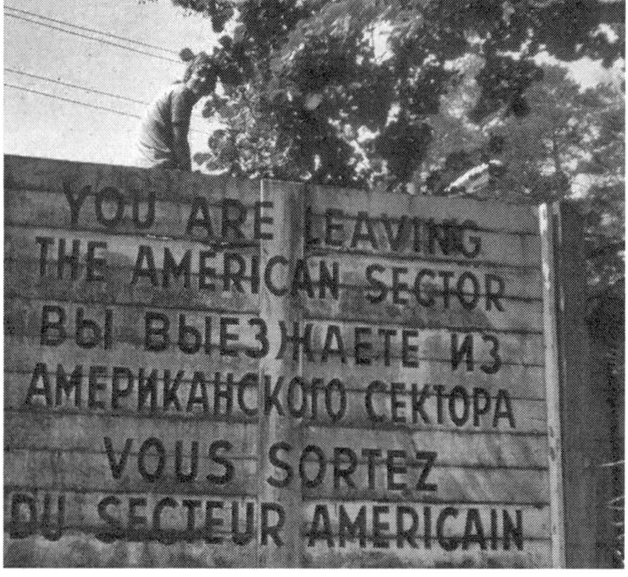

Thumbing his nose at danger: Bill Charlton '79 sits atop the border sign

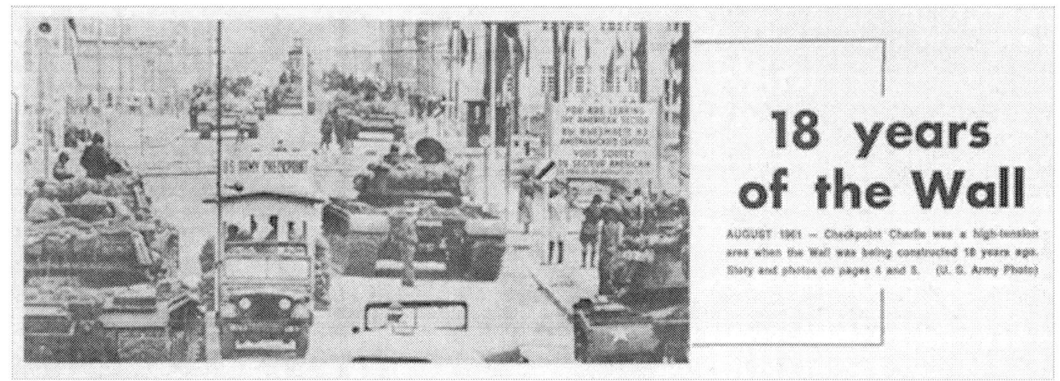

18 years of the Wall

AUGUST 1961 — Checkpoint Charlie was a high-tension area when the Wall was being constructed 18 years ago. Story and photos on pages 4 and 5. (U. S. Army Photo)

Showdown at Checkpoint Charlie: Remembering the 16-hour standoff between US and Soviet tanks on Oct. 28, 1961

Over the Wall: no guard towers on this quiet street, possibly occupied by KGB or high-level Party officials.

Dark Green Soviet cars like this one drove slowly through the American Sector regularly; always occupied by four uniformed Soviet guards

Brandenburg Gate, gateway between East and West Berlin; John Freeman '71, with Polizei; Soldier erecting border sign

A Vibrant City Restored and Reunified

Street performers at the Brandenburg Gate

Bode Museum, Museum Island, Berlin

Brandenburg Gate at night

Deutsches Historisches Museum

Spree River, near the Bode Museum

Nazi planes abandoned at Tempelhof Airport, 1946

Tempelhof Airport, 2009

Reichstag after Allied bombing, 1946

Reichstag with newly restored glass dome, 2008

Olympiastadion

Inside the newly refurbished Olympic Stadium, 2009

The Sony Center's ultra-modern color-changing roof

The city night lights

Memorial to the Murdered Jews of Europe

The Outpost Theater, now part of the Allied Museum

The new Hauptbahnhof (main train station), near the Reichstag building

Gendarmenmarkt: German Cathedral and Konzerthaus

Timeline of the Cold War in Berlin

1940

1945

February 4-11: ***President Franklin D. Roosevelt, British Prime Minister Winston Churchill and Soviet leader Joseph Stalin meet at Yalta to confirm a plan to divide both Germany and Berlin into American, British, French, and Russian zones.***

March 7: U.S. forces capture a bridge across the Rhine River and enter Germany.

April 12: Roosevelt dies; Harry Truman becomes president.

April 21: The Red Army of the Soviet Union reaches Berlin.

April 25-26: Soviet and American forces link up at the River Elbe.

April 30: German leader Adolf Hitler commits suicide.

May 2: Russian forces take control of Berlin.

May 7: The Germans unconditionally surrender at General Dwight D. Eisenhower's headquarters in Reims, France.

May 8: ***V-E Day; another surrender ceremony occurs in Berlin.***

June 5: The Allied Control Council (ACC), with representatives from each Allied power, announces the division of Germany.

June 29: Eisenhower's deputy, Lieutenant General Lucius Clay, meets with his Russian and British counterparts in Berlin to discuss Western access to the city, which lies 110 miles inside the Soviet zone. One highway and railroad are set aside for Western use.

July 3: British and American soldiers take over their Berlin zones.

July 7: The ACC creates a governing body for Berlin-- the Kommandatura; Russian say that the Soviets will not supply food for the Western sectors of Berlin.

July 17: Truman, Churchill and Stalin convene the Potsdam

November 20: The war crimes trials of Nazi leaders begin at Nuremberg.

November 30: The ACC approves three air corridors securing Western access to Berlin; each is 20 miles wide.

1946

March 5: In a famous speech at Westminster College in Missouri, Churchill declares that an "iron curtain" has fallen across Eastern Europe.

School News: 4 May: *Dependents School Division (DSD) was formally established. Its purpose was two-fold: (1) to organize and maintain schools on both the elementary and secondary levels in military communities in Germany, and (2) to supply German educators with a model American school system in action, from which to draw inspiration for the reorganization and democratization of the German educational program.*

School News: October 14: *The original Student Body assembled and Thomas A. Roberts School of Berlin opened its doors to American dependent pupils and children of the Allied Military Missions. From a low of thirty-three the school grew to around eighty students by the end of the year.*

1947

March 12: President Truman announces his "Truman Doctrine" pledging support to any country threatened by communism.

March 15: Clay replaces Eisenhower as military governor of the American zone of Germany.

1948

June 18: The Western powers announce plans for a new deutschmark to replace the former German currency which had become worthless. Russia refuses to go along and announces its own currency introduction four days later.

June 23: The Western deutschmark appears in Berlin. Just before midnight, the Soviets cut power to West Berlin and then begin a blockade of the city.

June 24: All rail, road, and water access from the Western zones to Berlin is halted. The next day, the Soviets declare they will not send any supplies to West Berlin, which has only enough food for 36 days and coal for 45 days. In response, the Western Allies impose a counter-blockade on Soviet areas.

June 26: ***The Berlin Airlift begins with 32 flights by American C-47 aircraft in West Germany to the Tempelhof airport in Berlin. Eighty tons of provisions are delivered that first day. The American attempt to supply Berlin's 2.5 million people is dubbed "Operation Vittles," while the British effort becomes known as "Operation Plainfare."***

July 1: The Soviets officially quit the Kommandatura.

July 17: Airlift pilot Gail Halvorsen strikes up a conversation with a group of children watching the planes arrive at Tempelhof and gives them some of his gum, promising to drop more from his aircraft the next day. Soon word of Halvorsen's efforts has spread, and by January what he dubs "Operation Little Vittles" will have dropped some 250,000 candy-laden parachutes into the city.

August 5: Work begins on a new Berlin airport, Tegel, in the French Sector. At its height the site will employ some 18,000 German workers.

December 20: "Operation Santa Claus" : Christmas gifts for 10,000 Berlin children.

1949

January 1949: "Operation Vittles": A cookbook compiled by *The American Women in Blockaded BERLIN* is published.

April 4: The U.S. and Western European governments sign the North Atlantic Treaty in Washington. This treaty establishes the North Atlantic Treaty Organization and commits its members to mutual defense in the event of a Soviet attack.

May 4: Delegates from the original four Allied powers announce an agreement to end the blockade in eight days. Clay, whose retirement has been announced by Truman on the 3rd, is saluted by 11,000 U.S. soldiers and dozens of airplanes. Once home, he will receive a ticker-tape parade in New York, address Congress, and get a medal from Truman.

May 12: At one minute after midnight, the Soviets lift their barricades and restore access from West Germany to Berlin. A British convoy immediately drives through, and the first train from the West reaches Berlin at 5:32 that morning. Later that day an enormous crowd celebrates the end of the blockade by Berlin's City Hall and pays tribute to Clay.

May 23: The Federal Republic of Germany is established in the country's Western zones.

October 7: The Soviets respond to the creation of the Federal Republic of Germany by announcing their own German Democratic Republic in the East.

1950s

1950

October 1: The new West Berlin constitution comes into effect, defining the city as part of the Federal Republic of Germany.

1953

<u>**School News**</u>: **September 9**: A ribbon cutting ceremony marked the opening of the Thomas A. Roberts School (TAR) on Hüttenweg. TAR served as the elementary school for the military community until US troop pull-out in 1994.

1960s

1961

August 13: ***Just after midnight, the Soviets and German Democratic Republic block movement by East Berliners into the West by beginning construction of a Berlin Wall dividing the two parts of the city.***

July 29- August 6: First Annual German-American Volksfest. During the last night of the festival, Soviet and E. German guards had begun erecting the Wall. Many families where separated that night, some trapped on the East side, others in the West as they were enjoying the festival.

1963

June 26: ***During a visit to the city, President John F. Kennedy famously declares, "Ich bin ein Berliner."***

November 22: ***President John F. Kennedy is assassinated in Dallas, Texas.***

1964

School News: November 30: Groundbreaking ceremony for Berlin American High School

1965

School News: August 25: Berlin American High School opens its doors at Am Hegenwinkel 2a. BAHS was one of the first five American schools opened in Germany. Following the withdrawal of U.S. troops from BERLIN in 1994, the Wilma Rudolph Oberschule moved into the building. ***NOTE: Alumni and faculty references to TAR after August 1965 are referencing the elementary school. Prior to this, TAR references apply to all grade levels.***

1967

April 6: Vice-President Hubert Humphrey visits W. Berlin.

1969

January 23: Jimi Hendrix rocks out at the Sportpalast (demolished in 1973).

February 27: President Richard Nixon visits Berlin. Students bussed to Tempelhof Airport to see him.

December 17: Bob Hope visits-- brings the *Bob Hope Christmas Show* to Berlin.

1970s

1976

School News: The Cubs become the Bears: Student Council President Vennie Gore '76 proposed and led a school mascot change at a Student Council meeting. BAHS Cubs were now the Berlin Bears. ***Note: Therefore, stories and news clippings reference the Berlin Cubs prior to 1976, and the Berlin Bears in subsequent references to the school mascot/persona.***

May 13-14 – Vice President Nelson A. Rockefeller visits Berlin.

1978

April 16: Gen. Clay dies. By his West Point grave, a memorial from the people of Berlin reads: "*Wir danken dem Bewahrer unserer Freiheit,*":"We thank the defender of our freedom."

Spring: Former heavyweight boxing champion Muhammad Ali visits BAHS.

July 15: President Jimmy Carter visited West Berlin on 15 July 1978.

1980s

1982

June 11: President Ronald Reagan visits West Berlin, speaks at Tempelhof Airport.

1983

January 31- February 1: Vice President George Bush visits Berlin to read an "open letter" to Europe (directed towards General Secretary Adropov) from President Reagan concerning intermediate-range nuclear ballistic missiles.

School News: VP Bush visits BAHS student body-- school assembly held at the Coles Sport Center on Hüttenweg.

1986

April 5: La Belle Nightclub bombing by the Libyans. Post goes on lock down. Curfew instituted for all US citizens.

1987

12 June: President Ronald Reagan visited West Berlin. Delivers his famous words: "Mr. Gorbachev, Tear Down This Wall."

School News: After he visited the Wall, President Reagan visited Tempelhof and congratulated the Berlin American High School's graduating class of '87. At the gala for the celebration **of Berlin's 750th Anniversary** as a city, BAHS student Jasper Kump '87 sang for President Reagan, the First Lady and 4,000 others in the Tempelhof atrium.

1989

November 9: After huge public demonstrations, the Berlin Wall comes down.

1990s

1990

October 3: East and West Germany are reunified.

1994

1 June: Berlin American High School closes, the summer the American Allied Forces left BERLIN.

6 July: Berlin Brigade officially deactivated by President Bill Clinton.

12 July : President Bill Clinton visits Berlin.

9 September : ***Allied Forces officially pull out of Berlin. The city bids farewell to the Allied troops amidst great fanfare which included a military parade, speeches and concerts. Those who entered as conquerors grew to be seen as protectors.***

Glossary of Terms

1K Zone- The Inner German Border between East and West Germany, 1949 – 1990.

Allies/Allied Forces- A group of countries comprised of Great Britain, France, the United States and Russia during the Cold War.

AYA - Allied Youth Activities, provided a teen club and extra-curriculars.

Berlin Brigade- Brigade size forces located in Berlin comprised of American and British forces. French forces were called Françaises à Berlin.

Berlin Brigade HQ- Brigade of US Army located in Berlin. They used the Allied forces patch, with Berlin in an arch on top of it. Headquarters were located on the Clay Compound on Clayallee, both named after General Lucius D. Clay.

Checkpoint Alpha- Border crossing at Helmstedt-Marienborn on the border between East Germany and West Germany.

Checkpoint Bravo– Border crossing between W. Berlin and E. Germany or the German Democratic Republic (GDR). The only Autobahn access for Allied personnel through E. Germany to W. Germany via Checkpoint Alpha.

Checkpoint Charlie- Border crossing between East and West Berlin.

Commissary- Military base/post grocery store; groceries sold at subsidized prices.

Dahlem- Quiet area in Berlin where the Freie University is located. Was part of the American Sector during the Cold War.

Deutsche Mark (DM)- Currency of West Germany during the Cold War.

DoDDS- Dept. of Defense Dependent Schools or DoDEA (Dept of Defense Educational Activity) as they are called now.

Duty Officer- Rotating position assigned to a Junior Officer. It is a duty or watch position.

DYA- Dependent Youth Activities. Youth center for Military Dependents a place to gather for fun, sports and after school activities (formerly the AYA).

East Germany- During the Cold War the German Democratic Republic (GDR) was part of the Russian Republic.

"Economy"- Living on the 'economy' meant you did not have military base housing, so you lived off base.

Flag Orders- Flag Orders were needed for military personnel and their dependents to travel by rail or car between W. Berlin through the E. Germany, to W. Germany.

Funny Money- A slang name given to money that was used in East Germany.

During the late 70s -early 80s the rate was 8 East German dollars to 1 US Dollar!

GDR (German Democratic Republic)- Also called DDR (Deutsche Demokratische Republik) or East Germany

German-American Volksfest - A large festival that celebrates the American way of life and the close friendship they have with Germany, held annually in Berlin, Germany in the former Truman Plaza complex in Dahlem. The first Volksfest was held in 1961.

Glienicke Brücke - A bridge across the Havel River that connects the Wannsee District of Berlin with the Brandenburg Capital, Potsdam

Grunewald - A forest located in Berlin on the East side of the Havel on the Western side of Berlin.

Gruney Man - Fictional character made famous by US military dependents, said to reside in the Grunewald Forest.

Harnack House - Located in the Dahlem District of Berlin, it was an Officers Club and Visitors Center during the Cold War; it is now a conference center with guest accommodations.

Host Nation Teacher- "Host Nation Teachers were hired locally by DoDDs to supplement the American school's teaching staff. They were to enrich us culturally...in addition to their various teaching topic." Additionally, students participate in activities which build appreciation and understanding of the culture of the country in which they reside. (www.dodea.edu**).**

Imbiss Stand-
Ku'damm (Kudamm)- A main avenue in Berlin, the Kurfürstendamm is Berlin's most popular shopping street and promenade. It is the Champs-Élysées of Berlin. The Brandenburg Gate, which was closed for so long, was the center of this avenue dividing East Berlin from West Berlin.

No Man's Land or Death Strip- Area between the inner and outer Walls surrounding Berlin. Contained rows of Czech hedgehogs (anti-tank obstacles) and sanded areas concealing land mines.

Oberammergau Passion Play- every ten years since 1634, the whole town of Oberammergau, Germany puts on a Passion Play to celebrate the life, death and resurrection of Jesus Christ. This is to fulfill a vow the town took to thank God for sparing their hamlet during the Great Plague.

Potsdam- Potsdam was the primary residency of the Prussian Kings in the 18th Century. Frederick the Great transformed the area into one of grandeur, building Sanssouci Palace. Although much of the area was damaged by Allied bombing raids in World War II, the leaders of the Allies, Churchill, Truman and Stalin met at the Cecilienhof Palace to sign the accord, the Potsdam Agreement.

Provost Marshall - Officer who is in charge of the Military Police.

Pückler- US military housing area north of BB Housing Area, housed officers and enlisted soldiers with large families.

PX (Post Exchange)- on any military post or base, this is similar to a department store, which sold clothing, shoes, housewares and electronics.

RTO- (Rail Transport Office) Railway station for the US Army Duty Train.

School buses/green buses- School buses for children were Army green, as were the regular busses that provided transportation for all military personnel and their families living in the American Sector of W. Berlin.

Sectors- Berlin was divided into four sectors: British, American, Soviet and French.

TDY- Temporary duty: It is defined as duty at a location(s), other than the permanent duty station.

Templehof- Airport in the western American Sector (hof means airport); largest and grandest airport ever made.

Tour of duty- The length of time that a Serviceman is assigned at a Post or Base.

Wannsee- The Wannsee is a beautiful suburb of Berlin near Potsdam. Palatial lake homes and villas populate the area. During World War II the Wannsee Conference took place here where the Final Solution was drafted.

West Berlin Air Corridor- During the Cold War, this comprised three airway areas that stretched between West Berlin and West Germany, over East Germany's Air Space

Zones- Germany was divided into four zones of occupation: British, American, Soviet and French.

Things to know: *German laws on the consumption of alcohol are some of the least restrictive in the world. It is legal to drink beer and wine at age 14 when accompanied by an adult and at age 16 without one. This is why there are references to teen drinking in some of the stories--students could legally patronize local beer halls and pubs. The easy availability of mass transit meant that parents had no fear of students being killed while drinking and driving. This, along with the belief that we were in a city doomed-- constantly on the verge of sudden annihilation, made it difficult for parents to prevent; therefore many just urged their students to use moderation.*

List of Contributors

Chapter 1 Post-war to 1949

Chapter 2: The 1950s

Chapter 3: The 1960s

Chapter 4: The 1970s

Chapter 5: 1980s

Chapter 6: Fall of the Wall to 1994

Photo Credits

Chapter 1: Post-war to 1949

1.	James Miller '83	Cover Photo
2.	Anastasia Lowe, Brat daughter	p. viii
3.	Marianna Lieurance Mounsey '50	p. 6
4.	Linda Ehrlich Packard '70	pp. 6-8
5.	John Thomas Wynn '56	pp. 10, 13
6.	Sandra Serbin Dresdner '56	pp. 16,18,20-22
7.	Merillan Murray Thomas '48	p. 26
8.	Anna Worrell Anderson '52	p. 30
9.	Dan Bunting '49	pp. 31-32, 34-37, 44
10.	Curtis Carter, Brat parent	p. 39
11.	Col. Gail Halvorsen, Candy Bomber	pp. 41-43

Chapter 2: The 1950s

1.	Gail Rybaltowski-Karppinen '63	p. 50
2.	Bill 'Toby' West '53	pp. 60, 64
3.	Alexander Longolius, FAC	p. 61
4.	John Gilliam '52	p. 63
5.	Anna Worrell Anderson '52	p. 64

Chapter 3: The 1960s

1.	Pat Willams '65	pp. 66, 68
2.	Jim Branson '64	pp. 72, 74
3.	Bill "Toby" West '53	pp. 77, 85, 92-93,97,100, 106
4.	Danica Charlton Lehner '82	p. 88
5.	Linda Ehrlich Packard '70	pp. 95, 141
6.	Jules DeNitto '63	pp. 108, 123-124
7.	Jim Polley '64	pp. 115, 117
8.	Maggie Ellithorpe Stafsnes '63	p. 119
9.	Robert Riddick '65	pp. 129, 131, 133
10.	Ruth Donnocker, FAC	pp. 141, 143
11.	Lewis D. Walls Jr. '74	pp. 146-149
12.	Daniel Jenkins '65, Wiesbaden	p. 151
13.	Ross Calvert '74	pp. 166, 172
14.	Ruchia (Roo) Eargle Moran '73	p. 178
15.	Jeri Polansky Glass '72	p. 186
16.	Deb Brian Clark '74	pp. 190, 192, 193
17.	Melvin De Vilbiss '71	pp. 197-199, 202-203

Chapter 4: The 1970s

1.	Patricia Simurra Price '76	pp. 208-210, 224
2.	James Miller '83	p. 221, 292, 379
3.	John Freeman '71	pp. 226, 419, 467
4.	Jeri Polanksi Glass '72	p. 238
5.	Linda Ehrlich Packard '70	pp. 241, 421, 469
6.	Rose Hanson Neel '84	pp. 243, 322, 352, 365, 380-385, 405, 467
7.	Bill Burhans Jr. '76	p. 245
8.	Col. Gail Halvorsen	pp. 263, 266
9.	Clarence L. Jaynes, Brat parent	pp. 280-281
10.	Danica Charlton Lehner '82	pp. 286, 419, 466-467,
11.	Daniel Jenkins '65, Wiesbaden	pp. 288-290
13.	Trisha A. Lindsey '82	p. 298

Chapter 5: The 1980s

1.	Peter Stein '80	pp. 301-302
2.	Yoshika Loftin Lowe '83	pp. 304, 315-316, 320, 327, 346, 374, 376, 378, 383-385
3.	Kath Kottke Sturgeon '86	pp. 307, 311, 409
4.	Carolyn Lindsey Grobes '80	p. 319
5.	Rose Hanson Neel '84	pp. 320, 322, 323, 343, 352, 371, 386-391, 411
6.	Trisha A. Lindsey '82	pp. 324, 326, 331, 333-334
7.	Richard Carmer, Brat photographer	p. 343
8.	Angela Ott '80	p. 349
9.	Johnny Hubbard '86	p. 364
10.	James Miller '83	pp. 367, 408
11.	Juli-Jay Hamilton Wollam '86	p. 381
12.	Mark Millen '83	p. 381
13.	Michelle Estes '90	pp. 397-398
14.	Anne Marie Carey-Neal '89	p. 424
15	John Freeman '71	p. 425
16.	Danica Charlton Lehner '82	p. 423, 425
17.	Linda Ehrlich Packard '70	p. 427
18.	Charles Bluem, Faculty '70-'94	p. 428

Chapter 6: Fall of the Wall to 1994

1.	Deb Brians Clarks '74	p. 430, 434
2.	Peter Stein '80	p. 435, 442, 444, 452-453, 457, 472- 474
3.	Justin Clark Mallon, Brat son	p. 439
4.	Gary Kelb, Faculty '86-92	p. 445
5.	Kath Kottke Sturgeon '86	p. 452, 470
6.	Joachim Kundert Jensen '94	p. 460, 464
7.	Danica Charlton Lehner '82	p. 470-471

8. Rose Hanson Neel '84 p. 471
9. John Freeman '71 p. 471

Joe Morasco '75 creator of the Berlin Observer Archive online- Thanks to Joe for all Observer news clippings. Additionally, all ephemera not otherwise credited.

Resources and Brat Publications

Berlin Observer Online Archive, created by Joe Morasco '75
www.theberlinobserverarchive.com

The Young Ambassadors by Dan Bunting '49

The Berlin Candy Bomber by Gail Halvorsen

Mercedes and the Chocolate Pilot by Margo Theis Raven

The Candy Bombers by Anrei Cherny

Candy Bomber by Michael Tunnell

PBS The American Experience: The Berlin Airlift www.pbs.org/wgbh/amex/airlift

The Wall Series*: Candy Bombers, Beetle Bunker, Smuggler's Treasure* by Robert Elmer

The Berlin Wall Memorial Bernauer Straße 119, 13355 Berlin;
www.berliner-mauer-gedenkstaette.de

The Cold War Museum, *7172* Lineweaver Rd, Warrenton, VA 20187
www.coldwar.org

Berlin Brigade: www.berlinbrigade.com by David Guerra

The Harnack House, mentioned by Rose Neel: www.harnack-house.us-berlin.com

Maps of U.S. Housing Areas in West Berlin: housing-areas.berlin-brigade.com

United States Army Transportation Museum, 300 Washington Boulevard, Besson Hall Fort Eustis, Virginia; 757-878-1115

Stop Train 349 (1963) starring Sean Flynn, Jose Ferrer, Nicole Courcel.
Movie made about the Duty Train Incident in 1963
The movie Stop Train 349 has been uploaded to YouTube. Can be seen playing on the Duty Train on exhibit at the Transportation Museum in Ft. Eustis, VA

History of JFK 50 Mile Hike – search for the JFK library online, then type in JFK 50 Mile in the search box. www.jfklibrary.org/JFK/JFK-Legacy/JFK-50-Race

Military Spouse Journey: Discover the Possibilities & Live Your Dreams and
1001 Things to Love About Military Life by Kathie Hightower '71
www.militaryspousejourney.com

Lincoln's Battle with God by Stephen Mansfield '76

ABOUT THE AUTHORS

Photo credit: Anastasia Lowe

Yoshika Loftin Lowe is a retired Homeschool Mom, who homeschooled her four children from birth through high school. All four of her children have either completed college or are presently in college. In retirement Yoshika finds pleasure in writing part-time and working full-time as a high school math teacher. She also teaches part-time at the local community college.

Growing up as a military brat was challenging—she attended 22 schools from pre-K through college. But she cherishes her time at BAHS and the friendships gained therein. After graduating from BAHS, Yoshika obtained her degree in applied and theoretical mathematics from the University of Houston. She met and married her husband Ivan in college, and they began a family.

This is Yoshika's first published book, she is also currently completing a Christmas devotional and family activity book entitled *An Advent Celebration.* The companion website, *An Advent Celebration,* is available every year during the advent season–beginning the fourth Sunday prior to Christmas through Christmas Eve. [anadventcelebration.blogspot.com]

Trisha A. Lindsey aka Ronin Schtihl Daire, is a published author. She is disabled and speaks her books into being with speech to text software; modern technology has freed her muse! It takes a lot of time for her to craft her books.

An Air Force Brat who grew up mostly overseas in Madrid, Spain and Berlin, Germany her ideas come from history and folklore. Writing in a five-book series format allows her the liberty to build layers in her characters fleshing them out fully.

There is always some component of Christianity in her works, as it is an integral part of her life. Her characters are real, gritty and they face real life situations that are found in everyday life. Readers may find a bit of themselves in one of her series. She is a graduate of Berlin American High School in what was formerly West Berlin, East Germany. She attended college at Tennessee State University, and was the first writer/editor of the Hubble Space Telescope Newsletter. She has been a Stay at Home Mom for these many years to her son Kiernan, niece Jasmine and daughter Kaylin. She is the author of over 10 books, 4 of which are available in softcover at Amazon.com.
[www.trishaalindsey.wix.com/trishaalindsey]

Coming Soon:

Anastasia Lowe is an aspiring filmmaker fresh from the Los Angles Film Studies Center. She is a director, writer and producer; she has been involved multiple projects in film and television.

Anastasia will be producing a documentary on the making of the Brats Overseas Book, *Cold War Memories: A Retrospective on Living in Berlin, A City Divided-Memoirs of U.S. Dependents in Berlin.* The documentary will contain video interviews that were later transcribed for inclusion in the book and other footage. Please check back on our website for updates as to its availability in the near future.

Contact Information

You can contact the Authors in the following ways:

Website: www.bratsoverseas1.wix.com/bratsoverseas

Facebook: Brats Overseas Book Project

Twitter: @Bratsoverseas

LinkedIn: Yoshika Lowe

Trisha A Lindsey

Instagram: Bratsoverseas

Pinterest: Yoshika Lowe

Trisha Lindsey

Bratsoverseas Book Project

Please make requests for interviews via contact on ***Linkedin*** if at all possible.

You may contact Anastasia at:

Website: http://alow63.wix.com/anastasialowe

LinkedIn: Anastasia Lowe